THE PENTECOSTAL PASTOR'S MANUAL

A GUIDE FOR AFRICAN PASTORS

Denzil R. Miller, Editor
Jeffery Nelson, Associate Editor
Todd Churchill, Associate Editor

The Pentecostal Pastor's Manual: A Guide for African Pastors
© Copyright 2022 by Africa's Hope, Springfield, Missouri, USA. All rights reserved. No part of this book may be reproduced, stored in a retrieval system, or transmitted in any form or by any means (electronic, mechanical, photocopy, recording or otherwise) without the prior written permission of the copyright owner, except brief quotations used in connection with reviews in magazines, newspapers, and reviews.

All Scripture quotations, unless otherwise indicated, are from THE HOLY BIBLE, NEW INTERNATIONAL VERSION®, NIV® Copyright © 1973, 1978, 1984, 2011 by Biblica, Inc.™ Used by permission. All rights reserved worldwide.

Editorial Committee:
    Denzil R. Miller, DMin, Editor
    Jeffery Nelson, PhD, Associate Editor
    Todd Churchill, Associate Editor

Cataloging Data:
    Miller, Denzil R., editor, 1946
    The Pentecostal Pastor's Manual: A Guide for African Pastors / Denzil R. Miller with Jeffery Nelson and Todd Churchill

    1. Practical Theology. 2. Pastoral Theology. 3. Handbooks. 4. Manuals

BV4016.M55 2022
253.088 MIL 2022

ISBN: 9798449228031

Published by Africa's Hope
580 West Central Street
Springfield, Missouri, USA 65802

Printed in the United States of America

Table of Contents

Contributor List 7
Foreword by Randel Tarr 11
Foreword by Dr. Barnabas Mtokambali 13

Introduction 15

PART 1: THE QUALIFICATIONS OF THE PENTECOSTAL PASTOR

Chapter 1: A Person of Experience 23
Chapter 2: A Person of the Spirit 33
Chapter 3: A Person of Good Character 43
Chapter 4: A Person Who Is Well Prepared 53

PART 2: THE PRIORITIES OF THE PENTECOSTAL PASTOR

Chapter 5: Ministerial Priorities 65
Chapter 6: Personal Priorities 75
Chapter 7: Family Priorities 85
Chapter 8: The Priority of Prayer 95

PART 3: THE BELIEFS OF THE PENTECOSTAL PASTOR

Chapter 9: Believes the Bible 107
Chapter 10: Upholds Pentecostal Truth 117
Chapter 11: Promotes Pentecostal Experience and Practice 127
Chapter 12: Appreciates Pentecostal Heritage 137

Table of Contents

PART 4: THE PERSONAL LIFE OF THE PENTECOSTAL PASTOR

Chapter 13: A Well-Managed Life 149
Chapter 14: Healthy Relationships 1599
Chapter 15: A Strong Devotional Habit 169

PART 5: THE PUBLIC MINISTRY OF THE PENTECOSTAL PASTOR

Chapter 16: Spirit-Anointed Preaching 181
Chapter 17: Effective Teaching 191
Chapter 18: Leading the Church in Worship 201
Chapter 19: Leading a Church into Pentecostal Revival 211
Chapter 20: Guiding Believers into Spirit Baptism 221
Chapter 21: Ministering in the Spirit's Power 231
Chapter 22: Engaging in Spiritual Warfare 241

PART 6: THE PENTECOSTAL PASTOR AS SHEPHERD

Chapter 23: Understanding Pastoral Ministry 253
Chapter 24: Caring for the Sheep 263
Chapter 25: Strengthening the Body 271
Chapter 26: Counseling God's People 281
Chapter 27: Guarding the Flock 293

PART 7: THE PENTECOSTAL PASTOR AS LEADER

Chapter 28: Pentecostal Leadership 305
Chapter 29: Servant Leadership 315
Chapter 30: Visionary Leadership 325
Chapter 31: Missional Leadership 335

Table of Contents

PART 8: THE PENTECOSTAL PASTOR AS ADMINISTRATOR

Chapter 32: Managing Records, Finances, and Properties 347
Chapter 33: Mobilizing Lay Leaders 357
Chapter 34: Directing Church Departments 367
Chapter 35: Overseeing Church Membership 379

PART 9: THE PENTECOSTAL PASTOR IN MISSION

Chapter 36: Understanding New Testament Strategy 391
Chapter 37: Evangelizing the Lost 401
Chapter 38: Serving the Community 413
Chapter 39: Planting New Churches 423
Chapter 40: Developing a Local Church Missions Program 433

PART 10: THE PENTECOSTAL PASTOR AND CEREMONIES AND SACRAMENTS

Chapter 41: Performing Weddings and Funerals 445
Chapter 42: Conducting Sacraments, Dedications, and
    Installations 455

APPENDICES

Appendix 1: WAGF Statement of Faith 467
Appendix 2: The Manifestation Gifts of 1 Corinthians 12 471
Appendix 3: Bible Book Abbreviations 473

Contributors List

Below is a list of contributors to this book. The number(s) in parentheses as the end of each reference indicates the chapter(s) to which this person is the major contributor.

Adade, Ayi, PhD. Secretary General, Togo Assemblies of God (29)

Ama, UcheChukwu. Deputy Chairman, Africa Assemblies of God Alliance World Missions Commission (40)

Banda, Lipenga. General Superintendent, Assemblies of God in Zambia (33)

Bogere, Richard, PhD. Co-Founder, Christ Chapel International, Kampala, Uganda; Teaching faculty member, Pan Africa Theological Seminary (6)

Bomboko, Cécile, PhD. Central Africa Regional Representative, Association for Pentecostal Theological Education in Africa (APTEA) (14, 32)

Bomboko, Marcel, PhD. Chairman, Board of Governors, West Africa Advanced School of Theology, Lomé, Togo (14, 32)

Chipao, Lawrence, PhD. Dean of Theology Faculty and Ministerial Formation, Malawi Assemblies of God University (34)

Churchill, Todd. AGWM Missionary to DR Congo, Africa's Hope (30)

Daplex Ouentchist, Honoré, PhD. President, Evangelical Church of the Assemblies of God, Cotê d'Ivoire (10)

Djakouti, Mitré. President, Togo Assemblies of God; Former President, Africa Assemblies of God Alliance (15)

Contributor's List

Dube, Andrew, PhD. President, Malawi Assemblies of God (11)

Flindja, Douti Lallebili, PhD. Academic Dean, West Africa Advanced School of Theology, Lomé, Togo (27)

Frimpong-Manso, Paul, PhD. General Superintendent, Assemblies of God, Ghana (37)

Gnanchou, Désiré Béchié, PhD. Former President, Evangelical Assemblies of God, Coté d'Ivoire; Director, Theological and Pastoral Institute of Katadji (23)

Kitoto, Dinah. Wife of Philip Kitoto, General Superintendent, Kenya Assemblies of God (7)

Kitoto, Philip. General Superintendent, Kenya Assemblies of God; Chancellor, KAG East University (7)

Kuoh, Jimmy, PhD. General Superintendent Emeritus, Assemblies of God Liberia; President, Liberia Assemblies of God Bible College (21, 41)

Lebelo, Gordon, PhD. General President, International Assemblies of God, South Africa (26)

Lwesya, Enson, DMin. Vice Chancellor, Malawi Assemblies of God University (28)

Mba, Arthur, PhD. First Vice President, Assemblies of God, Gabon (2, 18)

Mbiwan, Daniel. General Superintendent, Full Gospel Mission, Cameroon (25)

Miller, Denzil R., DMin. AGWM Missionary; Director, Acts in Africa Initiative (1, 3, 8, 16, 20, 36)

N'sembe Loyela, Israël. Pastor, Ark of the Covenant Evangelistic Center, Kinshasa; Former General Superintendent, Assemblies of God, DR Congo (22)

Contributor's List

Ndayisaba, Jérôme. President, Burundi Assemblies of God Fellowship (24)

Nelson, Jeffery, PhD. AGWM Missionary; Former Vice Chancellor, KAG East University, Nairobi, Kenya (5, 12, 39)

Ngabonziza, Emmanuel. Vice General Superintendent, Pentecostal Assemblies of God, Rwanda (38)

Niba, Felix, PhD. Director of Foreign Missions, Full Gospel Mission, Cameroon (13)

Oganya, Ngozi Cecilia, PhD. Coordinator of Theological Education by Extension (TEE), Assemblies of God Divinity School, Umuahia, Nigeria (17)

Sawadogo, Jephté, DMin. Vice President, Burkina Faso Assemblies of God; Director, Koubri Bible School (4, 42)

Sebastião, Francisco. President, Angola Assemblies of God (9)

Smith, Bernard, MA. AGWM Missionary to Togo (15)

Swai, Ron. General Treasurer, Tanzania Assemblies of God (35)

Turney, Mark, MA. AGWM Missionary; President, West Africa Advanced School of Theology, Lomé, Togo (19)

Watt, C. Peter, ThD. Chairman, Assemblies of God, South Africa (31)

Contributor's List

Foreword by Randel Tarr

The Pentecostal Pastor's Manual promises to serve as a significant resource for African pastors for years to come. The Church in Africa has long needed such a resource, one that addresses the unique challenges faced by Pentecostal pastors in Africa.

In this work, Dr. Denzil R. Miller and his editorial team, Dr. Jeffery Nelson and Todd Churchill, have assembled a truly impressive list of African leaders to address many of the issues faced by Pentecostal pastors in Africa today. As the "Contributors List" at the front of the book reveals, these leaders include national church officials, lead pastors, Bible school and seminary administrators and teachers, missions leaders, church planters, evangelists, and more.

The depth of experience and knowledge of these leaders adds to the great value of this work. Having served with several of these men and women, I can personally vouch for their integrity as leaders, their passion for Christ and His mission, and their desire to see the Church planted in every corner of Africa. Further, the editorial team itself brings a wealth of knowledge of Africa and its peoples to the development of this book. Each one has served for many years as a missionary in Southern, East, or Central Africa.

This book promises to strengthen the ministries of those who are already leading local churches across Africa, as well as those who are still in Bible school and extension training programs preparing for future ministry. It is filled with practical helps that will assist the Pentecostal pastor to succeed in ministry and bear fruit that will last.

One especially valuable emphasis of this book is its call to the Pentecostal pastor in Africa to be a man or woman of the highest character. Another important emphasis is the book's constant appeal to the African pastor to remain full of the Holy Spirit and to stay focused on the Church's God-given mission to see that every man, woman, and child in Africa be given an opportunity to hear the good news and come to faith in Jesus Christ. In a day when the so-called "prosperity gospel" has led so many churches in Africa away from God's mission to a quest for personal blessing, it is encouraging to see the strong missional focus of this book. The contributors to this book are true practitioners of the Word, men and women of God who seek to live out the focus of Christ's Great Commission in their daily lives.

For the past six decades I have been associated with the Church in Africa, first as a child growing up in Africa and later as a missionary in West Africa for more than 35 years. It is incredible to see what God has done through the work of thousands of African men and women who have consecrated their lives to win the lost at any cost. I believe this book will serve to enhance their effectiveness in ministry. My prayer is that, as this book is placed in the hands of thousands of pastors and Bible school students across Africa, the kingdom of God will come to the continent in an even greater way.

Spirit-empowered, biblically trained leaders are truly the hope of Africa!

~ Rev. Randel Tarr
Executive Director
Africa's Hope

Foreword by Dr. Barnabas Mtokambali

Most Pentecostal pastors in Africa can identify with Paul's state of mind when he wrote to the believers in Corinth:

> "I have been constantly on the move. I have been in danger....I have labored and toiled and have often gone without sleep; I have known hunger and thirst and have often gone without food; I have been cold and naked. Besides everything else, I face daily the pressure of my concern for all the churches." (2 Cor. 11:26-28)

While their individual circumstances may differ from Paul's, most Pentecostal pastors in Africa can identify with his feeling of being "hard pressed on every side" (4:8).

Few vocations are more challenging than pastoring a Pentecostal church in Africa. Think of the many areas of life and ministry in which the Pentecostal pastor must demonstrate competence. He or she must be able to capably care for the flock of God, while also being able to manage their own personal and family affairs. They must be competent preachers, teachers, counselors, and administrators—all at the same time. And all along, they must be able to lead their churches in fulfilling the command of our Lord to make disciples of all nations. The list could continue. That is why the emergence of this Pentecostal pastor's manual is so welcomed.

For a long time I have seen the need for a comprehensive pastor's guide written from an African and a Pentecostal point of view. I am therefore deeply grateful for the work done by Africa's Hope to produce this book. What is especially encouraging is that this manual has been written by mature Pentecostal pastors and leaders from across the continent. It is, at the same time, theologically sound, missionally focused, and practically useful. This manual provides Pentecostal pastors with many priceless insights into Pentecostal life and ministry. It will help to guide Pentecostal pastors across the continent into more productive ministry. And by strengthening the hands of our pastors, it will ultimately strengthen the churches they lead.

I expect that *The Pentecostal Pastor's Manual* will be especially useful during the Africa Assemblies of God Alliance (AAGA) "Decade of Revival" emphasis from 2021 to 2030. During these ten years, Assemblies of God churches across Africa have committed themselves to seek God for a powerful outpouring of the Holy Spirit on the Church, resulting in the greatest revival ever seen in Africa, empowering believers to take the gospel to every tribe, nation, and people before the soon coming of Christ.

During the Decade of Revival, Assemblies of God churches will focus on Holy Spirit empowerment, godly living, discipleship training, evangelism, church planting, and cross-cultural missions among the unreached peoples of the continent—especially in North Africa and the Horn of Africa. I believe that *The Pentecostal Pastor's Manual* will serve as an invaluable tool, helping pastors to lead their churches to fulfill this great mission. Then, should the Lord Jesus delay His coming, the book will continue to serve the Pentecostal church in Africa for many years to come.

I happily recommend this book to Pentecostal pastors and ministers across Africa.

~ Dr. Barnabas Mtokambali
Chairman
Africa Assemblies of God Alliance

Introduction

Noting how the church in Africa is growing, one African leader exclaimed, "God is blessing the African church so the African church can bless the nations!" We at the Africa's Hope Acts 1:8 Initiative wholeheartedly agree with this sentiment. We believe God has called the African church into the Kingdom for such a time as this (cf. Est. 4:14). The Pentecostal church in Africa has a great missionary destiny. During these final days of time, the Lord of the Harvest is pouring out His Spirit on His people to empower them to fully participate in fulfilling His Great Commission before He returns from heaven (Matt. 24:14; Acts 1:8-11).

To do this, the African church will need to be strong. And to be strong, it must have strong leadership. *The Pentecostal Pastor's Manual* was developed to address this need. It has been designed to equip Pentecostal pastors in Africa to do their part in fulfilling God's purpose for the church. Our sincere hope is that this book will become a treasured tool in the hands of Pentecostal pastors across the continent. It has been developed with six guiding principles in mind:

1. It is biblical in perspective. The writers and developers of this manual believe that the Bible is God's revealed Word to humanity. It is the Christian's all-sufficient guide to life and mission. Therefore, the book's developers have sought to base every concept in this manual firmly on Scripture.

2. It is Pentecostal in emphasis. The book has been written *by* Pentecostal pastors *for* Pentecostal pastors. It unapologetically seeks to address the unique concerns of Pentecostal pastors from a Pentecostal point of view. Every contributor to the book is a mature Pentecostal leader with a proven ministry. Because of their experience with the Spirit, and their understanding of Scripture, these men and women embrace a distinctively Pentecostal approach to life and ministry. This approach is reflected throughout this work.

Introduction

3. It is missional in focus. The developers of this manual believe that Christ has commissioned every Pentecostal pastor and church to fully participate in God's mission. God's mission is to redeem and call unto himself a people from every tribe, language, and nation on earth before Jesus returns (Matt. 24:14; Rev. 5:9). Christ summarized God's mission in His Great Commission (Matt. 28:18-20; Mark 16:15-17; Luke 24:47-49; John 20:21-22; Acts 1:8). This missional emphasis is promoted throughout the book.

4. It is African in orientation. The target audience for the *Pentecostal Pastor's Manual* is the Pentecostal pastor in Africa. The writers understand that African pastors carry out their ministries in a uniquely African context, and they do so with uniquely African challenges and concerns. Every chapter has been written with this context in mind.

5. It is comprehensive in scope. This book has been designed to address a wide range of issues faced by Pentecostal pastors in Africa today. The developers hope it will become an indispensable resource in the hands of pastors across the continent.

6. It is practical in application. While this manual necessarily addresses issues of pastoral theology and theory, the lessons taught herein are designed to be highly practical. They discuss, not only *what* the Pentecostal pastor must do, and *why* he or she must do it, they further discuss *how* they may effectively carry out their ministries.

Writing Process

The Pentecostal Pastor's Manual was first envisioned by Dr. John Easter, then Executive Director of Africa's Hope. He commissioned a working committee to produce this manual. When Dr. Easter was succeeded by Randy Tarr, the ministry's new director wholeheartedly embraced the project.

The committee's first task was to compile a comprehensive list of those topics the book would address. This was a large undertaking involving extensive research and many hours of frank discussion. The list of topics was further vetted by key African leaders and educators

Introduction

from across the continent. Eventually, the forty-two topics that became the chapters of this book were selected. Once the chapter topics had been determined, the committee grouped them into ten categories, which became the ten sections of the book.

Having decided what topics would be covered, and where they would appear in the book, the committee selected key Assemblies of God pastors, educators, and church leaders from across Africa to write individual chapters. A few American missionaries who have lived and ministered extensively in Africa were also invited to write. The names of these writers, along with a brief biographical sketch on each one, appear in the "Contributors List" near the front of the book.

Once a writer had completed his or her task, they submitted their work to the committee for evaluation and editing. The committee then examined each chapter for content and connection with other chapters. Their goal was to ensure that each chapter contributed to the Pentecostal and missional intent of the book, and to ensure that the writing style remained consistent throughout the work. Once the editorial process was completed, the chapter was included in the book.

Pronoun Usage

A word needs to be said about the use of the phrase "he or she" in this book when referring to Pentecostal pastors in Africa. This practice was followed to ensure that the growing number of women pastors in Pentecostal churches across Africa know that their ministries are esteemed and appreciated.

From its inception, the Pentecostal Movement has valued the place of women in ministry. Pentecostals believe that the same Spirit who qualifies men for ministry also qualifies women. They base this belief on Jesus' promise of Acts 1:8, where He promises the Holy Spirit to all believers, both men and women. Everyone who receives the Spirit, including women, receives power to witness for Christ. This witness necessarily includes the proclamation of the gospel.

Pentecostals also cite the promise of the prophet Joel quoted by Peter on the Day of Pentecost: "In the last days, God says, I will pour

Introduction

out my Spirit on *all people*. Your sons *and daughters* will prophesy....Even on my servants, both men *and women,* I will pour out my Spirit in those days, and they will prophesy" (Acts 2:17-18, emphasis added; cf. Joel 2:28-29). Pentecostals take this statement as a universal principle to be believed and acted upon during this "Age of the Spirit" when God is graciously pouring out His Spirit on all people.

Historically, English writers have used the pronouns "he" or "him" generically when referring to both men and women. To avoid any confusion, the editors have chosen to use the more inclusive terms "he or she" and "him or her" when referring to Pentecostal pastors. For readability reasons, this requires that the plural pronoun "they" sometimes be used as a substitute for the singular "he" or "she." This is a widely accepted practice among English writers today, and it is the practice of the New International Version Bible, 2011 edition, that is used in this book.

How to Use This Book

As its name implies, this book has been designed as a manual, or handbook, for Pentecostal pastors in Africa. You can use the book in several helpful ways. To begin with, you will want to read the book through from beginning to end. This exercise will give you a broad overview of the concepts discussed in the book. It will also help you gain broad insight into the many-sided work of the Pentecostal pastor in Africa.

As you move through the book, you should keep a pen and notebook nearby so you can jot down insights that strike you as being particularly applicable to your own life and ministry. You will also want to write down your personal thoughts on the topic. You should note certain improvements you should make in the way you are presently doing ministry. Finally, and most importantly, as you read, you will want to listen to the voice of the Spirit, noting what He says to you. You will then want to use your notebook as a prayer guide and as a road map for personal and ministerial development.

Introduction

You can also use this manual as a reference work. When a special occasion presents itself, such as a wedding, funeral, counseling session, leadership meeting, or other event, you can review the pertinent chapter or chapters to gain fresh insights and helpful guidelines. Or when you are seeking help in solving a pressing problem or approaching a new ministerial task, you can search the Table of Contents for chapters addressing that issue.

Finally, this book can be used by teachers in Bible colleges and seminaries as a textbook or as a supplemental reader for a pastoral ministries class. The book can be especially helpful in intensive short-term schools such as extension or church planting schools.

We, the managing committee for *The Pentecostal Pastor's Manual* thus commend this work to the Pentecostal pastors of Africa. It is our sincere prayer that God will use it to bless African pastors for decades to come, and that this book will serve as a useful tool in advancing God's kingdom in Africa, and through the African church, in the nations.

Respectfully,

~ Dr. Denzil R. Miller, editor
~ Dr. Jeffery Nelson, associate editor
~ Rev. Todd Churchill, associate editor

Introduction

~ Part 1 ~

The Qualifications of the Pentecostal Pastor

~ Chapter 1 ~

A Person of Experience

Imagine a man who studied medicine at a prestigious university. He attended lectures on surgery and read the best books on the subject. However, he never actually operated on anyone. Would you want this man to perform surgery on you? Of course not. If one aspires to become a surgeon, he or she must gain practical experience by performing many surgeries under the supervision of a skilled surgeon.

In like manner, before one enters into pastoral ministry, he or she must acquire experience. This experience must be both spiritual and practical. In this chapter, we will investigate the experience required of anyone who wants to be a Pentecostal pastor.

SPIRITUAL EXPERIENCE

Experience with God is the essential starting point for any Pentecostal pastor. Above all else, he or she must have a deep personal relationship with Christ. When Jesus chose the Twelve, He did so "that they might be with him" (Mark 3:14). He knew that, as they walked and talked with Him, they would become more like Him. Jesus said, "Everyone when he is fully trained will be like his teacher"

Chapter 1: A Person of Experience

(Luke 6:40). It is the same for us today, as we spend time with Christ in His Word and in prayer, we become ever more like Him (2 Cor. 3:18). Before we can minister *for* Him, we must become *like* Him, and to become like Him, we must spend time *with* Him.

The Pentecostal movement was formed out of the conviction that believers today can have the same life-changing spiritual experiences as did the apostles and other disciples in the New Testament. Pentecostals teach that, while right doctrine is essential, it is not enough. More than anything else, as a Pentecostal pastor, you must have an ongoing relationship with Jesus Christ. Without such a relationship, you are disqualified from ministry. This relationship is formed through spiritual experience.

Throughout the Bible, those who ministered to others began their journey by encountering God. Abraham heard the voice of God (Gen. 12:1-3). Moses met God in the burning bush (Exod. 3:1-4). Isaiah saw God in the temple, high and lifted up (Isa. 6:1-5). The disciples walked with Jesus (Mark 3:13-14). And Paul encountered the risen Christ on the road to Damascus (Acts 9:1-5).

In similar fashion, everyone who wants to be a Pentecostal pastor must have four essential encounters with God:

The New Birth

Nicodemus was a religious leader. He was a devout Pharisee and a member of the Jewish ruling council. None of this, however, was enough. Jesus informed Nicodemus, "You must be born again" (John 3:7). Jesus told him that he could not "enter," or even "see" the kingdom of God unless he experienced a spiritual rebirth (vv. 3-5).

Every Pentecostal pastor must be truly born again. He or she must be able to testify of a time in their life when they encountered Jesus, repented of their sins, and received Him as their Lord and Savior. At that moment, Jesus assumed His rightful place on the throne of their lives, and they were regenerated. Paul wrote, "If anyone is in Christ, that person is a new creation. The old has gone, the new is here!" (2 Cor. 5:17, margin).

Part 1: The Qualifications of the Pentecostal Pastor

Have you been born again? Has your very being been transformed from the inside out? If not, you can be right now. Turn from your sins and pray, asking God to forgive you. Put your full trust in Christ alone for salvation, and invite Him to take His rightful place as Lord of your life. To receive Christ as your Savior, believe with all your heart, and sincerely pray this prayer:

> "Jesus, I truly believe that You are the Son of God, the Savior of the world. I believe that You died for my sins and rose again. I know I am a sinner, and apart from faith in You, I am eternally lost. Please forgive me of my sins and become my Savior and Lord. I now forsake all to follow You. I will serve You all the days of my life. Come into my heart and be the Lord of my life. In Your name I pray. Amen."

The Baptism in the Holy Spirit

Just before Jesus ascended into heaven, He commanded His disciples, "Stay in the city until you have been clothed with power from on high" (Luke 24:19). They were to wait in Jerusalem until they had been baptized in the Holy Spirit (Acts 1:4). These men had been born again. They had sat under Jesus' teaching, and they had witnessed His miracles. He had commissioned them to preach the gospel in all the world. And yet, they were still not ready.

The task Jesus had given them was too big for them to do in their own strength. They needed to be filled with God's power. Jesus promised them, "You will receive power when the Holy Spirit comes on you; and you will be my witnesses in Jerusalem, and in all Judea and Samaria, and to the ends of the earth" (Acts 1:8).

The Spirit first came upon the disciples and filled them on the Day of Pentecost. In that moment, they spoke in tongues and received the power and boldness they needed to effectively proclaim Christ, even in the face of strong opposition. Anyone who desires to follow the Lord in ministry should be baptized in the Holy Spirit.

Jesus told us how we can be baptized in the Holy Spirit. He promised, "The Heavenly Father [will] give the Holy Spirit to those who ask him!" (Luke 11:13). Anyone can receive the Spirit's power by

Chapter 1: A Person of Experience

simply asking in faith. This asking involves three simple steps of faith:

1. Ask in faith. Begin by asking God for the Spirit. Speaking of the gift of the Spirit, Jesus promised, "Ask, and it will be given to you; seek, and you will find; knock, and it will be opened to you" (Luke 11:9). As you ask, believe that God is hearing and answering your prayer, and that He is, at this very moment, filling you with the Holy Spirit. Open wide your heart to God, and sense the Spirit's coming upon you. Once you sense the Spirit upon you, you are ready to take the second step of faith.

2. Receive by faith. Jesus further promised, "Everyone who asks receives" (Luke 11:10). On another occasion He taught, "Whatever you ask in prayer, believe that you have received it, and it will be yours" (Mark 11:24). Believe that God is answering your prayer and filling you with the Holy Spirit. As you do, sense the Spirit's presence deep inside, in your innermost being (John 7:38). Once this happens, take your third step of faith.

3. Speak in faith. The Bible says that on the Day of Pentecost "they were all filled with the Holy Spirit and *began to speak* in other tongues as the Spirit gave them utterance" (Acts 2:4, emphasis added). The words you speak will not be your own; they will come from God. They will come from deep inside, out of your spirit (1 Cor. 14:2). And they will be in a language you do not understand. This is God's sign to you, and to the church, that He has empowered you to speak for Him. Praise the Lord! You have been baptized in the Holy Spirit.

A Divine Call

Being a Pentecostal pastor is more than a career choice; it is a calling from God. Speaking of Jesus, Paul wrote, "It was he who gave some to be apostles, some to be prophets, some to be evangelists, and some to be pastors and teachers" (Eph. 4:11). Along with the four other ministry roles, pastors are a gift given by Christ to His Church. The Lord himself chooses whom He will appoint as a pastor. He

Part 1: The Qualifications of the Pentecostal Pastor

chooses, then He calls, then He deploys. Jesus told His twelve disciples, "You did not choose me, but I chose you and appointed you to go and bear fruit—fruit that will last" (John 15:16).

The Lord thus revealed three important truths concerning the call of God: First, He revealed that it is God alone who does the choosing. The authentic Pentecostal pastor is not self-chosen. He or she is chosen by Christ. Jesus further revealed that it is He who assigns ministry tasks. He continued, "I chose you, and I appointed you." Christ not only chooses who will serve, He writes the job descriptions and assigns workers to fulfill those jobs.

Finally, those He chooses and appoints, He deploys. Jesus finished His statement, "[I] appointed you to go and bear fruit." He is the Lord of the Harvest, and it is He who commands us, "Go into all the world and proclaim the gospel to the whole creation" (Mark 16:15). In other words, true Pentecostal pastors are neither self-chosen, self-appointed, nor self-sent. Rather, they are God-chosen, God-appointed, and God-sent. Our part is to hear His voice, submit to His authority, and obey His call.

God's call can come in various ways. It can come dramatically, as with Samuel who heard God audibly call his name (1 Sam. 3:1-11). More often, however, God's call comes as a gentle nudge in the deep parts of one's being. This was the experience of Elijah. The prophet did not hear God's voice in the powerful wind, the earthquake, or the fire. He rather heard God's voice as a "gentle whisper" (1 Kings 19:12).

This gentle prompting is often accompanied by an "inner knowing" that God is speaking. Over time, it grows in intensity, resulting in a sense of urgency. The boy Jesus must have felt this way when He told His parents, "I had to be in my Father's house" (Luke 2:49). Paul expressed this inner urgency to the Corinthians. "For necessity is laid upon me," he wrote, "woe to me if I do not preach the gospel!" (1 Cor. 9:16). The prophet Micah described this deep inner conviction from God: "But as for me, I am filled with power, with the Spirit of the Lord, and with justice and might, to declare to Jacob his transgression and to Israel his sin" (Mic. 3:8).

Chapter 1: A Person of Experience

As we respond in faith and obedience to the voice of the Spirit, the conviction grows until we know for sure that God has called us to devote our lives to proclaiming the gospel.

A Living Relationship

Finally, the Pentecostal pastor must have an ongoing, living relationship with God. Experience with God should not be thought of as a one-time event. One experience, no matter how dramatic, cannot sustain the Christian life. Even the first disciples, who experienced the Spirit on the Day of Pentecost, needed repeated fillings with the Spirit (Acts 4:8, 31; 5:8).

As a Pentecostal pastor, you must learn to cultivate an ongoing, personal walk with God. Paul wrote to the new Christians in Galatia: "Since we live by the Spirit, let us keep in step with the Spirit" (Gal. 2:25). In the same letter, he reproved them, "Are you so foolish? After beginning by means of the Spirit, are you now trying to finish by means of the flesh?" (Gal. 3:2). It is not enough to have been once filled with the Spirit, you must remain "full of the Spirit" (Luke 4:1; Acts 6:3; 7:55; 11:24).

Jesus described this relationship as remaining, or abiding, in Him (John 15:4). Abiding in Christ involves living in His Word and in His love (vv. 7, 9). It also involves keeping His commandments (v. 10) and living in the Spirit (1 John 2:27; 4:13).

PRACTICAL EXPERIENCE

Some skills cannot be learned from books. A man may read a magazine article on how to swim; however, he would be foolish to plunge into the depths before he first practiced his skills in the shallows. The same holds true for Pentecostal ministry. By itself, no amount of academic study can adequately prepare you for pastoral ministry. Before entering into ministry you must acquire practical experience. You can gain such experience only by participating in actual hands-on ministry.

Part 1: The Qualifications of the Pentecostal Pastor

In one Bible school in Southern Africa, prospective students are required to submit an "Application for Admission." The administration uses the knowledge gained from this form to help determine the applicant's fitness for admission into the school. Along with the usual personal and academic questions, the applicant is asked to write out in their own handwriting their personal testimony. In this testimony, the applicant is asked to address four issues: (1) tell how you came to know Christ as your Savior; (2) tell about your baptism in the Holy Spirit and how this experience has affected your life; (3) describe your call into ministry; and (4) describe how you have been active in the ministry of your local church.

The school administrator explained, "We ask the last question because we believe that practical experience is an essential component of effective ministerial training. Here at our school, we do not train *for* ministry, we train *in* ministry." While formal training is important, it alone will never prepare you for pastoral ministry. You must gain practical experience by being actively involved in ministry.

You would be very unwise to try to lead a congregation as pastor until you have gained practical experience. You can best gain such experience in a local church under the guidance of a mature, Spirit-filled pastor. Paul told Timothy that an overseer, or pastor, "must not be a recent convert" (1 Tim. 3:6). He added that the pastor must have "a good reputation with outsiders" (v. 7). Four essential areas of practical experience in ministry are experience in witnessing, experience in preaching and teaching, experience in giving, and experience in prayer, as follows:

Experience in Witnessing

First, in preparing for pastoral ministry, you must acquire experience in witnessing. You must become skilled at sharing the gospel with others. Such witness is the natural result of your having been baptized in the Holy Spirit, as discussed above. Speaking of himself, Jesus said that the Shepherd "goes ahead of [his sheep], and his sheep follow him" (John 10:4). As a Pentecostal pastor, the same is true of

Chapter 1: A Person of Experience

you. If you will go ahead of your sheep winning souls to Christ, they will follow. However, if you fail to witness, so will your people.

A related responsibility of any Pentecostal pastor is to lead his or her congregation in planting new churches in places where no Spirit-empowered missionary church exists. It is therefore important that you have participated in one or more church planting campaigns before assuming the leadership of a local assembly. This could have been an effort of your home church, the Bible school you attended, or some other ministry. This practical experience will help you know how to mobilize your own church to plant other churches.[1]

Experience in Preaching and Teaching

Further, anyone who aims to become a Pentecostal pastor must acquire experience in preaching and teaching the Word of God. For how can one effectively lead a Pentecostal church if he or she is not skilled in communicating the Word of God to others? Paul reminded Timothy that a pastor must be "able to teach" (1 Tim. 3:2). He further admonished his son in the faith to be prepared to preach the word at all times (2 Tim. 4:2).

One way you can gain teaching and preaching experience is to volunteer to teach a Sunday school or Bible class in your home church. Another way is to lead a home cell group. In these ways, you can, under your pastor's guidance, practice putting together and delivering biblical messages. Another good way to acquire preaching experience is to preach in open-air services. You can do this by organizing a group of faithful church members and going into market areas and other public places near your church to conduct open-air evangelistic services.[2]

---

[1] These issues are discussed in more detail in Chapter 37: "Evangelizing the Lost" and Chapter 39: "Planting New Churches."

[2] For more insight on preaching and teaching, see Chapter 16: "Spirit-Anointed Preaching" and Chapter 17: "Effective Teaching."

Part 1: The Qualifications of the Pentecostal Pastor

Experience in Giving

Third, the person wanting to be a Pentecostal pastor must have a history of faithful tithing and generous giving to the work of God. A miserly, tightfisted person can never represent a generous, open-handed God. Jesus encouraged His disciples, "Freely you have received; freely give" (Matt. 10:8). In similar manner, Paul admonished the Corinthian believers, "Follow my example, as I follow the example of Christ" (1 Cor. 11:1). As church members observe your faith-filled generosity, they too will be encouraged to give generously to God's work, trusting Him to supply all their needs (Phil. 4:19). As a result, the work of God will prosper.

Experience in Prayer

Finally, the one desiring to become a Pentecostal pastor must have practical experience in prayer. Prayer forms the foundation for all Pentecostal ministry. One's experience in prayer begins with a disciplined prayer life. The Bible tells how "Jesus often withdrew to lonely places and prayed" (Luke 5:16). To be an effective Pentecostal pastor you must do the same. You must learn to set aside time each day for communion with your Heavenly Father.[3]

You will also want to join with others in prayer. You can do this by participating in prayer groups, prayer retreats, and overnight prayer meetings. Through these practices, you can prepare yourself to pray for others. Two other areas where a you must gain experience are in praying for the sick and afflicted to be healed and in praying with believers to be filled with the Holy Spirit.[4]

---

[3] For more on the Pentecostal pastor's devotional life, see Chapter 8: "The Priority of Prayer" and Chapter 15: "A Strong Devotional Habit."

[4] These practices are covered in more detail in Chapter 19: "Guiding Believers into Spirit Baptism" and Chapter 21: "Ministering in the Spirit's Power."

Chapter 1: A Person of Experience

~ Chapter 2 ~

A Person of the Spirit

In a certain African country, a young man sensed the call of God on his life. He told his pastor what he was feeling. The pastor also recognized God's call on the young man's life, so he assigned him to a branch church in a nearby town. He told the young man, "You are to develop this church and plant other churches in the area." Filled with enthusiasm, the young man moved his family to the town and set himself to the task. He worked hard and did his very best. However, he had little success. The young man then said to himself, "I need more knowledge and training." So he enrolled in Bible school.

In the Bible school, the young man studied the Word of God. The more he learned, the more confident he became. He also learned about a biblical experience called the baptism in the Holy Spirit. The young man diligently sought for the Spirit, and was soon filled, just as the 120 disciples were on the Day of Pentecost (Acts 2:1-4).

His teachers then taught him how to walk in the Spirit's power. When he returned to his church, things changed. He now ministered with power and conviction. People were healed and delivered, and many came to Christ. As a result, the church grew and became strong.

Chapter 2: A Person of the Spirit

Within a short time, it was able to plant other churches. This story illustrates why it is so important for every Pentecostal pastor to become a true man or woman of the Spirit.

The last chapter discussed how the Pentecostal pastor must be a person of both spiritual and practical experience. This chapter will expand on these issues. It will discuss the Pentecostal pastor's basic understanding of the Spirit and His work. It will also address his or her personal walk and ministry in the Spirit.

UNDERSTANDS THE SPIRIT

If you, as a Pentecostal pastor, are to become a true person of the Spirit, you will need to understand four things:

Who the Spirit Is

First, you will need to understand who the Spirit is. Far too many Christians today, including Pentecostals, have no clear idea of who the Holy Spirit is. Many wrongly view Him as some vague impersonal force coming from God. The Pentecostal pastor, however, must understand and teach that the Holy Spirit is, in fact, God. He is the third person of the Holy Trinity (Matt. 28:19; 2 Cor. 13:14). Just as the Father is God, and the Son is God, the Holy Spirit is God. As God, the Spirit thinks (Acts 15:28), speaks (Acts 1:16), leads (Rom. 8:14), and can be grieved (Eph. 4:30). Because the Holy Spirit is a person, every follower of Christ can have a personal relationship with Him (John 14:16-18; 2 Cor. 13:14).

Further, as a Pentecostal pastor, you must understand and teach that the Holy Spirit is the Spirit of Missions. He is that member of the Trinity who, in this Age of the Spirit, carries out God's redemptive mission in the earth. He further empowers, inspires, and guides God's people to join Him in this mission (Acts 1:8).

How the Spirit Works

In addition to knowing *who* the Holy Spirit is, you must know *how* He works. The Spirit works in and through God's missionary

Part 1: The Qualifications of the Pentecostal Pastor

people, the Church, to fulfill God's mission in the earth. He empowered Jesus to accomplish His work (Luke 4:17-19; Acts 10:38). In the same way, He will empower Jesus' followers to accomplish their work (Acts 1:8; John 14:12). As a Pentecostal pastor, you must clearly understand and persuasively teach these truths.[1]

To properly grasp the Spirit's work in this age, you must understand three biblical concepts:

1. The mission of God. First, you must understand that the Bible presents God as a missionary God. His mission is sometimes referred to as the *missio Dei,* which is simply Latin for the mission of God. God's mission is to redeem, and call unto himself, a people from every tribe, and language, and nation on earth (Rev. 5:9). The Church exists as God's instrument to fulfill His mission.

Jesus had God's mission in mind when He gave His Great Commission: "Therefore go and make disciples of all nations, baptizing them in the name of the Father and of the Son and of the Holy Spirit, and teaching them to obey everything I have commanded you" (Matt. 28:19-20; cf. Mark 16:15-16; John 20:21).

As a true Pentecostal pastor, you must commit yourself to teaching God's people about His mission. You must also teach them about their role in fulfilling that mission.

2. The missional nature of Spirit baptism. In addition to understanding God's mission, as an authentic Pentecostal pastor, you must understand the essential role of Spirit baptism in fulfilling the mission. You must understand that God baptizes His people in His Spirit to enable them to accomplish His mission (Luke 24:49). Jesus began His ministry only after He had been empowered by the Holy Spirit (Luke 3:21-23; 4:17-19; Acts 10:38). He expects His disciples to do the same today (Acts 1:4-8).

3. Mobilizing for mission. Further, as a Pentecostal pastor, you must understand that, in leading your people into Spirit baptism, you

---

[1] For more on this topic, see Chapter 10: "Upholds Pentecostal Truth" and Chapter 11: "Promotes Pentecostal Experience and Practice."

are preparing them for Spirit-empowered mission. When Jesus commanded His disciples, "Stay in the city until you have been clothed with power from on high" (Luke 24:49), He was getting them ready for the mission that lay ahead (vv. 47-48). And when Paul asked the twelve Ephesian disciples, "Did you receive the Holy Spirit when you believed?" (Acts 19:2), he was inquiring into their readiness to join him in the mission of evangelizing Ephesus and the rest of Asia Minor (v. 10).

It must be the same with us today. We must understand that, by leading our people into Spirit baptism, we are preparing them for Spirit-empowered witness, church planting, and missions.

Interpreting the Book of Acts

Third, as an authentic Pentecostal pastor in Africa, you must grasp the missional nature and purpose of the book of Acts. One thing that distinguishes Pentecostals from non-Pentecostals is how each group interprets the book of Acts. Non-Pentecostals generally view Acts as the ancient story of how the Church began and carried out its mission. In their thinking, Acts recounts how God worked *then and there,* in the distant past. Pentecostals, however, see the book of Acts as a lasting pattern of how God wants to work in and through the Church *here and now,* in the immediate present.

The Pentecostal pastor understands that Acts is much more than a book of ancient history. It is rather a divinely inspired strategy manual for end-time mission. In Acts, the Holy Spirit has provided the Church with a model, the means, and a strategy to accomplish God's mission. That strategy is summed up in Jesus' final promise to the Church: "But you will receive power when the Holy Spirit comes on you; and you will be my witnesses in Jerusalem, and in all Judea and Samaria, and to the ends of the earth" (Acts 1:8).

This verse reveals an *empowerment-witness* pattern that is repeated throughout the book. Without exception, every outpouring of the Spirit in Acts resulted in Spirit-empowered witness. Grasping this concept is a key to your understanding the book of Acts and to your mobilizing your church for Spirit-empowered mission.

Part 1: The Qualifications of the Pentecostal Pastor

What It Means to Be Pentecostal

Finally, as a Pentecostal pastor, you must have a clear understanding of what it really means to be Pentecostal. True Pentecostalism is much more than an alternative worship style or an orientation to the supernatural. God raised up the Pentecostal church as a last-days Spirit-empowered missionary movement. The true Pentecostal pastor is thus committed to following the pattern of ministry laid down by Jesus in the gospels and copied by the apostles and other disciples in the book of Acts. He or she is committed to four biblical practices:

1. Same message. First, the authentic Pentecostal pastor is committed to faithfully proclaiming the same message as did the apostles and evangelists in the book of Acts. That message is the gospel. It is illustrated in the ministry of Philip who "went down to a city in Samaria and proclaimed the Messiah [or Christ] there" (Acts 8:5; cf. v. 12). Throughout Acts, the Church never wavered from proclaiming the message of Christ's atoning death and resurrection (cf. 2:22-24; 3:15; 4:10-12). In addition, they consistently called on the people to repent and believe the gospel (cf. 2:38; 16:31; 20:21; 26:20). We must do the same today.

2. Same mission. Second, the authentic Pentecostal pastor is committed to pursuing the same mission as did the Church in the book of Acts. As mentioned above, that mission is best summarized in Acts 1:8, where Jesus said, "But you will receive power when the Holy Spirit comes on you; and you will be my witnesses…to the ends of the earth." The book of Acts presents the Church as continually pressing the frontiers, moving into new territories, and preaching the good news in the power of the Spirit. As a true Pentecostal pastor, you must lead your church to do the same.

3. Same experiences. Third, the authentic Pentecostal pastor promotes the same spiritual experiences as did the apostles in the book of Acts. Those experiences include life-changing conversions (cf. Acts 2:41; 8:5-6; 9:1-8), water baptism by immersion (cf. 2:41; 8:13, 36-38; 9:17-19; 16:33), baptism in the Holy Spirit evidenced by speaking in tongues (cf. 2:4; 10:44-46; 19:6), miracles of healing (cf.

Chapter 2: A Person of the Spirit

3:1-10; 5:12-16; 20:7-12), and miracles of deliverance from demonic possession (cf. 8:7; 16:16-18). By the same measure, the Pentecostal pastor will reject any professed miracle or spiritual experience not supported by Scripture.

4. Same methods. Finally, the authentic Pentecostal pastor will employ the same methods used by the apostles and others in the book of Acts. These methods include Spirit-anointed proclamation of the gospel producing deep conviction, faith, and repentance (cf. Acts 2:14-41; 8:13). The Pentecostal pastor further expects God to confirm the word with signs, including miracles of speech, healing, and deliverance (cf. 5:12-16; 10:44-47; 14:6-10).[2]

In addition, the authentic Pentecostal pastor expects the Holy Spirit to guide them in the mission (cf. Acts 8:29; 10:9-20; 16:6-10). This guidance can come through inner impressions (cf. 8:29; 10:19), dreams (cf. 2:17; 16:9), and visions (cf. 9:10-16; 10:9-20). The principal evangelistic method used by the apostles in the book of Acts was planting Spirit-empowered missionary churches that would reach out to the surrounding area with the message of Christ.[3]

WALKS WITH THE SPIRIT

Not only must the Pentecostal pastor understand who the Spirit is, and how He works, he or she must learn to live under the Spirit's direction. Paul challenged the new believers in Galatia, "After beginning by means of the Spirit, are you now trying to finish by means of the flesh?" (Gal. 3:3). He was reminding them how they had begun their Christian walk. They had begun by being born of the Spirit and filled with the Spirit. Now, they were to "keep in step with the Spirit" (5:25). This must be the sincere aim of every Pentecostal pastor in Africa.

---

[2] For more on these topics, see Chapter 16: "Spirit-anointed Preaching" and Chapter 21: "Ministering in the Spirit's Power."

[3] For more on planting Spirit-empowered missionary churches, see Chapter 39: "Planting New Churches."

Part 1: The Qualifications of the Pentecostal Pastor

Two important ways you can do this is by praying in the Spirit and by cultivating the fruit of the Spirit, as follows:

Prayer in the Spirit

The Bible speaks of many kinds of prayer, including intercession, petition, confession, supplication, worship, thanksgiving, and more. Prayer in the Spirit, however, is especially suited to sustaining the Spirit-filled walk. Paul speaks of this kind of prayer in Ephesians 6:18. Further, in Romans 8:26, he describes how prayer in the Spirit works: "The Spirit helps us in our weakness. We do not know what we ought to pray for, but the Spirit himself intercedes for us through wordless groans." While prayer in the Spirit can be any prayer that is Spirit-initiated, Spirit-anointed, and Spirit-directed, it is more often prayer in tongues (1 Cor. 14:14-15). As a wise Pentecostal pastor, you should make frequent use of this powerful spiritual weapon (2 Cor. 10:4-5).[4]

Fruit of the Spirit

Another important way you can strengthen your spiritual walk is to cultivate the fruit of the Spirit. Paul identifies this fruit as "love, joy, peace, forbearance, kindness, goodness, faithfulness, gentleness and self-control" (Gal. 5:22-23).

As a Pentecostal pastor, not only must you know Jesus' power, your life must reflect His character. Gifts without fruit become "a resounding gong or a clanging cymbal" (1 Cor. 13:1). Many who cannot be won to Christ through demonstrations of power can be persuaded by acts of love. You can develop spiritual fruit in your life by walking in the Spirit (Gal. 5:16) and by abiding in Christ (John 15:4).

MINISTERS IN THE SPIRIT

Jesus testified, "The Spirit of the Lord is on me, because he has anointed me to proclaim good news" (Luke 4:18). Following his

---

[4] For more on the Pentecostal pastor's prayer life, see Chapter 8: "The Priority of Prayer."

Chapter 2: A Person of the Spirit

Lord's example, Paul described his own ministry as a "demonstration of the Spirit's power" (1 Cor. 2:4). In like manner, you, as a Pentecostal pastor, must commit yourself to carrying out your ministry in the power of the Holy Spirit. Like Paul, you must strive to become a competent minister of the Spirit (2 Cor. 3:6).

As such, you should be ever conscious of the Spirit's working (or failure to work) in your life and ministry, and among the people you lead. You must firmly reject any empty religious form devoid of the Spirit's power and presence (2 Tim. 3:5), and you must strongly contend for genuine Pentecostal doctrine, experience, and practice (cf. Jude 1:3).[5] Three ways you can do this is by pursuing the Spirit's anointing, by seeking the Spirit's guidance, and by contending for the Spirit's gifts, as follows:

Pursuing the Spirit's Anointing

As a true Pentecostal pastor, you must eagerly pursue the Spirit's anointing. You must seek to always preach, teach, and minister under the manifest presence of God. That is, you must pray and yield yourself to the Spirit, expecting Him to rest on your life, enabling you to minister with increased power and authority. The anointing of the Spirit will convince even the hardest of hearts, causing them to turn to God and proclaim, "Jesus is Lord!"

Seeking the Spirit's Guidance

Further, you must trust the Spirit of the Lord to guide you in ministry. This was the practice of Jesus and the apostles. The wise Pentecostal pastor understands that the Holy Spirit is truly the director of God's mission. He alone understands the needs and priorities of the mission.

The Spirit directed Philip to the Ethiopian eunuch (Acts 8:26-38), Peter to the household of Cornelius (10:9-25), and Paul and his missionary team into Western Europe (16:6-40). He will do the same for

---

[5] You can read more about Spirit-empowered ministry in Chapter 21: "Ministry in the Spirit's Power."

Part 1: The Qualifications of the Pentecostal Pastor

us today. If we will remain open and attuned to His voice, the Spirit of the Lord will guide us in our work for Christ.

Contending for the Spirit's Gifts

Paul urged the Corinthian believers to "eagerly desire gifts of the Spirit" (1 Cor. 14:1). As a faithful Pentecostal pastor, you must heed the apostle's instruction by cultivating the operation of spiritual gifts in your own life and in the life of the church you pastor. It is through these gifts that the anointing received at Spirit baptism is released in ministry. Paul discusses the working of the gifts in 1 Corinthians 12-14. Luke does the same in the book of Acts. Paul focuses on the operation of gifts in the church gathered for worship (1 Cor. 14:23-26), while Luke shows how the gifts function in frontline evangelism and church planting.[6]

In his last message to Timothy, Paul urged his son in the faith to "fan into flame the gift of God" which was in him through the laying on of the apostle's hands (2 Tim. 1:6). He was urging Timothy to be a man of the Spirit. Every Pentecostal pastor in Africa would do well to follow Paul's counsel to Timothy. They must closely guard the "good deposit" of the Holy Spirit entrusted to them (2 Tim. 1:14). In doing this, they must ensure that they remain full of the Holy Spirit and committed to God's mission. And they must strive to discharge their ministries in the power and anointing of the Holy Spirit.

---

[6] The gifts of the Spirit are discussed further in Chapter 19: "Ministering in the Spirit's Power." They are listed and defined in Appendix 2: "The Manifestation Gifts of 1 Corinthians 12:8-10."

Chapter 2: A Person of the Spirit

~ Chapter 3 ~

A Person of Good Character

"PROPHET ARRESTED FOR IMPREGNATING YOUNG GIRLS." This disturbing headline appeared prominently in a Southern Africa newspaper. The article went on to tell how several young girls, some as young as fourteen years old, had been impregnated by a well-known "Christian prophet." The girls had gone together to the authorities to report the preacher's illicit behavior. Sadly, as with scandals past, the church was shamed, the work of God stained, and the name of Christ dishonored.

However, it is not such openly scandalous sins that most hinder the progress of the church; it is the small hidden ones. Achan sinned in secret, but his sin affected the entire congregation (Josh. 7:1-12). In similar manner, a pastor's secret transgressions can affect an entire congregation. Because of their lack of character, many otherwise anointed servants of God have brought shame on the work of God and disqualified themselves from ministry.

Good character is the foundation on which an authentic Pentecostal ministry is built. Without this foundation, all else will eventually teeter and fall. An enduring ministry can never be built on talent, charm, social status, educational achievement, or even charismatic anointing. It must be built solidly on the foundation of character. Above all else, the people of God must be able to trust their pastor.

THE IMPORTANCE OF CHARACTER

The Pentecostal pastor must be a man or woman of high character. Paul wrote to Timothy, who was serving as pastor of the church in Ephesus, urging him to live an exemplary life:

> "An overseer must be above reproach, the husband of one wife, sober-minded, self-controlled, respectable, hospitable, able to teach, not a drunkard, not violent but gentle, not quarrelsome, not a lover of money." (1 Tim. 3:2-3)

Paul also exhorted Titus concerning a pastor's character:

> "An overseer, as God's steward, must be above reproach. He must not be arrogant or quick-tempered or a drunkard or violent or greedy for gain, but hospitable, a lover of good, self-controlled, upright, holy, and disciplined." (Titus 1:7-8)

Notice how, in both lists, Paul primarily addresses issues of character rather than competence. While competence is important for the Pentecostal pastor, character is of supreme importance.

THE MEANING OF CHARACTER

What then is meant by the word character? Character speaks of one's moral compass. It is the person we are on the inside. For the Christian, character is Christlikeness. Character determines how a person acts (or reacts) when pressed. It is who we are when no one else is watching. Another word for character is integrity. Integrity speaks of moral soundness or wholeness.

As Pentecostal pastors, we should be more concerned with our character than with our reputation. This is because our reputation is what others think we are, while our character is what we really are. Remember God's warning to Samuel when he was tempted to anoint David's older brother as king over Israel. The prophet said, "People

Part 1: The Qualifications of the Pentecostal Pastor

look at the outward appearance, but the Lord looks at the heart" (1 Sam. 16:7). Samuel ultimately anointed David as king because he was a man who sought to please God (1 Sam. 13:14; Acts 13:22).

Godly character manifests itself in three critical areas in the life and actions of the Pentecostal pastor, as follows:

Truthfulness

The true Pentecostal pastor chooses to follow in the footsteps of Jesus, who "committed no sin, and no deceit was found in his mouth" (1 Pet. 2:22). He or she is truthful in all of their communications with others. Put another way, the faithful Pentecostal pastor refuses to lie—even when telling a lie seems to be the most painless way out of a difficult situation. Paul exhorted the Ephesian Christians to "put off falsehood and speak truthfully" (Eph. 4:25).

As a Pentecostal pastor, you must strive to have such a reputation in the community that whenever you speak, people know they are hearing the truth. If they cannot believe you when you speak in the marketplace, how can they believe you when you speak from the pulpit? You must be known as someone who always "[speaks] the truth in love" (Eph. 4:15).

Financial Honesty

As a faithful Pentecostal pastor, you must be truthful in all of your communications, and you must be completely honest in all of your financial dealings. This includes your financial dealings with God, with the church, and with those outside the church. You do this because you know that God is watching. And, above all else, you want to please Him. Therefore, you refuse to rob God of your tithes and offerings (Mal. 3:8).

Some pastors demand that their church members pay tithes to the church, while they refuse to do so themselves. In doing this, they not only rob God, they reveal the deceitfulness of their own hearts. If you are such a person, repent and do what you know to be right (cf. Acts 26:20).

Further, you must be honorable in your handling of church funds. The fact that you are a pastor does not give you the right to use church monies as you please. You must diligently safeguard all offerings received by the church. And you must ensure that all funds are used only for the purpose for which they were given. For example, you must not use money given to missions to purchase a car, or money given for evangelism to repair the church building. Even worse, you must never take money given to help the poor, and like Judas, who pilfered from the moneybag, use it for your own benefit (cf. John 12:6).

In addition, as a faithful Pentecostal pastor, you must be honest in your financial dealings with those outside the church. You must be known as a person of the highest integrity. You must never steal, cheat others, or fail to promptly pay back any money you have borrowed. To do otherwise will bring disrepute on the church and cause people to turn from the message of Christ.

Sexual Purity

As a Pentecostal pastor, not only must you be truthful in your communications, and honest in your financial dealings, you must, at all times, behave honorably with those of the opposite sex. You must be faithful to your marriage vows and "reject every kind of evil" (1 Thess. 5:22).

You must treat "older women as mothers, and younger women as sisters, with absolute purity" (1 Tim. 5:2). In doing this, you must ensure that you are never alone with a woman other than your wife. You must also guard against emotional bonding with any woman other than your wife through careless conversation or activity. The same, of course, applies to women pastors in their dealings with men.

As a servant of Christ, you will thus take seriously the admonition of Paul: "But among you there must not be even a hint of sexual immorality, or of any kind of impurity, or of greed, because these are improper for God's holy people" (Eph. 5:3).

Part 1: The Qualifications of the Pentecostal Pastor

OTHER NEEDED CHARACTER TRAITS

As God's representative, you should seek to cultivate other godly character traits as well. Five qualities that deserve mentioning are courage, dependability, humility, compassion, and generosity, as follows:

Courage

Courage is the moral strength to do what is right even in the face of threat, difficulty, or danger. It is the boldness to take a risk, to stand firm for what is good, and to trust God when there seems to be no way forward. Nelson Mandela wrote in his autobiography, "I learned that courage was not the absence of fear, but the triumph over it. The brave man is not he who does not feel afraid, but he who conquers that fear."

Courage is the opposite of cowardice. Cowardice is the child of inflated self-concern; courage is born of concern for others. Cowardice short-circuits one's ability to do or say what is right; courage emboldens one to remain true in the face of danger. Moses was courageous when he stood before Pharaoh demanding that the Egyptian king free God's people (Exod. 5:7). Jesus was courageous when He humbly submitted to the shame and agony of the cross (Heb. 12:2). And Stephen was courageous when he told the Jewish leaders that they had murdered their Messiah (Acts 7:51-52).

If we will yield to the indwelling Holy Spirit, He will give us the courage we need to stand for Christ and declare His name to all. When threatened, Peter and John prayed, "Now, Lord, consider their threats and enable your servants to speak your word with great boldness." In response to their prayer, God filled them with the Spirit, and they "spoke the word of God boldly" (Acts 4:29-31). As a Pentecostal pastor, you too must seek to remain full of the Spirit and dependent on God to give you the courage you need to faithfully fulfill your calling.

Dependability

Further, as a steward, or manager, of Christ's Church, you must be dependable. The Lord must be able to place His full trust in you

(Titus 1:7; 1 Pet. 4:10). Paul wrote, "It is required that those who have been given a trust must prove faithful" (1 Cor. 4:2). Your life must therefore exhibit such character traits as dependability, punctuality, diligence, and perseverance. Such behaviors are fruits of the Spirit-filled walk (Gal. 5:22).

Paul exhorted the Ephesian elders, "Keep watch over yourselves and all the flock of which the Holy Spirit has made you overseers. Be shepherds of the church of God, which he bought with his own blood" (Acts 20:28). As pastors, the Lord has entrusted us with the very souls of men and women. And one day we will give account to God concerning our faithfulness in this matter (Heb. 13:17). James solemnly warns, "Not many of you should become teachers, my fellow believers, because you know that we who teach will be judged more strictly" (James 3:1).

Humility

As an imitator of Christ, the Pentecostal pastor must be humble (Eph. 5:1). Jesus told His disciples, "Whoever wants to become great among you must be your servant, and whoever wants to be first must be your slave—just as the Son of Man did not come to be served, but to serve, and to give his life as a ransom for many" (Matt. 20:26-28).

How disturbing to observe a Pentecostal pastor filled with pride and self-interest, demanding to be served by others rather than serving them. Such an attitude is the very opposite of the humility displayed by our Lord. Paul wrote to the Philippian Christians, "In your relationships with one another, have the same mindset as Christ Jesus: Who, being in very nature God, did not consider equality with God something to be used to his own advantage; rather, he made himself nothing by taking the very nature of a servant, being made in human likeness. And being found in appearance as a man, he humbled himself by becoming obedient to death—even death on a cross!" (Phil. 2:5-8). The arrogant chieftain demands to be served; the godly pastor delights in humbly serving others.

Part 1: The Qualifications of the Pentecostal Pastor

Compassion

As a true Pentecostal pastor, you must be a person of compassion. Compassion is love in action. It manifests itself in concern for those in need. It is an outward expression of a heart filled with God's love. The Bible says about Jesus, "When he saw the crowds, he had compassion on them, because they were harassed and helpless, like sheep without a shepherd" (Matt. 9:36).

Jesus' compassion moved Him to care for the spiritual and physical needs of others. As shepherds of God's flock, we too must exhibit loving concern for His people, and for those who do not know Christ. Compassion will cause us to care for others in their time of need, and it will move us to proclaim the gospel to all.

As men and women of God, our ongoing walk with the Spirit should motivate us to love and care for others. Paul explained, "God's love has been poured out into our hearts through the Holy Spirit, who has been given to us" (Rom. 5:5). Of all people, we who claim to be full of Christ's Spirit should demonstrate Christ's compassion toward others.

Generosity

A final essential character trait for an authentic Pentecostal pastor is generosity. As a result of being filled with the Spirit at Pentecost, the first believers were possessed by a spirit of generosity. The Bible says about them, "All the believers were together and had everything in common. They sold property and possessions to give to anyone who had need" (Acts 2:44-45). In like manner, as a Spirit-filled pastor, you must be quick to share what you have with others. You must be openhanded with God, the church, and with those in need.

When sending out the Twelve, Jesus exhorted them, "Heal the sick, raise the dead, cleanse those who have leprosy, drive out demons. Freely you have received; freely give" (Matt. 10:8). Such generosity is contagious. As the people see their pastor's liberality, they too will be encouraged to open their hearts and their purses and be generous. This culture of generosity will powerfully impact the

BUILDING CHARACTER

The question arises: How can a Pentecostal pastor develop the godly character described above? We do this by following the example of Jesus. He is our model for life and ministry. John wrote, "Whoever claims to live in him must walk as Jesus did" (1 John 2:6).

In the words of Paul, we are to "clothe ourselves with Christ" (cf. Col. 3:12-17; Rom. 13:14). When Jesus ordered His disciples, "Follow me" (Mark 4:19), He was telling them to watch Him and pattern their lives after His. As they did this, they would be transformed into His image (Rom. 8:29; 2 Cor. 3:18). Gradually, their lives would become like His. By the Spirit's power, they would begin to live as He lived, think as He thought, and love as He loved (2 Pet. 1:3-4). If you want to be an authentic Pentecostal pastor, resolve to become like Jesus.

As the Twelve followed Jesus, they became more than they were before. Before, they were mere fishermen. However, as they followed Him, they became fishers of men, just like their Master. In other words, they took on the character of Jesus. Bible scholars sometimes call this process spiritual formation.

We must not suppose, however, that we can achieve a Christ-like character through self-effort or will power. We must have God's help. We can acquire His help by practicing three spiritual disciplines:

Abiding in Christ

First, we can acquire Christ's aid in developing a godly character by abiding, or remaining, in Him. Only through abiding in Christ can we become like Him. Jesus said, "No branch can bear fruit by itself; it must remain in the vine. Neither can you bear fruit unless you remain in me" (John 15:4). To remain in Christ is to draw life from Him by continuing in His Word and in His presence. We do this through committed prayer, regular contemplative Bible study, and by fully trusting Him to provide for all of our needs.

Drawing Near to God

We further develop the character of Christ by daily drawing near to Him. James assures us, "Come near to God and he will come near to you" (James 4:8). Just as with abiding in Christ, we draw near to God through prayer, worship, and faithful service. As we draw near to Christ, we are changed into His likeness. Paul wrote, "We all, who with unveiled faces contemplate the Lord's glory, are being transformed into his image with ever-increasing glory, which comes from the Lord, who is the Spirit" (2 Cor. 3:18).

Walking in the Spirit

Finally, we develop the character of Christ by walking in the Spirit. To walk in the Spirit is to live one's life in submission to the Holy Spirit. It is to obey His commands. Paul said that we are "sanctified by the Holy Spirit" (Rom. 15:16). This means that the Spirit of God gives us the power we need to live like Jesus. Paul encouraged the Galatian Christians, "Walk by the Spirit, and you will not gratify the desires of the flesh" (Gal. 5:16).

Solomon wrote, "Though it cost all you have, get understanding. Cherish her, and she will exalt you; embrace her, and she will honor you" (Prov. 4:7-8). Much the same can be said to the Pentecostal pastor. Though it costs you all you have, get character; cherish it, and it will exalt you; embrace it, and it will bring you honor. Above all else, the Pentecostal pastor must be a man or woman of character.

Chapter 3: A Person of Good Character

~ Chapter 4 ~

A Person Who Is Well Prepared

As with any organization, the church should be led by those who are well prepared for the task. An internationally known evangelist once said, "If I knew I had only three years to preach the gospel, I would spend the first two in preparation." A successful pastor wisely observed, "Success occurs when opportunity meets preparation." Both men were emphasizing the importance of preparation in gospel ministry.

Paul wrote to Timothy, whom he had appointed as pastor of the church in Ephesus, "Whoever aspires to be an overseer [pastor] desires a noble task" (1 Tim. 3:1). Paul then cited several preconditions for serving in the role of pastor. One of those conditions was, "He must not be a recent convert" (v. 6).

The Greek word translated "recent convert" in this passage is *neophytos,* which literally means "newly planted" or "one who is a

Chapter 4: A Person Who is Well Prepared

beginner." This is in contrast to another designation Paul uses for pastor, that is, "elder," or *presbyteros* in Greek. This word speaks of experience and maturity, and it implies preparation (1 Tim. 5:17-19; Titus 1:5). Paul is saying that a pastor must not be a novice in his or her walk with Christ. On the contrary, he or she must be a person who is mature in the faith and well prepared for the work of ministry.

A young Pentecostal preacher once told the principal of a Bible school, "I don't need training; all I need is to be empowered by the Spirit like the disciples on the Day of Pentecost." This, however, is a foolish statement. What the young preacher failed to realize is that, before the Day of Pentecost, the twelve disciples had spent three years with Jesus learning from Him. While the young minister was right in his assessment of the need to be empowered by the Holy Spirit, he was wrong in his view of the necessity of spiritual, intellectual, and practical preparation for ministry.

Jesus chose His twelve disciples "that they might be with him and that he might send them out to preach" (Mark 3:14). Before He commissioned them to go into all the world and preach the gospel, He spent countless hours with them preparing them for the task.

This chapter discusses the importance of the Pentecostal pastor being well prepared. It identifies some areas in which preparation is needed. It then talks about how the Pentecostal pastor can acquire and maintain the needed preparation.

AREAS OF PREPARATION

Pastoral preparation allows the aspiring minister to develop the essential skills and attitudes needed to successfully fulfill their calling. It can be thought of as the pastor's toolbox or survival kit. Adequate preparation will not only equip you to do your job effectively, it will protect you from failure during times of stress or peril. As a Pentecostal pastor, you must be well prepared in at least five ways:

Part 1: The Qualifications of the Pentecostal Pastor

Spiritually Prepared

Above all else, as a Pentecostal pastor, you must be spiritually prepared for the job. For how can you effectively communicate God's grace to others if you have never experienced His grace yourself? Therefore, to be a Pentecostal pastor, you must have been truly born again (John 3:3-7) and genuinely filled with the Holy Spirit (Acts 1:8; Eph. 5:18). Further, you must be faithfully living a Christ-honoring life (1 John 2:6), and fully committed to Christ and His mission (Matt. 16:24).

Paul reminded Timothy that "physical training is of some value, but godliness has value for all things" (1 Tim. 4:8). Paul used this training metaphor to illustrate the spiritual discipline required in preparing for pastoral ministry (cf. 1 Cor. 9:24-27). He was saying to Timothy that, just as an athlete must train well to prepare himself or herself for a race, the pastor must spiritually prepare himself or herself for the work of ministry. The footballer who refuses to train will disqualify himself from the team. In like manner, the pastor who refuses to exercise spiritual discipline will exclude himself or herself from ministry.

Biblically Prepared

Secondly, to be an effective Pentecostal pastor, you must be biblically prepared. That is, you must have a thorough understanding of Scripture. A chief duty of any pastor is to feed the flock of God by faithfully teaching them God's Word. Effective biblical instruction will cause the saints to mature in Christ (1 Pet. 2:2), arm them against false teachers (Acts 20:28-29), and equip them for Christian service (Eph. 4:11-12). No wonder Paul twice told Timothy that a pastor must be "able to teach" (1 Tim. 3:2; 2 Tim. 2:24). An effective teaching ministry can only be built on a foundation of broad biblical knowledge. To properly teach God's people, you must know how to correctly interpret and apply "the word of truth" (2 Tim. 2:15).

Chapter 4: A Person Who is Well Prepared

Morally Prepared

Next, as a Pentecostal pastor, you must be morally prepared for ministry. You must live a holy, Christ-honoring life. Paul wrote that an overseer, or pastor, "must be blameless,...not given to drunkenness, not violent, not pursuing dishonest gain" (Titus 1:7). He added that a pastor must be "upright, holy, and disciplined" (v. 8). In similar manner, he told Timothy that an overseer must "be above reproach, faithful to his wife,...not a lover of money" (1 Tim. 3:2). Anyone who has not gained victory in these areas of life has disqualified himself or herself from ministry. That person must immediately withdraw themselves from ministry until he or she has gained victory over these moral vices.

As a Pentecostal pastor, you must vigilantly guard against three great sins that have ensnared and disqualified so many religious leaders. Those three great vices are greed (the love of money), lust (illicit desire), and worldly ambition (the need to be admired by and to control others). No amount of charisma or anointing can make up for failure in these areas.

In Paul's letter to the Galatian believers, he warned them against yielding to the desires of the sinful nature (Gal. 5:19-21). They should rather cultivate the fruit of the Spirit (vv. 22-23). Paul then revealed to them the pathway from moral defeat to moral victory: "Those who belong to Christ Jesus have crucified the flesh with its passions and desires. Since we live by the Spirit, let us keep in step with the Spirit" (vv. 24-25). The apostle further exhorted the Galatians, "Walk by the Spirit, and you will not gratify the desires of the flesh" (v. 16).

Intellectually and Emotionally Prepared

Finally, to effectively carry out your ministry you must be intellectually and emotionally prepared for the job. In other words, you must be able to think rationally, and you must be able to control your emotions and respond appropriately to the challenges you encounter.

Paul wrote to Titus, "Since an overseer manages God's household, he must be blameless—not overbearing, not quick-tempered,... not violent.... Rather, he must be...self-controlled...and disciplined"

Part 1: The Qualifications of the Pentecostal Pastor

(Titus 1:7-8). In his first letter to Timothy, the apostle added, "The overseer is to be...temperate, self-controlled,...not violent but gentle, not quarrelsome" (1 Tim. 3:2). Note how each of the above selected character traits speak of intellectual and emotional maturity. As a Pentecostal pastor, you must strive to cultivate these traits in your own life and ministry.

A pastor who is intellectually astute and emotionally mature will exhibit confidence in exercising his or her God-given gifts and abilities. This confidence will aid them in responding to difficult situations and making important decisions. It will further protect them from shirking difficult responsibilities such as announcing bad news, defending the church from false teachers, and other difficult tasks.

MEANS OF PREPARATION

Knowing the value of good preparation, the wise Pentecostal pastor will make every effort to prepare himself or herself for ministry. Let's look at three ways you can accomplish this:

Through Practical Experience

First, you can prepare yourself for ministry by seeking practical experience. Three useful ways to gain experience are as follows:

1. Working in a local church. The local assembly is the natural place to begin your ministry. Paul and Barnabas were involved in ministry in the church in Antioch when the Holy Spirit directed them into missionary service (Acts 11:25-26; 13:1-3). Paul further recruited many of his missionary associates from those active in local churches. For example, he recruited Timothy from the church in Lystra (16:1-2), Sopater from Berea, Aristarchus and Secundus from Thessalonica, and Gaius from Derbe (20:4). These men learned how to minister in their local churches. Once they had proved themselves, they were chosen for broader ministry.

Therefore, as an aspiring Pentecostal pastor, you should seek opportunities to serve in your home church. You should be ready to volunteer when opportunities for service arise. By participating in the

Chapter 4: A Person Who is Well Prepared

ministries of the local assembly, you will gain valuable experience, your spiritual gifts will be revealed, your character will be strengthened, and your calling to broader ministry will be confirmed.

2. Serving under an experienced pastor. Another effective form of preparation for Pentecostal ministry is mentorship training. Mentorship training occurs when a novice preacher walks alongside a veteran pastor and learns from him or her. This is the way Jesus trained His disciples (Mark 3:14-15). He told them, "Come, follow me...and I will send you out to fish for people" (Mark 1:17). As they walked and ministered with Jesus, they learned to minister as He ministered. He explained, "Everyone who is fully trained will be like their teacher" (Luke 6:40).

Other biblical examples of mentorship training are Moses and Joshua (Exod. 24:12-13), Eli and Samuel (1 Sam. 2:11), Elijah and Elisha (1 Kings 19:19-21), and Paul and his missionary associates—including Timothy, Titus, Luke, and others. Serving under an experienced pastor will allow you to gain insight into church life and to learn about pastoral work.

3. Partnering with others. You can also gain invaluable experience by partnering with others in ministry teams. These teams can include intercessory prayer teams, evangelism teams, church planting teams, and others. One benefit of working with others in teams is that it will help you to learn how to work in harmony with your co-laborers in ministry.

Through Non-formal Learning

Another way you can prepare yourself for ministry is through "non-formal learning." Non-formal learning is learning that occurs outside of a structured classroom environment. While non-formal learning is unstructured, it should not be thought of as being careless or haphazard. It can be deliberate and effective. Non-formal learning can include personal Bible study, reading books and articles, attending conferences, and learning by extension, as follows:

1. Personal Bible study. One valuable means of non-formal training is personal Bible study. Reading the Bible through each year is a

Part 1: The Qualifications of the Pentecostal Pastor

worthwhile practice. It can help familiarize you with the overall flow of Scripture. Another valuable way to read the Bible is by repeatedly reading a particular book of the Bible. One Bible scholar said, "The secret to knowing the Bible is not reading it but *rereading* it." As you read a book several times, you will gain greater insight into the many truths taught therein.

Beyond mere Bible reading, you will want to develop the habit of systematic Bible study. If possible, you should acquire a good study Bible containing maps, book outlines and introductions, text commentary, articles, and charts.[1]

2. Reading books and articles. Another valuable means of non-formal training available to every Pentecostal pastor is the thoughtful reading of selected books and articles. Someone has rightly noted, "Leaders are readers." You should therefore become an avid reader. Daily reading will help to stimulate your brain, expand your mind, and enhance your thinking skills. It will also give you new insights into the challenges of life and ministry. Further, the reading habit will help you to increase your vocabulary, thus enhancing your speaking ability.

You must, however, exercise care in your choice of reading materials. Many books and articles available in Africa today promote unscriptural concepts and bogus practices (cf. 1 Tim. 4:7; 2 John 1:7-8). You should shun such reading materials.

3. Attending conferences and seminars. You can further develop your ministry skills by attending pastors' conferences and seminars. These meetings are often planned to help pastors improve their ministerial skills. They further serve to inspire discouraged pastors and help them to gain new insights into Scripture and church work. Seminars also inform pastors of denominational initiatives, and they help develop a needed sense of teamwork among colleagues in ministry.

---

[1] An excellent Pentecostal study Bible is the *Full Life Study Bible,* also known as the *Life in the Spirit Study Bible,* or the "Fire Bible." This Bible has been translated into a number of languages.

Chapter 4: A Person Who is Well Prepared

Through Formal Training

Finally, if at all possible, as an aspiring Pentecostal pastor, you should get formal training. Formal training is training offered through resident and non-resident schools and institutions. Opportunities for formal training include the following:

1. Secular education. Primary, secondary, and possibly post-secondary education is crucial for the Pentecostal pastor in Africa. These institutions help prepare students for life in the modern world. In them, the students learn to read, write, and do arithmetic. There, they learn about history, geography, and other important subjects. For the aspiring Pentecostal pastor, the benefit of school studies is immense. They help to arouse their curiosity, broaden their thinking, and make them aware of current trends in society.

2. Bible institutes and colleges. It is further crucial that, if possible, you should study at a reputable Bible institute or college. How foolish an aspiring medical doctor would be to discount formal medical training! In the same way, the one who aims to be a Pentecostal pastor would be foolish to dismiss formal ministerial training. Many national churches require their pastors to attend a Bible school. Whether or not the church requires such study, the wise Pentecostal pastor will pursue formal ministerial training.

3. Extension studies. Some Bible schools offer extension and correspondence courses. These courses may be delivered in person, by mail, or through the internet. They allow the pastor to study while remaining at home and engaged in ministry. They are an excellent way for a pastor to enhance his or her knowledge and skills.

At present, Assemblies of God churches throughout Africa operate more than 300 ministerial training institutions. These schools offer training to both Assemblies of God and non-Assemblies of God students. The local Assemblies of God pastor in your area can help you locate the school (or schools) in your country.

4. Graduate studies. Some Pentecostal ministers in Africa will want to pursue graduate or seminary studies. This is especially true for those teaching in Bible colleges and seminaries. It is essential,

Part 1: The Qualifications of the Pentecostal Pastor

however, that one pursue graduate studies in an accredited Pentecostal seminary. A number of Assemblies of God national churches in Africa operate Master's level schools. Doctoral studies are offered through Pan-Africa Theological Seminary (PAThS). PAThS is a fully accredited seminary, operated by the Assemblies of God in Lomé, Togo, with extensions in other African countries. Studies are offered in English and French.

ONGOING PREPARATION

In truth, as a Pentecostal pastor, your preparation for ministry never ends. You must become a lifelong learner. Your life must be characterized by a continual quest for excellence. Paul testified to this quest in his own life when he wrote, "Not that I have already obtained all this, or have already arrived at my goal, but I press on to take hold of that for which Christ Jesus took hold of me" (Phi. 3:12).

This quest for excellence must continue throughout your life. You must continue to prepare yourself *spiritually* by seeking to remain full of the Holy Spirit and through the practice of the spiritual disciplines of prayer, fasting, worship, and Scripture meditation.[2] You should further continue to prepare yourself *biblically* through a disciplined study of Scripture, and if the Spirit directs, through a pursuit of advanced training.[3]

Further, you must continually seek to improve yourself *morally*. In the words of Solomon, you must diligently guard your heart from evil, giving careful thought to the path of your feet (Pro. 4:23-27).[4]

Finally, as a wise Pentecostal pastor, you must continue to prepare yourself *intellectually* and *emotionally*. You can do this through disciplined reading and study, and by allowing the Spirit and the

---

[2] For more on spiritual preparation, see Chapter 15: "A Strong Devotional Habit."

[3] For more on the Pentecostal pastor's relationship to the Bible, see Chapter 9: "Believes the Bible."

[4] For more on moral preparation, see Chapter 3: "A Person of Character."

Chapter 4: A Person Who is Well Prepared

Word of God to work mightily in your life, shaping you into the image of Christ (2 Cor. 3:18).

~ Part 2 ~

The Priorities of the Pentecostal Pastor

~ Chapter 5 ~

Ministerial Priorities

A veteran pastor sat with a group of eager Bible school students. One student asked him, "Sir, how were you able to build such a strong church? And to what do you attribute your success in ministry?" His answer surprised the students. "To do the best," he said, "you must give up the good." Seeing the puzzled looks on the students' faces, he explained, "In life, there are many good things you can do. The world will place many demands on you. Your church members and elders will have expectations of you. Other pastors will do certain things, and they will expect you to do the same."

The veteran pastor continued, "All of these things may be good. But as a man or woman of God, you will need to ask Him, 'Lord, what do *You* want me to do?' Then, once you hear God's voice, you must do what He says. The other things may be good, but what God tells you to do is best. God will bring people into your church to help you do those other things. You, however, must always focus on doing what God has told you to do."

The veteran pastor was talking about establishing ministerial priorities. A priority is something of utmost importance. It is the thing one does before doing other less important things.

Chapter 5: Ministerial Priorities

BIBLICAL PRIORITIES

Jesus and His disciples were on their way from Judea to Galilee. Pausing on the road, Jesus told them, "I must go through Samaria" (John 4:4). This must have puzzled the disciples, because they would have to go out of their way to get there. When they arrived in the town of Sychar, they learned why Jesus had to go through Samaria. There were some lost people there who were ready to receive the message of salvation. And He wanted to teach His disciples a lesson on reaping the harvest.

On another occasion, Jesus told His disciples, "I will build my church" (Matt. 16:18). He later commanded them, "Go and make disciples of all nations" (Matt. 28:19). In each of these instances, Jesus was speaking of priorities that He had set for himself and for them.

Following the example of their Lord, the apostles also established ministerial priorities. Their priorities were to do the work Christ had given them. One day, a group of church members came to the apostles with a complaint. Their widows were being neglected in the daily distribution of food, and they wanted the apostles to take care of the problem. The apostles, however, had already established their priorities, so they answered the people, "It would not be right for us to neglect the ministry of the word of God in order to wait on tables" (Acts 6:2).

While caring for the neglected widows was a good and necessary thing, it was not what Christ had commanded His apostles to do. So they asked the church to select deacons to take care of this need while they prioritized prayer and preaching. As a result, "the word of God spread. The number of disciples in Jerusalem increased rapidly, and a large number of priests became obedient to the faith" (v. 7).

This chapter will address the important issue of ministerial priorities for the Pentecostal pastor in Africa today.

DETERMINING MINISTERIAL PRIORITIES

What priorities should a Pentecostal pastor have? While there are many good things he or she *could* do, there are a few things they *must*

Part 2: The Priorities of the Pentecostal Pastor

do. Seven of these priorities are (1) serving God's mission, (2) fulfilling God's call, (3) reaching the lost, (4) proclaiming God's Word, (5) praying, (6) upholding Pentecostal values, and (7) equipping God's people for ministry. Let's look more closely at each of these ministerial priorities:

Serving God's Mission

First, the Pentecostal pastor must prioritize serving God's mission. After His wilderness temptation, Jesus returned to Galilee. There, He entered the synagogue in Nazareth and began to read from the scroll of Isaiah: "The Spirit of the Lord is upon me, because he has anointed me to proclaim good news to the poor...to proclaim the year of the Lord's favor" (Luke 4:18-19). Jesus knew His Father's priorities for His life and ministry. He understood that the Father had sent Him to serve His mission. He had also sent His Son to give His life as a ransom for all people (Matt. 20:28).

Like Jesus, as a Pentecostal pastor, you must commit yourself to serving God's mission. Jesus told His disciples, "As the Father has sent me, I am sending you" (John 20:21). Just as God sent Jesus into the world to serve His mission, Jesus now sends you into the world to do the same. God's mission, sometimes referred to as the *missio Dei,* is to redeem and call unto himself a people from every tribe and language and nation on earth (Rev. 5:9).[1]

Fulfilling God's Call

Second, the Pentecostal pastor must prioritize fulfilling God's call on his or her life. Jesus never lost focus of what the Father had called Him to do. In His darkest hour, He prayed to His Father, "Not my will, but yours be done" (Luke 22:42). In the same way, the Pentecostal pastor in Africa must understand God's call on his or her life, and they must strive to fulfill that calling. God has marked out a path for each of His ministers to run. Every Pentecostal pastor m ·+ find

---

[1] For more on the Pentecostal pastor's role in fulfilling G
see Chapter 31: "Missional Leadership" and Chapter 40: "De'
sions Program in a Local Church."

Chapter 5: Ministerial Priorities

that path. And they must stay on that path until they finish their course (Heb. 12:1-2; 2 Tim. 4:7).

Reaching the Lost

Third, the Pentecostal pastor must prioritize reaching the lost. This was a priority for Jesus. He testified, "The Son of Man came to seek and to save the lost" (Luke 19:10). Reaching the lost must remain a priority for everyone who seeks to follow Christ. Jesus commanded, "Go into all the world and preach the gospel to all creation" (Mark 16:15).

This command of Christ will remain in force until He returns from heaven (Matt. 24:14). As a faithful Pentecostal pastor, you must lead the way in mobilizing the church for Spirit-empowered evangelism and missions. You can do this in two ways:

First, you must be an example to the church by actively sharing the gospel with others, seeking to lead them to the Lord. As your church members see you witnessing, they will be encouraged to witness too. Second, you must demonstrate your concern for the lost by giving generously to missions, and by fervently praying for the unreached tribes of Africa and beyond. You must mobilize the church to do the same. You must make evangelism and missions a top priority in the church's programming and budgeting.[2]

Preaching the Word

Fourth, the Pentecostal pastor must prioritize the proclamation of God's Word. Paul exhorted Timothy, his son in the faith, "Preach the word; be prepared in season and out of season; correct, rebuke and encourage—with great patience and careful instruction" (2 Tim. 4:2). Preaching the Word involves both proclaiming the gospel to the lost and instructing and encouraging believers in the ways of the Lord. Jesus commanded, "Go into all the world and preach the gospel" (Mark 16:15). He also commanded, "Feed my sheep" (John 21:17).

---

[2] For more on reaching the lost, see Chapter 37: "Evangelizing the ost."

Part 2: The Priorities of the Pentecostal Pastor

To preach well, you must be committed to correctly handling the Word of Truth (2 Tim. 2:15). To do this, you must become an eager student of God's Word.[3]

Praying

Fifth, the Pentecostal pastor must prioritize prayer. By living a life of committed prayer, you demonstrate your dependence on God. You are further following in the footsteps of Jesus and the apostles. The Bible says of Jesus that, during the days of His life on earth, "he offered up prayers and petitions with fervent cries and tears" (Heb. 5:7; cf. Mark 1:35; Luke 5:16). It says of the apostles that they were "constantly in prayer" (Acts 1:14; cf. 3:1; 6:2-4; 10:9).

Prayer not only changes the situation, it changes the one who is praying. The reformer, Martin Luther, understood the value of prayer. It is said of him that he once exclaimed, "I have so much to do today that I shall spend the first three hours in prayer!" In the same way, prayer must be a priority in the life of every Pentecostal pastor.[4]

Upholding Pentecostal Values

Sixth, the Pentecostal pastor must strive to uphold Pentecostal values in his or her ministry. Pentecostal values are those strongly held beliefs and commitments that define a person as an authentic Pentecostal believer. Three core values a Pentecostal pastor must uphold are a commitment to sound biblical doctrine, a strong allegiance to God and His mission, and an openness to the moving of God's Spirit.

This openness to the moving of God's Spirit includes an emphasis on seeing believers baptized in the Holy Spirit.[5] Both Jesus and

---

[3] For more on the Pentecostal pastor's preaching ministry, see Chapter 16: "Spirit-Anointed Preaching."

[4] For more on the Pentecostal pastor's prayer life, see Chapter 8: "The Priority of Prayer."

[5] For more on Pentecostal values, see Chapter 10: "Upholds Pentecostal Truth"; Chapter 11: "Promotes Pentecostal Experience and Practice"; and Chapter 12: "Appreciates Pentecostal Heritage."

Chapter 5: Ministerial Priorities

the apostles emphasized this need. Before returning to heaven, Jesus commanded His followers, "Do not leave Jerusalem, but wait for the gift my Father promised...in a few days you will be baptized with the Holy Spirit" (Acts 1:4-5; cf. Luke 24:49). Years later, when Paul met the twelve disciples in Ephesus, his first question to them was, "Did you receive the Holy Spirit when you believed?" (Acts 19:2).

Jesus and the apostles insisted that all believers be baptized in the Holy Spirit because they knew this experience would empower them to be Christ's witnesses "in Jerusalem, and in all Judea and Samaria, and to the ends of the earth" (Acts 1:8).

Equipping God's People

Finally, the Pentecostal pastor must prioritize training God's people for ministry. The wise Pentecostal pastor understands that one of his or her primary roles as pastor is to "equip [Christ's] people for works of service" (Eph. 4:12). This means that you as a pastor are to do more than care for the sheep, you are to develop God's people into useful members of the kingdom. You must therefore make the development of disciples a priority in ministry.[6]

PURSUING MINISTERIAL PRIORITIES

Having examined these seven biblical priorities for Pentecostal pastors, you must now decide whether you will adopt them as your own. It is one thing to read about these priorities in a book. It is quite another to allow God's Spirit to write them on the pages of your heart. For this to happen, you will need to commit to a process of turning these principles into priorities, and then turning those priorities into ministerial practices. Let's look at this process.

Establishing Priorities

You begin the process by recognizing that becoming a competent Pentecostal pastor requires effort. Ministerial competence is the end

---

[6] For more on developing God's people, see Chapter 16: "Effective Teaching" and Chapter 25: "Strengthening the Body."

Part 2: The Priorities of the Pentecostal Pastor

point of a long journey. And, as with any journey, this journey begins by choosing a destination. It continues by developing and executing a plan to arrive at that destination. To establish the above seven priorities in your own ministry, and into the ministries of your church, you will need to commit to the journey.

You can begin the journey by taking the seven ministerial priorities and recording them in a notebook. You can then use this list as a daily prayer guide. As you pray through this list each day, ask God to embed these biblical concepts into your spirit. If you will do this, a change will occur. The Holy Spirit will begin to write these priorities on the tablets of your heart. Rather than remaining theoretical concepts, in time, they will develop into ministerial priorities.

As you pray, ask yourself, "What are my present ministerial priorities?" Your present ministerial priorities are those practices in which you invest the most time and energy. List those priorities. Then ask, "How do these priorities align with the priorities of Jesus and the apostles? Now, based on your self-evaluation, ask yourself the following questions:

- How well am I doing in serving God's mission?
- How well am I doing in fulfilling God's call on my life and on the life of the church I lead?
- How well am I doing in reaching the lost in my locale and around the world?
- How well am I doing in preaching the Word of God?
- How effective is my personal prayer life and the prayer ministry of the church I lead?
- How well am I doing in promoting Pentecostal values in my church?
- How well am I doing in equipping God's people for ministry?

Write your answers in your notebook. Now ask yourself, "What must I do differently to better achieve each of these priorities in my life and ministry?" Again, write your answers in your notebook, and continue to pray over them each day.

Chapter 5: Ministerial Priorities

Implementing Priorities

Once you have embraced these ministerial priorities as your own, you should begin to implement them into your own ministry and into the ministries of the church. To do this you may want to use the following strategies:

1. Increase your understanding. You will need to increase your understanding of what the Bible teaches about each of these seven ministerial priorities. You can do this by searching the Scriptures and looking for insights on these topics. Jesus instructs us to "study the Scriptures diligently" in our search for truth (John 5:39). As you read, ask yourself, "What is the Spirit saying to me?" Write your new insights in your notebook. If possible, you will want to acquire and read good books on these topics.[7]

Another way to increase your understanding of these subjects is to preach and teach about them often. This strategy will not only increase your understanding of the topics, it will prepare your members for the next step, the implementation of these priorities into the life of the church.

2. Develop a plan. Next, you will want to develop a plan to implement these priorities into your own ministry and into the ministries of the church. To do this you will need to increase the church's understanding of each of the seven priorities. You can begin by answering the following questions:

- What must I do to guide my church to better serve God's mission?
- What must I do to better fulfill God's call on my life and on the church He has called me to lead?
- What must I do to lead the church into more effectively reaching the lost?
- What must I do to better preach and teach the Word of God in the church?

---

[7] An excellent book on the mission of God is *A Biblical Theology of Missions,* by Paul York, published by Africa's Hope Discovery Series.

Part 2: The Priorities of the Pentecostal Pastor

- What must I do to better promote prayer in the church?
- What must I do to lead the church into greater Pentecostal experience and practice?
- What must I do to better equip God's people for ministry?

Write you answers in your notebook and review them often.

3. Work your plan. You must now work your plan. This means that you will need to move forward to implement the strategies you have developed. As you move forward with your plan, you will want to constantly evaluate and reevaluate your progress. When necessary, make any needed adjustments to the plan.

Remember, you will not achieve success overnight. It will take time, and when difficulties come, you will need to persevere. If you will do this, in time, your church will begin to change. It will become the powerful church Christ intends for it to be. Let the apostle's words encourage you: "Let us not become weary in doing good, for at the proper time we will reap a harvest if we do not give up" (Gal. 6:9).

Every Pentecostal pastor in Africa must align his or her ministerial priorities with those of Jesus and the apostles. They must then allow these priorities to guide their ministries. While this process may be a struggle, it is worth the effort. Through devotion to Christ, commitment to God's will, and the quickening power of the Holy Spirit, the Pentecostal pastor can achieve his or her ministerial goals.

Chapter 5: Ministerial Priorities

~ Chapter 6 ~

Personal Priorities

"My mother's sons were angry with me and made me take care of the vineyards; my own vineyard I had to neglect" (Song 1:6). These are the sad words of the Shulamite maiden. She had been so busy taking care of the fields of others that she had not tended to her own. She, however, was not talking about physical vineyards; she was talking about her life. She had invested so much time in others that her own life had become overgrown with weeds.

Sadly, this same condition could describe the lives of many Pentecostal pastors in Africa today. They have spent so much time tending to the affairs of ministry, and ministering to the needs of others, they have failed to care for themselves. As a result, both have suffered. Their own spiritual lives have been drained, and the churches they lead have been weakened.

Paul appointed Timothy to care for the church in Ephesus. He later wrote to his young colleague, cautioning him, "Watch your life and doctrine closely. Persevere in them, because if you do, you will save both yourself and your hearers" (1 Tim. 4:16). Paul thus advised Timothy, not only to attend to his public ministry, but to his private life as well. A prudent pastor will not only prioritize his or her ministry to others, as was discussed in Chapter 5, they will also prioritize self-care. This chapter will examine six personal priorities of the Pentecostal pastor.

THE PRIORITY OF KNOWING CHRIST

Above all else, the Pentecostal pastor must prioritize his or her relationship with Christ. Before a pastor can make Him known to others, they must themselves know Him well. How can one introduce someone to a person they do not know?

As a Pentecostal pastor, you must know Christ both intellectually and experientially. In other words, you must understand who Jesus is and what He has done. And you must have met Him personally, having a close relationship with Him.

Knowing Who He Is

To know Christ intellectually is to know the truth about Him. It is to understand what the Bible says about who He is and why He came to earth. The Bible teaches the following about who Christ is:

- He is the eternal Word of God, the Creator of all things (John 1:1-4).
- He is God manifested in the flesh (1 Tim. 3:16).
- He is "the Messiah, the Son of the living God" (Matt. 16:16).
- He is "the way the truth and the life," the only way to the Father (John 14:6).

The Bible also tells why Christ came to earth:

- He came "to seek and to save the lost" (Luke 19:10; cf. 1 Tim. 1:15).
- He came "to serve, and to give his life as a ransom for many" (Mark 10:45; cf. John 12:27; Titus 2:13-14).
- He came "to destroy the devil's work" (1 John 3:8; cf. Heb. 2:14).
- He came "that [we] may have life, and have it to the full" (John 10:10).

Part 2: The Priorities of the Pentecostal Pastor

Knowing Him Personally

While it is vital that the Pentecostal pastor knows who Jesus is and why He came, that is not enough. As a Pentecostal pastor, you must know Christ personally. You must have personally met the Lord, and you must have an ongoing relationship with Him.

Paul spoke of this priority in his own life. He wrote to the believers in Philippi, "I want to know Christ—yes, to know the power of his resurrection and participation in his sufferings, becoming like him in his death" (Phi. 3:10). Paul's desire to know Christ was so great that he was prepared, not only to triumph with Him, but to share in His sufferings. He was even ready to die for Him. The Pentecostal pastor must share Paul's passion for knowing Christ.

Getting to Know Him

You can pursue the priority of knowing Christ in three ways:

1. Through a personal encounter. One first gets to know Christ through a personal encounter with Him. This applies to everyone, even the Pentecostal pastor. Saul of Tarsus knew about Christ; however, he did not know Him personally until he encountered Him on the Damascus Road (Acts 9:1-9). There, Saul cried out, "Who are you, Lord?" Jesus answered, "I am Jesus, whom you are persecuting" (v. 5). Saul's life was turned around. He came to know Christ as his Lord and Savior. In a moment, the Church's worst persecutor became its greatest promoter.

Reflecting on this experience, Paul wrote, "Therefore, if anyone is in Christ, the new creation has come: The old has gone, the new is here!" (2 Cor. 5:17). Anyone who aspires to be a Pentecostal pastor must begin here. Jesus declared, "Very truly I tell you, no one can see the kingdom of God unless they are born again" (John 3:3).

2. Through the Word of God. A second way the Pentecostal pastor can get to know Christ better is by encountering Him in the Bible—especially in the gospels and epistles. The gospels tell of His life, His works, and His teaching. The epistles explain their meaning. By reading the gospels, you can walk the dusty roads of Galilee with Jesus.

You can sit at His feet and listen to His teaching. You can stand and watch Him die on the cross. And you can peer into the empty tomb of your Savior and hear the angel shout, "He is not here. He is risen!"

A young Pentecostal pastor once said to himself, "Jesus' disciples spent three years walking with Him and learning from Him. Their lives were transformed. I'm going to do the same. I will spend the next three years reading and rereading the four gospels." True to his commitment, the young preacher spent the next three years reading the gospels. Hour upon hour he spent pouring over the story of Jesus. After that, His life and ministry were never the same.

3. Through prayer. A third way the Pentecostal pastor can get to know Jesus is through prayer. The Bible speaks of many kinds of prayer, including petition, confession, intercession, thanksgiving, and prayer in the Spirit. However, the kind of prayer that will help the pastor know Jesus better is communion prayer. James spoke of this kind of prayer. "Come near to God," he exhorted, "and he will come near to you" (James 4:8). Moses also practiced communion prayer. The Bible says that he talked with God "face to face, as one speaks to a friend" (Exod. 33:11).

Mary, the sister of Martha, is a good illustration of this kind of prayer. When Jesus visited her home, she sat at His feet listening closely to every word He spoke. Her sister complained, accusing her of being lazy. However, Jesus commended Mary, saying, "[She] has chosen what is better, and it will not be taken away from her" (Luke 10:38-42). Getting to know Jesus must become the priority of every Pentecostal pastor. This practice will dramatically impact his or her life and ministry as no other.

THE PRIORITY OF WALKING IN THE SPIRIT

Not only must the Pentecostal pastor prioritize knowing Christ, he or she must prioritize walking and living in the Spirit. Paul admonished the Christians in Galatia, "Since we live by the Spirit, let us keep in step with the Spirit" (Gal. 5:25).

Part 2: The Priorities of the Pentecostal Pastor

What it Means to Walk in the Spirit

To walk in the Spirit means at least three things:

1. Filled with the Spirit. First, to walk in the Spirit means to be filled with the Spirit (Acts 1:4-8). In other words, before one can walk in the Spirit, he or she must first be filled with the Holy Spirit as were the disciples on the Day of Pentecost (Acts 2:1-4). After they received the Spirit, the disciples began to live and minister in the Spirit's power. The book of Acts tells the exciting story of their Spirit-empowered ministry. Every Pentecostal pastor must have this vital experience.

2. Led by the Spirit. Second, to walk in the Spirit is to be led by the Spirit. The Pentecostal pastor must keep his or her ear open to the voice of the Holy Spirit. Then, when the Spirit speaks, they must obey. This is what Jesus did. First, He was filled with the Holy Spirit. Then, He was led by the Spirit (Luke 3:21-22 with 4:1). Paul and his missionary team were also guided by the Holy Spirit (Acts 16:6-10). The same is true for Pentecostal pastors today. Like Jesus and Paul, they too must be guided by the Holy Spirit.

3. Ministry in the Spirit. Finally, to walk in the Spirit means to minister in the Spirit's power. Jesus promised, "You will receive power when the Holy Spirit comes on you; and you will be my witnesses in Jerusalem, and in all Judea and Samaria, and to the ends of the earth" (Acts 1:8). This is what happened to Jesus and the apostles. They were filled with the Holy Spirit and began to minister in the Spirit's power (e.g., Luke 3:21-22 with 4:14; Acts 4:31-33). As you walk in the Spirit, you too can expect the Spirit to empower your ministry.

How to Walk in the Spirit

The question arises, as a Pentecostal pastor, what must you do to ensure that you are living and walking in the Spirit? First, as discussed above, you must ensure that you have been genuinely filled with the Spirit. When you are filled with the Spirit, you can expect two biblical evidences: The first is that you will speak in tongues as the Spirit gives utterance (Acts 2:4; 10:44-46; 19:6). The second is that you will receive supernatural power to witness for Christ (Acts 1:8; 4:31).

Once you have been filled with the Holy Spirit, you must keep your heart tuned to the Spirit's promptings. This is what Christians did in the book of Acts. During the first Jerusalem council, the apostles and elders made a decision concerning the inclusion of Gentile believers into the church. They began their letter by saying, "It seemed good to the Holy Spirit and to us" (Acts 15:28). They wanted their readers to know that they had listened to the voice of the Spirit before making their decision. One practice that can help you to walk and live in the Spirit is to spend time each day praying in the Holy Spirit (Rom. 8:26-27; Eph. 6:18).[1]

THE PRIORITY OF PERSONAL GROWTH AND DEVELOPMENT

In addition to knowing Christ and walking in the Spirit, the Pentecostal pastor must prioritize personal growth and development. He or she must constantly strive to be the best they can be for the Lord.

Comparing life to a race, Paul urged the Christians in Corinth to pursue excellence. He reminded them, "Do you not know that in a race all the runners run, but only one gets the prize?" He then urged them, "Run in such a way as to get the prize" (1 Cor. 9:24). In a similar manner, he urged the Colossians, "Whatever you do, work at it with all your heart, as working for the Lord" (Col. 3:23).

Such an attitude of excellence is neither inherited from one's ancestors, nor is it imparted by the laying on of hands. Achieving excellence in ministry requires focus, determination, and discipline. The pursuit of excellence is not trying to be better than somebody else. Rather, it is being the best you can be in serving the Lord.

---

[1] For more on the Pentecostal pastor's prayer life, see Chapter 8: "The Priority of Prayer."

Part 2: The Priorities of the Pentecostal Pastor

One area in which the Pentecostal pastor must pursue excellence is in his or her study habits. Unfortunately, however, there is a tendency among some Pentecostal pastors to scorn study. While placing a premium on imparted knowledge, they downplay the pursuit of acquired knowledge. The Bible, however, teaches that "the heart of the discerning acquires knowledge, for the ears of the wise seek it out" (Prov. 18:15).

Therefore, as a faithful Pentecostal pastor, you must tirelessly seek to increase your knowledge of Scripture. At the same time, you must strive to keep abreast of current trends in society. You will then be able to combine the two, prophetically applying biblical truth to current trends. Further, you must make it your habit to read good books by reputable authors. This practice will enhance your thinking skills. Excellence in study will help to produce excellence in ministry.

THE PRIORITY OF SELF-CARE

Once, a Pentecostal pastor was experiencing extreme fatigue and body pains. He went to the doctor, fearing that he had contracted some deadly disease. However, after examining him, the doctor told him that his symptoms were caused by stress. The doctor prescribed rest and a healthy diet. It worked! Very soon the pastor regained his vigor in ministry.

African pastors are known to be hard workers. This is good. However, they should beware of trying to be everything to everyone. An exhausted pastor can become a liability both to their family and to their church. Stress can cripple the pastor's ability to pray, study, and preach. It can further affect his or her public behavior, causing them to seem distracted and unconcerned about people. This, in turn, can cause discontent in the congregation, creating even more stress for the pastor.

Pentecostal pastors sometimes shun rest. They feel that, if they take time to rest, they are being unfaithful to their calling. Jesus, however, understood the need for rest. He once told His disciples, "Come with me by yourselves to a quiet place and get some rest" (Mark 6:31).

The zealous pastor needs to remember that even God himself rested on the seventh day of creation (Gen. 2:2). He did this, not because He was tired, but to provide an example for humanity. Jesus said, "The Sabbath was made for man, not man for the Sabbath" (Mark 2:27). God provided the Sabbath as a means for His people to honor their Creator, and as a time to gain the strength they need to face the demands of life. If the principle of Sabbath rest is violated, it will cause inefficiency in ministry.

The Pentecostal pastor must therefore set aside one day each week for rest and recuperation. He or she should then let the people know that this is the pastor's day off, his or her Sabbath. The pastor should spend the day in leisure enjoying time with his or her spouse and children.[2]

THE PRIORITY OF PERSONAL HOLINESS

An article appeared in a newspaper in East Africa telling of a prominent pastor who divorced his wife because of her adulterous behavior. He refused to forgive her and chose to remarry. Seeing what this pastor had done, a man said to his wife, "If the pastor divorced his wife, who do you think you are?" He too left his wife for another woman. As a pastor, your actions will inevitably affect the actions of those you lead, either for good or bad.

As a Pentecostal pastor, God calls you to exemplary living. Peter wrote, "Just as he who called you is holy, so be holy in all you do; for it is written: 'Be holy, because I am holy'" (1 Pet. 1:15-16). Paul wrote that an overseer must live a life "above reproach, faithful to his wife, temperate, self-controlled, respectable,...not given to drunkenness" (1 Tim. 3:2-3). He added that an overseer "must also have a good reputation with outsiders" (v. 7). To Titus, the apostle said that

---

[2] For more on self-care, see Chapter 13: "The Well-Managed Life."

Part 2: The Priorities of the Pentecostal Pastor

an elder "must be blameless...one who loves what is good, who is self-controlled, upright, holy and disciplined" (Titus 1:7-8).

In Africa, pastors are held in high esteem. They influence people both directly and indirectly. They influence them directly with their words—by what they say. They influence them indirectly with their lives—by what they do. What pastors do is often more influential than what they say. A member once told his pastor, "What you do speaks so loudly I cannot hear what you are saying." Therefore, as a Pentecostal pastor, you must make living a life of holiness one of your highest priorities.

THE PRIORITY OF TIME MANAGEMENT

Pentecostals value spontaneity and self-expression in worship. They prize the unrehearsed intervention of the Spirit. These values are good, and they should never be abandoned. However, the Pentecostal pastor should never use them as an excuse for poor time management. Just as you are a steward of the money God has placed in your hands, you are steward of the time God has given you. You must therefore commit yourself to effective time management.

Some pastors are undisciplined with their time, and are habitually late for meetings and appointments. These pastors set a negative pattern for the churches they lead. Their careless behavior lessens their credibility with the people. It becomes part of the organizational culture of the church and hinders its progress.

On the other hand, good time management will enable you to lead the church more effectively. You will be able to set aside time for study, administrative activity, visitation, counseling, and family matters. Effective time management includes such activities as daily goal setting, creating a workable to-do list, prioritizing tasks based on importance and urgency, and setting a time limit to complete each task.

As a Pentecostal pastor, you must be purposeful about the way you live your life and conduct your ministry. You must intentionally

Chapter 6: Personal Priorities

establish personal priorities. You must then consciously go about living up to these priorities. If you will do these things, you will be blessed, and so will the people you lead.

~ Chapter 7 ~

Family Priorities

The pastor of a large urban church in East Africa shared the heartbreaking story of his maternal grandfather. For several years, his grandfather pastored a Pentecostal church. However, the day came when he abandoned his family and his faith and took to himself three wives. Because of this tragic failure, none of his children followed the Lord. None, that is, except the pastor's mother. The pastor now testifies, "I am a product of my mother's faithfulness. She is the one who influenced me to follow the Lord." Today, this pastor is known for his teaching and preaching on family matters.

The sad truth is that even Pentecostal pastors sometimes struggle in their marriages and with their children. For this reason, they must place the highest priority on nurturing their relationship with their families. For the pastor, to succeed in his or her home life is to succeed wonderfully; to fail is to fail utterly. The two previous chapters dealt with the Pentecostal pastor's ministry and personal priorities. This chapter will address their family priorities.

Chapter 7: Family Priorities

RELATIONSHIPS IN THE FAMILY

The Bible speaks about the pastor's relationship to his family. Paul wrote concerning the pastor, "He must manage his own family well and see that his children obey him, and he must do so in a manner worthy of full respect." The apostle then asked rhetorically, "If anyone does not know how to manage his own family, how can he take care of God's church?" (1 Tim. 3:4-5). The Bible's various instructions to husbands, wives, and children also apply to the pastor's household (cf. Gen. 2:24; Mark 10:6-9; 1 Cor. 11:3; Eph. 5:22-33; 6:1-4; Col. 3:18-21; 1 Pet. 3:1-7).

Biblical Order

As a Pentecostal pastor, your home life must be ordered according to Scripture. When culture opposes Scripture, you must always submit to the latter, ensuring that your dealings with your spouse and children are in full harmony with the teachings of God's Word.

For example, most African cultures view the husband as the unchallenged ruler of the family. His word, no matter how irrational, must never be questioned. Jesus, however, demonstrated a different kind of leadership. Speaking of himself, He declared, "The Son of Man did not come to be served, but to serve, and to give his life as a ransom for many" (Mark 10:45).

The Lord thus modeled the kind of leadership He expects from you as a Christian husband. Your leadership in the family should be defined by humility and selfless concern for your wife and children. Paul expounded on this servant-leadership theme, exhorting husbands, "Love your wives, just as Christ loved the church and gave himself up for her" (Eph. 5:25).

Paul described how the Christian home should be ordered: "For the husband is the head of the wife as Christ is the head of the church, his body, of which he is the Savior" (Eph. 5:23). In another place, the apostle wrote, "Husbands, love your wives and do not be harsh with them. Children, obey your parents in everything, for this pleases the

Lord. Fathers, do not embitter your children, or they will become discouraged" (Col. 3:19-21). In such a well-ordered environment, your marriage can grow and your children can thrive.

Mutual Submission

The Bible teaches that the relationship between the husband and wife must be one of mutual submission. Paul wrote that husbands and wives must "submit to one another out of reverence for Christ" (Eph. 5:21). Though the husband is the head of the wife, he must, like Jesus, willingly submit himself to her needs and humbly serve her. She must do the same with him. Rather than reduce your status as pastor, this kind of humble service to the family will enhance your standing in the church and community.

Love and Respect

Furthermore, your relationship with your family should be characterized by mutual love and respect. Paul exhorted husbands, "Love your wives, just as Christ loved the church and gave himself up for her" (Eph. 5:25). Later he added, "Each one of you also must love his wife as he loves himself, and the wife must respect her husband" (v. 33). The reverse is also true; the wife must love her husband, and the husband must respect his wife. In doing these things, the pastoral family will become a model for others.

Authenticity

Further, your relationship with your family must be characterized by authenticity. This means that you must be the same person at home that you are in public. You must demonstrate a sincere interest in what is happening in the lives of your spouse and children. When at home, the children must hear the voice of their father or mother, not the voice of a preacher who is far removed from the reality of their lives.

CHALLENGES FOR FEMALE PASTORS

A word to female pastors and their families is in order here. Married women pastors in Africa find themselves in a unique and challenging position. God has called them to lead a church; however, in matters concerning the home, He has called them to respect their husbands and submit to his authority. This can be a difficult situation to manage.

In addition, most African cultures resist female leadership, although, thankfully, in many places this attitude is changing. As a result, some church members are reluctant to follow a female pastor's leadership or allow her to perform certain pastoral duties.

It is therefore particularly important that the pastor's husband support his wife in her ministry. At times, he must be willing to humble himself and support her in many ways that seem contrary to popular culture. For instance, at times, because of the demands of her work, the husband should be willing to humble himself, pitch in, and help out in any way he can. On the other hand, the woman pastor should not use her ministerial duties as an excuse to neglect her domestic obligations to her husband and children.

This will require an exceptional level of maturity and flexibility on the part of both the female pastor and her husband. They must prioritize their relationship with one another above all else, and they must learn to communicate well with one another.

MANAGING THE FAMILY WELL

Not only must the Pentecostal pastor properly manage his church, he must properly manage his family. As noted above, Paul reminded Timothy that an overseer "must manage his own family well" (1 Tim. 3:4). He later wrote to Titus, "An elder must be blameless, faithful to his wife, a man whose children believe and are not open to the charge of being wild and disobedient" (Titus 1:6).

This important responsibility includes leading, protecting, and caring for his wife and children. The Bible teaches that a man should relate to his wife as Christ relates to the church (Eph. 5:25-27). Further, he is to watch over his children with the same loving concern that his Heavenly Father watches over him. The wise man advised,

Part 2: The Priorities of the Pentecostal Pastor

"Start children off on the way they should go, and even when they are old they will not turn from it" (Pro. 22:6).

As a Pentecostal pastor, your leadership of your family involves at least three activities:

Spiritual Development

First, you must concern yourself with your family's spiritual development. Like Job, you must purposefully lead your family in spiritual matters (Job 1:4-5). One way you can do this is by conducting regular devotions with your family. In these devotional times, you should teach your children to pray and to read and memorize Scripture. You must further ensure that your children come to know Christ as Savior, and that they have been baptized in the Holy Spirit.

Personal Development

Second, you must oversee your family's personal development. You and your spouse should aim at molding your children into mature adults, committed Christians, and productive citizens. In addition, you should teach your children how to handle money wisely. As your children grow and become more mature, you should allow them to assist in managing the household finances. In this way, they can learn to differentiate wants from needs.

Social Development

Finally, you and your spouse should tend to your children's social development. The family's home life should provide the right environment for the children to grow in their social skills. You must teach them to recognize the difference between good and bad company. You must further teach them how to relate to others in various social settings.

PRIORITIES TOWARD ONE'S SPOUSE

The Bible speaks frankly about the husband's responsibilities toward his wife. These responsibilities of course apply to the Pentecostal pastor. As a godly man, your duties towards your wife include the following:

Express Love

Paul wrote that a husband is to "love [his] wife just as Christ loved the church" (Eph. 5:25). Christ's love for the church was sacrificial and selfless. Your love for your wife should be the same. You should declare your love for your wife both in private and in public. When alone with her, you should often tell her, "I love you." When in public, you should openly express your love for your wife. For instance, you could announce to the church, "I'm blessed to have my wife with me here today. She is an amazing wife and a wonderful mother to our children. I love her very much."

These and other similar actions will help you bond both to your wife and to your church. You should also demonstrate your love for your wife with your actions, that is, by speaking kindly to her, preferring her before yourself, and by helping her with her responsibilities.

Offer Support

A second responsibility you, as a Pentecostal pastor, have concerning your wife and children is to provide them with due consideration and support. Peter wrote to husbands, "Be considerate as you live with your wives, and treat them with respect" (1 Pet. 3:7).

As a Christian man, you are required to support your wife and children materially by providing them with adequate shelter, food, and clothing. Although your wife and older children may help out in this area, you, as the man of the house, bear the primary responsibility.

Another important way you can support your wife is by helping her to fulfill her personal calling in ministry. Your motto should be, "If I cannot help my wife reach her potential, how will I help my church do the same?" To do this, you will need to freely acknowledge that God has a calling on your wife's life, just as He has a calling on your life. You must then walk with her with prayer and counsel, helping her to discern and follow God's will for her life.

Part 2: The Priorities of the Pentecostal Pastor

Provide Protection

A third responsibility you have concerning your wife is to protect her from physical, emotional, and spiritual attack. On the most basic level, you must protect her physically. The Bible calls the wife the "weaker partner" in the marital relationship (1 Pet. 3:7). As the physically stronger partner, you should stand guard over your wife at all times, ever ready to protect her from physical attack. Knowing this will make her feel safe and valued.

Further, you must protect your wife from emotional harm. Unfortunately, the pastor's wife is often a favorite target of criticism. In-laws and carnal church members often criticize her and her children. Others fail to show their appreciation for all she does. This can be very hurtful to her. You should be aware of this dynamic in the church, and you should protect your wife and provide her with the emotional support she needs.

Finally, since the pastor's wife is a prime target of Satan, you must protect her spiritually. You can do this by building a hedge of prayer around her. Also, when necessary, you must stand in the gap between her and the enemy (Ezek. 22:30).

PRIORITIES TOWARD HIS CHILDREN

The Pentecostal pastor must also prioritize his children. Next only to his responsibility to love and care for his wife, he is responsible to love and care for his children. He should care for them just as his Heavenly Father cares for him. He is to "bring them up in the training and instruction of the Lord" (Eph. 6:4).

As a godly man and a Christian father, you have three primary responsibilities toward your children:

Model God's Love

First, you must model God's love toward your children. Children develop many of their concepts about God by watching their father. If their earthly father is kind and loving, they will view their Heavenly

Father as kind and loving. If their earthly father is a tyrant, the children will view God in the same way. When you model godly attributes like love, respect, service, and trust, your children will be able to embrace your instruction and correction in the home. The Bible describes the true nature of love:

> "Love is patient, love is kind. It does not envy, it does not boast, it is not proud. It does not dishonor others, it is not self-seeking, it is not easily angered, it keeps no record of wrongs. Love does not delight in evil but rejoices with the truth. It always protects, always trusts, always hopes, always perseveres. Love never fails." (1 Cor. 13:4-8)

This is the kind of love you should show your children.

Lead Them to Christ

In addition to showing them the love of God, you must lead your children into a personal relationship with Jesus Christ. A good time to do this is during family devotions. In these devotions, you can present the plan of salvation to your children. Then, when the time is right, you can pray with them to receive Christ as their Savior. After this, it will be important for the children to publicly proclaim their commitment to Christ through testimony and water baptism. You should also look for opportunities to lead your children into the baptism in the Holy Spirit. You should then encourage them to share their faith with their friends.[1]

Shape Their Character

You should have a clear plan for shaping your children's character. You and your spouse must teach them right from wrong and how to "reject every kind of evil" (1 Thess. 5:22). You should also teach your children to be polite, kind, and respectful of authority, along with the importance of honesty and hard work. This instruction will go a long way in helping them succeed in life.

---

[1] For insights on how to do this, see Chapter 20: "Guiding Believers into Spirit Baptism."

Part 2: The Priorities of the Pentecostal Pastor

You can do these things by modeling holy living in the home, and by thoughtfully discussing moral issues with your children. When your children see their parents sincerely practicing righteousness, they will naturally want to follow you. At times you will need to lovingly discipline your children to turn them away from foolish and hurtful practices (Pro. 29:15).

HELPING THE EXTENDED FAMILY

You must also show loving concern for your and your spouse's extended families. These extended family members may include parents, brothers and sisters, nieces and nephews, and possibly others. Paul wrote, "Anyone who does not provide for their relatives, and especially for their own household, has denied the faith and is worse than an unbeliever" (1 Tim. 5:8).

However, there are times when the demands of extended family members may run contrary to Scripture. For instance, your families may seek to impose unbiblical practices on your family such as ritual circumcision or the naming of a new baby. On such occasions, you must lovingly, yet firmly, reject these proposals.

Another way extended family members may place unrealistic demands on you and your family is by moving into your house for long periods of time. As a result, they become a drain on your family's financial, mental, and emotional resources. The greatest demands are often placed on the pastor's wife. She can be pressed, even to the point of exhaustion. In such instances, as head of the house, you must take charge of the situation and establish healthy boundaries.

You should remember Paul's admonition to Timothy, as stated above, that one must care for his relatives, *"especially for their own household."* As a Christian man, your primary responsibility is not to your extended family but to your wife and children. It may therefore be necessary to remind the offending relative of the Bible's injunctions to "keep away from every believer who is idle and disruptive" (2 Thess. 3:6), and that "the one who is unwilling to work shall not eat" (v. 10).

Chapter 7: Family Priorities

Rather than constantly reacting to the demands of extended family members, you and your spouse should proactively determine the kind of help you will offer them. In doing this, you will need to agree on guidelines, such as: Who will determine for either side of the extended family who will be helped? And, for how long will that help be offered?

Your chief aim toward your extended family members is to be salt and light to them. It is possible to bend so much to culture that you become ineffective in ministry. You should therefore seek to strike a compassionate balance between helping and refusing to help. Nevertheless, at all times, your family should seek to be a witness to your extended family members.

As a Pentecostal pastor, God has called you to lead the church in fulfilling God's mission. However, in doing this, you must not neglect your own family. You must never have to confess, "I have won the lost to Christ; yet I have lost my own family."

~ Chapter 8 ~

The Priority of Prayer

As was his custom, Moses went outside the camp to the tent of meeting to pray. Each time the people saw him do this, they stopped what they were doing and watched until he entered the tent. While Moses was inside the tent praying, a pillar of cloud would come down and hover at its entrance. When the people saw this, they were filled with wonder, and they bowed down to worship God. They were encouraged, knowing that their leader often spoke with God. This practice of Moses especially affected his young assistant, Joshua. He would often follow Moses to the tent, and he would remain there long after Moses left. He very much wanted to be like his mentor (cf. Exod. 33:8-11).

Nothing uplifts a congregation like a praying pastor. The devil does not fear our academic degrees. Nor does he fear our large church budgets or our magnificent buildings. What the devil does fear, however, is our prayers. He and his demonic hordes tremble when God's people fall to their knees in Spirit-anointed, faith-filled prayer. If a

Chapter 8: The Priority of Prayer

Pentecostal pastor excels in nothing else, he or she must excel in the practice of prayer.

LIFESTYLE OF PRAYER

The great Protestant reformer, Martin Luther, once said, "To be a Christian without prayer is no more possible than to be alive without breathing." What is true for every believer in Christ is doubly true for the Pentecostal pastor. One cannot minister as a true Pentecostal pastor without a lifestyle of committed prayer. Jesus taught His disciples that they "should always pray and not give up" (Luke 18:1).

As a Pentecostal pastor, you must take Jesus as your example. The Lord's entire life and ministry were bathed in prayer. Luke writes that "Jesus often withdrew to lonely places and prayed" (Luke 5:16). On one occasion, He "went out to a mountainside to pray, and spent the night praying to God" (6:12). On yet another occasion, He took Peter, John, and James and "went up onto a mountain to pray" (9:28). In fact, Jesus prayed at every opportunity. Like Jesus, to lead God's people, you must be a man or woman of constant prayer. No one can minister in the Spirit's power without a persistent prayer habit.

Through prayer, you prepare yourself for ministry. While waiting in prayer, you draw near to God (James 4:8; cf. Heb. 10:22). In addition, you gain the spiritual strength you need to live for Christ, and the power you need to effectively carry out your ministry (Isa. 40:31; Psa. 40:1-3).

The Bible urges, "Walk by the Spirit, and you will not gratify the desires of the flesh" (Gal. 5:16). To do this you will need to live in constant communion with God. Such communion is achieved through prayer. During seasons of prayer, the Spirit will speak to you and give you encouragement and direction. Spirit-anointed prayer will further prepare you for spiritual battle (Eph. 6:12, 18).

THE MINISTRY OF PRAYER

In addition to developing your personal prayer life, as a Pentecostal pastor, you must view prayer as a means of ministering to others. There are three ways you can minister to others through prayer:

Ministering through Private Prayer

First, you can minister to others through private prayer. Jesus called this kind of prayer secret prayer. He taught, "When you pray, go into your room, close the door and pray to your Father, who is unseen" (Matt. 6:6). There in the secret place, you must spend time interceding for the needs of others. As you pray, you can petition God with confidence, knowing that God sees your labor of love and that He will answer your prayers. In the same passage, Jesus promised, "Your Father, who sees what is done in secret, will reward you." Your times of secret prayer can take at least three forms:

1. Devotional prayer. First, you should pray devotionally. In other words, you should spend time in prayer drawing near to God. This practice will strengthen your relationship with the Lord. As you pray in the Holy Spirit, your faith will be built up, and you will be kept in the love of God (Jude 20-21; cf. Rom. 5:5). Out of this relationship with God you will be able to successfully fulfill your ministry.[1]

2. Intercessory prayer. Next, as mentioned above, as a Pentecostal pastor, you should spend time before God petitioning Him for the needs of others—especially for the needs of those connected with your church. Jesus often prayed for His disciples (John 17:9). For example, He prayed for them that their faith would remain strong (Luke 22:32). He further prayed that God would protect them (John 17:11-12, 15), and that they would have joy (v. 13). He also prayed for their sanctification (vv. 17-19) and that they would remain unified (vv. 21-23).

In like manner, the apostle Paul continually prayed for God's people. He wrote to the believers in Rome, "Constantly I remember

---

[1] For more on drawing near to God, see Chapter 15: "A Strong Devotional Habit."

you in my prayers at all times" (Rom. 1:9-10). He told the Ephesians, "I have not stopped giving thanks for you, remembering you in my prayers" (Eph. 1:16; cf. Col. 1:9). As Pentecostal pastors we must follow the examples of Jesus and Paul and spend much time in prayer, interceding for others.[2]

3. Prayer with fasting. Finally, as a Pentecostal pastor, you should often pray with fasting. The spiritual disciplines of prayer and fasting will help you to bring your spirit in tune with the Spirit of God. As you spend time in prayer and fasting, your flesh will be brought into submission, and your spirit will be prepared to more clearly discern the voice of the Spirit (cf. Gal. 5:16-17).

Ministering through Person-to-Person Prayer

Further, you will often be called upon to minister in person-to-person prayer. Person-to-person prayer occurs when you pray for someone you are with. This kind of prayer often happens during prayer times in front of the church. It may also occur in a home or hospital during a pastoral visit. Or it may even take place in the marketplace during times of evangelistic outreach. Such prayer often includes the laying on of hands or anointing with oil (cf. Acts 19:6; James 5:14). It always involves praying in faith (James 5:15).

Four examples of person-to-person prayer are praying with people to be saved, praying with people to be healed, praying with people to be delivered from demonic bondage, and praying with people to be filled with the Holy Spirit. You must become proficient in each of these areas of ministry. In each situation, you must demonstrate confidence in God's Word, speak words of faith and encouragement, and show sincere concern for the individuals with whom you are praying.[3]

---

[3] For more information on praying for individuals, see Chapter 20: "Guiding Believers into Spirit Baptism"; Chapter 21: "Ministering in the Spirit's Power"; and Chapter 22: "Engaging in Spiritual Warfare." Also, see the book, *Power Encounter: Ministering in the Power and Anointing of the Holy Spirit,* by Denzil R. Miller, which offers helpful advice in praying with

Part 2: The Priorities of the Pentecostal Pastor

Ministering through Public Prayer

At times you will be called on to pray public prayers. Some pastors offer a pastoral prayer over their congregations each Sunday morning. In addition, the Pentecostal pastor is often called on to pray at public gatherings such as funerals and weddings. When asked to pray on such occasions, you must offer your prayer with dignity and grace. Your public prayer, however, must never be offered for mere show or ceremony. You should always pray sincerely. Jesus warned, "When you pray, do not be like the hypocrites, for they love to pray standing in the synagogues and on the street corners to be seen by others" (Matt. 6:5).

LEADING THE CHURCH IN PRAYER

Not only must the Pentecostal pastor develop his or her own personal prayer life, he or she must develop a strong prayer ministry in the local church where they pastor.

Preaching and Teaching on Prayer

One important key to developing a strong prayer ministry in the church is to preach and teach often on the topic. In doing this, you will again be following the example of Jesus, who himself taught much on the subject of prayer (cf. Luke 18:1; Matt. 6:5-15).

You can encourage Christians to pray by sharing testimonies with them of how God has answered prayers in the past. These testimonies can be drawn from the Bible, from history, or from contemporary life. You must further take time to teach practical lessons on the benefits and practice of prayer.[4]

---

people to be healed, filled with the Spirit, and delivered from demonic bondage. It can be downloaded for free in e-book format (PDF) at DecadeofPentecost.org.

[4] Preaching and teaching outlines on prayer can be found in the book, *Interceding for the Nations: 100 Sermon Outlines on Missional Prayer*, which can be downloaded for free in e-book format (PDF) at DecadeofPentecost.org.

Chapter 8: The Priority of Prayer

Modeling Prayer

Not only must you teach about prayer, you must show believers how to pray. Again, this was how Jesus taught His disciples. He not only taught them with words, He showed them with His life. He modeled a lifestyle of prayer before them. Jesus' disciples noticed how He walked in constant communion with His Heavenly Father. On one occasion, after watching Him pray, they asked Him, "Lord, teach us to pray, just as John taught his disciples" (Luke 11:1). As a Pentecostal pastor, you should live such a lifestyle of prayer that your members will ask you, "Pastor, teach us to pray, just as Jesus taught His disciples."

Organizing for Prayer

Further, you must organize your church for prayer. You can do this by forming prayer groups and by scheduling prayer events, as follows:

Forming prayer groups. You will want to encourage the formation of specialized prayer groups in the church. These groups can be formed as auxiliaries of existing ministries such as men's ministries, women's ministries, youth ministries, and others. They can also be formed to address particular needs in the church, community, nation, or world. These needs could be social or spiritual, local or global. For instance, some members may want to pray for revival in the church, while others may want to pray for peace in the country. Many other needs could be identified that require prayer.

Scheduling prayer events. You will also want to include numerous prayer events on the church's calendar of activities. You should, of course, schedule regular ongoing prayer services for the church, such as a midweek prayer meeting. You will also want to schedule special prayer events such as prayer retreats or weeks of special prayer.

For example, one Pentecostal pastor scheduled a week of intense prayer and fasting twice each year in January and July. In preparation for these events, he encouraged members to gather prayer requests from their family members, friends, neighbors, and coworkers. They

Part 2: The Priorities of the Pentecostal Pastor

would then write these requests on specially prepared forms and distribute them to members to be prayed over during morning and evening prayer meetings. Great blessing came to the church and the community through this practice.

Many Pentecostal churches schedule a series of prayer meetings leading up to Pentecost Sunday each year. (Pentecost Sunday always comes seven weeks after Easter Sunday.) In these special meetings, members call on God to pour out His Spirit on the church. They also pray that during their Pentecost celebrations many Christians will be empowered by the Holy Spirit (Acts 1:8; 2:4). And they pray that many will come to the Lord as happened on the original Day of Pentecost (2:41).

You may also want to schedule an annual prayer retreat with the church staff and leaders. You should diligently seek the Lord's guidance as to which prayer emphases you should schedule for the church.

Praying for God's Mission

One prayer emphasis should be present in every Pentecostal church in Africa. The Pentecostal pastor must ensure that his or her church prays regularly for the advancement of God's mission in the earth. This was Jesus' prayer request, and it must not be neglected (Matt. 9:37-38). You should therefore lead your church in committed prayer for the progress of God's kingdom in your community, nation, continent, and the world. You should lead them in prayer for the missionaries sent out by your national church, as well as those supported by your local assembly. And you should pray often for the thousands of unreached people groups (UPGs) in the world.[5]

---

[5] Information on unreached people groups (UPGs) can be found on the Internet at www.JoshuaProject.net.

Chapter 8: The Priority of Prayer

LEADING A PRAYER MEETING

The Pentecostal pastor must know how to properly conduct a prayer meeting. Here are some practical guidelines for leading an effective prayer meeting.

Plan Ahead

As with any important event in the church, you will need to plan ahead for an effective prayer meeting. You will need to choose the time and venue of the meeting. You will further need to determine the purpose of the prayer meeting and what its emphasis will be. And you will need to make a list of prayer points to be covered in the meeting. You may also need to gather pertinent information about those prayer items. You will then share this information with the participants at the appropriate time in the prayer meeting.

Keep Time—Stay Focused

When leading a prayer meeting, you will need to keep time and stay focused. In other words, you should start and end the prayer meeting at the appointed times. Some people are busy, and they will appreciate how you respect their time. As a result, they will be more likely to attend the prayer meetings.

Further, when leading the prayer meeting, you should stay focused. This means that you will not allow the prayer meeting to wander here and there, but you will stay on target. A brief devotion and a short time of singing are appropriate at the beginning of the prayer meeting. However, the bulk of the meeting should remain focused on prayer.

Be Open to the Spirit

While the prayer meeting should be well organized and focused, the leader of the meeting should at all times remain open to the moving of the Holy Spirit. He or she should encourage the people to pray in the Spirit (Rom. 8:26-27; 1 Cor. 14:15: Eph. 6:18) and remain open to the guidance of the Spirit and the manifestation of spiritual gifts (1 Cor. 14:26).

Part 2: The Priorities of the Pentecostal Pastor

A MODEL PRAYER MEETING

Someone may ask, "What should a Pentecostal prayer meeting look like?" The answer to this question is found in the Bible. The book of Acts gives us an example of a typical prayer meeting in the early church. This prayer meeting happened soon after the Day of Pentecost.

The church was undergoing great persecution. The Jewish leaders captured Peter and John. They then threatened them and commanded them to stop preaching in Jesus' name. When they let the two apostles go, they returned to the church and reported what had happened to them. The Christians began to pray. Their prayer and the results of their prayer are recorded in Acts 4:23-31. From this prayer meeting, we learn three important lessons about how we should conduct our prayer meetings today:

The Nature of Our Praying

First, we learn about the nature of our praying, *or how we should pray*. The Bible says of those early Christians that "they raised their voices together in prayer to God" (Acts 4:24). Thus, their praying was fervent ("they raised their voices") and it was unified ("they raised their voices together"). When we come together to pray, we too should seek God fervently, and we must pray in unity. In addition, our prayers should be offered in faith (Mark 11:24). Those who prayed that day in Jerusalem fully expected God to hear and answer their prayer. And so must we today.

The Content of Our Prayers

Next, we learn about the content of our prayers, or *what we should pray for*. Those early Christians did not focus their praying on their problems, though they had many. They rather focused their attention on the power and greatness of God (Acts 4:24-25). And they prayed for God's will to be done (vv. 26-28). They further asked God to empower them and give them boldness to proclaim the gospel, even in the midst of persecution (vv. 29-30). By asking God to

Chapter 8: The Priority of Prayer

"stretch out His hand," they were asking Him to move powerfully by His Spirit (cf. Ezek. 37:1; Luke 11:20 with Matt. 12:28; Acts 11:21).

The Results of Our Prayers

Finally, we learn what we can expect to happen when we pray. If we will pray like those early believers, we too can expect God to make His presence known in our prayer meetings. The Bible says, "After they prayed, the place where they were meeting was shaken. And they were all filled with the Holy Spirit and spoke the word of God boldly" (Acts 4:31). If we will pray as they did, we can expect God to respond to our prayers in the same way he responded to theirs. We can expect Him to fill us with the Holy Spirit and empower us as Christ's witnesses to the lost.

~ Part 3 ~

The Beliefs of the Pentecostal Pastor

~ Chapter 9 ~

Believes the Bible

Mounted on the front wall of the Africa's Hope headquarters building in Springfield, Missouri, USA, is a large map of Africa. Superimposed over the map is the image of an African man with his arm outstretched before him. In the man's hand is a Bible. He is preaching the gospel. This image represents thousands of Pentecostal preachers across Africa who faithfully proclaim God's Word to all who will hear. It further represents the Pentecostal pastor's special relationship to his or her Bible.

The Bible is like no other book in the world. Although it accurately relates history, it is more than a history book. While it teaches right behavior, it is more than a book of ethics. Philosophers marvel at the depths of its concepts, yet the Bible is more than a book of philosophy. The Bible contains the "very words of God" (Rom. 3:2). It reveals the sinful state of humanity, and it shows the way to salvation through Christ. This chapter will examine the Pentecostal pastor's special relationship to the Bible as the Word of God.

Chapter 9: Believes the Bible

HOW THE PENTECOSTAL PASTOR VIEWS THE BIBLE

Pentecostal pastors hold the Bible in highest esteem. They believe it to be God's message to mankind—the eternal Word of God. For the Pentecostal pastor, the Bible serves as the foundation for all ministry and practice. Article 1 of the "Statement of Faith of the World Assemblies of God Fellowship," entitled "The Inspiration of the Scriptures," summarizes the Pentecostal pastor's view of the Bible: "The Scriptures, both the Old and New Testaments, are verbally inspired of God and are the revelation of God to man, the infallible, authoritative rule of faith and conduct (2 Tim. 3:15-17; 1 Thess. 2:13; 2 Pet. 1:21)."[1] To get a better idea of what this statement means, let's break it down into its four parts:

Verbally Inspired

First, the Pentecostal pastor believes that "the Scriptures, both the Old and New Testaments, are verbally inspired of God." When we say that the Scriptures are *inspired of God,* we mean that God sovereignly moved upon the prophets and apostles of old, supernaturally guiding them to write down the thoughts and ideas He chose. Paul affirmed this truth when he wrote, "All Scripture is God-breathed" (2 Tim. 3:16). Peter described this supernatural process in more detail: "Above all, you must understand that no prophecy of Scripture came about by the prophet's own interpretation of things. For prophecy never had its origin in the human will, but prophets, though human, spoke from God as they were carried along by the Holy Spirit" (2 Pet. 1:20-21).

When we say that the Bible is *verbally inspired* by God, we mean that divine inspiration extends to the very words of the text. God did not only inspire the thoughts of Scripture, He oversaw the process, choosing the very words in which these thoughts were expressed. Jesus affirmed this truth when He said, "It is easier for heaven and earth

---

[1] See Appendix 1: "Statement of Faith of the World Assemblies of God Fellowship."

to disappear than for the least stroke of a pen to drop out of the Law" (Luke 16:17). Verbal inspiration thus means that every word in Scripture is Holy Spirit inspired. It is there because God wanted it there.

Because the Bible is inspired, it is rightly called God's Word. In fact, the Bible refers to itself as the "Word of God" or the "Word of the Lord" more than forty times.

The Revelation of God

The Pentecostal pastor further believes the Bible is "the revelation of God to man." This means that God has revealed His will for humanity through the words of Scripture. He inspired the Bible so people would come to know Him, His works, and His ways. By giving us the Bible, God has shown himself to be a self-revealing God. The Bible is proof that God wants all men and women everywhere to know Him and His plan of salvation.

Infallible

Further, the Pentecostal pastor believes that the Bible is infallible. To say that the Bible is infallible is to say that it is without error. Since the words of Scripture are inspired by God, its concepts are true and its statements are accurate. The Psalmist declared, "The Lord's word is flawless" (Psa. 18:30). Jesus affirmed this truth when He stated, "Heaven and earth will pass away, but my words will never pass away" (Matt. 24:35).

It is important that the Pentecostal pastor understands that when we speak of the Bible being infallible, we are not referring to any particular translation of the Bible. We are referring to Scripture as it appeared in its original manuscripts. Bible translators work hard to ensure that they correctly translate the text. Nevertheless, because they are human, it is inevitable that mistakes are made. These mistakes, however, are minor. Today, we can be confident that our Bibles accurately reflect the words of God as they were revealed to the original writers.

The Authoritative Rule of Faith and Conduct

Finally, the Pentecostal pastor believes that the Bible is the believer's "authoritative rule of faith and conduct." The Bible tells the man or woman of God what they ought to believe and how they ought to live. Because the Bible is the Word of God, it is authoritative. This means that its teachings must be believed, and its commands must be obeyed. King David understood this truth. He called God's Word "a lamp for my feet, a light on my path" (Psa. 119:105).

HOW THE PENTECOSTAL PASTOR REGARDS THE BIBLE

How then should the Pentecostal pastor regard the Bible? What attitudes and opinions should he or she hold concerning Scripture? Believing that the Bible is indeed God's Word, the Pentecostal pastor should approach the Bible with three attitudes:

Holy Reverence

Because the words of Scripture flow from the heart of a holy God, the Bible itself is holy. And because the Bible is holy, the Pentecostal pastor must hold it in the highest regard. He or she must respect the Word of God and treat it with holy reverence. Paul commended the Christians in Thessalonica for such an attitude: "When you received the word of God,...you accepted it not as a human word, but as it actually is, the word of God, which is indeed at work in you who believe" (1 Thess. 2:13). Because the Pentecostal pastor reveres the Bible as the very words of God, he or she will refrain from distorting its teachings in an attempt to make it say what they want it to say. Peter warns that those who do this do it "to their own destruction" (2 Pet. 3:16).

Deep Love

Not only must the Pentecostal pastor revere the Bible, he or she must possess a sincere love for its teachings. The writer of the 119th Psalm exhibits such a love for God's Word. With 176 verses, this

Psalm qualifies as the longest chapter in the Bible. It is an extended prayer to God.

In this magnificent prayer, the author repeatedly expresses his love for God's Word. For instance, he tells God, "I delight in your commands because I love them" (v. 47). And he reminds God of how His words have affected his life: "My soul is consumed with longing for your laws at all times....Your statutes are my delight; they are my counselors" (vv. 20, 24). Like the Psalmist, the Pentecostal pastor must cultivate a sincere affection for God's Word.

Strong Confidence

Further, because the Pentecostal pastor truly believes the Bible is God-breathed, he or she approaches it with strong confidence. They know that they can believe its pronouncements, and they can trust its promises. Because the Pentecostal pastor fully trusts the Bible, like Abraham, he or she is fully persuaded that what God has promised He will surely perform (Rom. 4:21).

Not only does the Pentecostal pastor believe the Bible is true, he or she understands that it is powerful. It was through the Word of God that the universe was created (John 1:1-3). The Bible says of itself, "The word of God is alive and active. [It is] sharper than any double-edged sword" (Heb. 4:12). Paul described the gospel as "the power of God that brings salvation" (Rom. 1:16). These and many other passages speak of the power of God's Word. For example, speaking through the prophet Isaiah, God said of His Word, "As the rain and the snow come down from heaven, and do not return to it without watering the earth and making it bud and flourish,...so is my word that goes out from my mouth: It will not return to me empty, but will accomplish what I desire and achieve the purpose for which I sent it" (Isa. 55:10-11).

In addition, the Bible tells us that God's Word shows the way (Psa. 119:105), saves the soul (James 1:21), creates faith (Rom. 10:17), regenerates (1 Pet. 1:23), sanctifies (John 17:17), builds up (Acts 20:32), heals and rescues (Psa. 107:20), cleanses (John 15:3), prospers (Josh. 1:8), creates joy (Jer. 15:16), and much more. Because

Chapter 9: Believes the Bible

of these powerful truths, the Pentecostal pastor has strong confidence in God's Word.

THE PENTECOSTAL PASTOR'S RESPONSIBILITIES CONCERNING THE BIBLE

As a Pentecostal pastor you bear certain responsibilities toward God's Word. Here are six of those responsibilities:

To Know the Bible

First, you must have a broad knowledge of Scripture. Nothing qualifies the Pentecostal pastor for service more than a thorough knowledge of the Bible. And nothing disqualifies him or her more than a shallow, superficial knowledge of Scripture. You must therefore commit yourself to a lifelong quest of understanding the Scriptures. You can do this in three ways:

1. Daily reading. You can acquire a knowledge of God's Word through daily Bible reading. You should therefore develop the discipline of Scripture reading.[2] You can complete the Bible in one year by reading an average of just fifteen minutes per day. If you will adopt this practice, day by day, your knowledge of the Bible will increase.

2. Systematic study. You can increase your knowledge of Scripture through systematic Bible study. The Bible speaks of this practice among the Jewish believers in Berea. It says, "They received the message [of the gospel] with great eagerness and examined the Scriptures every day to see if what Paul said was true" (Acts 17:11). You would be wise to copy the Bereans' practice of carefully examining God's Word.

You will also want to build a personal reference library to aid you in your study of the Scriptures. This library should include Bible reference books such as concordances, commentaries, and other Bible studies. It should further include a good study Bible. An excellent

---

[2] For more on this topic, see Chapter 15: "A Strong Devotional Habit."

Part 3: The Beliefs of the Pentecostal Pastor

Pentecostal study Bible is the *Full Life Study Bible,* published by Life Publishers in Springfield, Missouri, USA.[3]

If at all possible, you should complete a course of study at a Pentecostal Bible school. This will greatly increase your knowledge of Scripture and ministerial skills. The Africa Assemblies of God have an extensive system of ministerial training institutions across the continent. These institutions include both residential and non-residential schools. At least one Assemblies of God Bible school can be found in almost every country in Sub-Saharan Africa and the Indian Ocean Basin. These schools offer training to both Assemblies of God and non-Assemblies of God ministers.[4]

3. Memorization. You should also systematically memorize Scripture. A good goal is to memorize at least one new scripture or scripture passage per week. In addition, it is a good practice to memorize any text or passage of Scripture you are to teach or preach from. This practice will allow you more freedom in your preaching. It will also greatly increase your supply of memorized scriptures.

To Live by Its Standards

Second, as a Pentecostal pastor, you must live by the Bible's standards. It is not enough to know what the Bible teaches, you must allow its teachings to shape your life and ministry. The Bible exhorts, "Do not merely listen to the word, and so deceive yourselves. Do what it says" (James 1:22; cf. Rom. 2:13). With the Psalmist, you must be able to honestly pray, "I have chosen the way of faithfulness; I have set my heart on your laws. I hold fast to your statutes, Lord" (Psa. 119:30-31).

---

[3] This Bible also goes by the name, *Life in the Spirit Study Bible.* It is popularly known as "The Fire Bible," and it has been published in more than sixty languages around the world. For more information, see https://www.firebible.org/.

[4] A list of Assemblies of God Bible schools in Africa can be found at the Africa Theological Training Service (ATTS) website: https://africaatts.org/.

Chapter 9: Believes the Bible

To Correctly Handle the Word of Truth

Third, as a Pentecostal pastor, you must commit yourself to correctly handling "the word of truth" (2 Tim. 2:15). Because you believe the Bible is God's eternal Word to humanity, you must resist any temptation to willfully twist the Scriptures to suit your own ideas. You will rather heed Peter's warning to "ignorant and unstable people" who distort the Scriptures to their own destruction and the destruction of others (2 Pet. 3:16). And you must carefully obey the command of Scripture to "teach what is appropriate to sound doctrine" (Titus 2:1).

To Faithfully Advance Its Mission

Fourth, you must commit yourself to clearly understanding and zealously advancing God's mission as revealed in Scripture. The Bible reveals that God is a missionary God and that He is working to fulfill His mission in the earth. This mission is sometimes referred to as the *missio Dei*. God is on mission to redeem and call unto himself a people from every tribe, tongue, and nation on earth (Rev. 5:9).[5]

As a true Pentecostal pastor, you must lead your church to join God in this mission (Matt. 24:14). To do this, you must clearly understand what the Bible teaches about God's mission. And you must commit yourself to leading your church to do its part in fulfilling that mission.

To Preach and Teach the Word

Fifth, as a Pentecostal pastor, you must faithfully preach and teach the Word of God to your people. In doing this, you will help them to "grow in the grace and knowledge of [the] Lord" (2 Pet. 3:18). And you will ensure that God's people have been "thoroughly equipped for every good work" (2 Tim. 3:17). This is one important reason Paul urged Timothy, his son in the faith, "Preach the word; be

---

[5] For more on God's mission, see the Africa's Hope Discovery Series textbook, *A Biblical Theology of Missions,* by Paul York.

prepared in season and out of season; correct, rebuke and encourage—with great patience and careful instruction" (2 Tim. 4:2).

The Pentecostal pastor who faithfully teaches God's Word will be rewarded (Matt. 24:45-47). The one who fails in this duty will be severely judged (James 3:1).

To Stoutly Defend the Truth It Reveals

Finally, as a true Pentecostal pastor, you must be prepared to defend the truth revealed in Scripture. Like Paul, you must be set "for defense of the gospel" (Phi. 1:16). In the words of the apostle, you "must hold firmly to the trustworthy message as it has been taught, so that [you] can encourage others by sound doctrine and refute those who oppose it" (Titus 1:9).

With this in mind, you must diligently watch over the flock of God to protect the saints from false teachers and false teachings (Acts 20:28-31). You can do this by faithfully teaching sound biblical doctrine to the church. And you can protect the flock by exposing and opposing any deviation from the truth of God's Word.[6]

The Pentecostal pastor should be known as a man or woman of the Book. They must be persuaded that the Bible is inspired by God. Because of this, they should cherish the Bible and hold it in the highest regard. They should know the Word of God and diligently teach and preach its precepts to God's people.

---

[6] For more on protecting the flock, see Chapter 27: "Guarding the Flock."

Chapter 9: Believes the Bible

~ Chapter 10 ~

Upholds Pentecostal Truth

Every Pentecostal pastor in Africa must faithfully uphold Pentecostal truth in the church he or she pastors. To do this, they must clearly understand the biblical truths that define Pentecostalism as a movement. And they must be able to defend these truths.

The issue involves more than just being able to win a theological debate. It involves the successful fulfillment of the Great Commission. How one views the work of the Holy Spirit in the lives of believers will profoundly affect the way he or she seeks to fulfill Christ's command to make disciples of all nations (Matt. 28:18-20). Without a clear understanding of the empowering work of the Holy Spirit, the fulfillment of the Great Commission will be impossible.

Imagine a pair of scissors with one of its blades missing. No matter how sharp the blade, by itself it is useless. However, when the two blades are united, the scissors become a valuable tool. So it is with the biblical teaching on the work of the Holy Spirit. If one emphasizes only the regenerative work of the Holy Spirit (as found in Paul's letters), to the exclusion of His empowering work (as found in Acts),

Chapter 10: Upholds Pentecostal Truth

the Spirit's activity in the lives of believers is diminished, and the work of the kingdom is impaired. However, when both concepts are brought together, a more complete understanding of the work of the Spirit emerges. As a result, God's people experience God's Spirit as He intended. And they are enabled to more effectively advance God's kingdom in the earth.

This chapter is about the Pentecostal pastor's responsibility to uphold Pentecostal truth in the church. By Pentecostal truth we mean those biblical doctrines and practices uniquely emphasized by Pentecostal scholars. These truths concern the person and work of the Spirit in the lives of believers.

If the Pentecostal movement in Africa is to retain its evangelistic and missionary fervor, Pentecostal pastors must faithfully promote Pentecostal doctrine and practice in their churches. If they fail in this effort, the movement will surely falter and wane, as have other movements before. Their churches may retain the external trappings of Pentecostalism; however, they will eventually lose their spiritual vitality and missionary zeal. They will become yet another historic church with a noble past but a powerless present (2 Tim. 3:5).

UNDERSTANDING THE FOUNDATION

Pentecostal scholars look to all of Scripture as a foundation for their teachings. However, their primary source for understanding the empowering work of the Holy Spirit is the New Testament book of Acts. In this book, they find inspiration and understanding about how the Holy Spirit fills, empowers, and uses people for kingdom service.

The theological position that distinguishes Pentecostal scholarship from non-Pentecostal scholarship is the way each approaches the book of Acts. The non-Pentecostal reads Acts as sacred history. For them, the book tells the divinely inspired story of how the Church began in first-century Jerusalem and then spread across the Roman Empire. In other words, for the non-Pentecostal, the book of Acts is viewed as mere history, recounting the stories of what happened *then and there* in the first century.

Part 3: The Beliefs of the Pentecostal Pastor

Pentecostals, however, view Acts much differently. They agree with other evangelicals that the book accurately recounts the history of the early Church. However, they see the book as more than sacred history. Pentecostals believe Luke wrote the book of Acts to provide the Church with a lasting model of how it should behave until Christ returns. Acts thus provides us with an enduring example of how Christians should live and minister *here and now*. From Acts we learn that the Church exists to bear Spirit-empowered witness to Christ at home and to the ends of the earth (Acts 1:8).

The book of Acts further tells the story of how Christ's first disciples were baptized in the Holy Spirit, and how that experience dramatically transformed their lives and ministries. It portrays the Church as fulfilling its mission in the power of the Holy Spirit with miraculous signs following (5:12-16; 6:8; 15:12). In Acts, the Spirit calls, empowers, and sends Christ's servants to the nations to boldly proclaim the message of salvation. As they obey, the Spirit strategically directs them on their way. Their missionary work is accompanied by powerful outpourings of the Holy Spirit (2:4; 4:31).

The missionary activity of the Holy Spirit in Acts thus provides the Pentecostal pastor with a clear picture of what a Pentecostal church should look like today.

PROMOTING PENTECOSTAL "DISTINCTIVES"

Pentecostals further maintain that the book of Acts provides the Church with an enduring pattern of how one receives the Holy Spirit. The experience of Spirit baptism is received subsequent to the new birth. And its reception is accompanied by the missional sign of speaking in tongues as the Spirit enables. Let's briefly review these distinctive Pentecostal doctrines.

The Doctrine of Subsequence

The doctrine of subsequence holds that the baptism in the Holy Spirit is an experience "distinct from and subsequent to the new

Chapter 10: Upholds Pentecostal Truth

birth."[1] Non-Pentecostals see regeneration and Spirit baptism as two parts of the one experience of salvation. Pentecostals, however, see them as distinct and separate experiences. Pentecostals point to how this truth is clearly shown on three occasions in the book of Acts:

1. Receiving the Spirit in Samaria (Acts 8:4-17). In this story, Philip went down to Samaria and preached Christ to them. The people listened closely to his words, believed the message, were delivered from demonic bondage, experienced great joy, and were baptized in water (vv. 5-8, 12). However, it was not until Peter and John arrived some days later and placed their hands on them that they received the Holy Spirit (vv. 14-17).

2. Saul (Paul) receives the Spirit (Acts 9:1-19). Saul encountered Jesus on the road to Damascus. At that moment, he believed on Jesus and twice called Him "Lord" (v. 5; 22:8-10). He later wrote, "No one can say, 'Jesus is Lord,' except by the Holy Spirit" (1 Cor. 12:3). Saul immediately submitted himself to Christ and obeyed his new Lord's command to go into the city (vv. 6-9). There, he met Ananias, who called him "brother Saul" (v. 17; 22:13). Three days later, when Ananias laid hands on him, Saul received the Holy Spirit (vv. 17-18).

3. Twelve Ephesian disciples receive the Spirit (Acts 19:1-7). These men were likely members of the emerging church in Ephesus (18:27). The text calls them "disciples" (v. 1). They had believed the message of John the Baptist concerning the Lord Jesus, and they had put their faith in Christ for salvation. Paul, therefore, baptized them in water (v. 5). It was after all of this that "Paul placed his hands on them, the Holy Spirit came on them, and they spoke in tongues and prophesied" (v. 6).

In all three instances, there was a clear period of time between the people's conversion and their being baptized in the Holy Spirit. Further, the empowering purpose of Spirit baptism logically requires

---

[1] From the World Assemblies of God Fellowship Statement of Faith, Statement 9: "The Baptism in the Holy Spirit" (see Appendix 2).

Part 3: The Beliefs of the Pentecostal Pastor

that the experience be separate from and subsequent to the new birth (Acts 1:8).

The Doctrine of Evidential Tongues

Pentecostals further teach that the baptism in the Holy Spirit "is received by faith, and is accompanied by the manifestation of speaking in tongues as the Spirit gives utterance as the initial evidence."[2] As with the doctrine of subsequence, Pentecostals derive their doctrine of evidential tongues from an inductive study of the book of Acts.

Five times the book tells of people being initially filled with, or baptized in, the Holy Spirit. On three of these occasions, the text explicitly states that those receiving the Spirit spoke in tongues as a result of their being filled with the Spirit. The first instance occurred on the Day of Pentecost when about 120 disciples "were filled with the Holy Spirit and began to speak in other tongues as the Spirit enabled them" (Acts 2:4). The second instance took place at the household of Cornelius in the coastal city of Caesarea. The Bible says that those in attendance "were astonished that the gift of the Holy Spirit had been poured out even on Gentiles. For they heard them speaking in tongues and praising God" (10:45-46). The third instance took place in the city of Ephesus, where Paul encountered twelve disciples. The Bible says, "When Paul placed his hands on them, the Holy Spirit came on them, and they spoke in tongues and prophesied" (19:6).

In the two remaining instances of people being initially filled with the Holy Spirit in Acts, the text strongly implies that the recipients of the gift spoke in tongues. In the first instance, the new believers in Samaria received the Spirit when the apostles, Peter and John, placed their hands on them (Acts 8:17). While Luke does not explicitly state that they spoke in tongues, the text reveals that something very dramatic and convincing occurred. Simon the Sorcerer was

---

[2] From the World Assemblies of God Fellowship Statement of Faith, Statement 9: "The Baptism in the Holy Spirit" (see Appendix 2).

Chapter 10: Upholds Pentecostal Truth

so impressed that he asked to purchase the gift. Bible scholars agree that the sign Simon saw was these new believers speaking in tongues, since this is the only sign of receiving the Spirit mentioned elsewhere in Acts.

The final instance of someone being initially filled with the Spirit in Acts was when a disciple named Ananias laid hands on Saul of Tarsus and prayed with him to be filled with the Spirit (Acts 9:17-18). While the text does not state the Saul spoke in tongues at this moment, Paul later testified that he did pray in tongues often (1 Cor. 14:18). It is likely that he began speaking in tongues on this occasion.

For these and other reasons, Pentecostal scholars insist that anyone seeking the empowering of the Holy Spirit should expect to speak in tongues when initially filled.

PROCLAIMING THE "FULL GOSPEL"

One effective way a Pentecostal pastor can promote Pentecostal truth in his or her church is by consistently emphasizing the "Full Gospel" in his or her teaching and preaching. The term Full Gospel refers to a theological concept embraced by early Pentecostals. This concept is also known as the "Fourfold Gospel" or the "Foursquare Gospel." Early Pentecostal leaders developed it to help emphasize what they believed to be the core message of the Church.

The four pillars of the Full Gospel are summed up in four concise statements: Jesus saves; Jesus heals; Jesus baptizes in the Holy Spirit; and Jesus is coming again. Early Pentecostals felt that these four key doctrines were being neglected by the churches, and they needed to be emphasized. The great strength of this model is that it keeps Jesus at the center of our preaching and teaching. During this time when many Pentecostal churches across Africa seem to have lost their way, it would be good for Pentecostals to return to these four emphases:

Jesus Saves

The first pillar of the Full Gospel is the truth that Jesus saves. He alone is the Son of God and Savior of the world (John 20:31; 1 John

4:14). Pentecostals thus believe that mankind's only hope of salvation is through the shed blood of Jesus on the cross (Acts 4:12; Col. 1:20). Every true Pentecostal pastor will preach often on the cross of Christ, calling on people to "repent and believe the good news!" (Mark 1:15).

Jesus Heals

The second pillar of the Full Gospel is the truth that Jesus heals. Pentecostals believe that the promise of divine healing lies at the heart of the gospel. They believe that both salvation from sin and deliverance from sickness are provided for in the Atonement. Healing is thus the privilege of all believers (Isa. 53:4-5; Matt. 8:16-17). Because of this, they boldly proclaim, "Jesus Christ is the same yesterday and today and forever" (Heb. 13:8). Just as He saved and healed people in the Bible, He saves and heals people today.

Jesus Baptizes in the Holy Spirit

The third pillar of the Full Gospel is the truth that Jesus baptizes believers in the Holy Spirit, empowering them as His witnesses to the lost (Acts 1:8). Pentecostals boldly proclaim that all believers are entitled to and should ardently seek to be baptized in the Holy Spirit according to Christ's command (vv. 4-5; cf. Luke 24:49).

As discussed above, this experience is distinct from the new birth, and it is confirmed by the initial physical evidence of speaking in tongues as the Spirit of God gives utterance (Acts 2:4). Every Pentecostal pastor should preach often on the baptism in the Holy Spirit. And they should pray with their people to be filled.[3]

Jesus is Coming Again

The fourth pillar of the Full Gospel is the truth that Jesus is coming again. Jesus promised that He would return from heaven to take His people to be with Him (John 14:3). At His coming, the dead in Christ will be raised first. Then, those who are still alive will be

---

[3] For more information on praying with believers to be filled with the Spirit, see Chapter 20: "Guiding Believers into Spirit Baptism."

caught up together with them to meet the Lord (1 Thess. 4:16-17; 1 Cor. 15:51-52). This is the blessed hope of the Church (Titus 2:13).

Those who know Christ as their Savior, and are living lives of faithful obedience, receive the message of Christ's coming with joy. However, those who reject Christ, receive it with dread. The Pentecostal pastor must boldly declare the message of Christ's coming to all, calling on them to renounce all sin and worldliness and pursue lives of holiness. Knowing that Christ is coming soon inspires Pentecostal Christians to work to see lost people come to Christ.

PENTECOSTAL MINISTRY

The wise Pentecostal pastor understands that Pentecostal life and ministry are a natural outgrowth of a firm adherence to Pentecostal truth. He or she understands that the people's trust must never "rest on human wisdom, but on God's power" (1 Cor. 2:4-5). Right belief should lead to right experience, and right belief and experience should lead to right practice. Let's look at five examples of Pentecostal life and ministry that emerge from an adherence to Pentecostal truth:

Spirit-filled Living

Spirit-filled living is the natural result of one's embracing Pentecostal truth. As you preach and pray with your people to be filled with the Spirit, the Spirit of God will begin to work powerfully in their lives. He will begin to mold them into effective workers for Christ. You must then make the most of this situation by guiding the people into the Spirit-filled walk.[4]

Spirit-Directed Prayer

Preaching and teaching Pentecostal truth from the pulpit will lead to Spirit-directed prayer in the church. As you lead your members into the Spirit-filled life, and teach them how to pray in the Spirit,

---

[4] The book, *In Step with the Spirit,* by Denzil R. Miller, is available for free download from www.decadeofpentecost.org.

their prayer habits will change. They will begin to pray powerful, Spirit-directed prayers. Paul talked of such prayer in Romans 8:26-27 (cf. 1 Cor. 14:14-15; Eph. 6:18).[5]

Powerful Witness

Jesus promised, "You will receive power when the Holy Spirit comes on you; and you will be my witnesses" (Acts 1:8). As people are filled with the Spirit and directed to the harvest, they will begin to witness with greater zeal and power than ever before. Again, you must make the most of the situation by leading the people in witnessing, church planting, and other evangelistic activities.

Spiritual Gifts

The faithful teaching of Pentecostal truth in the church will also encourage the manifestation of spiritual gifts. As a Pentecostal pastor, you should encourage this practice in the church by teaching on the subject.[6] In addition, you should allow time for the manifestation of the gifts in church services. You can further promote the operation of spiritual gifts by allowing the Spirit to work in and through you. The operation of spiritual gifts in the church will result in more people being saved, healed, and filled with the Spirit.

Missionary Vision

Finally, as you faithfully teach Pentecostal truth to your people, a missions vision will be created in the church. As church members are filled with the Spirit and taught about their responsibility to make disciples of all nations, their hearts will be ignited with a passion for the salvation of people everywhere. You must then promote this vision by developing a strong missions program in the church.[7]

---

[5] For more on teaching church members how to pray, see Chapter 8: "The Priority of Prayer."

[6] See Appendix 2: "The Manifestation Gifts of 1 Corinthians 12:8-10."

[7] For more information on this subject, see Chapter 40: "Developing a Local Church Missions Program."

Chapter 10: Upholds Pentecostal Truth

    The Pentecostal church today looks to the church in the book of Acts as its model for Spirit-anointed ministry and practice. It is inspired by the great missionary zeal of the first Church and draws from it a powerful strategy for reaching the lost with the gospel. In these final days before Jesus returns, Pentecostal pastors must be truly Pentecostal in belief, experience, and practice. And they must teach their people to be the same.

~ Chapter 11 ~

Promotes Pentecostal Experience and Practice

A wise Pentecostal pastor once observed, "It is one thing to be a Pentecostal preacher; it is quite another thing to be a preacher of Pentecost." The important point the pastor was making is that a preacher can be Pentecostal in name without being Pentecostal in practice. A pastor may sincerely identify himself or herself with a Pentecostal denomination while at the same time disregarding Pentecostal experience and practice. However, a true Pentecostal pastor will faithfully promote Pentecostal experience and practice in the church he or she leads.

In the last chapter, we examined the Pentecostal pastor's duty to uphold Pentecostal truth. In this chapter, we will discuss his or her obligation to promote Pentecostal experience and practice.

PROMOTES PENTECOSTAL EXPERIENCE

Pentecostals universally maintain that, while believing in God is essential, this alone is not enough. They often point to the words of

Chapter 11: Promotes Pentecostal Experience and Practice

James: "You believe that there is one God. Good! Even the demons believe that—and shudder" (James 2:19).

Pentecostals teach that, beyond mere belief in God, one must enjoy a personal relationship with Him. That relationship is established and maintained through personal experiences with God. Three of these essential experiences are the new birth, Spirit baptism, and daily communion with Christ. Let's look more closely at each of these three experiences and how you, as a Pentecostal pastor, must promote these experiences in the church Christ has appointed you to lead:

New Birth

First, you must emphasize the need to be born again in your preaching and teaching. You must require that every church member has been truly born from above. And you must ensure that everyone who attends your church is challenged to receive Christ as Savior. This is what Jesus did with Nicodemus. He challenged the religious leader, "You must be born again" (John 3:7). These words of Jesus should frequently be on your lips as you teach and preach.

To be born again is to be "born of God" (John 1:13; cf. 3:5, 8). A person is born of God when they humbly come to Christ, acknowledge Him as Lord and Savior, repent of their sins, and place their total trust in Him for forgiveness and cleansing. At that moment, a life-changing spiritual conversion occurs. Christ enters their life, and the Holy Spirit transforms them from the inside out. Paul wrote, "Therefore, if anyone is in Christ, that person is a new creation: The old has gone, the new is here!" (2 Cor. 5:17, margin).

Spirit Baptism

In addition to leading people into the new birth, as a faithful Pentecostal pastor, you must challenge all who receive Christ as Savior to immediately be baptized in the Holy Spirit. This was the practice of the early Church. When the apostles in Jerusalem heard that people were being saved in Samaria, they immediately sent Peter and John to pray with them to receive the Holy Spirit (Acts 8:14-17). Years later, when Paul arrived in Ephesus, the first question he asked the

Part 3: The Beliefs of the Pentecostal Pastor

disciples there was, "Did you receive the Holy Spirit when you believed?" (19:2). When the apostle discovered that they had not received the Spirit, he immediately laid hands on them, and "the Holy Spirit came on them, and they spoke in tongues and prophesied" (v. 6).

As a Pentecostal pastor, you must follow the example of the apostles and work hard to ensure that every new Christian is immediately baptized in the Holy Spirit. You must further ensure that everyone who receives the Spirit has a clear understanding of why God baptizes believers in the Holy Spirit. He gives them His Spirit to empower them as Christ's witnesses (Acts 1:8). You will therefore want to challenge newly Spirit-baptized believers to boldly share Christ with their family and friends.

To develop a truly Spirit-empowered missionary church, you will need to preach and teach often on the need for every believer to be baptized in the Holy Spirit. Your teaching on Spirit baptism should clearly answer three questions: (1) What is the baptism in the Holy Spirit? (2) Why must every believer be baptized in the Holy Spirit? and (3) How can a person receive the Holy Spirit?[1]

Further, you will need to provide church attenders with frequent opportunities to be filled or refilled with the Holy Spirit. This means that you will need to make space in church services for believers to seek God and ask Him for the Holy Spirit (cf. Luke 11:13). In addition, you will need to carefully cultivate an atmosphere in church services where people can readily receive the Spirit. Such an atmosphere will include the manifest presence of God and a sense of expectant faith in the hearts of God's people.[2]

---

[1] For a sermon outline on this topic, see the book, *Proclaiming Pentecost: 100 Sermon Outlines on the Power of the Holy Spirit,* Sermon 2: "The Baptism in the Holy Spirit." This book is available in e-book format (PDF) at www.DecadeofPentecost.org.

[2] For more information on preparing believers to receive the Holy Spirit, see the book, *Mobilizing for Mission,* Chapter 7: "How to Preach on the

Chapter 11: Promotes Pentecostal Experience and Practice

Daily Communion

Finally, you must ensure that your church members are living in daily communion with Christ. Jesus referred to this practice as abiding, or remaining, in Christ (John 15:4-7). Paul called it walking "in step with the Spirit" (Gal. 5:25). You must therefore teach the people that it is not enough to be born again, or even to be filled with the Spirit. Christians must commit themselves to living in unbroken fellowship with Christ through the Holy Spirit (cf. John 14:16-18, 23; 1 John 1:3).

Through word and example you must teach God's people how to do the following:

- Walk "in step with the Spirit" (Gal. 5:25).
- "Live in accordance with the Spirit" by having "their minds set on what the Spirit desires" (Rom. 8:5-6).
- Welcome God's Spirit to walk with them as their Advocate, Helper, and Comforter (John 14:16).
- "Pray in the Spirit on all occasions with all kinds of prayers and requests" (Eph. 6:18; cf. Rom. 8:26; Jude 20).
- Depend on the Holy Spirit to enlighten their minds and stir their hearts as they meditate on Scripture (John 16:13).
- Cultivate spiritual fruit in their lives (Gal. 5:22-23).

To accomplish these goals, you will need to diligently teach God's people what the Scriptures say about the Spirit-empowered life. You will also need to model these practices in your own life and ministry.

PROMOTES PENTECOSTAL PRACTICE

Along with leading God's people into Pentecostal experience, you, as a Pentecostal pastor, must lead them into authentic Pentecostal practice. To do this, you must commit yourself to promoting ten core Pentecostal practices in your church:

Baptism in the Holy Spirit." It is available for free download at www.DecadeofPentecost.org.

Part 3: The Beliefs of the Pentecostal Pastor

Anointed Proclamation

First, as a Pentecostal pastor, you must commit yourself to anointed proclamation of the Word of God. The anointing is the manifest presence of God that comes to rest on a Spirit-filled disciple, enabling him or her to minister with greater power and effectiveness. In seeking the anointing, you will be following the example of Jesus and the apostles. Jesus said of His own preaching, "The Spirit of the Lord is on me, because he has anointed me to proclaim good news" (Luke 4:18). The apostles also preached under an anointing of the Holy Spirit (Acts 2:14-18; 4:8; 13:8-12).

You can ensure the Spirit's anointing by inviting Him to come upon you as you minister the Word of God. Then, when He comes, you will need to respond in faith by boldly proclaiming the Word of God (Acts 4:31). Jesus has promised to confirm the anointed proclamation of the Word with miraculous signs (Mark 16:15-18).

Prayer for the Sick

Second, as an authentic Pentecostal pastor, you must commit yourself to praying for the sick and afflicted, believing God for divine healing. Jesus sent out His twelve disciples with the command: "Heal the sick, raise the dead, cleanse those who have leprosy, drive out demons. Freely you have received; freely give" (Matt. 10:8). James instructed church leaders, "Is anyone among you sick? Let them call the elders of the church to pray over them and anoint them with oil in the name of the Lord. And the prayer offered in faith will make the sick person well; the Lord will raise them up" (James 5:14-15).[3]

Missions Involvement

Third, as a true Pentecostal pastor, you must ensure that missions remains at the top of your church's agenda. Enthusiastic missions involvement is at the core of what it means to be truly Pentecostal. Jesus

---

[3] For more insight on this topic, see the Africa's Hope Discovery Series textbook, *Power Ministry: How to Minister in the Spirit's Power,* Chapter 11: "How to Heal the Sick."

Chapter 11: Promotes Pentecostal Experience and Practice

joined Pentecost to missions when He told His disciples, "You will receive power when the Holy Spirit comes on you; and you will be my witnesses in Jerusalem, and in all Judea and Samaria, and to the ends of the earth" (Acts 1:8). A church cannot legitimately call itself Pentecostal while at the same time avoiding missions. As a Pentecostal pastor, you are therefore obligated to establish an active missions program in the church.

To do this, you will need to preach and teach often on God's mission. God's mission is His plan to redeem and call to himself a people from every tongue, tribe, and nation on earth before Jesus returns (cf. Matt. 24:14; Rev. 5:9). You must ensure that every church member understands his or her obligation to participate in fulfilling God's mission.

You will also need to create opportunities for church members to become personally involved in missions. You can do this by leading the people on short-term missions trips, open-air crusades, street evangelism, and other similar outreaches. In addition, you will want to plan frequent missions awareness events where members are challenged to make their financial commitments to the missions program of the church. Every Pentecostal church should adopt missionaries to support with their finances and prayers.[4]

The Call of God

Fourth, as a Pentecostal pastor, you must emphasize God's call into ministry. The call of God is His choosing and calling people to himself and to His purposes. Jesus, who was himself sent by God, now calls and sends others into the harvest (Matt. 4:19; John 20:21). He told His disciples, "You did not choose me, but I chose you and appointed you so that you might go and bear fruit" (John 15:16).

If the Pentecostal church is to continually expand (as God intends for it to do), it must have a steady supply of new church planters, pastors, missionaries, evangelists, and other full-time ministers of the

---

[4] For more insight on this topic, see Chapter 40: "Developing a Local Church Missions Program."

gospel. These people must come from our Pentecostal churches. Therefore, you must encourage your people to listen for God's call. And when He speaks, like the prophet of old, they should respond, "Here am I. Send me!" (Isa. 6:8).[5]

Spiritual Warfare

Fifth, as a Pentecostal pastor in Africa, you must be prepared to engage in spiritual warfare. You must at all times be ready to confront and defeat demonic powers when they manifest themselves. This is what Jesus and the apostles did (Mark 1:21-28; Acts 16:16-18). You must prepare your members to do the same.[6]

Vibrant Worship

Sixth, you must ensure that your church practices vibrant, Spirit-anointed worship. Such worship is a hallmark of Pentecostal spirituality. Pentecostals are known for their free and open worship services. Their services include enthusiastic singing, hand clapping, dancing, and the lifting of hands. However, it is not enough that your church's worship be enthusiastic. It must be anointed. And it must be authentic. Jesus instructed His disciples, "God is spirit, and his worshipers must worship in the Spirit and in truth" (John 4:24). Paul added, "Where the Spirit of the Lord is, there is freedom" (2 Cor. 3:17).

---

[5] For more on the divine call into ministry, see Chapter 1: "A Person of Experience." Twelve sermon outlines on the call of God can be found in the book, *Proclaiming Christ to the Nations: 100 Sermon Outlines on Spirit-Empowered Missions,* Section 5: "The Call of God." These outlines are available in e-book format at www.DecadeofPentecost.org.

[6] For more insight on this topic, see Chapter 20: "Engaging in Spiritual Warfare." See also the Africa's Hope Discovery Series book, *Power Ministry: How to Minister in the Spirit's Power,* Chapter 12: "Casting Out Demons."

Chapter 11: Promotes Pentecostal Experience and Practice

During worship times, you should encourage every worshiper to focus their attention on God and His greatness. And you should instruct God's people to open their hearts to the moving of God's Spirit.[7]

Personal Testimony

Seventh, you should encourage your church members to share their testimonies with others. God's people should at all times be prepared to share the story of what God has done in their lives (1 Pet. 3:15). The Bible exhorts, "Let the redeemed of the Lord tell their story" (Psa. 107:2).

Testimony is at the heart of what it means to be Christ's witness. It is a simple but powerful way for believers to share the gospel with the lost. You should therefore encourage this practice among church members. And you should make room in church services for God's people to share testimonies of how the Spirit is working in their lives.

Spiritual Gifts

Eighth, as a Pentecostal pastor, you must contend for the moving of the Spirit in church services resulting in the manifestation of spiritual gifts. This was the practice of the early Church, and it should be the practice of every Pentecostal church today (e.g., Acts 11:28-30; 13:1-2; 21:10-14). In 1 Corinthians 12:8-10, Paul speaks of nine spiritual gifts:

> "To one there is given through the Spirit a message of wisdom, to another a message of knowledge by means of the same Spirit, to another faith by the same Spirit, to another gifts of healing by that one Spirit, to another miraculous powers, to another prophecy, to another distinguishing between spirits, to another speaking in different kinds of tongues, and to still another the interpretation of tongues. All these are the work of one and the

---

[7] For more information on this topic, see Chapter 18: "Leading the Church in Worship."

Part 3: The Beliefs of the Pentecostal Pastor

same Spirit, and he distributes them to each one, just as he determines."[8]

As you teach the people to minister in these gifts, the church will be edified, God will be glorified, and His kingdom will be advanced.

You must know, however, that the manifestation of spiritual gifts is not automatic. The gifts must be desired, and they must be encouraged (1 Cor. 12:31; 14:1). You must therefore covet the manifestation of spiritual gifts in your own life, and you must inspire their manifestation in the lives of others. You can do this by teaching and preaching on the subject. You should also model the proper operation of gifts. You can further encourage the manifestation of spiritual gifts by making room for them in church services (14:26) and by guarding against their misuse (14:39-40).[9]

Intercessory Prayer

Ninth, you must lead your church into committed intercessory prayer. Like the church in the book of Acts, the Pentecostal church in Africa today must be committed to prayer (Acts 1:14; 4:23-32; 12:5; 13:2). Just as Jesus taught His disciples how to pray, you must teach your people the same (Luke 11:1-13). You can do this by preaching and teaching often on prayer, and by faithfully modeling a lifestyle of prayer before the church. As the people observe their pastor praying, they too will be encouraged to pray (Luke 11:1; Exod. 33:10).[10]

Holy Living

Finally, as a faithful Pentecostal pastor, you must require that church members live holy, God-honoring lives (1 John 2:6). Holy living is a mandate of Scripture and a universal practice of true

---

[8] See Appendix 2: "The Manifestation Gifts of 1 Corinthians 12:8-10."
[9] For more information on this topic, see Chapter 21: "Ministering in the Spirit's Power."
[10] For more information on this topic, see Chapter 8: "The Priority of Prayer."

Chapter 11: Promotes Pentecostal Experience and Practice

Pentecostal believers (1 Pet. 1:16). As the title *Christian* implies, followers of Christ must strive to be like Him. They must be holy because the God they represent is holy. Paul exhorted the Philippian Christians to "become blameless and pure, 'children of God without fault in a warped and crooked generation'" (Phi. 2:15).

You must therefore show your people how to live Christlike lives. To do this, you will need to teach and preach often on the requirement for Christians to live holy and pure lives. You must further show the people what such a life looks like. Paul reminded the believers in Philippi, "You are witnesses, and so is God, of how holy, righteous and blameless we were among you who believed" (1 Thess. 2:10). He further exhorted believers, "Follow my example, as I follow the example of Christ" (1 Cor. 11:1). You must be able to say the same words to your church members.

True Pentecostalism can never be reduced to a set of religious beliefs, no matter how true those beliefs may be. At its essence, Pentecostalism is a way of life that seeks to conform itself to the experiences and practices of first-century believers as described in the book of Acts and the writings of the apostles. Every Pentecostal pastor must therefore aim at leading his or her church into authentic Pentecostal experience and practice.

~ Chapter 12 ~

Appreciates Pentecostal Heritage

Leila McKinney was likely the first Pentecostal missionary to children in Africa. She was filled with the Spirit in the early days of the Azusa Street Outpouring in Los Angeles, California, USA, from 1906 to 1908. A zeal for missions filled the revival, and Leila, along with her aunt Julia Hutchins and others, were moved to go to Africa to preach the gospel. Leila wrote in *The Apostolic Faith* newspaper published by the mission, "I am willing to trust Him through to Africa. I know the Lord wants me to go there. I want to testify to the people and teach the children about the blessed Lord, and to work for the Lord. I am willing to forsake all my loved ones for His sake." The story of Leila McKinney is but one of millions surrounding the Pentecostal revival in Africa.

It is crucial that the Pentecostal pastor in Africa understand and appreciate how the message of Pentecost came to the continent. An African pastor once remarked, "If we do not know where we came from, we do not know who we are, or where we are going." When we

Chapter 12: Appreciates Pentecostal Heritage

do not understand our past, we are like a boat without a sail. We run the risk of drifting aimlessly with no clear direction or purpose. However, if we know where we came from and why we are here, we can confidently move forward into the future.

This chapter will answer several important questions about the beginnings of Pentecostalism in Africa: What are the origins of the modern Pentecostal movement? When and how did it come to Africa? How did Pentecost spread across the continent? What challenges does the Pentecostal church in Africa face today? What is the future of Pentecostalism in Africa?

THE MOVEMENT BEGINS

In late December 1900, in a small Bible school in Topeka, Kansas, USA, Charles Fox Parham gave his students a research assignment. He told them to search the Scriptures to discover the "Bible evidence" of the baptism in the Holy Spirit. After a time of intensive study, the students presented their findings to Parham. They had concluded that the biblical evidence of Spirit baptism was speaking in tongues as the Spirit gives utterance.

They then began a prayer meeting that continued for several days. Soon after midnight on January 1, 1901, the Holy Spirit came powerfully on a woman named Agnes Ozman. Miraculously, she began to speak in tongues as the Spirit gave the utterance. Within days, many others, including Parham, were baptized in the Holy Spirit, evidenced by speaking in tongues. As a result of being filled with the Spirit, Parham and his students began preaching the gospel with great power and authority, much like the believers in the book of Acts. Their hearts were captured by a great missionary zeal. Parham believed that God was pouring out His Spirit to empower the church to reach the nations with the good news about Christ before His soon return.

In 1905, Parham moved his school to Houston, Texas, USA, where he continued to teach about the baptism in the Holy Spirit. Soon, Lucy Farrow joined the movement. She then introduced Parham to William J. Seymour, an African American holiness preacher.

Part 3: The Beliefs of the Pentecostal Pastor

Seymour listened to Parham teach, and he too accepted the Pentecostal message.

A short time later, Seymour received an invitation from a small holiness church in Los Angeles, California, to come and be their pastor. Seymour accepted the invitation and journeyed to Los Angeles. In his first sermon in the church, he preached a message on the baptism in the Holy Spirit with the evidence of speaking in tongues. Julia Hutchins, the pastor, rejected the message and locked Seymour out of the mission.

Seymour then began preaching the Pentecostal message in the homes of some church members. As he preached and the people prayed, many were filled with the Spirit. The crowds became so large that they were forced to purchase an old rundown church building on Azusa Street. God continued to pour out His Spirit, and over a period of three years, from 1906 to 1908, thousands came from all over the world and were filled with the Holy Spirit. They returned to their homes with the message that Pentecost had come.

Pentecostal missionaries went out from Azusa Street to more than 25 nations in two years, including China, India, Japan, Egypt, Liberia, Angola, and South Africa. The mighty Azusa Street Revival did more to spread Pentecost around the world than any other. Today, at least 26 different Pentecostal denominations trace their origins to Azusa Street, including the Assemblies of God.[1]

During those same years, God was pouring out His Spirit in other places around the world. Other early centers of Pentecostal outpouring were Wales (1904), India (1905), England (1907), Korea (1907), Chile (1909), and other places. God was fulfilling the promise He made to the prophet Joel: "In the last days, God says, I will pour out my Spirit on all people" (Acts 2:17; cf. Joel 2:28).

---

[1] For more on how the Azusa Street Revival impacted Africa, see the book, *From Azusa to Africa to the Nations*, Second Edition, by Denzil R. Miller, available for free at www.DecadeofPentecost.org.

Chapter 12: Appreciates Pentecostal Heritage

PENTECOST ARRIVES IN AFRICA

Let's now look at how the message of Pentecost came to Africa and how it spread across the continent.

Pentecost Comes to Africa

The first Pentecostal missionaries from America to Africa came directly from the Azusa Street mission. They arrived in Liberia in 1907. Their group included Lucy Farrow, J. W. and Julia Hutchins, their niece, Leila McKinney, and later that year, Edward McCauley. A total of about a dozen African American men, women, and children went from Azusa to Liberia that year in two groups. Within weeks, seven of them died of malaria or blackwater fever. Nevertheless, they saw many Liberians come to the Lord and be baptized in the Holy Spirit. The first permanent Pentecostal church in Africa was planted in Monrovia in 1907. Missionaries from Azusa also traveled to South Africa and Angola.

God also used indigenous Africans to spread the Pentecostal message. Two exciting stories are those of Elias Letwaba of South Africa and William Wadé Harris of Liberia. These men helped launch movements that impacted several African nations in Southern and West Africa, resulting in hundreds of thousands coming to Christ.

Elias Letwaba (1870-1959) has been called the most influential African Pentecostal preacher in South African history. In around 1870, while Elias was still in his mother's womb, she received a vision from God. The Spirit told her that God would one day use her son as His instrument to establish many churches. Letwaba thus grew up with a great hunger to know God and be used by Him.

In 1908, he met John G. Lake, an American missionary who, before coming to South Africa, had received the Holy Spirit under the ministry of Charles Parham. Lake had also attended the Azusa Street Revival in Los Angeles. Letwaba and Lake traveled together in ministry until 1913, when Lake returned to the USA.

As God had revealed to Letwaba's mother, he became a powerful Pentecostal preacher and educator, leading many into salvation and

Part 3: The Beliefs of the Pentecostal Pastor

the baptism in the Holy Spirit. He saw thousands healed and thousands more saved in his ministry in South Africa and Rhodesia (Zimbabwe). Letwaba was affiliated with the Apostolic Faith Mission in South Africa. He founded the Patmos Bible School, South Africa's first black-run seminary. Letwaba preached tirelessly until his death in 1959.

William Wadé Harris (c. 1860-1929) was used by God to spread the gospel throughout West Africa. He has been called "Africa's most successful evangelist." During his early adult years, he was affiliated with the Methodist and Episcopal churches in Liberia. He lived in Monrovia during the time the Azusa Street missionaries were there. Some believe that these African American missionaries were the source of Harris' Pentecostal theology.

Harris testified that the angel, Gabriel, appeared to him in a vision telling him that many would come to Christ through his prophetic ministry. Following that vision, Harris journeyed throughout Liberia, Côte d'Ivoire, Ghana, and Sierra Leone, telling people to forsake their sins and turn to Christ. He ministered in the Spirit's power, driving out demons, healing the sick, and speaking in tongues. He further insisted that people give up their fetishes, believe in Jesus, and wait for white men to come with their Bibles to teach them the Word of God. It is estimated that more than one hundred thousand people were converted through his ministry.

Letwaba and Harris are but two examples of the thousands of African pastors, evangelists, teachers, and missionaries who have preached the Full Gospel in Africa, proclaiming that Jesus saves, heals, baptizes in the Holy Spirit, and is coming soon.

Pentecost Spreads across Africa

The story of the spread of Pentecost across Africa through the Assemblies of God (AG) is a story of the Spirit working through western missionaries and African ministers to plant the church in Africa. While the AG is only one of many Pentecostal churches on the continent, God has used the movement mightily to spread the message of Christ. Let us look at two such stories.

Chapter 12: Appreciates Pentecostal Heritage

Liberia. In 1908, Jasper Klabioh Toe prayed, "If there is a creator God, help me find Him." God spoke to Toe, telling him to "walk to the ocean." At the same time, the Spirit had been dealing with American missionary, John Moore Perkins. Perkins had been baptized in the Holy Spirit while attending a Pentecostal revival in Toronto, Canada. Later, God directed him to take the message of Christ to Liberia.

While sailing along the coast of Liberia, Perkins heard the Spirit tell him to go ashore at a certain location. The ship's captain warned him, "This is not a safe place." Perkins, however, insisted on stopping. He and his team thus disembarked at the very place where the Spirit had led Toe. It was Christmas Day 1908. Perkins shared the gospel with Toe, who quickly received Christ. The work that Toe and Perkins began developed into the Liberia Assemblies of God. Today the church is the largest Pentecostal group in the country.

Nigeria. In the early 1930s, Augustine Ehurieiwe Wogu of Port-Harcourt, Nigeria, came across a copy of the *Pentecostal Evangel,* a magazine published by the Assemblies of God, USA. Wogu was drawn to what he read in the magazine about divine healing and the baptism in the Holy Spirit. As a result, he began praying for the sick and leading people into Spirit baptism. When the church he was attending refused to accept his Pentecostal teachings, Wogu and a few others left to begin an independent Pentecostal church they named the Church of Jesus Christ.

Several years later, in 1939, Wogu encountered some American AG missionaries in Port Harcourt. They had come to Nigeria to investigate the possibility of the AG starting a work there. Wogu asked them to send missionaries to help him. The mission agreed and sent a team led by W. Lloyd Shirer to work with Wogu. They agreed to call the church the Assemblies of God Nigeria. Today, it is the largest AG national church in Africa with more than three million members and adherents.

These are just two of the hundreds of stories that could be told. They do, however, help to convey the story of how God's Spirit swept across Africa through the cooperation of Africans and those whom the Spirit sent to Africa. Other stories could be told of how the flame

Part 3: The Beliefs of the Pentecostal Pastor

of Pentecost was ignited in other church fellowships across the continent, such as the Church of Pentecost in Ghana and the Full Gospel Believers' Church in Ethiopia.

Africa Assemblies of God. When the Pentecostal message first came to Liberia in 1906, there were no Pentecostal churches or believers anywhere in Africa. God, however, was beginning to pour out His Spirit on the continent. The growth of the Assemblies of God is a shining example of how God has blessed the continent. By 1948, the Assemblies of God in Africa had grown to 40,000 believers, meeting in about 700 churches in 11 African nations.

In 1989, the AG formed the Africa Assemblies of God Alliance (AAGA), composed of participating national churches across the continent. The next year, AAGA launched their "Decade of Harvest" emphasis, continuing from 1991 to 2000. The emphasis was on Spirit-empowered church planting and missions. During those ten years the church grew from 2.1 million adherents meeting in 11,688 churches in 31 countries, to 6.3 million adherents meeting in 24,019 churches in 39 countries. The momentum gained during the Decade of Harvest continued through the next decade. By 2010, the Africa AG had grown to 16.6 million adherents meeting in 67,827 churches.

In January 2010, AAGA launched a second decadal initiative, called the "Decade of Pentecost" (2010-2020). Like the Decade of Harvest, the Decade of Pentecost emphasized church planting and missions. An additional goal was to see 10 million church members baptized in the Holy Spirit and mobilized as Spirit-empowered witnesses. By the end of 2019, the Africa AG had grown to 18.7 million adherents meeting in 87,741 churches in Sub-Saharan Africa and the Indian Ocean Basin.

In January 2021, AAGA launched a third decadal emphasis called the "Decade of Revival." In this decade, the church will continue its emphasis on evangelism, Spirit baptism, church planting, and missions. One unique emphasis of the Decade of Revival is that the Africa AG are targeting North Africa, with a goal of launching Spirit-empowered church planting movements in this previously neglected region.

Chapter 12: Appreciates Pentecostal Heritage

THE IMPACT OF PENTECOST

Pentecostalism has changed the face of the African church in many ways. The growth of the movement has been remarkable. In 2015, the *Oxford Research Encyclopedia* reported that there were 202 million Pentecostals (Renewalists) in Africa, making up 35% of the continent's Christian population and 17% of its total population. In varying degrees, virtually every African denomination has been affected. Many traditional churches have adopted such outward expressions of Pentecostalism as joyous singing, expressive worship, and fervent prayer. Several have even embraced some of Pentecostalism's more fundamental practices such as being born again, speaking in tongues, and power ministry.

Pentecostal Christianity has also affected Africa's broader culture. One way they have done this is through a phenomenon known as "redemption and lift." When people become committed Christians, their lives are changed, and they are "lifted" out of their sin and degradation. As a result, they become better people and more productive citizens. They begin to treat their families with love and respect, thus producing more productive offspring. Moreover, dedicated Christians often pursue higher education, work harder, get better jobs, and seek to practice financial integrity. They often reach out in compassion to care for those who are struggling with life. In addition, some Pentecostal Christians are taking their values into the political arena and are making a difference there. These actions and more contribute to a better society. While not all Pentecostal Christians live up to the ideals of Christ in society, those who strive to do so are making a positive impact.

FACING THE FUTURE

Today's Pentecostal church in Africa stands at a crossroads. As it reflects on its past, it can boast of many successes, as we have discussed in this chapter. However, as African Pentecostalism looks to the future, it faces many challenges. Three of those challenges are the threats of doctrinal perversion, spiritual stagnation, and self-centeredness.

Part 3: The Beliefs of the Pentecostal Pastor

In response, as a Pentecostal pastor, you would do well to ask yourself three probing questions:

- Will I remain true to Scripture, or will I lead my church into doctrinal error?
- Will I guide my church into authentic Pentecostal revival, or will I allow it to sink into spiritual stagnation, "having a form of godliness but denying its power"? (2 Tim. 3:5).
- Will I guide my people to seek the lost in the power of the Holy Spirit, or will I lead them into a vain, self-centered pursuit of personal prosperity and blessing?

The future of the Pentecostal church in Africa depends largely on how you and thousands of other Pentecostal pastors answer these questions.

If Pentecostal pastors across the continent will wholeheartedly commit themselves to be true to their Pentecostal heritage and remain authentically Pentecostal in doctrine, experience, and practice, the future is bright. However, if they decide to forsake their heritage and become like those around them, the future of Pentecostalism in Africa stands in peril. It is therefore crucial that Pentecostal pastors across Africa eagerly follow the godly examples of their forefathers.

This Pentecostal heritage is a sacred trust. Authentic Pentecostal revival is the world's last great hope. If the gift of Pentecost is cherished and fanned into flame, it can erupt into a blazing fire, spreading from Africa to the nations of the world. However, if it is neglected or abused, it can flicker and die. Pentecostal pastors across Africa must therefore give heed to Paul's words to Timothy, his young Pentecostal colleague and pastor of the church in Ephesus: "I remind you to fan into flame the gift of God, which is in you through the laying on of my hands" (2 Tim. 1:5). Paul added, "Guard the good deposit that was entrusted to you—guard it with the help of the Holy Spirit who lives in us" (v. 14).

As Pentecostal pastors in Africa, we too must cherish and fan into flame the gift of God that has been passed to us by our Pentecostal

Chapter 12: Appreciates Pentecostal Heritage

forebearers. And like them, we must faithfully preserve what has been entrusted to us by the Holy Spirit who indwells and empowers us.

~ PART 4 ~

THE PERSONAL LIFE OF THE PENTECOSTAL PASTOR

~ Chapter 13 ~

A Well-Managed Life

The young pastor sat at his desk with his head buried in his hands. The demands of pastoral ministry were becoming more than he could bear. He was considering leaving the ministry and returning to his secular job. What this young pastor did not realize, however, is that he was not alone in his anguish. Across Africa, hundreds of Pentecostal pastors find themselves in similar circumstances. They feel they cannot continue to cope with the many pressures of ministry.

One reason these pastors feel so overwhelmed is that they have not learned to manage their lives well. They live such poorly managed lives that each new challenge catches them off guard, knocking them off balance.

While it is unrealistic for a Pentecostal pastor to think he or she can escape all the pressures of life and ministry, it is not unrealistic for them to believe they can effectively cope with these challenges. This chapter will offer advice on how you, as a Pentecostal pastor, can achieve a well-managed life.

Chapter 13: A Well-Managed Life

THE IMPORTANCE OF A WELL-MANAGED LIFE

One biblical title for a pastor is *overseer* (1 Tim. 3:1-2). Paul instructed the Ephesian elders, "Keep watch over yourselves and all the flock of which the Holy Spirit has made you overseers" (Acts 20:28). As an overseer, a pastor "manages God's household" (Titus 1:7). The Pentecostal pastor thus bears the responsibility of effectively managing the affairs of a local church. However, before he or she can successfully manage a church, they must first be able to manage their own lives well.

A Well-Managed Life

While a well-managed life is not without stress, neither is it cluttered with unnecessary disorder and confusion. A well-managed life will provide you with the confidence you need to progress in ministry. It will allow you to be more productive—to do more with less effort. And it will help you to cope well with life's emergencies. Let's look at four features of a well-managed life:

1. Purpose. A well-managed life is a life lived with clear purpose. Paul referred to God's purpose as His "good, pleasing, and perfect will" (Rom. 12:2). The more clearly you understand God's purpose for your life, the more effective you will be in ordering your life around that purpose.

Broadly speaking, you, as a Pentecostal pastor—like every other follower of Christ—live to glorify God and to do His will. While you may accept this truth, you must not stop here. You must strive to know God's perfect, or complete, will for your life. You must seek to understand why God has placed you in your particular church at this particular time. You must seek God in prayer asking Him, "Lord, why have You brought me to this place?" and "What do You want me to accomplish here for Your glory?"

2. Priority. Once you clearly understand God's purpose for your being in your particular church at this particular time, you can begin to formulate your personal and ministerial priorities. Your priorities are those things you consider most important. They are the issues on

Part 4: The Personal Life of the Pentecostal Pastor

which you focus the greater part of your time and energy. Christ spoke of His life's priorities when He said, "I have come down from heaven not to do my will but to do the will of him who sent me" (John 6:38).

As a Pentecostal pastor, you can use your understanding of God's will to guide you in making your ministry and life decisions. You can ask of each possible alternative, "How does this activity help me to fulfill God's purpose for my life?" Any activity that furthers God's purpose should be embraced. Any activity that does not further God's purpose should be avoided or discontinued.[1]

3. Balance. Further, a well-managed life is a balanced life. A balanced life is one that budgets the appropriate time and energy for each of life's essential activities. A man trying to cross a stream on the trunk of a fallen tree must carefully maintain his balance. If he leans too far to the left or right, he will fall into the water. The same is true for the Pentecostal pastor. If he or she focuses all of their attention on just one or two aspects of life or ministry, they are in danger of getting out of balance and failing in some other critical area.

For instance, you as a pastor could spend so much time taking care of church members that you neglect your own family. Or you could be so committed to sermon preparation that you neglect prayer or reaching out to the lost. As a faithful Pentecostal pastor, you must strive to maintain balance in various areas of life, such as

- a balance between doing and being,
- a balance between work and rest,
- a balance between ministry and family,
- a balance between caring for others and self-care.

Jesus' words to the Pharisees apply here. He challenged them concerning their overemphasis on tithing, while neglecting other

---

[1] For more on the Pentecostal pastor's personal and ministerial priorities, see Chapter 4: "Personal Priorities," and Chapter 5: "Ministerial Priorities."

more important practices. He said, "You should have practiced the latter without leaving the former undone" (Luke 11:42).

4. Direction. Finally, for a Pentecostal pastor, a well-managed life is a life directed by the Spirit of God. The more closely you follow the guidance of the Holy Spirit, the more ordered your life will become.

Paul encouraged the believers in Galatia, "Walk by the Spirit, and you will not gratify the desires of the flesh" (Gal. 5:16). He then listed several "acts of the flesh." Consider how each of these acts could be cited as fruit of a poorly managed or undisciplined life: "sexual immorality, impurity and debauchery; idolatry and witchcraft; hatred, discord, jealousy, fits of rage, selfish ambition, dissensions, factions and envy; drunkenness, orgies, and the like" (Gal. 5:19-21).

On the other hand, to be led by the Holy Spirit is to live a life submitted to God. Such a life seeks to cultivate the "fruit of the Spirit." Paul identifies this fruit as "love, joy, peace, forbearance, kindness, goodness, faithfulness, gentleness and self-control" (Gal. 5:22-23). Consider how each of these virtues could be cited as a quality of a well-managed life. They are produced by remaining in Christ (John 15:5) and walking in the Spirit (Gal. 5:24-25).

Our Model of a Well-Managed Life

Jesus is our perfect model of one who lived a well-managed life. Jesus ordered His life around His Father's agenda, and He walked in step with His Father's schedule. Because of this, He was able to stay focused on His mission. Notice how Jesus' life exemplifies the four above-mentioned characteristics of a well-managed life:

- *Purpose.* Jesus knew His purpose in coming, and He stayed true to His life's mission. That is why, as His ministry was coming to an end, He was able to pray to His Father, "I have brought you glory on earth by finishing the work you gave me to do" (John 17:4).
- *Priority.* Jesus always put first things first. For instance, He prioritized maintaining a strong relationship with His Father. Mark wrote of Him, "Very early in the morning, while it was

Part 4: The Personal Life of the Pentecostal Pastor

still dark, Jesus got up, left the house and went off to a solitary place, where he prayed" (Mark. 1:35).
- *Balance.* Jesus lived a perfectly balanced life. He balanced being with doing and work with rest (Mark 6:31-32). Because He lived a balanced life, He was never flustered and never hurried. He was always in the right place at the right time doing the right thing.
- *Direction.* Jesus lived His life under the direction of the Holy Spirit. He was full of the Spirit (Luke 4:18-19), and He always did as the Spirit directed (Matt. 4:1; Luke 4:1). He said of himself, "The Son can do nothing by himself; he can do only what he sees his Father doing, because whatever the Father does the Son also does" (John 5:19).

As a Pentecostal pastor, you must make it your aim to follow Jesus' example (1 John 2:6).

Benefits of a Well-Managed Life

While achieving a well-managed life requires effort, for the Pentecostal pastor, it is effort well spent. The pastor who manages his or her life well will experience greater productivity in ministry. Because their time is well managed, they are able to do more with less effort.

Further, a well-managed life results in greater peace of mind. Effective life management tends toward order, and order tends toward peace. Throughout His life, Jesus exhibited an uncommon peace of mind. When others panicked, He remained calm. For example, when His disciples panicked in the storm, He slept peacefully in the stern of the boat (Matt. 8:23-27). Much the same happened with Paul on his voyage to Rome (Acts 27:27-38).

A well-managed life also promises greater longevity in ministry. A poorly managed life results in stress, and stress results in burnout. However, a well-managed life produces peace, which contributes to greater endurance in ministry.

Chapter 13: A Well-Managed Life

THREE ASPECTS OF A WELL-MANAGED LIFE

As a Pentecostal pastor, you must be able to successfully manage three aspects of life and ministry, as follows:

Managing Finances

First, you must learn to administer your personal finances well. You can begin this process by reminding yourself that everything you possess ultimately belongs to God (Psa. 24:1; 1 Cor. 4:7). You must realize that you are a mere manager of God's property, and one day you will give an account to Him about how you have handled your finances (Luke 16:2).

A good money management plan is to divide your income into three broad categories: First, you give to God; then, you save for the future; and finally, you spend wisely on present needs. Let's look more closely at this three-part plan for godly financial management.

1. First, you give to God. As a Pentecostal pastor, generous giving is your first step in achieving financial well-being. Scripture repeatedly informs us that the firstfruits of everything we receive belongs to God (cf. Exod. 13:1; 34:26; Lev. 2:14; Pro. 3:9). Thus, the starting point in managing your finances is to faithfully give your tithes and offerings to God. You must further fulfill any other financial commitments you have made to Him or His church, such as missions and building fund pledges. God promises to abundantly bless those who are generous with Him (Mal 3:10-11; Luke 6:38).

2. Then, you save for the future. After giving to God, you must save for future and emergency needs. You can do this by placing a set amount of money into a savings account in each week. As this account grows, it can serve as a safety net for emergencies, and it can be a source of funds for larger purchases.

3. Finally, you spend wisely. What remains after giving to God and investing in savings can be used to meet the ongoing necessities of the family, such as food, housing, and other needs. Because this money also belongs to God, you must spend it wisely. The best way to do this is to develop a workable budget, or financial plan. This plan will serve as a guide for spending, and it will help to bring your purchases into line. Well-managed finances will help bring peace and stability into your home. And they will help you and your family to achieve your goals.

Managing Time

Second, in your pursuit of a well-managed life, you must learn to manage your time. Because of cultural influences, many African pastors find time management to be a challenge. Time, however, is a person's most valuable resource. While we can replace lost money, we can never call back lost time. The Bible exhorts us to redeem the time by making the most of every opportunity (Eph. 5:15-16; Col. 4:5).

As a faithful Pentecostal pastor, just as you must learn to budget your money, you must learn to budget your time. You must learn to allocate time for family, work, leisure, study, prayer, visitation, and other essential activities. This task will require your creating to-do lists, organizing workspace, developing daily and weekly routines, and avoiding procrastination.

Practicing Self-care

Third, in seeking a well-managed life, you must learn how to practice self-care. Self-care is the exercise of tending to our own spiritual, emotional, and physical needs. We do this, not for selfish reasons, but for godly reasons. We care for ourselves so that we might better serve God and others.

When God created humans, He created them with spirit, soul, and body (1 Thess. 5:23). The spirit is the part of a man or woman that communes with God. The soul is the part that thinks, feels, and chooses. And the body is the physical part of humans. It is the house in which our spirit and soul dwell. Self-care involves caring for all three.

You can care for your spirit and soul by practicing the spiritual disciplines of meditation on the Word, worship, prayer, and fasting.[2] Further, you must continually yield your thoughts, emotions, and will to the lordship of Christ. The Bible instructs us, "Do not conform to the pattern of this world, but be transformed by the renewing of your mind. Then you will be able to test and approve what God's will is—his good, pleasing and perfect will" (Rom. 12:2). The Bible further teaches us how we should regulate our thought lives:

> "Whatever is true, whatever is noble, whatever is right, whatever is pure, whatever is lovely, whatever is admirable—if anything is excellent or praiseworthy—think about such things." (Phi. 4:8)

Caring for our bodies is important because our bodies are temples of the Holy Spirit. We should therefore honor God with our bodies (1 Cor. 6:19-20). A healthy body enables us to better fulfill God's calling on our lives. It makes it possible for us to live life to the full (John 10:10). We should therefore care for our bodies by eating well, exercising regularly, getting enough sleep, and having regular medical checkups.

PURSUING A WELL-MANAGED LIFE

You may be asking, "How can I, as a Pentecostal pastor, go about pursuing a well-managed life?"

Make a Decision

You begin your quest for a well-managed life with a decision. Jesus told the story of the Prodigal Son. In this story, the rebellious son demanded from his father his inheritance and left home. Soon, because of his self-indulgent lifestyle, the young man found himself in the fields feeding pigs. At that point, the boy came to his senses and said to himself, "I will set out and go back to my father and say to him: Father, I have sinned against heaven and against you. I am no longer worthy to be called your son; make me like one of your hired

---

[2] This topic is dealt with in Chapter 15: "A Strong Devotional Habit."

servants" (Luke 15:18-19). With that decision, he arose and began his journey home.

It is much the same in seeking a well-managed life. Your journey to a more productive lifestyle must begin with a firm decision. You must look at your present condition and determine that there is a better way to live and minister. You must then say to yourself, "I will arise and pursue a more productive lifestyle."

Create a Plan

While a decision to pursue a well-managed life is essential, it is not enough. Your decision must be followed by a workable plan. This plan will involve three steps, as follows:

1. Self-assessment. You begin your journey to a well-managed life with self-assessment. In this self-assessment, you will examine your current lifestyle to determine where it needs improvement. You can do this by honestly answering such questions as these:

- How well am I doing in managing my finances?
- How well am I doing in managing my time?
- How well am I doing in caring for my spirit, soul, and body?
- How can I do better in each of these areas?

Carefully answer these questions, and write your answers in a notebook.

2. Setting goals. Once you have identified the areas in which you need improvement, set your personal developmental goals. You can do this by asking and thoughtfully answering the following questions:

- In what ways do I want to improve my financial management skills?
- In what ways do I want to improve my time management skills?
- In what ways do I want to improve my skills in caring for my spirit, soul, and body?

Again, write your answers in your notebook. Be specific.

3. Developing a plan. Once you have set your goals, you must develop a plan for reaching these goals. Focus on only one or two issues at a time, and develop a plan for achieving each goal. In your plan, you will want to identify specific steps you can take to achieve your goals. For example, you may want to improve your financial skills by developing and following a family budget. Or, you may want to improve your time management skills by making a to-do list each morning, and then using this list to guide your day's activities.

Move into Action

Once you have developed your plan, you must move into action. You must begin to execute your plan. Be persistent; stick with your plan. Then, at the end of three to six months, evaluate your progress. Identify where you have done well and where you have not done well. Then, adjust the plan and repeat the process. You may want to continue to work on the same goals, or you may choose to work on other goals.

Achieving a well-managed life is a life-long process. It is a goal worth pursuing, and will bring many blessings into the life of the Pentecostal pastor.

~ Chapter 14 ~

Healthy Relationships

An expert in the Law of Moses approached Jesus with a question. "Teacher," he asked, "which is the greatest commandment in the Law?" Without hesitation, Jesus answered him, "'Love the Lord your God with all your heart and with all your soul and with all your mind.' This is the first and greatest commandment. And the second is like it: 'Love your neighbor as yourself'" (Matt. 22:36-39). Thus, according to Jesus, relationships are at the heart of what it means to serve God.

Christianity is more than a religion; it is a personal relationship with God through Jesus Christ. It is not a matter of simply adhering to certain beliefs or performing certain rituals. Rather, it is a matter of loving God and others. This idea of a loving relationship with God and with people distinguishes Christianity from other religions.

Pastoral ministry must be performed up close. Just as a shepherd cannot tend his sheep from a distance, a Pentecostal pastor cannot care for his or her people from afar. To be successful in ministry, the Pentecostal pastor must understand the importance of building strong, healthy relationships. And they must know how these relationships are developed and maintained.

UNDERSTANDING RELATIONSHIPS

Relationships are the connections we make with each other. They are the ways we relate to one another. Relationships can be close or distant, strong or weak, genuine or superficial, healthy or destructive. As a Pentecostal pastor, you must know how to build healthy relationships with family members, church members, friends, and other pastors. And you must be able to teach others to do the same.

Healthy relationships allow God's people to live together in harmony. They bless people and build them up. They help them to feel secure, respected, and accepted. Healthy relationships also bring God's people together in productive enterprise. They cause a church to prosper and grow strong. On the other hand, unhealthy relationships cause people to fall into arguments and resentments. Such relationships cause a church to become weak and ineffective.

Paul therefore exhorted the early Christians to develop healthy relationships with one another. He wrote to the Christians in Ephesus, "Make every effort to keep the unity of the Spirit through the bond of peace" (Eph. 4:3). He counseled the believers in Rome, "Live in harmony with one another. Do not be proud, but be willing to associate with people of low position" (Rom. 12:16). Paul understood that healthy relationships form the basis for effective ministry both inside and outside the assembly.

TYPES OF RELATIONSHIPS

As a Pentecostal pastor, it is important that you be aware of the various types, or levels, of relationships you encounter in life. This understanding will help you better prioritize which relationships you should invest in more heavily.

Part 4: The Personal Life of the Pentecostal Pastor

The Primary Relationship

Your most important relationship in life is your relationship with God. All other relationships must be built on this primary relationship. You must therefore give your relationship with God top priority. If you get this relationship right, all other relationships will fall into place. The opposite is also true; if you bungle this relationship, all other relationships will be negatively affected.

Your relationship with God must be one of deep love (Matt. 22:37). This love for God will express itself in devoted obedience to His commandments (John 14:15, 21) and in loving concern for others (John 15:12).

Family Relationships

Second only to your relationship with God is your relationship with your spouse. The Bible says that God has made the husband and wife one flesh (Gen. 2:24). The husband must therefore love his wife as he loves his own body, even as Christ loves the church. And the wife must respect her husband and submit to his authority in the home (Eph. 5:21-33). You and your spouse must therefore cherish this relationship above all other human relationships. And you must invest ample time and effort into strengthening this relationship.

Your third most important relationship is with your children. You must love your children deeply, and you must tenderly care for them. The Bible says that parents must bring up their children in the instruction of the Lord (Eph. 6:4). Therefore, you must never neglect your children—even in the pursuit of your pastoral duties. Rather, you must make time to form a bond of friendship with each one of them. This will produce an atmosphere of loving friendship in the home. This atmosphere will allow you to go about your work in peace, and it will increase your productivity in ministry. It will also serve as a testimony to the church and community. Most importantly, you must seek to lead your children into a personal relationship with Christ. And you must ensure that each child has been filled with the Holy Spirit.

Chapter 14: Healthy Relationships

In addition, you must cultivate a loving relationship with your extended family. You should show the proper Christian love and respect for your parents, your brothers and sisters, your cousins, and other family members. You must, however, keep all things in their proper order. You must never prefer your extended family members above your spouse and children. Paul wrote to Timothy, "Anyone who does not provide for their relatives, and especially for their own household, has denied the faith and is worse than an unbeliever" (1 Tim. 5:8).[1]

Ministerial Relationships

In addition to your relationships with God and your family members, as a Pentecostal pastor, you must carefully tend to your ministerial relationships. These relationships include both those *to* whom you minister and those *with* whom you minister. They include your church members, your community, and your denomination or national church. Each of these relationships is unique, and each should be handled slightly differently. To a large degree, your success or failure in ministry will depend on how you manage these relationships.

Further you will need to build a strong personal and professional relationship with both the pastoral and lay staff members of your church. When Jesus chose the twelve apostles, He sent them out to preach and cast out demons. However, He first called them to spend time with Him (Mark 3:13-15). Our Lord knew that the bond He would build with them while they were together would serve as a foundation for their ministry when they were apart. The same is true of the church you lead. Your bond with your pastoral and lay staff will serve as a foundation for all ministry in the local church.[2]

---

[1] For more on this topic, see Chapter 7: "Family Priorities."
[2] For more on this topic, see Chapter 5: "Ministerial Priorities."

Part 4: The Personal Life of the Pentecostal Pastor

Three Risky Relationships

Some relationships come with a level of risk. Three of those relationships are your relationship with the world, your relationship with those of the opposite sex, and your choice of close friends. As a Pentecostal pastor, you must navigate each of these relationships very carefully, as follows:

1. Your relationship with the world. You must be vigilant in your relationship with the world. The world is composed of the many earthly systems controlled by Satan and those who serve him (1 John 5:19). Jesus told His disciples, "You do not belong to the world, but I have chosen you out of the world" (John 15:19). The Bible explains that, while the follower of Christ must live in the world, he or she must not be engrossed with the things of the world (1 Cor. 7:31). They must not set their affections on worldly things (1 John 2:15). Neither must they pattern their lives after the ways of the world (Rom. 12:2).

2. Your relationship with the opposite sex. Further, as a Pentecostal pastor, you must closely monitor your relationship with those of the opposite sex. Because some pastors have failed to keep boundaries in this relationship, they have fallen into disgrace and have brought shame to the work of God. Paul warned Timothy, "Flee the evil desires of youth and pursue righteousness" (2 Tim. 2:22). He further instructed his son in the faith, "[Treat] older women as mothers, and younger women as sisters, with absolute purity" (1 Tim. 5:2).

You must relate to those of the opposite sex with absolute propriety. Other than your spouse, you should never find yourself alone with a person of the opposite sex. You should also guard your thought life. Every adulterous affair begins in one's imagination. Therefore, you must never allow your thoughts to wander from your spouse to another person (Matt. 5:28). The Bible admonishes, "Above all else, guard your heart, for everything you do flows from it" (Pro. 4:23).

3. Your choice of friends. One's choice of friends can bring great blessing or great harm into his or her life. You must therefore use wisdom in choosing your friends. The Bible tells us, "The righteous choose their friends carefully, but the way of the wicked leads them astray" (Pro. 12:26). Paul adds, "Do not be misled: Bad company corrupts good character" (1 Cor. 15:33). As a Pentecostal pastor, you should form strong bonds of friendships only with those who will encourage you to draw close to God and live a life that is pleasing to Him.

CHARACTERISTICS OF HEALTHY RELATIONSHIPS

Africans recognize that the quality of one's life is largely determined by the quality of his or her relationships. What then are some benchmarks the Pentecostal pastor can use to guide them in building and maintaining healthy relationships in their homes, churches, and communities? As a Pentecostal pastor, your relationships should exhibit five characteristics:

Love

The first characteristic that must define your relationships with others is sacrificial love. You must love your spouse, your children, and God's people with the same passion that Christ loves you. Jesus commanded His disciples, "As I have loved you, so you must love one another" (John 13:34). He was telling them that selfless love must define their relationships with one another. Jesus was willing to lay down His life for them. Now, they must be willing to lay down their lives for one another (John 15:12-13). Peter thus urges us, "Love one another deeply, from the heart" (1 Pet. 1:22).

Open Communication

The second characteristic that should define your relationship with others is open, honest communication. Paul advised the Christians in Ephesus to speak the truth in love. If they would do this, they would grow and mature as His body (Eph. 4:15). The apostle further admonished the Colossian believers, "Let your conversation be always full of grace, seasoned with salt, so that you may know how to answer everyone" (Col. 4:6).

Part 4: The Personal Life of the Pentecostal Pastor

As a Pentecostal pastor, you must carefully weigh your words before speaking, remembering the words of Scripture: "Those who guard their lips preserve their lives, but those who speak rashly will come to ruin" (Pro. 13:3). Your communication with others should be characterized by friendliness, confidence, and sincerity. Your words should be frank without being harsh, honest without being unkind. And you must learn to listen closely to what others say. The Bible admonishes, "To answer before listening—that is folly and shame" (Pro. 18:13).

Mutual Trust

A third characteristic that should define your relationship with your family and church members is mutual trust. Trust is the confidence people have in one another. Mutual trust is the shared belief that all parties in the relationship will be truthful and that they will remain committed to the relationship. For mutual trust to occur, all parties in the relationship must demonstrate their devotion to one another.

As a Pentecostal pastor, you must prove yourself to be worthy of the people's trust. People must feel safe around their pastor. They must feel secure in confiding their deepest secrets with him or her. And they must know that their pastor will not share these secrets with anyone else.

Respect

A fourth characteristic that should define your relationship with others is mutual respect. Respect is the high regard one has for the feelings, rights, and dignity of others. Peter urged Christians, "Show proper respect to everyone" (1 Pet. 2:17). Wives should respect their husbands and husbands should respect their wives. Children should respect their parents, and parents should respect their children. Church members should respect their pastor, and their pastor must respect them.

Because all people bear the image of their Creator, you must value every person regardless of their race, tribe, or social standing.

Chapter 14: Healthy Relationships

Paul urged the Christians in Rome to "be devoted to one another" and to "honor one another above yourselves" (Rom. 12:10). He added, "Live in harmony with one another. Do not be proud, but be willing to associate with people of low position. Do not be conceited" (v. 16).

Humility

Finally, your relationship with others should be marked by humility. Humility is the opposite of arrogance and self-promotion. It is freedom from pride and conceit. Humility is a person's ability to see himself as God sees him. In other words, a humble person is able to see himself as he really is. Humility is an expression of true love. Paul wrote, "Love...does not boast, it is not proud. It does not dishonor others, it is not self-seeking" (1 Cor. 13:4-5).

Pride closes the door to deep, lasting relationships. Humility opens it wide (Rom. 12:16). As a humble pastor, you will be a man or woman of the people. You will be accessible. Rather than building walls between yourself and people, you will build bridges.

MAINTAINING HEALTHY RELATIONSHIPS

Here are three practices that will help you to build and maintain healthy, God-honoring relationships with others:

Be Purposeful

First, you must be purposeful about building and maintaining healthy relationships with your family members, church members, and ministerial associates. You must take the initiative and actively pursue these relationships. This is what Jesus did. He chose to walk among the people. He took time to listen to them and hear their cries. His enemies noticed this, and they accused him of being "a friend of tax collectors and sinners" (Matt. 11:19). As a Pentecostal pastor, you must strive to be like Jesus and actively seek to build strong relationships with others.

Part 4: The Personal Life of the Pentecostal Pastor

Nurture Relationships

Further, you must work hard to nurture healthy relationships. You must be willing to invest the time and effort needed to build strong, lasting bonds with your family, your church members, and your ministerial associates. To do this, you will need to spend time with them, listening to their stories, laughing at their jokes, and crying over their heartaches and failures (Rom. 12:15). If you will do this, in time, a strong bond of affection will form between you and your people.

Practice Forgiveness

Finally, if you are to build and maintain strong, lasting relationships with others, you must learn to ask for and offer forgiveness. It is inevitable; people will offend, and they will be offended. Misunderstandings will occur and feelings will be hurt. If relationships are to be preserved, forgiveness must occur.

The coin of forgiveness has two sides. One side is the guilty person asking for forgiveness. The other side is the offended person granting forgiveness. You must be prepared to do both (Matt. 5:22-26). You must be quick to ask for forgiveness when you have offended. And you must be willing to grant forgiveness when someone asks for it. Forgiveness liberates both the offender and the offended. It opens the door to reconciliation and makes the way for broken relationships to be mended.

Effective ministry is built on strong, healthy relationships. The wise Pentecostal pastor will invest heavily in building these relationships.

Chapter 14: Healthy Relationships

~ Chapter 15 ~

A Strong Devotional Habit

"I consider everything a loss because of the surpassing worth of knowing Christ Jesus my Lord" (Phi. 3:8). These are the words of the apostle Paul. Second only to Jesus, he is believed to be the greatest missionary who ever lived. He preached with power, worked miracles, and planted churches throughout the Roman Empire. God used him to open the door of salvation to the Gentiles (Acts 14:27). Yet, in all of this, he felt that His greatest achievement in life was simply knowing Jesus. His constant prayer was, "I want to know Christ" (Phi. 3:10).

Like Paul, you as a Pentecostal pastor are a leader. As such, you have many responsibilities. You have been called to develop believers into disciples and to advance God's kingdom in the earth. These are big jobs, and you must faithfully perform these duties. However, if you want to go far in ministry, like Paul, you must prioritize your relationship with Christ. You must dedicate yourself to knowing Christ and learning to live in constant communion with Him.

To do this, you will need to develop a strong devotional habit. No amount of labor, no matter how diligent or effective, will make up for lack of fellowship with the Lord. This chapter will deal with the devotional habit of the Pentecostal pastor.

THE DEVOTIONAL HABIT

We will begin our investigation of the devotional habit with some definitions.

Understanding the Term

A habit is something a person does regularly. It is a recurring behavior that has become second nature. Like a man brushing his teeth every morning, habits are developed through repetition. At the beginning, a person has to remind himself or herself of the need to do the activity. And sometimes they have to discipline themselves to do it. However, over time, the activity becomes habitual.

What then is the devotional habit? The devotional habit is the Christian discipline of maintaining a daily time of communion with Christ. It is the time that the faithful servant of Christ sets aside each day to nurture his or her relationship with God. It is a habit because, over time, it becomes routine. It is devotional because its purpose is to nurture one's relationship with God and to increase their commitment to Him and His mission.

Benefits of the Devotional Habit

If you will develop and faithfully maintain a strong devotional habit, many benefits will come into your life and ministry. Let's look at four of those benefits:

1. Knowing Christ. The first benefit of your developing a strong devotional habit is that it will cause you to grow in your relationship with Christ. The writer of Hebrews urges us, "Let us draw near to God with a sincere heart" (Heb. 10:22). James adds a promise to the command: "Come near to God and he will come near to you" (James 4:8). As you pray and meditate on Scripture, you will enter into the Most Holy Place (Heb. 10:19). There, in the presence of God, you, like Moses of old, will find yourself communing with God "face to face, as one speaks to a friend" (Exod. 33:11).

Part 4: The Personal Life of the Pentecostal Pastor

2. Discerning God's will. A second benefit of your developing a strong devotional habit is that you will come to better understand God's will for your life. As you pray, read God's Word, and apply its teachings to your life, your mind will be transformed. When this happens, you "will be able to test and approve what God's will is—his good, pleasing and perfect will" (Rom. 12:2).

3. Developing a biblical worldview. A third benefit of your developing a strong devotional habit is that the practice will help you to develop a biblical worldview. As you prayerfully search the Scriptures, you will begin to see the world as God sees it. You will begin to understand His plan for humanity. And you will be able to discern your place in fulfilling that plan.

4. Staying in tune with the Spirit. A fourth benefit of maintaining a strong devotional habit is that you will learn to live in close fellowship with the Holy Spirit (2 Cor. 13:14). Paul urged Christians to "keep in step with the Spirit" (Gal. 5:25). He further admonished them, "Be continually filled with the Holy Spirit" (literal translation of Ephesians 5:18). In an atmosphere of devotion, the Holy Spirit will make His power and presence known. It is like the current from the power source to the light bulb. As long as the cord is plugged into the socket, the bulb glows. However, if the plug is pulled out, the power ceases to flow and the bulb goes out. Through a faithful devotional habit, you can stay plugged into the power source. You can remain full of God's Spirit.

DEVOTIONAL PRIORITIES AND PRACTICES

Two questions arise: "How can you, as a Pentecostal pastor, develop a strong devotional habit?" and "What must you do to get the most out of the practice?"

Three Important Issues

To establish a strong devotional habit, you will need to address three related issues:

Chapter 15: A Strong Devotional Habit

1. Priorities. Your first step in forming a devotional habit is determining your priorities. A priority is something a person considers most important. It is the thing that he or she does first. You must decide that your relationship with God is a top priority. And you must see the devotional habit as a means of strengthening that relationship. To do this, you will need to guard against the so-called "tyranny of the urgent." That is, you must not allow the many urgent activities of life to crowd out those practices that are most important.

As a busy pastor, you encounter many urgent needs every day, duties that make constant demands on your time. While you cannot ignore these demands, you must learn to put them in their proper order. You must guard your relationship with God. And you must keep that relationship at the top of your priority list. That's what Jesus did. He did not allow His many responsibilities to keep Him from communion with His Heavenly Father. The Bible tells us that He "often withdrew to lonely places and prayed" (Luke 5:16). He knew that He needed this time alone with His Father to sustain Him in ministry.

The story of Mary and Martha further illustrates this point. Mary prioritized sitting at Jesus' feet and listening to Him teach. However, Martha was distracted by all the work that needed to be done. Jesus told Martha, "You are worried and upset about many things, but few things are needed—or indeed only one. Mary has chosen what is better, and it will not be taken away from her" (Luke 10:41-42). Martha had been distracted by the tyranny of the urgent. However, Mary had prioritized the best thing, communion with the Lord. Every Pentecostal pastor must learn to do the same.

You may be tempted to say, "I cannot read the Bible and pray today. I have too many urgent things to do." However, if you say this today, and then the next day, and then the next, you will fall into a pattern that is difficult to escape. But if you will view your time of daily devotion as an appointment with God, and if you will faithfully keep that appointment, you will develop a hunger for God's presence. You will begin to approach your devotional time with joy.

2. Time management. The second issue a Pentecostal pastor must address in developing a devotional habit is time management. Time

Part 4: The Personal Life of the Pentecostal Pastor

management is the practice of organizing one's daily schedule to ensure that the proper amount of time is allotted to each of the day's activities. Effective pastors understand that time is a gift from God, and they must manage it well. In scheduling your day, you must ensure that you reserve adequate time for personal devotion.[1]

One mature pastor spoke of how he scheduled his devotional time. "I set a time each morning for devotional prayer and Bible study," he said. "I let my people know what my schedule is. Then, if during that time someone calls and says to me, 'I want to see you,' I make them wait until I have finished my devotions. When I am finished, I come out and meet with them. Of course, there are emergencies I must respond to. However, these are the exceptions. The rule is that I give priority to the time I spend with God."

3. Self-discipline. The third issue in developing a strong devotional habit is self-discipline. For what good is it if a Pentecostal pastor establishes priorities and organizes his or her time and then lacks the self-discipline needed to follow through with their plan? You must therefore discipline yourself to keep your appointment with God each day. As a pastor, you have no one to tell you, "It is time to pray. It is time to read the Bible." Therefore, you must discipline yourself. Paul told Timothy that an overseer, or pastor, must have self-control (1 Tim. 3:2). He further taught that self-control, or self-discipline, is a fruit of the Holy Spirit (Gal. 5:23).

Two Devotional Practices

As we have already indicated in this chapter, the two primary practices of the devotional habit are prayer and Bible study. Let's look more closely at each of these devotional practices:

1. Devotional prayer. The Pentecostal pastor should incorporate devotional prayer into his or her times of devotion. Devotional prayer is different from petitioning prayer or intercessory prayer. In petitioning prayer, the seeker asks the Lord to meet a need in his or her own

---

[1] For more on the Pentecostal pastor and time management, see Chapter 13: "A Well-Managed Life."

Chapter 15: A Strong Devotional Habit

life. In intercessory prayer, he or she prays for the needs of others. However, in devotional prayer, the worshiper commits his or her way to God, seeking to draw near to Him. David prayed a devotional prayer when he asked God, "Show me your ways, Lord, teach me your paths" (Psa. 25:4).

Devotional prayer further includes times of singing, worship, and thanksgiving to God. Sometimes it includes repentance, as when David prayed, "Against you, you only, have I sinned and done what is evil in your sight....Cleanse me with hyssop, and I will be clean; wash me, and I will be whiter than snow" (Psa. 51:4, 7). God's Word promises, "If we confess our sins, he is faithful and just and will forgive us our sins and purify us from all unrighteousness" (1 John 1:9).

During your devotional times, you will want to pray for your family, that they will be in good physical and spiritual health. You will also want to pray for your church, that the Holy Spirit will empower and direct its affairs, and that all who are part of the church will be filled with the Spirit. Further, you will want to pray that the church will be in good health and that the gifts and fruit of the Spirit are present in the church.

2. Devotional Bible study. Your devotional times should include Bible study. It is important, however, that you understand the difference between devotional and professional Bible study. Professional Bible study is the study that a pastor does to prepare for ministry. This kind of Bible study occurs when he or she studies the Bible to prepare a sermon or Bible lesson. For the Pentecostal pastor, professional Bible study is essential. However, it is not the kind of Bible study you should do during your times of devotion.

Devotional Bible study occurs when you read the Bible for personal spiritual growth. Your aim is not to prepare a sermon but to better understand God's Word, and to allow God's words to shape your life. The purpose of devotional Bible study is to encounter God in His Word. Its purpose is to know God better, to draw closer to Christ, and to serve Him more perfectly. Job spoke of his own devotional response to Scripture when he said, "I have not departed from the commands of his lips; I have treasured the words of his mouth more than my daily bread" (Job 23:12).

Some have suggested four steps in devotional Bible study. The first step is to read the passage slowly and thoughtfully. The second step is to reflect on the text, asking such questions as, "What is God saying to me through this passage?' and "How must I respond to God's message in this passage?" The third step is to pray, "Lord, what do you want me to do?" And the final step is to obey what God has said in His Word and to put its principles into practice.

FURTHER INSIGHTS INTO THE DEVOTIONAL HABIT

In closing, let's look at three additional insights into how you can enhance your devotional habit and strengthen your relationship with God.

Using the Lord's Prayer

Occasionally, you will want to use the Lord's Prayer as a guide during your times of devotion. This prayer is found in Matthew 6:9-13. Jesus gave it to His disciples as a model, or outline, for effective prayer. Using this prayer as a guide, your devotional session will proceed as follows:

1. *Begin with praise:* "Our Father in heaven, hallowed be your name" (v. 9). Spend a few moments singing and worshipping God. Praise Him for who He is, and thank Him for all He has done.
2. *Pray for God's will to be done:* "Your kingdom come, your will be done on earth, as it is in heaven" (v. 10). Pray that God's kingdom will come into people's lives. Pray that they will be born again and begin to follow Christ (John 3:3-8). Pray that they will be healed and delivered from demonic bondage (Matt. 12:28; Luke 11:20). Pray for them to be filled with the Holy Spirit (Mark 9:1; Acts 1:3-8). And pray for Jesus' soon coming (Luke 22:18; Rev. 12:10; 22:20).
3. *Petition God:* "Give us today our daily bread" (v. 11). Ask God to supply all your needs "according to the riches of his

glory in Christ Jesus" (Phi. 4:19). Intercede for the needs of others.
4. *Ask for and give forgiveness:* "And forgive us our debts, as we also have forgiven our debtors" (v. 12). Humble yourself before God, asking for His forgiveness and granting forgiveness to others.
5. *Ask for God's guidance and protection:* "And lead us not into temptation, but deliver us from the evil one" (v. 13). Ask God for His direction in your life and ministry and for His protection from the devil and his demonic forces.

Continuous Prayer

In addition to maintaining a daily time of devotion, the Pentecostal pastor must learn to "pray continually" (1 Thess. 5:17). This, of course, does not mean that you should remain in the prayer closet all day every day. It rather means that you should never stop praying. You should learn to live in a continuous state of communion with God. As you go about your daily activities, a prayer should continually be on your lips (Psa. 34:1; Heb. 13:15). This practice will be enhanced if your day begins with a time of devotion as described above. Prayer without ceasing is essential to living a life in step with the Spirit of God (Gal. 5:25).

Journaling

Finally, it is a good practice for a Pentecostal pastor to keep a daily prayer journal. A prayer journal is a notebook in which the pastor keeps a record of what transpires during his or her times of devotion. In this journal, you record the requests you have made of God, along with God's answers to those requests. As you observe God's faithfulness in answering your prayers, your faith will be strengthened.

You will also want to record any words or impressions you may receive from the Holy Spirit. These impressions may later serve as guideposts, helping you to discern God's direction for your life and ministry. In addition, you may want to write down any insights you receive when reading the Bible. Some of these insights may later be

Part 4: The Personal Life of the Pentecostal Pastor

developed into messages for the congregation. You will occasionally want to review what you have written in your journal, asking God to impress on your heart those things He wants you to remember.

For the Pentecostal pastor, a daily devotional habit is not an option; it is a necessity. Such a habit will powerfully enrich his or her life and ministry in many ways. It will provide them with the direction and spiritual strength they need to fulfill God's calling on their lives.

Chapter 15: A Strong Devotional Habit

~ PART 5 ~

THE PUBLIC MINISTRY OF THE PENTECOSTAL PASTOR

~ Chapter 16 ~

Spirit-Anointed Preaching

A non-Pentecostal pastor doubted the reality of the baptism in the Holy Spirit. He often expressed his skepticism concerning the experience. Then one day, while reading Acts 2 and reflecting on the events of the Day of Pentecost, he asked for and received the Pentecostal experience. He later testified, "In the short time since I have received the Holy Spirit, my preaching has produced more results than in all my previous years of preaching!"

Historically, powerful, Spirit-anointed preaching has been a hallmark of Pentecostal ministry. Since the beginning of the twentieth century, the Pentecostal movement has produced a vast army of preachers empowered by the Holy Spirit, zealously declaring the message of salvation to the nations.

This chapter will address the topic of Pentecostal preaching. It will focus on the role of the Holy Spirit in anointing the preacher. It will also offer recommendations on sermon preparation and delivery.

Chapter 16: Spirit-Anointed Preaching

PENTECOSTAL PREACHING

Jesus commanded His disciples, "Go into all the world and preach the gospel to all creation" (Mark 16:15). Preaching is the impassioned proclamation of the Word of God with the intent of persuading people to follow Christ and do His will. It is a prominent theme in the New Testament where some form of the words *preach* or *proclaim* appears nearly 150 times. The ability to preach effective, Spirit-anointed messages is a primary responsibility of every Pentecostal pastor.

The Book of Acts Model

Pentecostals believe that the preaching of the apostles and others in the book of Acts is meant to serve as a model for preachers today. In Acts, Luke records the contents of several sermons preached by the apostles and other preachers (e.g., Peter: Acts 2:14-40; 3:12-26; 10:28-47; Stephen: Acts 7:1-53; Paul: Acts 13:16-41; 17:22-31). The large amount of space Luke gives to these sermons in Acts shows the importance he places on them. He wanted his readers to know how the apostles preached so they could do the same.

A careful examination of the sermons in Acts reveals at least five important features of apostolic preaching:

1. *Centered on Jesus.* The person and work of Christ is at the center of every message preached in Acts. The New Testament preachers consistently announced that Jesus was the fulfilment of Old Testament prophecy, and that He was the only way to salvation (cf. Acts 2:22-24, 30-32; 3:13-20; 4:10-12; 5:30-31; 8:5; and others).
2. *Appealed to Scripture.* The preachers in the book of Acts consistently appealed to Scripture to support their claims (cf. Acts 2:17-21; 3:22-23; 4:11, 25-26; and others).
3. *Anointed by the Holy Spirit.* The preachers in Acts were filled with, and thus anointed by, the Holy Spirit (cf. Acts 2:4, 14; 4:8; and others).
4. *Supernatural confirmation.* In Acts, the proclamation of the gospel was often accompanied by confirming signs and wonders (cf. Acts 3:1-8; 8:4-7; 14:8-10; and others).

Part 5: The Public Ministry of the Pentecostal Pastor

5. *A call to repentance and faith.* The preachers in the book of Acts normally concluded their sermons with a call to repentance and faith (cf. Acts 2:38; 3:19; 8:22; and others).

These same characteristics should be at the heart of Pentecostal preaching in Africa today. You would do well to memorize this list and use it as a standard for evaluating your own preaching ministry.

THE ANOINTING OF THE HOLY SPIRIT

In the Old Testament, prophets, priests, and kings were anointed with oil when they were installed into office (cf. Exod. 28:41; 1 Sam. 9:16; 16:11-13; 1 Kings 1:34; 19:16). This anointing served as a sign of their calling, and it symbolized their God-given authority to function in their offices. It further symbolized the presence of God's Spirit on them to enable them to perform the functions of their office (Isa. 61:1-2).

As mentioned above, one feature of preaching in the book of Acts is that the preachers were anointed by the Holy Spirit. Let's take a closer look at this idea.

Jesus' Anointed Ministry

Jesus began His ministry by announcing, "The Spirit of the Lord is on me, because he has anointed me to proclaim good news" (Luke 4:18). He thus described the Spirit's anointing as the Spirit being on Him. He used this term to describe the powerful working of the Holy Spirit in and through Him, enabling Him to carry out His messianic ministry.

The Apostles' Anointed Ministry

Much the same happened to the 120 disciples on the Day of Pentecost. First, the Spirit came on them (Acts 2:3). Then, He filled them. And finally, He began to speak through them (vv. 4, 14). All of this occurred in fulfilment of Jesus' promise in Acts 1:8: "But you will receive power when the Holy Spirit comes on you; and you will be my witnesses...to the ends of the earth."

Chapter 16: Spirit-Anointed Preaching

Thus, to be anointed is to be filled with and empowered by the Holy Spirit. Just as the Spirit came on Jesus and the early disciples, anointing them for ministry, the Spirit will come on the yielded disciple today, anointing him or her for ministry.

Anointing Described

The anointing is the powerful working of the Holy Spirit in, on, and through individuals who have fully yielded themselves to God. It is the manifest presence of God that comes to rest on a Spirit-filled disciple, enabling him or her to minister with increased power and effectiveness.

In the book of Acts, the terms *filled with* and *full of* the Holy Spirit are sometimes used to describe the Spirit's anointing. The term, *filled with* the Holy Spirit, describes the Spirit's coming on, filling, and anointing an individual to act and speak with power and authority (Acts 4:8, 31; 13:9-12). The term, *full of* the Holy Spirit, describes the ongoing state of being anointed by the Holy Spirit (Acts 6:3, 5; 7:55). This could be "the anointing that remains" spoken of by John (1 John 2:27). The anointing remains on us as long as we remain in Christ (John 15:4-7). Separation from sin is an essential condition for the anointing to remain (John 14:15-16). This anointing must be a priority in the life of every Pentecostal pastor.

Anointed Preaching

Spirit-anointed preaching should not be confused with mere eloquence, natural charisma, or the ability to move a crowd emotionally. Neither should it be confused with the enthusiastic delivery of a sermon. While Spirit-anointed preaching may exhibit these characteristics, it is much more. Spirit-anointed preaching is Spirit-infused preaching. It is the kind of preaching modeled by Jesus and the apostles.

Luke illustrates this truth with the story of Apollos. He explains, "Apollos...was a learned man, with a thorough knowledge of the Scriptures. He had been instructed in the way of the Lord, and he spoke with great fervor and taught about Jesus accurately" (Acts

Part 5: The Public Ministry of the Pentecostal Pastor

18:24-25). Apollos was thus an eloquent and intellectually competent preacher. Yet he "knew only the baptism of John" (v. 25). He lacked the experience of Pentecost. However, after Priscilla and Aquila "explained to him the way of God more adequately," he was evidently filled with the Holy Spirit. He then journeyed to Achaia where he was "a great help to those who by grace had believed" (v. 27).

Jesus said of His own anointed preaching and teaching, "The words I have spoken to you—they are full of the Spirit and life" (John 6:63). The Bible describes the apostles' preaching: "With great power the apostles continued to testify to the resurrection of the Lord Jesus. And God's grace was so powerfully at work in them all" (Acts 4:33). The phrase, *God's grace was so powerfully at work in them all,* aptly describes the anointing of the Holy Spirit. In Acts, the Spirit's anointing on a preacher deeply affected those who listened (Acts 2:4, 14 with 1 Cor. 2:4; Acts 2:37 with 1 Cor. 2:5).

Paul spoke of his own Spirit-anointed preaching in his epistles. He reminded the Corinthian believers of how he had first preached the gospel to them. "My message and my preaching," he wrote, "were not with wise and persuasive words, but with a demonstration of the Spirit's power" (1 Cor. 2:4-5). He described his ministry to the believers in Romans: "By the power of signs and wonders, through the power of the Spirit of God...I have fully proclaimed the gospel of Christ" (Rom. 15:19). He reminded the believers in Thessalonica, "Our gospel came to you not simply with words but also with power, with the Holy Spirit and deep conviction" (1 Thess. 1:5).

The Holy Spirit stands ready to anoint our preaching today just as He anointed Jesus and the apostles in the first century. But what is the source of the anointing, and how may it be attained?

THE SOURCE OF THE ANOINTING

To be able to preach with the Spirit's anointing, the Pentecostal pastor must understand its source. The source of the anointing is the indwelling and empowering presence of the Holy Spirit. It is the Spirit *inside* and *upon* the preacher (John 14:17; Acts 1:8). This

Chapter 16: Spirit-Anointed Preaching

power of the Holy Spirit is received when one is baptized in and filled with the Holy Spirit (Acts 2:4). The anointing remains as one walks "in step with the Spirit" (Gal. 5:25). This truth is demonstrated in the ministries of Jesus and the apostles.

The Source of Jesus' Anointing

Jesus affirmed that the source of His anointing was the Spirit of the Lord (Luke 4:18). Although He was truly the incarnate Son of God, He chose to empty himself of His divine power and privileges and to carry out His ministry in the Spirit's power (Phi. 2:5-8). Jesus' Spirit-anointed ministry would thus serve as a model for all who would follow Him.

Jesus did not begin His ministry until He was first anointed by the Spirit. His Spirit baptism occurred immediately after John baptized Him in water. The Bible says, "As [Jesus] was praying, heaven was opened and the Holy Spirit descended on him in bodily form like a dove" (Luke 3:21-22). Jesus then "began his ministry" (v. 23). He started to move and minister in the Spirit's power (Luke 4:1, 14). He announced, "The Spirit of the Lord is on me, because he has anointed me to proclaim the good news" (Luke 4:18). Later, when the people heard Jesus speak, they "were amazed at the gracious words that came from his lips" (v. 22). And they were astonished "because his words had authority" (v. 32; cf. Matt. 7:28-29).

The Source of the Apostles' Anointing

Just as the Holy Spirit was the source of Jesus' anointed ministry, He was also the source of the apostles' anointed ministry. Like Jesus, the apostles were first baptized in the Holy Spirit. They then began to preach with power.

Peter is possibly the best example of this spiritual dynamic. Before Pentecost, He was afraid to confess Jesus to a servant girl (Matt. 26:69-72). However, once He was filled with the Holy Spirit, He preached with power, and His words deeply affected his hearers (Acts 2:37). As a result, three thousand people came to Christ. This scenario is repeated several times in Acts (4:8, 31-33).

Part 5: The Public Ministry of the Pentecostal Pastor

The same anointing that was on Jesus and the apostles enabling them to preach with power is available to us today.

EXPERIENCING THE ANOINTING

The questions arise, "How can one truly experience the anointing of the Holy Spirit today? How is the anointing received? How is it manifested in ministry? How can it be maintained?"

Receiving the Anointing

The anointing is received today just as it was received by Jesus and the early disciples. It is initially received when one is baptized in the Holy Spirit. As explained above, Jesus received the Holy Spirit at His baptism. He then began to minister with power. The same was true for the disciples. They first received the Spirit at Pentecost, and like Jesus, they too began to minister with power.

Jesus gave clear instructions concerning how one may receive the Spirit. He told His disciples, "Your Father in heaven [will] give the Holy Spirit to those who ask him!" (Luke 11:13). He explained, "Ask and it will be given to you; seek and you will find; knock and the door will be opened to you. For everyone who asks receives; the one who seeks finds; and to the one who knocks, the door will be opened" (vv. 9-10). The Spirit is thus received by asking in faith (v. 9), receiving by faith (v. 10 with Mark 11:24), and speaking in faith (Acts 2:4).[1]

Manifesting the Anointing

The anointing received at Spirit baptism is manifested in ministry primarily through the operation of spiritual gifts. Truly Spirit-anointed preaching is, in fact, a manifestation of the gift of prophecy. It is Spirit-initiated, Spirit-inspired utterance. Spirit-anointed preaching may also include the manifestation of the revelation gifts such as words of knowledge and words of wisdom. In addition, Spirit-

---

[1] More is said about receiving the Holy Spirit in Chapter 20: "Guiding Believers into Spirit Baptism."

Chapter 16: Spirit-Anointed Preaching

anointed preaching is often accompanied by a manifestation of a power gift, as happened with Paul in Lystra (Acts 14:8-10).[2]

You can acquire the anointing by asking for, and responding in faith to, the presence of the Holy Spirit. As you approach the pulpit, you should pray, "O Holy Spirit, come now and anoint me to minister your Word." You must then move with faith, believing that God has heard your prayer. Once you sense the Spirit's presence, respond in faith, yielding to His leading and trusting Him to enable and empower your preaching.

Maintaining the Anointing

The anointing is maintained by living and walking in the Spirit (Gal. 5:25). The Spirit-filled walk is a life of submission to God and His mission. Prayer, including prayer in the Spirit, is a key element to maintaining the anointing (Rom. 8:26-27; 1 Thess. 5:17).

ANOINTED PREPARATION AND DELIVERY

Any Pentecostal pastor intent on becoming an effective, Spirit-anointed preacher will need to apply himself or herself to both the preparation and delivery of the sermon. He or she must ensure that the Holy Spirit is present, anointing and guiding each activity.

Sermon Preparation

A close examination of the preaching in Acts reveals two significant truths: the apostles' messages were filled with Scripture, and they were anointed by the Holy Spirit. The preachers in Acts exhibited a broad knowledge of Scripture. They often quoted Scripture in their messages. For example, Peter's Pentecost sermon contains four Old Testament citations (cf. Acts 2:16-21, 25-28, 31, 34-35). Similarly, Stephen's message to the Jewish Sanhedrin contains eight citations (cf. Acts 7:3, 6-7, 28, 32-35, 37, 40, 42-43, 49). Other sermons in Acts follow the same pattern. These early preachers

---

[2] See Appendix 2: "The Manifestation Gifts of 1 Corinthians 12:8-10."

understood Scripture, and they based their messages on that understanding.

Pentecostal pastors in Africa today must do the same. Like our apostolic counterparts, we must ground our preaching solidly in Scripture. To do this, we must dedicate ourselves to disciplined Bible study. We must allow sufficient time each week for serious Bible reading and sermon preparation. As we prepare, we must look to the Holy Spirit to anoint and inspire our thoughts, realizing that the anointing of the Holy Spirit does not rule out preparation; it rather enhances it.

Further, in Acts the preachers prayed in anticipation of being filled with and anointed by the Holy Spirit. The book of Acts consistently connects the coming of the Holy Spirit with prayer. For instance, the disciples were praying before the outpouring at Pentecost (Acts 1:14; 2:1-4); the Jerusalem believers were praying before the second outpouring of the Spirit in the city (Acts 4:23-31); and Paul and Ananias were praying before Paul was filled with the Spirit (Acts 9:5, 10-15). More examples could be cited.

We Pentecostal pastors who want the Holy Spirit to anoint our preaching must commit ourselves to prayer. Such committed prayer will ensure the Spirit's anointing, profoundly affecting both the content and delivery of our sermons.

Sermon Delivery

The goal of sermon delivery is not to impress the hearers but to enhance the people's understanding of the message. Everything that is said or done should be aimed at directing people into an encounter with God. Any techniques or mannerisms that contribute to this goal should be cultivated. Any that distract from the goal should be discarded.

Therefore, as Pentecostal preachers, our demeanor should be authentic and unaffected. We should avoid mumbling, hollering, aimless pacing, and wild arm waving. Rather, our gestures should be spontaneous and unrehearsed. Our movements should spring naturally from the inner working of the Spirit and the content of the

Chapter 16: Spirit-Anointed Preaching

message. If we will mentally and emotionally engage with the message, appropriate gestures will naturally follow.

The altar call is particularly important. During this critical stage of the sermon, it is essential that the preacher be led by the Holy Spirit. The altar call is no time to introduce new ideas into the message. The preacher must remain focused and not go off on tangents. Rather, he or she must stay on point and give clear instructions about what he or she is asking the people to do.

Pentecostal pastors are unique among preachers in that we value and seek the anointing of the Holy Spirit on our preaching. In doing this, we seek to follow the example of Jesus and the New Testament preachers. "Lord, fill and anoint me for ministry" should be our persistent prayer.

~ Chapter 17 ~

Effective Teaching

"My people are destroyed from lack of knowledge" (Hos. 4:6). These words from God were spoken through the prophet Hosea to the priests of Israel. Because these spiritual leaders had failed to teach God's people the truth, they had believed lies. As a result, they had wandered deep into sin. The prophet described their sad condition: "There is no faithfulness, no love, no acknowledgment of God in the land. There is only cursing, lying and murder, stealing and adultery" (vv. 1-2).

Sadly, many Pentecostal Christians across Africa find themselves in a similar situation. They lack a clear understanding of God's Word. Therefore, their spiritual growth has been stunted. As a result, they have become easy prey to false teachers. As a faithful Pentecostal pastor, you must ensure that such a condition does not exist in any church you have been called to pastor.

THE PASTOR'S RESPONSIBILITY

Every Pentecostal pastor bears the awesome responsibility of feeding the flock of God. In his final meeting with the pastors of the

Chapter 17: Effective Teaching

church in Ephesus, Paul urged them, "Keep watch over yourselves and all the flock of which the Holy Spirit has made you overseers" (Acts 20:28). He then charged these pastors, "Be shepherds of [or "feed"] the church of God, which he bought with his own blood." Paul knew that by teaching God's people the Word of God, the Ephesian pastors would help them to become spiritually strong. This would prepare them to resist the "savage wolves" who would soon enter the church, distort the truth, and seek to draw the people away from Christ (vv. 29-30).

Teaching is thus at the core of what it means to be a Pentecostal pastor. Paul wrote about five ministry gifts that Christ has given to the church: "So Christ himself gave the apostles, the prophets, the evangelists, the pastors and teachers, to equip his people for works of service, so that the body of Christ may be built up" (Eph. 4:11-12).

Notice how, in this passage, Paul joins the last two ministry gifts into one. Rather than saying "the pastors and the teachers," as he had done with the first three gifts, Paul simply says "the pastors and teachers." Because of this, some scholars have referred to this gift as "the pastor-teacher." The point is this: For a man or woman to be a pastor, he or she must also be a teacher. Whom God calls to pastor, He gifts to teach.

To properly care for the sheep, you must be able to effectively nourish God's people, feeding them the Word of God. The Bible compares God's Word to nutritious foods like bread (Matt. 4:4), milk (1 Pet. 2:2), and solid food (Heb. 5:12-14). Any pastor who fails to feed his or her people the Word of God is an unfaithful shepherd, and God will hold them accountable for this failure (James 3:1; Eze. 34:1-6).

However, if you will faithfully teach the people the Word of God, you will be honored by God (Matt. 24:45-47). More importantly, God's people will be made strong. They "will no longer be infants, tossed back and forth by the waves, and blown here and there by every wind of teaching and by the cunning and craftiness of people in their deceitful scheming. Instead, speaking the truth in love, [they]

Part 5: The Public Ministry of the Pentecostal Pastor

will grow to become in every respect the mature body of him who is the head, that is, Christ" (Eph. 4:14-15).

Making Disciples

Jesus commanded His Church, "Go and make disciples of all nations" (Matt. 28:19). He was telling them that they should do with others what He had done with them. Jesus had walked with His disciples, taught them the truth, and showed them how to live. As Pentecostal pastors, we must do the same with our church members. It is not enough to make converts, we must make disciples. A disciple is a devoted follower of Christ. He or she is one who sits at the feet of Jesus and learns from Him. Not only must we call people to follow Christ, we must "teach them to obey" all of His commands (v. 20).

Preaching and Teaching

Many Pentecostal pastors in Africa see themselves as preachers, but they do not see themselves as teachers. As a pastor, however, God has called you to be both. You must be, at the same time, a skilled preacher and an effective teacher. To clearly understand your role as a teacher of God's people, you need to know the difference between preaching and teaching.

The Bible clearly distinguishes between these two tasks. For example, the Bible says that Jesus "went throughout Galilee, *teaching* in their synagogues, *proclaiming* the good news of the kingdom" (Matt. 4:23, emphasis added). It says of Paul and Barnabas that they "remained in Antioch, where they and many others *taught* and *preached* the word of the Lord" (Acts 15:35, emphasis added). Paul exhorted Timothy, pastor of the church in Ephesus, "Until I come, devote yourself to the public reading of Scripture, to *preaching* and to *teaching"* (1 Tim. 4:13, emphasis added). What then is the difference between preaching and teaching?

At its heart, preaching is the public proclamation of the gospel with the intent of calling people to faith in Christ. Teaching is explaining what it means to live for Christ. Preaching is announcing; teaching is instructing. Peaching is making a declaration; teaching is making disciples. The preacher calls wanderers to faith in Christ; the teacher explains to them the ways of the Lord. The teacher's purpose is to show God's people how to serve Him more perfectly. As a pastor-teacher, you must carefully explain the Scriptures to God's people. You must give them the information and insights they need to put into practice the word they have heard.

Following the Example of Jesus

As a Pentecostal pastor, you must strive to follow the example of Jesus, the greatest teacher who ever lived. Jesus often referred to himself as "Teacher" (Matt. 26:18; John 13:13-14). Others did the same (e.g., Matt. 8:19; 12:38; Luke 10:25; John 11:28). The gospels often speak of Jesus' teaching ministry. (e.g., Mark 1:21-22; Luke 4:31-32). And long passages of Scripture are dedicated to His teachings. These passages include the Sermon on the Mount (Matt. 5-7), the Olivet Discourse (Matt. 24-25), and the Upper Room Discourse (John 14-16). If Jesus took His teaching ministry so seriously, so must we today.

Much could be said about how Jesus fulfilled His teaching ministry. Books have been written about His teaching methods. Three features of His teaching method deserve mention:

1. He taught with authority. The Bible says of Jesus, "The people were amazed at his teaching, because he taught them as one who had authority, not as the teachers of the law" (Mark 1:22). Jesus taught with authority because He had been sent by God, and because He spoke the words God had given Him. He testified, "I do nothing on my own but speak just what the Father has taught me" (John 8:28). To teach with authority, like Jesus, you too must faithfully teach the Word of God.

2. He taught in love. Jesus deeply loved those He taught. His teaching was, in fact, an outflow of His love for people. On one occasion, Jesus encountered a large crowd of tired and hungry people. When He saw them, "He had compassion on them, because they were like sheep without a shepherd." Then, out of His great love for them, "He began teaching them many things" (Mark 6:34). He would later

Part 5: The Public Ministry of the Pentecostal Pastor

feed them natural food (vv. 35-44). But first, He ministered to their greatest need and fed them the Word of God.

On another occasion, Jesus met with His disciples in an upper room. The Bible says, "Jesus knew that the hour had come for him to leave this world and go to the Father. Having loved his own who were in the world, he loved them to the end" (John 13:1). Again, because of His deep love for them, and for those they themselves would soon lead, He taught them a powerful lesson on servant leadership (vv. 2-17).

On both occasions, Jesus' love for people moved Him to teach them. In like manner, as a Pentecostal pastor you must love those you have been called to lead. And this love must move you to faithfully teach them the Word of God. Without such love for your people, your words can become "a resounding gong or a clanging cymbal" (1 Cor. 13:1).

3. He taught in the Spirit's power. Jesus once explained to His disciples the nature of His teaching ministry. "The words I have spoken to you," He said, "they are full of the Spirit and life" (John 6:63). Jesus' words were full of the Spirit and life because He himself was full of the Spirit and life. He began His ministry by being anointed by the Holy Spirit (Luke 3:21-22; 4:18-19). He then carried out His teaching ministry in the power of the Spirit (Luke 4:14-15).

Jesus taught, not only with words, but with demonstrations of the Spirit's power (Luke 5:17). His words were so laden with the Spirit's power that, as He taught, demons cried out, "What do you want with us, Jesus of Nazareth? Have you come to destroy us? I know who you are—the Holy One of God!" (Mark 1:24). Jesus cast the demon out of the man, and the people responded, "What is this? A new teaching—and with authority! He even gives orders to impure spirits and they obey him" (v. 27).

Jesus passed on His teaching ministry to His disciples (Matt. 28:19-20). By watching Him, they learned how to teach others. As Pentecostal pastors, we must do the same. We must seek to imitate the teaching ministry of Jesus.

Chapter 17: Effective Teaching

THE PASTOR AS MASTER TEACHER

As the pastor, you should view yourself as the "master teacher" in the church you have been called to lead. In other words, not only must you become a skilled teacher of the Word yourself, you must diligently train others to do the same. This is what Jesus and the apostles did. As the master teacher, you have three primary responsibilities: (1) you must develop your own teaching ministry; (2) you must develop the teaching skills of others; and (3) you must organize the teaching ministry of the church. Let's look at each of these responsibilities:

Developing Yourself

First, as the master teacher in the church, you must strive to improve your own teaching ministry. Paul wrote to Timothy saying that an overseer, or pastor, must be "able to teach" (1 Tim. 3:2). Or, as one translation puts it, a pastor must be "skillful in teaching." In his letter to the Christians in Rome, Paul stated that those who have been gifted to teach must faithfully exercise this gift (Rom. 12:6-8). By implication, they should diligently strive to develop their skills as a teacher. Although the ability to teach may be given as a spiritual gift, it must be developed as a learned skill. As a Pentecostal pastor, you must become a lifelong student of God's Word. And you must work hard to develop your teaching skills (2 Tim. 2:15).

Someone has rightly observed that teaching is more than talking, and learning is more than listening. The ultimate aim of teaching is to produce change in the lives of the learners. Effective teaching thus involves frequent application of the truths being taught. Realizing this, we should never be content with knowing that our members have merely heard our words. We should only be satisfied when we see their lives being transformed. Therefore, we must not only explain what the Word of God means, we must help believers apply the truths of Scripture to their lives.

Further, as Pentecostal pastors, we must understand that we often teach more with our actions than we do with our words. Paul understood this truth. He thus called on the Corinthian Christians, "Follow

Part 5: The Public Ministry of the Pentecostal Pastor

my example, as I follow the example of Christ" (1 Cor. 11:1). Jesus was applying the same principle when He told His disciples, "The student is not above the teacher, but everyone who is fully trained will be like their teacher" (Luke 6:40). Therefore, as examples to the church, we must put into practice those things we teach to others.

Developing Others

Second, as the master teacher in the church, you must work to develop the teaching skills of other church leaders. As the church grows and matures, leaders will be needed to direct emerging ministries. To lead well, each one will need to develop some basic teaching skills. You must ensure that every new leader receives the training they need to lead well.

In doing this, you must teach lay leaders how to study and properly interpret the Bible. And you must show them how to prepare and teach God's Word to others. If you will do these things, the church will always have a steady supply of capable teachers. If you fail to teach lay leaders how to teach, the discipleship ministry of the church will flounder and the spiritual development of Christians will suffer.

ORGANIZING THE CHURCH TO TEACH

Finally, as the master teacher, you must be the congregation's chief advocate for Christian education. You must carefully organize and avidly promote the teaching ministries of the church. You must further ensure that the church's teaching ministries involve every person of every age in the congregation. Training programs in the church should include the following:

Sunday School

No training program in the church has greater potential than the Sunday School. The Sunday School is the only ministry in the church that reaches every person of every age grouping in the assembly. You must therefore work to ensure that the church you lead has a well-organized, well-funded Sunday School. You must further ensure that the Sunday School Department is led by a qualified person. Because of the great importance of this ministry, you should actively participate in the school. And you must constantly monitor its activities and strive to improve its effectiveness.[1]

Home Cells Groups

If done right, home cell groups are another effective means of discipleship training. These groups meet weekly in the homes of select church members for fellowship, prayer, and Bible study. As master teacher, you must ensure that every home group is led by a faithful, well-trained leader. Time should be allotted in each cell group meeting for open discussion on a chosen biblical topic. You, or someone you have delegated, should closely monitor what is being taught in each cell group. You may want to provide a set curriculum to be taught in the groups.[2]

Departmental Ministries

The church's departmental ministries should be viewed as a means of discipleship training. These departments include Men's Ministries, Women's Ministries, Youth Ministries, Children's Ministries, and others. Practical Bible lessons should be taught each time one of these groups meets.

School of Ministry

Every Pentecostal pastor should consider starting a School of Ministry in his or her church. A School of Ministry is a school aimed at "equipping the saints for works of service" (Eph. 4:12). Its purpose is to train workers for ministry in the local church. In this school, the pastor teaches courses dealing with practical issues such as preaching, teaching, prayer, soul winning, church planting, leadership skills,

---

[1] The Africa's Hope *Living the Truth* discipleship series is an adult Sunday School curriculum that takes students through the entire Bible in seven years. It is available for free download at https://africaatts.org/resources/.

[2] The Africa's Hope *Roots of Faith* series is a topical Bible study curriculum available for free download at https://africaatts.org/resources/.

and more. Such training will help to ensure that the church has a steady supply of qualified workers.

As the church grows and prospers, you may need to delegate part of your training responsibilities to others. However, as the church's master teacher, you must always remain actively engaged in the church's teaching and discipleship ministries.

Three times Jesus asked Peter, "Simon, son of John, do you love me?" And three times Peter answered, "Yes, Lord, you know that I love you." Each time Jesus responded, "Feed my lambs," or "Feed my sheep." (John 21:15-18). If Peter really loved Jesus, he would do what his Lord had commanded and faithfully feed the flock of God.

Today, Jesus is asking Pentecostal pastors across Africa the same question: "Do you love me?" And He is issuing the same command to them that He gave to Peter: "Feed my sheep." As proof of their love, Jesus commands these pastors to take seriously their God-given responsibility to care for God's people by faithfully teaching them the Word of God.

Chapter 17: Effective Teaching

~ Chapter 18 ~

Leading the Church in Worship

In a Central African country, a young intern was assigned to serve under an elderly pastor. The pastor asked the intern to lead the church in worship the following Sunday morning. The young man, however, was not pleased. He wished that the old pastor had asked him to preach. He felt that leading worship was beneath his dignity as a pastor. Further, because he had been filled with the Spirit in Bible school, he saw no need to pray or otherwise prepare for the event.

As might be expected, under his leadership on Sunday morning, the worship service did not go well. Had it not been for the skillful intervention of the old pastor, the service would have been a disaster. Since that time, the pastor has chosen his worship leaders very carefully. He now allows only mature, well-trained persons to serve as worship leaders.

Leading a church into true worship is a deeply spiritual task. It requires skill, preparation, and spiritual sensitivity. King David understood this. He therefore required that those who led the people in praise and worship be chosen only from among the Levites (cf. 1 Chr. 15:16). While a pastor may choose others to lead the church in worship, they can never relinquish their responsibility to ensure that the church practices scriptural, Spirit-led worship.

THE ESSENCE OF TRUE WORSHIP

In the Bible, both the Hebrew and Greek words for worship mean to bow down and pay homage to God. They convey the idea of humbly expressing one's gratitude to Him, and of exalting Him for His holiness, glory, and power (Isa. 6:1-3; Rev. 7:11-12).

Worship in Spirit and Truth

Jesus revealed the essence of true worship when He told the Samaritan woman, "A time is coming and has now come when the true worshipers will worship the Father in the Spirit and in truth, for they are the kind of worshipers the Father seeks. God is spirit, and his worshipers must worship in the Spirit and in truth" (John 4:23-24). In this passage, Jesus revealed four profound truths about true worship:

1. God is spirit. Being a divine spirit, God is not limited by time or location. He can therefore be worshiped at any time and in any place.

2. God is seeking true worshipers. He is looking for people who will worship Him from the depths of their hearts rather than with outward form and ritual (cf. Mark 12:33).

3. True worship must be done in the Spirit and in truth. Since God is spirit, those who worship Him must worship Him in the Spirit. Since He is absolute truth, they must worship Him in accordance with truth as revealed in Scripture.

4. Now is the time. The time to worship God in the Spirit and in truth is now.

Worship is the sacred act of appropriately responding to God's presence, as did the twenty-four elders in Revelation 4. Awed by Christ's presence, they "fall down before him who sits on the throne and worship him" (v. 10). As God's people worship Him, He further manifests His presence in their midst, stirring them to worship Him even more.

Pentecostal Expectations

As a Pentecostal pastor, it is essential that you understand the unique nature of Pentecostal worship. Pentecostal worship is unique in that it emphasizes a personal encounter with God through the Holy Spirit. Pentecostals thus enter into worship with a different set of expectations than most non-Pentecostals. Many non-Pentecostals enter worship with the aim of fulfilling a religious duty or of carrying out a set of religious rituals. The true Pentecostal, however, enters into worship with a different aim. His or her aim is to encounter the living Christ, and as a result of that encounter, to be transformed by His Spirit (2 Cor. 3:17-18).

This transformation could be small or great, subtle or dramatic. A subtle transformation could be that, as the believer encounters Christ in worship, they find renewed strength and joy in serving Him. A more dramatic transformation could be that the worshiper encounters the resurrected Christ and is miraculously healed or baptized in the Holy Spirit.

Such transformation is brought about by two means: by the Spirit and by the truth (cf. John 4:23). As worshipers draw near to God, He manifests His presence. As they encounter and respond in faith to God's manifest presence (worship in the Spirit) they are transformed into Christ's image (2 Cor. 3:17-18). Further, as they respond in faith to the proclaimed Word (worship in truth), they are transformed even more.

PREPARING THE CHURCH FOR WORSHIP

As pastor, it is your responsibility to prepare the church to truly worship God. You must ensure that the people know how to worship Him in the Spirit and in truth. You must further ensure that the people actually practice such worship. You can accomplish this in three ways:

Chapter 18: Leading the Church in Worship

By Teaching about Worship

First, you can teach the church what the Bible says about worship. You can do this through sermons, exhortations, and teaching series. One of the best ways the Pentecostal pastor can teach his or her people how to worship God in the Spirit and in truth is to show them. The people must observe their pastor earnestly worshiping God. A mature pastor once instructed a group of student pastors, "If you will sincerely worship God, your people will follow you, and they too will worship Him."

Further, you must show the people how to worship God with their lives. You can do this by living a lifestyle of holiness and by being a channel of the Spirit's blessings to others.

By Monitoring Worship Services

Second, in your role as an overseer, you must prayerfully monitor worship services to ensure that the people are being led to truly worship God in the Spirit and in truth. You must require that everything in the church service be done "in a fitting and orderly way" (1 Cor. 14:40). In other words, you must ensure that worship be practiced in a way that genuinely glorifies God and draws people closer to Christ (1 Cor. 10:31).

By Mentoring the Worship Team

A third way you can ensure that the church worships God in the Spirit and in truth is by lovingly mentoring the church's worship team. You must teach them that their role is to lead the congregation into truly Spirit-directed praise and worship. You must therefore spend time with them, teaching them how to truly worship God, and showing them how to lead others into authentic worship.

In addition, you must pray often with the worship team members, ensuring that they have been filled with the Holy Spirit and that they know how to follow the Spirit's guidance. You should also ensure that the team selects songs that are both spiritual and scriptural. As pastor, you must reserve the right to pre-approve all new songs before they are used in any worship service.

Part 5: The Public Ministry of the Pentecostal Pastor

Further, as pastor of the church you must be ever mindful that, second only to the Spirit himself, you are the church's chief worship leader. This does not mean that you will stand in front of the congregation leading the people in praise and worship. It does mean, however, that you must remain in charge of the service at all times. The worship team must understand that, as pastor, you may step up and take charge of the service at any moment. When this happens, the worship team must immediately relinquish the service to you.

When true worship in the Spirit and in truth occurs, powerful blessings come to the church: God is glorified, the Spirit's presence is manifested, and the body of Christ is strengthened.

LEADING THE CHURCH IN WORSHIP

The Pentecostal pastor who understands these truths will be passionate about guiding his or her church into Spirit-led worship. This means that, during worship times, you must remain attentive to the voice of the Spirit, and you must be quick to follow His promptings. Like Moses in the wilderness, you must be ready to direct the church to move when the cloud moves, and to stop when the cloud stops (cf. Exod. 40:34-38).

Encouraging Participation

As the church's spiritual leader, you should encourage every person in attendance to actively participate in worship. Urge them to express their praise to God by raising their hands, singing, shouting, testifying, clapping, dancing, kneeling, or any other scriptural expression of worship. You should further teach the people that they are worshiping God when they give their tithes and offerings. In doing this, they honor God with their wealth and the firstfruits of their harvest (Pro. 3:9).

By Developing Choirs

In addition, the Pentecostal pastor should encourage the development of choirs and music groups to minister in church services and evangelistic outreaches. Every group or choir should at all times remain amenable to the pastor or minister of music. You should therefore work with singing groups much the same way you work with the worship team, teaching them the difference between performing for the people and true ministry in the Spirit.

Nurturing Spiritual Gifts

As spiritual leader of the church, the Pentecostal pastor should also encourage the exercise of spiritual gifts in worship services. This was a common occurrence in the New Testament church, and it should be a common occurrence in worship services today (cf. Acts 11:27-28; 13:2).

Paul exhorted the Corinthian church to "eagerly desire gifts of the Spirit" (1 Cor. 14:1). He further instructed them, "When you come together, each of you has a hymn, or a word of instruction, a revelation, a tongue or an interpretation" (1 Cor. 14:26). Therefore, as pastor, you should teach the church about spiritual gifts. And you should make room for their manifestation in church services. At the same time, you must guard against the misuse of spiritual gifts (1 Cor. 14:26-33).[1]

The Role of Music

Music and singing play an important role in worship. The Psalmist urges God's people, "Sing joyfully to the Lord, you righteous; it is fitting for the upright to praise him. Praise the Lord with the harp; make music to him on the ten-stringed lyre. Sing to him a new song; play skillfully, and shout for joy" (Psa. 33:1-3).

According to Paul, music and singing serve at least four functions in worship: to glorify God, to express gratitude to Him, to teach scriptural truth, and to admonish believers to live for Him. The apostle emphasized the first two in his letter to the Ephesian church: "Sing and make music from your heart to the Lord, always giving thanks to God the Father for everything" (Eph. 5:19-20). He emphasized the

---

[1] See Appendix 2: "The Manifestation Gifts of 1 Corinthians 12:8-10."

second two in his letter to the Colossians: "Teach and admonish one another with all wisdom through psalms, hymns, and songs from the Spirit" (Col. 3:16).

A Timely Warning

A timely warning is in order here. People are often attracted to Pentecostal churches because of their enthusiastic singing. This is good, and you should encourage this practice. At the same time, however, you must never allow the church to offer up "strange fire" to the Lord (Lev. 10:1). In other words, you must ensure that the singing and dancing does not become an exhibition of the flesh rather than a response of sanctified hearts to the Spirit of God. Therefore, as pastor, you must never allow the music to become so loud and boisterous that it drowns out true heartfelt worship. Remember Paul's admonition: "No flesh should glory in God's presence" (1 Cor. 1:29, literal translation). May God never have to say to your church, "Away with the noise of your songs! I will not listen to the music of your harps" (Amos 5:23).

TWO WORSHIP CHALLENGES

Africa is a vast continent composed of more than 3,000 ethnic groups speaking more than 2,100 languages. It is therefore not unusual for a Pentecostal congregation in Africa to include individuals from several different tribes. In addition, each congregation is made up of various age groups. This diversity lends itself to different preferences in music and worship styles. If not handled wisely, it can be a source of disharmony in a congregation. Rather than promoting unity in the church, the church's worship services can become a source of division.

Two challenges stemming from this diversity are disagreements over worship styles and the challenge of employing multiple languages in worship services. As pastor, you must deal wisely with each of these challenges.

Chapter 18: Leading the Church in Worship

Music and Worship Styles

Many Pentecostal churches in Africa find members at odds with one another concerning music and worship styles. For instance, the church's young people may prefer a loud, energetic worship style, while the elderly members prefer a quieter, more reserved style. The one prefers contemporary songs while the other prefers traditional hymns. As pastor, you must use great wisdom in dealing with this issue. And you must be able to distinguish between style and substance in worship.

Style speaks of individual preferences concerning the outward forms of worship; substance speaks of its inner realities. Worship is whole-hearted adoration of God (cf. Mark 7:6-7). The truth is that a Christian can authentically worship God using various styles. No matter what style one employs, if it is done in the Spirit and in truth, it is accepted by God. If it is not done in the Spirit and in truth, it is rejected. You must therefore teach the people to respect one another's preferences in worship. You should "make every effort to do what leads to peace and to mutual edification" (Rom. 14:19).

The wise pastor will teach the elderly members to rejoice when they see the young people worshipping God in a manner that opens their hearts to God and draws them close to Him. Out of love for the young people, they should be willing to join them in their worship of God. In the same manner, you must teach the young people to respect the needs and preferences of their elders, and to wholeheartedly join them in their worship. You will also want to teach the young people to love and appreciate the great hymns of the faith.

The wise Pentecostal pastor will thus ensure that the worship services of the church contain a blend of both new and old songs, contemporary and traditional. He or she will keep in mind that the important thing is that every believer encounters God's Spirit in worship and that they sincerely express their heartfelt devotion to Christ.

Multiple Languages

As mentioned above, many Pentecostal churches across Africa are attended by people who speak different languages. This issue

Part 5: The Public Ministry of the Pentecostal Pastor

poses some significant challenges for the Pentecostal pastor. If the church chooses to conduct its worship services in just the dominant language of the region—while neglecting all others—it runs the risk of alienating people from other language groups. If, however, it employs multiple languages in worship, the church runs the risk of creating discontent among local believers. You must therefore manage this situation with wisdom. You must ensure that the church's worship services appeal to the prevailing culture, while at the same time, welcoming others.

You will need to seek God for His wisdom in dealing with this issue. You and your leadership team will need to prayerfully address such issues as these:

- Which will be the principal language the church will use in worship services?
- Which other languages will be used? When will these languages be used and in what context?
- Into which language will announcements, public prayers, and the sermon be translated?
- Which languages will be used in singing? When and how will these languages be used?
- What language groups in the church are presently being neglected? How can we help them to feel included?

While every congregation will have to find its own way in dealing with this issue, some broad principles apply. For example, in planning worship, you should seek to ensure that everyone who attends a service feels welcomed and included. Another aim is that all who attend be edified. In addition, the worship services should tend to unify rather than divide the congregation. Adhering to these principles will help to ensure that the right decisions are made.

Some urban churches, like international churches, will want to conduct their services in the common European language of the country. Other churches will want to use a regional African tongue. Some will want to translate the entire service. Others will translate only the sermon. Still others may want to go to multiple services with each service being conducted in a different language. Whatever strategy your church adopts, your goal must be to ensure that everyone who attends worship feels respected and included.

A primary responsibility of every Pentecostal pastor is to lead his or her church into authentic, Spirit-anointed worship. He or she can do this by teaching the people what it means to truly worship God in the Spirit and in truth, and by modeling in his or her own life what an authentic lifestyle of worship looks like.

~ Chapter 19 ~

Leading a Church into Pentecostal Revival

Someone described the outpouring of the Holy Spirit on the Day of Pentecost as the Church's first revival. It was on that day that God first poured out His Spirit on the Church, filling it with life and empowering it to fulfill its mission in the earth. The modern Pentecostal Movement derives its name and identity from what occurred on that day.

To be Pentecostal means that one embraces both the experience and purpose of Pentecost. The experience of Pentecost is a powerful spiritual experience the Bible describes as a baptism, or immersion, in the Holy Spirit (Luke 3:16; Acts 1:5). The purpose of Pentecost is empowerment for witness at home and to the ends of the earth (Acts 1:8).

Unlike non-Pentecostal churches, a Pentecostal church cannot remain true to its purpose and calling without repeated outpourings of the Holy Spirit. Just as the body will die if it stops breathing in air, a

Chapter 19: Leading a Church into Pentecostal Revival

Pentecostal church will die if it stops breathing in the Spirit of God. In other words, to be truly Pentecostal a church must experience Pentecostal revival. Jesus explained, "The Spirit gives life; the flesh counts for nothing" (John 6:63). This chapter will discuss how you, as a Pentecostal pastor, can lead your church into such revival.

UNDERSTANDING REVIVAL

Before a Pentecostal pastor can lead his or her church into revival, they must have in their minds a clear picture of what New Testament revival looks like. Unfortunately, however, many Pentecostal pastors have a distorted notion of revival. They have gotten their idea of revival, not from Scripture, but from popular church culture. As a result, they see revival as a church filled with people joyfully singing, dancing, and praising God. Or they think of revival as God showering material blessings and prosperity on His people. While some of these features may accompany revival, they do not describe true revival as pictured in the book of Acts.

Although the word *revival* is not found in the New Testament, the concept of spiritual renewal is (cf. Acts 3:19). Revival speaks of renewed life and implies the restoration of consciousness, vigor, and strength. What the Old Testament calls revival (Psa. 85:6; Hab. 3:2), the New Testament describes as an outpouring of the Spirit (Acts 2:17-18). In the first two chapters of Acts, the Bible identifies three essential elements of New Testament revival:

- First, God's people are baptized in, and thus empowered by, the Holy Spirit (Acts 1:8; 2:1-4).
- Next, God's people begin to boldly proclaim Christ to the lost in the power of the Holy Spirit (Acts 2:14-40; 4:31).
- Finally, lost people repent, put their faith in Christ, and they are saved (Acts 2:41, 47; 5:12-16).

Other outcomes of a genuine outpouring of the Holy Spirit as described in the book of Acts are miraculous healings, signs, and wonders (Acts 2:43; 5:12-16). These supernatural marvels often result in great joy, lively church gatherings, and church growth.

Nevertheless, three essential elements remain at the heart of true Pentecostal revival: spiritual empowerment, powerful witness, and people coming to Christ. If any one of these three elements is missing, true Pentecostal revival has not taken place.

A BIBLICAL EXAMPLE

Let's expand a bit on our definition of revival by looking more closely at what occurred on the Day of Pentecost. A close examination of Acts 2 reveals seven key elements of genuine New Testament revival:

People Seek God

The first key element of genuine New Testament revival is that God's people seek His face in prayer. The Bible tells us that, before the outpouring of the Spirit at Pentecost, the 120 disciples "stayed continually at the temple, praising God" (Luke 24:53). It also says that "they all joined together constantly in prayer" (Acts 1:14). The book of Acts consistently connects prayer with the outpouring of the Holy Spirit. The implication is clear: If a church wants to experience Pentecostal revival, the members must earnestly seek God in prayer.

God Pours Out His Spirit

The second element of New Testament revival is an outpouring of God's Spirit. At Pentecost, in response to the prayers of His people, God graciously poured out His Spirit on the Church. It happened like this:

"When the day of Pentecost came, they were all together in one place. Suddenly a sound like the blowing of a violent wind came from heaven and filled the whole house where they were sitting. They saw what seemed to be tongues of fire that separated and came to rest on each of them. All of them were filled with the Holy Spirit and began to speak in other tongues as the Spirit enabled them." (Acts 2:1-4).

Chapter 19: Leading a Church into Pentecostal Revival

Believers Receive the Spirit

A third element of New Testament revival is that believers are filled with the Holy Spirit. It is one thing for God to pour out His Spirit; it is quite another for His people to receive the Spirit. On the Day of Pentecost, the Holy Spirit not only came on each of them, "all of them were filled with the Holy Spirit and began to speak in other tongues as the Spirit enabled them" (Acts 2:4). The disciples were thus baptized in the Holy Spirit as Jesus had promised (Acts 1:4-5). At that moment, they received power to be Christ's witnesses at home and to the ends of the earth (Acts 1:8). God's people receiving the Spirit marks the beginning of true Pentecostal revival.

Outsiders Take Notice

The fourth element of revival in the New Testament is that outsiders take notice of what God is doing among His people. At Pentecost, those who witnessed the coming of the Spirit on the disciples and listened as they spoke in unlearned languages were "amazed and perplexed." They began asking one another, "What does this mean?" (Acts 2:12).

The Gospel is Proclaimed

The fifth element of authentic New Testament revival is bold, Spirit-inspired proclamation of the gospel. This is what happened at Pentecost. After Peter was filled with the Holy Spirit, he stood and courageously proclaimed the gospel to the gathering crowd. He told them about Jesus and called them to repentance and faith (Acts 2:14-40). All who were filled with the Spirit joined Peter in witnessing for Christ (v. 47).

Many Are Saved

A sixth element of New Testament revival is that many respond to the gospel and are saved. At Pentecost, because of the outpouring of the Holy Spirit and Peter's anointed proclamation of the gospel, many repented and came to the Lord. The Bible says that the listeners were "cut to the heart" and cried out to Peter, "What shall we do?" Peter responded, "Repent and be baptized, every one of you, in the name of Jesus Christ for the forgiveness of your sins. And you will receive the gift of the Holy Spirit" (Acts 2:37-38). As a result, 3,000 were saved, baptized in water, and added to the church (v. 41). In the days that followed, "the Lord added to their number daily those who were being saved" (v. 47).

The Church Expands

The seventh element of New Testament revival is the expansion of the church. Following Pentecost and other outpourings of the Spirit throughout the book of Acts, the church continued to grow numerically and expand geographically (cf. Acts 2:47; 4:31-35; 5:12-16; 9:31).

Other notable elements of revival revealed in Acts 2 are devotion to Scripture, prayer, and love for one another. As God performed wonders in their midst, the people lived with a sense of holy awe. The presence of God's Spirit further created in their hearts a spirit of generosity. All of these things resulted in the growth of the church (Acts 2:41, 47; 4:4; 5:14).

In summary, true Pentecostal revival happens as people believe the message about Jesus, are filled with the Spirit, and then go out to share the good news with others. Those who receive the gospel are then saved and filled with the Holy Spirit. They themselves then become faithful proclaimers of the gospel. As this process is repeated over and over, the revival spreads far and wide.

THE ROLE OF THE PASTOR

As a Pentecostal pastor, you are the key to revival in your local church. You can either be the channel that enables the flow of the Spirit or the dam that blocks its flow. Whatever you do—or fail to do—can determine whether or not your church experiences a true move of the Spirit. Further, as spiritual leader of the church, you will largely determine how effectively your church responds to an outpouring of the Spirit when it comes. You must take this awesome responsibility seriously.

Chapter 19: Leading a Church into Pentecostal Revival

Pentecostal revival usually begins with desire in the heart of the pastor. This desire for a move of the Spirit will motivate him or her to earnestly seek God for an outpouring of the Holy Spirit on the church. The pastor must then convey this desire for revival into the hearts of God's people. You can do this by preaching and teaching often on the topic.

You can further create such a desire in the hearts of your people by leading them in fervent prayer for revival. Speaking of the Holy Spirit, Jesus told His disciples, "I say to you: Ask and it will be given to you; seek and you will find; knock and the door will be opened to you" (Luke 11:9; cf. v. 13). A literal translation of Jesus' words would read, "I say to you: Keep asking, and it will be given to you. Keep seeking, and you will find. Keep knocking, and the door will be opened to you." The implication is clear: As long as we continue to ask for the Spirit, we will continue to receive from God. However, when we stop asking, we will stop receiving. The fires of Pentecostal revival must therefore be fueled by persistent prayer.

Further, as pastor, you must show your people how to pray in faith. You must lead them to believe that, if they will faithfully seek God, He will keep His promise to send revival (Mark 11:24). You will want to continually remind the people of Peter's prophetic declaration: "In the last days, God says, I *will* pour out my Spirit on all people" (Acts 2:17, emphasis added). As church members embrace this promise, they will be encouraged to believe Jesus' promise that the Heavenly Father will "give the Holy Spirit to those who ask him!" (Luke 11:13).

As a church pursues Pentecostal revival, it must, at the same time, pursue Pentecostal mission. This was Jesus' clear instruction in Acts 1:8. First, He promised revival: "You will receive power when the Holy Spirit comes on you." At the same time, He mandated mission: "And you will be my witnesses…to the ends of the earth."

Therefore, as pastor, the task of leading believers into Spirit baptism in preparation for Spirit-empowered witness must remain one of your top priorities. You must be ever mindful that one primary reason God placed you in your church is that you may raise up other Spirit-empowered disciples whom He can use to build His kingdom (Eph. 4:11-12).

ENCOURAGING PENTECOSTAL REVIVAL

A few weeks after the outpouring of the Spirit in Jerusalem on the Day of Pentecost, the Scriptures tell of another outpouring that occurred in Samaria, about 50 kilometers (30 miles) north of Jerusalem (Acts 8:1-25). This revival was led by Philip the evangelist with the aid of the apostles Peter and John. By observing the actions of these men, we discover seven practical ways to encourage revival in the church:

Be Filled with the Spirit

The first way you, as a Pentecostal pastor, can encourage revival in your church is to earnestly seek God to be personally filled or refilled with the Holy Spirit. Philip was one of the seven Spirit-filled "deacons" in the Jerusalem church (Acts 6:3-5). He was likely filled with the Spirit on the Day of Pentecost or soon thereafter. When he was driven out of the city by persecution, he remained full of the Holy Spirit. Upon arriving in Samaria, he ministered in the Spirit's power, igniting a mighty revival in the place.

He, along with the apostles Peter and John, who came down from Jerusalem to assist him (8:14-17), were able to inspire revival in Samaria because they themselves were full of the Holy Spirit. Pentecostal revival thus begins with you, the pastor, and other church leaders being filled or refilled with the Holy Spirit.[1]

Exercise Bold Faith

The second way you can encourage revival in the church is to exercise bold faith. When Philip arrived in Samaria, he acted in faith. As a result, God granted him miracles to confirm the message he preached, and many were won to the Lord (Acts 8:5-8).

---

[1] For more on the Pentecostal pastor's experience with the Spirit, see Chapter 1: "A Person of Experience."

Chapter 19: Leading a Church into Pentecostal Revival

Like Philip, you will need to believe that revival is possible. You must be fully persuaded that God is able to do what He has promised (cf. Rom. 4:18-21). And you will need to courageously act on the promises of God with full assurance that revival is coming. If you will do this, your faith will be contagious. As your members see their pastor acting with bold faith, they too will be encouraged to believe God for revival.

Proclaim Christ

A third way you can lead your church into Pentecostal revival is to faithfully proclaim the gospel of Christ. The Bible tells us, "Philip went down to a city in Samaria, and proclaimed the Messiah there" (Acts 8:5). This was the practice of Christians throughout the book of Acts. Wherever they went, they told people about Jesus (cf. Acts 2:22; 3:13; 4:2, 33; 9:22; 16:31). If you want to experience authentic New Testament revival in your church, you must do as Philip and the apostles did. You must faithfully proclaim Christ to all. And you must teach your people to do the same.[2]

Pray for the Sick

Fourth, you can lead your church into true New Testament revival by faithfully praying for the sick and afflicted, expecting God to supernaturally confirm His Word with miraculous signs following. In Samaria, "when the crowds heard Philip and saw the signs he performed, they all paid close attention to what he said" (Acts 8:6). These miraculous signs included powerful deliverances and miraculous healings. As a result, great joy came to the people, many were saved, and revival came to the city.[3]

---

[2] For more on the topic of preaching, see Chapter 16: "Spirit-Anointed Preaching."

[3] For more on ministry in the supernatural, see the Discovery Series book, *Power Ministry: How to Minister in the Spirit's Power*, by Denzil R. Miller, available from Africa Theological Training Service (ATTS), https://africaatts.org/.

Part 5: The Public Ministry of the Pentecostal Pastor

Emphasize Spirit Baptism

A fifth way you can encourage Pentecostal revival in your church is to frequently emphasize the need for members to be baptized in the Holy Spirit. When the apostles at Jerusalem heard that the Samaritans had received the gospel, they immediately sent Peter and John to pray with them to receive the Holy Spirit (Acts 8:14-17). Any Pentecostal pastor who wants his or her church to experience true Pentecostal revival must do the same. They must teach and preach often on Spirit baptism. And they must pray with their people to receive the Spirit. This will help prepare the church to fully participate in the revival and to spread the gospel to the lost.[4]

Lead in Witnessing

A sixth way you can encourage authentic Pentecostal revival is to lead your church in witnessing to the lost. Philip launched the Samaritan revival through bold Spirit-empowered witness to the lost people of Samaria. In doing this, he became an example to the church. We know the new Christians in Samaria followed his example in witnessing, for within a short time "the church throughout Judea, Galilee, and Samaria enjoyed a time of peace and was strengthened. Living in the fear of the Lord and encouraged by the Holy Spirit, it increased in numbers" (Acts 9:31).

If you, as a Pentecostal pastor, want genuine spiritual revival in your church, you will need to follow Philip's example. You must not only tell your people to witness, you must be an example of the true purpose of Pentecostal revival by being a witness yourself.[5]

---

[4] For more on praying with believers to receive the Spirit, see Chapter 11: "Promotes Pentecostal Experience and Practice" and Chapter 20: "Guiding Believers into Spirit Baptism."

[5] For more on leading the church into Spirit-empowered evangelism, see Chapter 36: "Understanding New Testament Strategy" and Chapter 37: "Evangelizing the Lost."

Chapter 19: Leading a Church into Pentecostal Revival

Persist in Prayer

Finally, you can lead your church into Pentecostal revival by showing the church how to pray, as discussed earlier in this chapter. When the apostles Peter and John arrived in Samaria, "they prayed for the new believers there that they might receive the Holy Spirit" (Acts 8:15). If you want to see authentic Pentecostal revival come to your church, you too must lead the people in prayer. And you must persist in prayer until the answer comes, remembering the words of Paul, "Let us not become weary in doing good, for at the proper time we will reap a harvest if we do not give up" (Gal. 6:9).[6]

To remain a vital witness in the community and in the world, every Pentecostal church must experience repeated outpourings of the Holy Spirit. The Pentecostal pastor must take the lead in this endeavor. He or she must set the example by earnestly pursuing revival, and they must teach the people to do the same. They can take encouragement from God's promise to Joel quoted by Peter on the Day of Pentecost:

> "In the last days, God says, I will pour out my Spirit on all people. Your sons and daughters will prophesy, your young men will see visions, your old men will dream dreams. Even on my servants, both men and women, I will pour out my Spirit in those days, and they will prophesy." (Acts 2:17-18)

---

[6] For more on leading the church in prayer, see Chapter 8: "The Priority of Prayer."

~ Chapter 20 ~

Guiding Believers into Spirit Baptism

Jesus was about to return to heaven. The work He had started He would leave with His Church. In preparation for His departure, He gathered His disciples on a mountaintop outside Jerusalem. There, He gave them a final command and a final promise.

His command was, "Do not leave Jerusalem, but wait for the gift my Father promised...For John baptized with water, but in a few days you will be baptized with the Holy Spirit" (Acts 1:4-5). His promise was, "But you will receive power when the Holy Spirit comes on you; and you will be my witnesses in Jerusalem, and in all Judea and Samaria, and to the ends of the earth" (v. 8). In issuing these instructions, Jesus was mobilizing His emerging Church to fulfil the mission He had given them.

In like manner, every Pentecostal pastor in Africa must mobilize his or her church to participate in Christ's redemptive mission. Like Jesus, they must ensure that their people have been baptized in the

Chapter 20: Guiding Believers into Spirit Baptism

Holy Spirit and empowered as Christ's witnesses to the lost. No church is ready to fully participate in God's mission until its leaders and members have received this promised power from on high (Luke 24:49). This chapter will address this important issue. It will help you to prepare yourself to guide your members into Spirit baptism.

WHAT IS THE BAPTISM IN THE HOLY SPIRIT?

The baptism in the Holy Spirit (sometimes referred to as Spirit baptism) is a powerful life-changing experience. It is an encounter with God in which His Spirit comes upon a follower of Jesus, clothing them and filling them with His presence and power. The baptism in the Holy Spirit is what happened to the 120 disciples on the Day of Pentecost. The Bible describes their experience like this:

> "When the day of Pentecost came, they were all together in one place. Suddenly a sound like the blowing of a violent wind came from heaven and filled the whole house where they were sitting. They saw what seemed to be tongues of fire that separated and came to rest on each of them. All of them were filled with the Holy Spirit and began to speak in other tongues as the Spirit enabled them." (Acts 2:1-4)

Think about what happened to the disciples on that occasion. First, the Holy Spirit came on them, just as Jesus had predicted in Acts 1:8. Next, the Spirit entered into them, filling them with His mighty power and presence. As a result, they began to speak in tongues as the Spirit enabled them. Finally, they began witnessing with extraordinary power and effectiveness (Acts 2:14-41). This pattern continued throughout the book of Acts. And we can expect it to continue today.

With these things in mind, we can affirm three things about Spirit baptism:

1. It is a powerful experience. Jesus described Spirit baptism as being "clothed with power from on high" (Luke 24:49). He promised, "You will receive power when the Holy Spirit comes on you" (Acts

1:8). When a person is filled with the Spirit, he or she encounters the mighty power of God.

2. It is a promise for all believers. Jesus said that the Heavenly Father would freely give the Holy Spirit to any child of His who would ask in faith (Luke 11:13; Mark 11:24). In his Pentecost sermon, Peter said of the experience, "The promise is for you and your children and for all who are far off—for all whom the Lord our God will call" (Act 2:39).

3. It is a command from God. Jesus commanded His disciples, "Do not leave Jerusalem, but wait for the gift my Father promised" (Acts 1:4). In similar manner, Paul charged the Ephesian believers to "be filled with the Spirit" (Eph. 5:18). Because every Christian has been commissioned as Christ's witness, every Christian must be empowered by the Holy Spirit (Luke 24:48-49; Acts 1:8; 5:32).

Spirit baptism further equips the Christian to live a life that pleases God (Gal. 5:16). It enhances his or her ability to pray (Rom. 8:26-27). And with Spirit baptism comes a greater probability that one will be used in the manifestation of spiritual gifts (1 Cor. 12:7-10). In addition, the experience engenders a greater sensitivity to the things of God (John 16: 8; 1 Cor. 2:12), a potential for greater spiritual understanding (John 3:8; 1 Cor. 2:14), a deeper love for God (Rom. 5:5), and a greater consecration to His work (Acts 4:20; 5:29). Every Christian needs to be baptized in the Holy Spirit.

ENCOURAGING SPIRIT BAPTISM

These things being true, the faithful Pentecostal pastor will work hard to inspire and guide his or her members into Spirit baptism. Here are five strategies you can use to encourage and assist your people to be baptized in the Holy Spirit:

1. Help them understand. First, you can encourage your people to be filled with the Spirit by helping them to understand the nature, purpose, and importance of the experience. You can do this by preaching and teaching often on the subject. As believers become more knowledgeable about the Spirit, they will be better prepared to respond to Him and be filled.[1]

2. Instill desire. Speaking of the Holy Spirit, Jesus declared, "Let anyone who is thirsty come to me and drink" (John 7:37). On another occasion He promised, "Blessed are those who hunger and thirst for righteousness, for they will be filled" (Matt. 5:6). Thus, hunger and thirst for God are essential prerequisites for receiving the Holy Spirit.

Knowing this, you will want to instill in your people a longing to be empowered by God's Spirit. One way you can do this is by helping them to visualize how being filled with the Spirit will bless their lives. These blessings include power to witness, a closer walk with Christ, assistance in prayer, victory over temptation, and much more.

You can further create a desire for the Spirit in the people's hearts by living out the Spirit-filled walk before them. As believers observe the gifts and fruit of the Spirit on display in their pastor's life, a desire to be filled with the Spirit will be birthed in their hearts.

3. Inspire faith. Again, speaking of the Spirit, Jesus declared, "Whoever believes in me…out of them will flow rivers of living water" (John 7:38). Paul explained, "By faith we…receive the promise of the Spirit" (Gal. 3:14). Since the Spirit is received by faith, it follows that you will want to prepare your people to receive the Spirit by building their faith in God's promises.

For example, you could remind them of Christ's words in Luke 11. There, Jesus promised, "I say to you: Ask and it *will* be given to you….For *everyone* who asks receives…" (vv. 9-10; cf. v. 13, emphases added). Point out that *everyone* in this passage means every child of God—including them. Other promises you can share with them are found in Mark 11:24 and Acts 2:39. In addition, you can build the people's faith by sharing with them testimonies of those whom God has filled with the Spirit and used for His glory.

---

[1] The e-book, *Proclaiming Pentecost: 100 Sermon Outlines on the Power of the Holy Spirit,* is available for free download from the DecadeofPentecost.org website. It is available in multiple languages.

Part 5: The Public Ministry Of The Pentecostal Pastor

4. Cultivate atmosphere. Another important way you can help your people be filled with the Spirit is by cultivating the proper atmosphere in church services. Spirit baptism is best received in an atmosphere where faith is high and the Spirit's presence is strong. Faith can be said to be high when God's people keenly anticipate a move of the Spirit. They expect God to immediately fulfill His promises. The Spirit's presence can be said to be strong when people sense the awesome nearness of God. Like Jacob, they can testify, "Surely the Lord is in this place" (Gen. 28:16).

Remember, on the Day of Pentecost, the Holy Spirit first filled the place; He then filled the people (Acts 2:3-4). First, the Presence is felt; then, the Spirit is received. The Spirit's presence can be cultivated through earnest prayer, obedience to the Word, anointed worship, and openness to the Spirit.

5. Provide opportunities. Finally, if you expect to see your members baptized in the Holy Spirit, you will need to provide them with frequent opportunities to receive. Prayer for the Spirit must become a regular event in your church's worship gatherings. In addition, you must give regular altar calls that include an invitation to be filled with the Spirit.

In planning your church's worship services, you must allow sufficient time at the end of services for prayer in the altars. This may mean that you will need to shorten the worship and the preaching time. Further, you will want to train altar workers how to lead seekers into Spirit baptism. In addition, you may want to dedicate certain prayer meetings and home cells to seeing believers empowered by the Spirit.

PRAYING WITH BELIEVERS TO RECEIVE

You have delivered your sermon, and believers have presented themselves to be filled with the Spirit. What should you do next? How can you most effectively lead these seekers into the experience of Spirit baptism?

Chapter 20: Guiding Believers into Spirit Baptism

First, it is important that you be aware of the spiritual dynamics about to occur in these believers' lives as they are being filled with the Spirit. As on the Day of Pentecost, the Spirit will first come upon them (Acts 2:3). He will then rush inside them, filling them with His power and presence (v. 4a). Finally, the Spirit will flow out of them in Spirit-inspired speech (v. 4b). You should look for these spiritual dynamics to occur in believers as they are being baptized in the Holy Spirit.

You should further keep in mind the fact that, throughout the entire process, the seekers will need to act in bold faith (Gal. 3:2, 5, 14). Remember, it is faith that will prepare their hearts to receive the Spirit; it is faith that will bring His presence; and it is faith that will release the Spirit's power in inspired speech. With these things in mind, let's look at how you, as a Pentecostal pastor, can lead seekers into Spirit baptism.

Three Steps of Faith

In Luke 11:9-13, Jesus teaches His disciples how they can ask for and receive the Holy Spirit. This passage, along with what happened to the 120 on the Day of Pentecost (Acts 2:1-4), suggests a three-step model for receiving the Holy Spirit. These three steps are asking in faith, receiving by faith, and speaking in faith. Here is how you can lead seekers in these three steps of faith:

Step 1: Asking in faith. First, lead the seekers in asking for the Spirit. Remember Jesus' promise: "Ask and it *will* be given to you" (Luke 11:9, emphasis added). Much as you would lead a sinner in the sinner's prayer, you can lead the seekers in a prayer asking to be filled with the Holy Spirit. Instruct them that, as they pray, they should consciously believe that God is hearing their prayer and that He is acting to answer their prayer. The prayer may proceed as follows, with the candidates repeating each line:

> "Lord, I come to be filled with the Holy Spirit... You promised that I would receive power when the Spirit came upon me... I need that power to be your witness... You also promised that everyone who asks receives... I am asking; therefore, I expect to

receive... When I receive, I will speak out in faith... I will not be afraid... I will begin to speak in tongues as Your Spirit gives me utterance... Holy Spirit, come upon me now."

Once you have prayed, assure the candidates that God has heard their prayer, and that He is ready now to fill them with the Holy Spirit. Encourage them to be sensitive to the Spirit's coming upon them. They should consciously sense His presence. You may want to take a few moments to worship the Lord together, responding to the coming of the Spirit.

Step 2: Receiving by faith. Now, lead the seekers in their step of faith. Jesus said, "Everyone who asks *receives*" (Luke 11:10, emphasis added). Jesus is speaking of an active rather than passive kind of receiving. He is saying, "Everyone who asks must then reach out to receive." Jesus told us how this is done. It is done by an act of faith. "Whatever you ask for in prayer," He said, "believe that you *have received* it, and it will be yours" (Mark 11:24, emphasis added).

To lead the seekers in their step of faith, ask them to lift their hands toward heaven, and in faith pray this simple prayer: "Lord, right now, in Jesus' name, I receive the Holy Spirit." This prayer will provide them with a definite point where they can release their faith to receive the Spirit. At that moment, they should "believe that they *have* received!" The moment they believe, the Spirit will rush inside them and fill them. Tell them to sense the Spirit's presence deep inside.

Step 3: Speaking in faith. Now, encourage the candidates to act in faith and begin to boldly speak out—not from their mind, but from deep within, from where they sense God's presence inside (John 7:38). As they yield to the Spirit flowing into and through their being, they will begin to speak words they do not understand (Acts 2:4; 10:46; 19:6). Their speaking could be compared to Peter's step of faith when, in obedience to Jesus' command, he stepped out of the boat and began walking on the water. His bold step of faith resulted in a miracle (Mark 14:28-29). And so will theirs! Encourage them not

Chapter 20: Guiding Believers into Spirit Baptism

to be fearful but to cooperate fully with the Spirit by continuing to speak in faith.

Speaking in Tongues

It may be helpful here to say a bit more about speaking in tongues, since this is often a new and perhaps strange phenomenon to those who have never experienced it. It is important to understand that, when a Spirit-filled believer speaks in tongues, the words they speak do not come from their minds, as in natural speech. The words come from deep inside, from their spirits. Jesus said, "He who believes in me, as the Scripture said, 'From his innermost being will flow rivers of living water'" (John 7:38, literal translation). Paul said, "Anyone who speaks in a tongue does not speak to people but to God. Indeed, no one understands them; they utter mysteries by the Spirit" (1 Cor. 14:2). Remind the seekers that their speaking will not be forced. It will be a natural flow of supernatural words. They should simply allow it to happen, and cooperate with the Spirit by boldly speaking out in faith.

After-Prayer Counsel

It is important that after-prayer counsel be given to the candidates. If they have been filled with the Spirit, you will give one kind of counsel; if they have not been filled, you will give another kind.

To those seekers who are filled with the Spirit and speak in tongues, give this advice: Tell them that receiving the Spirit is not an end in itself; it is rather a means to a greater end. The purpose for their receiving the Spirit is that they may receive strength to live for God and to be Christ's Spirit-empowered witnesses. You will also want to encourage them to spend time each day praying in the Spirit, that is, in praying in tongues. This practice will strengthen them spiritually, and it will remind them of the Spirit's presence within (1 Cor. 14:4).

To those candidates who, at this time, are not filled with the Spirit, give this advice: Tell them not to be discouraged, and assure them that the promise of Jesus is still true: "Ask and it *will* be given to you" (Luke 11:9, emphasis added). Tell them that they should keep asking, seeking, and knocking, as Jesus taught. As they do, they should keep in mind Jesus' promise: *"Everyone* who asks receives" (v. 10, emphasis added). You may want to ask them if they want to pray again. If they do, repeat the above procedure, encouraging them to act in bold faith.

MOBILIZING THOSE WHO RECEIVE

As a Pentecostal pastor, you should never lose sight of the primary reason Jesus baptizes His followers in the Holy Spirit. He baptizes them to empower them as His witnesses (Acts 1:8). You should therefore encourage those who have been filled with the Spirit to immediately begin to witness to their families and friends. You should also guide them into bold evangelism, church planting, and missions outreach. This is what Jesus and the apostles did in the Gospels and in Acts.[2]

As soon as Jesus was anointed by (baptized in) the Holy Spirit, He began to minister in power (Luke 3:22-23; 4:8; 14, 18-19; 5:17). Upon receiving the Spirit on the Day of Pentecost, Peter stood with the disciples and preached with such power that three thousand people came to the Lord (Acts 2:14-41). Those who came to Christ also witnessed with power. Because of their witness, "the Lord added to their number daily those who were being saved" (v. 47). A few days later, when God again poured out His Spirit on the disciples in Jerusalem, "they were all filled with the Holy Spirit and spoke the word of God boldly" (4:31). This pattern continued throughout the book of Acts, and it should continue in our Pentecostal churches today.

---

[2] For more on these subjects, see Chapter 37: "Evangelizing the Lost" and Chapter 39: "Planting New Churches."

Chapter 20: Guiding Believers into Spirit Baptism

~ Chapter 21 ~

Ministering in the Spirit's Power

Henry and his wife Ruth were serving as missionaries to the idol worshiping people of Glofaken village in southeastern Liberia. For a long time, Henry had been urging the people to forsake their idols and turn to Jesus, but few had responded.

One day, the village chief and his elders visited Henry. The chief said to Henry, "You have been challenging us to forsake the idols of our forefathers and turn to your God. You say your God is more powerful than our idols, but we have not witnessed the power of this God you boast about. If you can show us His power, we will consider abandoning our idols to serve Him."

Henry knew the chief was not only challenging him; he was challenging God! So Henry prayed, "Lord, show Your power to the people of Glofaken." God answered Henry's prayer, and He soon began to demonstrate His power through Henry's ministry.

Chapter 21: Ministering in the Spirit's Power

One morning, the chief's son asked Henry to pray that God would remove the cataracts that covered his eyes, preventing him from seeing clearly. Henry laid his hands on the man and prayed, asking God for a miracle. God immediately answered his prayer, and the man's cataracts disappeared!

After that, God continued to work miracles among the people of Glofaken. On one occasion, God spoke to Henry telling him to lay hands on a dead woman who was about to be buried. To the people's amazement, the woman's eyes opened, and her life was restored. Because of these and other miracles, the chief and his elders turned to God and put their faith in Jesus, along with many other people of Glofaken village. A strong Spirit-filled church was established.

In His Great Commission, Jesus commanded His Church, "Go into all the world and preach the gospel to all creation. Whoever believes and is baptized will be saved, but whoever does not believe will be condemned." To this command He added a promise: "And these signs will accompany those who believe: In my name they will drive out demons; they will speak in new tongues; they will pick up snakes with their hands; and when they drink deadly poison, it will not hurt them at all; they will place their hands on sick people, and they will get well" (Mark 16:15-18). Throughout the history of the Church, people have put their faith in Jesus as they heard the good news and witnessed such demonstrations of the Spirit's power.

This chapter will discuss the importance of the Pentecostal pastor ministering in the Spirit's power. In doing this, it will look at the manifestation gifts listed in 1 Corinthians 12:8-10, along with their purpose in ministry. It will further offer some biblical guidelines for the operation of spiritual gifts in the church.

MINISTRY IN THE SPIRIT'S POWER

Every Pentecostal pastor must know how to minister in the Spirit's power with signs following. Such ministry was the norm for ministry in the New Testament, and it remains the norm for ministry today.

Part 5: The Public Ministry Of The Pentecostal Pastor

Power ministry has its origin in the Spirit of God. It therefore stands to reason that anyone desiring to minister in the Spirit's power must be filled with the Holy Spirit. Jesus understood this. That is why, before ascending into heaven, He left His disciples with a final command: "Do not leave Jerusalem, but wait for the gift my Father promised, which you have heard me speak about. For John baptized in water, but in a few days you will be baptized in the Holy Spirit" (Acts 1:4-5). Jesus then promised them, "But you will receive power when the Holy Spirit comes on you; and you will be my witnesses in Jerusalem, and in all Judea and Samaria, and to the ends of the earth" (v. 8).

Sadly, many pastors in Africa today have not received the Spirit's empowering. Because these men and women are not full of the Holy Spirit, they see no manifestation of the Spirit's power in their ministries. This is tragic. If you have not been filled with the Holy Spirit, you need to seek God until you have been "clothed with power from on high" (Luke 24:49). God will fill you with the Spirit and empower you for ministry, just as He did those first disciples on the Day of Pentecost (Acts 2:1-4).[1]

Further, there are Pentecostal pastors who, although they have been filled with the Spirit, experience little of the Spirit's power in their ministries. Too many of these pastors think the only purpose of being filled with the Holy Spirit is to enable them to speak in tongues. They are like the village hunter who cleans his gun every morning, fires a few shots in the air, puts it away, and expects his wife to cook good meat. They make a lot of noise, but they accomplish very little.

While speaking in tongues is an essential manifestation of the Spirit, it is not the primary purpose for being filled with the Spirit. The primary purpose for being filled with the Spirit is empowerment for ministry (Acts 1:8). As Pentecostal pastors, we must move beyond merely speaking in tongues to Spirit-empowered ministry. We must

---

[1] For more on this topic, see Chapter 2: "A Person of the Spirit" and Chapter 20: "Guiding Believers into Spirit Baptism."

learn to minister in the Spirit's power accompanied by signs and wonders. Such a ministry will bring blessing to the people of God and draw sinners to Jesus.

EXAMPLES OF SPIRIT-EMPOWERED MINISTRY

The Pentecostal pastor can best learn how to minister in the Spirit's power by studying and imitating the ministry of Jesus in the gospels and of the early disciples in the book of Acts.

The Ministry of Jesus

Although Jesus was truly God manifested in the flesh, He chose to fulfill His ministry as a man full of the Holy Spirit. The Bible says He "emptied himself, by taking the form of a servant, being born in the likeness of men" (Phi. 2:7). Jesus thus became our prime example of Spirit-empowered ministry.

Centuries before Christ's coming, Isaiah predicted that the Messiah would fulfill His calling in the power of the Holy Spirit (Isa. 61:1-2). In fulfillment of Isaiah's prophecy, Jesus began His earthly ministry by announcing, "The Spirit of the Lord is upon me because he has anointed me to proclaim good news" (Luke 4:18). Peter described Jesus' Spirit-empowered ministry: "God anointed Jesus of Nazareth with the Holy Spirit and power, and he went around doing good and healing all who were under the power of the devil, because God was with him" (Acts 10:38). These and other passages in the New Testament show that Jesus performed His ministry in the power of the Holy Spirit (see Luke 4:1, 14; 5:17). The miracles, signs, and wonders that accompanied Jesus' ministry helped convince people to follow Him (see Matt. 4:23-25; 9:35-36; John 2:11).

Our Lord's voluntary dependence on the Spirit's power in ministry provides us with a great example. Like Jesus, we must be empowered by the Holy Spirit, and like Him, we must boldly declare the good news to all. At the same time, we must trust God to confirm the proclaimed word with signs and wonders performed in the power of the Holy Spirit.

Part 5: The Public Ministry Of The Pentecostal Pastor

The Ministries of the Apostles

Along with the ministry of Jesus, the ministries of the apostles and other disciples in the book of Acts provide excellent examples of ministry in the Spirit's power. These early disciples learned to minister in the Spirit's power by observing and imitating the Spirit-empowered ministry of Jesus. Virtually every miracle the disciples performed in the book of Acts has its root in a miracle performed by Jesus in the gospels.

The apostles followed Jesus' example of being filled with the Spirit. They knew that, before they could minister as He did, they needed to be empowered by the Spirit as He was. And like Jesus, they ensured that all who came to Christ were empowered by the Holy Spirit and mobilized for Spirit-empowered ministry (see Acts 2:38-39; 8:14-17; 9:17; 19:1-7).

These examples teach us that true New Testament ministry goes beyond natural knowledge, skill, and ability. It requires spiritual empowerment, which comes by being filled with the Holy Spirit. Under the anointing of the Holy Spirit, Jesus and the apostles declared the message of salvation with signs following.

THE ROLE OF SIGNS AND WONDERS

What then is the role of signs and wonders in gospel ministry today? Signs, wonders, and miracles demonstrate God's loving compassion for fallen humanity. They show that the gospel has power to change lives. Like road signs, they point people to Jesus as Healer, Deliverer, and Savior. John tells us, "A great crowd of people followed [Jesus] because they saw the signs he had performed by healing the sick" (John 6:2; see also John 20:30-31; Acts 3:1-10). God wants the same thing to occur in our ministries today.

Jesus further declared that the gates of hell, manned by demonic forces, would not prevail against His advancing Church (Matt. 16:18). He cast out demons to set the oppressed free and to demonstrate the dominion of His kingdom over the kingdom of the devil (Matt. 12:28-29; Luke 11:20-22). Jesus has given this same power

Chapter 21: Ministering in the Spirit's Power

and authority to all who will receive His Spirit and submit themselves to His authority (Matt. 10:1; Mark 3:14-15; Luke 9:1-2; Acts 1:8).

The Pentecostal pastor must further realize that the Spirit's power is available to every member of his or her church (Acts 2:39). God wants to fill each of them with His Holy Spirit, empower them for witness, and give them diverse gifts of the Spirit. He does this "for the common good" of the church (1 Cor. 12:7) and for the advancement of His kingdom in the earth (see Mark 16:20).[2]

SPIRITUAL GIFTS

The power of the Holy Spirit received at Spirit baptism is released in ministry primarily through the manifestation of spiritual gifts. In 1 Corinthians 12:8-10, Paul speaks of nine gifts of the Spirit that should be in operation in every church. These nine gifts are sometimes referred to as the *manifestation gifts,* since, in verse 7, Paul refers to them as "the manifestation of the Spirit." These gifts have been defined as supernatural anointings given by the Holy Spirit through Spirit-filled disciples to accomplish the will of the Father. The nine manifestation gifts can be grouped into three categories: The first category is *revelation gifts,* and includes a message of knowledge, a message of wisdom, and the distinguishing between spirits. The second category is *prophetic gifts,* and includes prophecy, different kinds of tongues, and the interpretation of tongues. The third category is *power gifts,* and includes gifts of healing, faith, and miraculous powers. It is mainly through the power gifts that signs and wonders are manifested.[3]

The Purpose of Spiritual Gifts

The Spirit imparts spiritual gifts for three reasons: First, He gives them to edify, or build up, the local church (1 Cor. 12:7; 14:12, 26).

---

[2] You can find out more about leading church members to be filled with the Spirit in Chapter 20: "Guiding Believers into Spirit Baptism."

[3] For a complete listing of these gifts along with their definitions and purposes, see Appendix 2: "The Manifestation Gifts of 1 Corinthians 12:8-10."

As a result of being strengthened, the church can more effectively prepare its members for service (Eph. 4:11-12).

Second, the Spirit bestows the gifts to enable the church to more effectively spread the gospel to the lost. This function of spiritual gifts is on display in the book of Acts where the gifts are manifested in frontline evangelism and missions.

Finally, the Holy Spirit imparts spiritual gifts to enable the church to expand and plant other Spirit-empowered churches. It is easier to establish a church where the gospel is preached with signs following than where there are no manifestations of God's power. The story of Henry and Ruth, told at the beginning of this chapter, illustrates this truth.

The Operation of Spiritual Gifts

Spiritual power is essential for the proper functioning of the church. Spiritual power, however, can be abused. Just as a governmental official can abuse political power, the Pentecostal Christian can abuse spiritual power. To guard against this, in 1 Corinthians 12-14 Paul laid down certain guidelines for the proper operation of spiritual gifts in the church.

In chapter 13, the apostle says that spiritual gifts should be understood as expressions of God's love through the believer. Loving concern for the welfare of others must therefore be the principle that guides every manifestation of the Spirit.

Then, in chapter 14, Paul lays down some specific rules for the proper manifestation of spiritual gifts in the local assembly, especially the gifts of prophecy, tongues, and the interpretation of tongues. He says that prophetic utterances should never cause confusion in the church. They should rather serve to strengthen, encourage, and comfort God's people (v. 3). Further, the prophetic gifts should always be delivered in an orderly manner (vv. 27-32). And finally, the spirit and content of prophetic utterances should always be "weighed carefully" before they are received as being from God (v. 29).

Chapter 21: Ministering in the Spirit's Power

Across Africa today, the prophetic gifts are being abused, and so are the power gifts. False prophets and false apostles have turned healing and miracles into a profit-making enterprise. These corrupt men and women unashamedly peddle their lying signs and wonders to gullible people who seek solutions to their problems. However, in all of Scripture, there is no instance of a miracle being sold to anyone.

As a faithful Pentecostal pastor, you must ensure that your church does not follow such ungodly practices. Rather, you should humbly trust God to perform signs and wonders through your ministry. And you should do this without yielding to the temptation of commercializing God's miracles. Jesus commanded His disciples, "Heal the sick, raise the dead, cleanse those who have leprosy, drive out demons." He then added, "Freely you have received; freely give" (Matt. 10:8). The godly Pentecostal pastor will always remember that spiritual gifts are not theirs to use as they see fit. Rather, they are gifts *of the Holy Spirit* and are to be used only "as he determines" (1 Cor. 12:11).

You can evaluate the manifestation of a spiritual gift in the church by asking the following questions:

1. Is the manifestation in line with the Word of God? If it does not line up with the clear teachings of Scripture, it should be rejected. God's Spirit will never contradict God's Word.

2. Does the manifestation of the gift glorify God? Spiritual gifts are not given to elevate the minister; they are given to glorify God and to point people to Jesus (Matt. 15:31; Mark 2:12). If the manifestation of a spiritual gift tends to exalt anyone other than God, it should be questioned (John 16:13-15; 1 Cor. 1:29).

3. Does the manifestation edify the church? Spiritual gifts are given to build up the church. If a manifestation causes confusion or weakens people's faith in Christ, it must be rejected.

4. Does the manifestation serve to advance the mission of God? Spiritual gifts are powerful tools for evangelism and church planting. Therefore, those who operate in the gifts should become effective witnesses for Christ. If a manifestation of the Spirit tends to distract or turn people away from God's mission, it must not be allowed.

Part 5: The Public Ministry Of The Pentecostal Pastor

Encouraging Spiritual Gifts

While you, as a Pentecostal pastor, must guard against the misuse of spiritual gifts in your church, this should not be your primary concern. Your primary concern should be to encourage the manifestation of the gifts. You must never be satisfied with mere discussions of signs and wonders. Rather, you must advocate for their frequent operation in the church and in the marketplace. You can do this in four ways:

First, you should teach your members about God's loving concern for all people, and how He wants to extend His hand of grace to save, bless, and heal them. You will further need to instruct members on how God wants to use them in Spirit-empowered ministry, and how they themselves can be used in manifesting spiritual gifts.

Second, you must model Spirit-empowered ministry before the people. The best way to encourage members to exercise spiritual gifts is to show them how it is done. This is what Jesus did with His disciples. He showed them how to minister in the Spirit's power by delivering a demon-possessed man (Luke 8:26-39) and by healing a sick woman and raising a dead girl (vv. 40-56). He then "sent them out to proclaim the kingdom of God and to heal the sick" (9:2). You must therefore allow God to fill and refill you with the Holy Spirit. Then, you must trust Him to use you to demonstrate spiritual gifts in your own life and ministry.

Third, you must encourage your members to respond to the promptings of the Holy Spirit and to act in faith to manifest spiritual gifts. You must also provide opportunities for the people to exercise gifts during times of worship and evangelism.

Finally, you must encourage the manifestation of spiritual gifts in the church by seeking to cultivate the appropriate atmosphere in church services. Such an atmosphere is marked by the manifest presence of God and expectant faith. God manifests His presence when His people open their hearts to Him in genuine praise and worship. Expectant faith is created when God's people are encouraged to reach out and expect God to manifest His presence "by signs, wonders and various miracles, and by gifts of the Holy Spirit distributed according to his will" (Heb. 2:4).

The true Pentecostal pastor will strive to be a man or woman of the Spirit. They will make it their aim to learn to minister in the power of the Holy Spirit with signs following, and they will teach their people to do the same.

~ Chapter 22 ~

Engaging in Spiritual Warfare

Jesus understood that He was involved in a great spiritual struggle with Satan and his legions. He once drove a demon out of a man who was blind and mute. The people watched in amazement as the man began to see and speak. Some asked, "Could this be the Son of David?" Others whispered, "It is only by Beelzebul, the prince of demons, that this fellow drives out demons" (Matt. 12:22-24).

Jesus knew what they were thinking and said to them, "Every kingdom divided against itself will be ruined, and every city or household divided against itself will not stand." He then explained to them what had just happened: "If it is by the Spirit of God that I drive out demons, then the kingdom of God has come upon you." He then added, "How can anyone enter a strong man's house and carry off his possessions unless he first ties up the strong man? Then he can plunder his house" (Matt. 12:25-29).

The same is true today; we too are involved in a great conflict with the forces of evil. Before we can set people free from the clutches of sin and Satan, we must often engage in spiritual warfare. We must first tie up the strong man. Then, we can plunder his house. This chapter will discuss the Pentecostal pastor's need to be competent in challenging and defeating demonic spirits.

UNDERSTANDING SPIRITUAL WARFARE

Before Jesus returned to heaven, He left His Church with a Great Commission. He ordered His followers, "Go and make disciples of all nations, baptizing them in the name of the Father and of the Son and of the Holy Spirit, and teaching them to obey everything I have commanded you" (Matt. 28:19-20). The book of Acts is the story of how Christ's first disciples began to fulfill His commission in the power of the Holy Spirit.

The Great Commission is still in effect today, and it will remain in effect "to the very end of the age" (v. 20). To effectively carry out this commission, the Church and its leadership must know how to confront and defeat Satan and his demonic forces.

The Reality of Spiritual Warfare

Spiritual warfare is real. There is a real enemy, and there are real spiritual battles that we as Pentecostal pastors must fight and win. In his letter to the Ephesians, Paul spoke of this spiritual warfare:

> "For our struggle is not against flesh and blood, but against the rulers, against the authorities, against the powers of this dark world and against the spiritual forces of evil in the heavenly realms." (Eph. 6:12)

The apostle further explained how Christ's servants have been given powerful spiritual weapons to use in this warfare against evil: "The weapons we fight with are not the weapons of the world. On the contrary, they have divine power to demolish strongholds" (2 Cor. 10:4).

Millions across Africa have not received an adequate witness of the gospel. These people live in places dominated by religious systems opposed to the spread of Christianity. These systems are controlled by powerful demonic rulers, who are themselves controlled by Satan, the "prince of demons" (Mark 3:22; cf. 1 John 5:19). To rescue these people, the strong man will have to be bound and evicted (Matt. 12:28-29). Thus, if the Church is to successfully fulfill Christ's mission, it must learn to move in the power of the Holy Spirit. And it must know how to engage and defeat demonic forces.

Jesus taught His disciples to pray, "Your kingdom come, your will be done, on earth as it is in heaven" (Matt. 6:10). He once said to them, "Truly I tell you, some who are standing here will not taste death before they see that the kingdom of God has come with power" (Mark 9:1). Jesus was referring to the Day of Pentecost, when His disciples would be "clothed with power from on high" (Luke 24:49; Acts 2:4).

Today, the kingdom of God comes in power each time someone is saved, healed, delivered, or filled with the Holy Spirit. The Pentecostal pastor should lead his or her people to pray often for God's kingdom to come in power.

The Nature of Spiritual Warfare

Spiritual warfare is the clash between good and evil, between that which is holy and that which is unholy. In this age, it is the ongoing struggle between Satan and his demons and the true Church of God.

The devil has marshalled all his resources to sabotage God's redemptive mission for the nations. He is a murderer and a liar and seeks to "steal, kill, and destroy" (John 8:44; 10:10). He and his demons work to blind people's minds to the truth of the gospel (2 Cor. 4:3-4). Because he hates God, the devil wants to strike out at Him and hurt Him. However, he knows he cannot hurt God. So he seeks to afflict and destroy those whom God loves, the human race.

Jesus announced that God's kingdom had come (Mark 1:14-15; Luke 8:1, 9:11). He boldly declared that He had come to overthrow the kingdom of Satan and to establish God's rule in the earth. The message of the kingdom of God was also at the heart of the preaching of Christ's disciples (cf. Acts 8:12; 19:8). Jesus sent them out to proclaim the kingdom of God and to demonstrate its power over "all the

Chapter 22: Engaging in Spiritual Warfare

power of the enemy" (Luke 10:19; cf. Matt. 10:7; Luke 9:1-2; 10:8-9).[1]

PREPARING FOR SPIRITUAL WARFARE

As a Pentecostal pastor, you must be ready at all times to challenge and defeat demonic spirits. And you must teach your church members to do the same. Here are some ways you can prepare yourself for spiritual warfare:

Be Filled with the Holy Spirit

First, ensure that you have been filled with the Holy Spirit (Acts 2:4; 4:31) and that you are presently walking and living "in step with the Spirit" (Gal. 5:25). Jesus himself was filled with the Spirit (Luke 3:21-22), and He lived and ministered in the Spirit's power (Luke 4:18-19; Acts 10:38). Jesus testified that it was by the power of the Holy Spirit that He drove out demons (Matt. 12:28). If we are to successfully engage in spiritual warfare, we too must be empowered by the Holy Spirit.

Realize What Christ Accomplished

Next, in preparing for spiritual warfare, you must realize all that Christ accomplished at Calvary. There, He paid the price for the redemption of humanity (Isa. 53:6; 1 John 2:2). He further destroyed the devil's dominion over the world (John 12:31). The Bible tells us that Christ "disarmed the powers and authorities, he made a public spectacle of them, triumphing over them by the cross" (Col. 2:15).

Now, because of Christ's mighty work at Calvary, Satan and his demons are defeated enemies (Heb. 2:14-15). If we will walk in the Spirit, and fully submit ourselves to Christ and His will, He will give

---

[1] For more on the coming of God's kingdom, see the Africa's Hope Discovery Series textbook, *The Kingdom of God: A Pentecostal Interpretation* by Denzil R. Miller, published by the Africa Theological Training Service (https://africaatts.org/).

us the power and authority we need to overcome Satan and his demons.

Remember Who You Are in Christ

Further, in preparation for spiritual warfare, you should remind yourself of who you are in Christ. Although you live here on earth, as God's child, you are a citizen of heaven (Phi. 3:20). If you will remember this truth, and choose to live as a true child of heaven, the Lord offers you all the resources, authority, and power of that realm. The more you learn to think and act as a citizen of God's kingdom, the more prepared you will be to proclaim the gospel of the kingdom to lost humanity, and the more able you will be to wage war in the spiritual realm.

Put On the Full Armor of God

Finally, Paul exhorts spiritual warriors to "be strong in the Lord and in his mighty power" (Eph. 6:10). One way we can do this is by putting on the full armor of God. Then, when the evil day comes, we will be able to stand our ground against the enemy (vv. 11, 13).

Paul then cites seven powerful spiritual weapons Christ has given to His servants. He also offers some insights into how each weapon may be used to wage spiritual warfare (Eph. 6:13-18). Let's look more closely at these seven spiritual armaments:

1. The belt of truth. First, we must arm ourselves with the "belt of truth" (Eph. 6:14). To put on the belt of truth means two things: It means that we arm ourselves with the truth of God's Word (John 17:17). It also means that we must wrap ourselves in truthfulness, that is, in absolute honesty and integrity. With this weapon we will be able to counter the lies of the devil (John 8:44).

2. The breastplate of righteousness. Next, we must prepare ourselves for spiritual battle by putting on the "breastplate of righteousness" (Eph. 6:14). We do this by ensuring that we are in right relationship with God, and that we live in unbroken fellowship with Jesus Christ (John 15:5). As a result of this relationship, we are enabled to live clean and holy lives (Titus 2:11-12).

3. Feet fitted with readiness. Third, we must arm ourselves with "readiness" (Eph. 6:15). In other words, we must constantly be on guard against the attacks of the enemy (1 Pet. 5:8). This readiness is produced by hearing and obeying the gospel. Also, as faithful shepherds of the flock of God, we must prepare God's people for the enemy's attacks, as Paul did with the Ephesian elders (Acts 20:28-31).

4. The shield of faith. Fourth, we must take up the "shield of faith" (Eph. 6:16). We can use this spiritual weapon as a defense against "all the flaming arrows of the evil one" (v. 16). These flaming arrows include various temptations of the devil such as unholy thoughts and desires and enticements to disobey God's commands. Our faith is built up by listening to and reading the Word of God (Rom. 10:17) and by praying in the Holy Spirit (Jude 20).

5. The helmet of salvation. A fifth weapon at our disposal is the "helmet of salvation" (Eph. 6:17). This salvation includes, not only salvation from sin and hell, but also any salvation or deliverance that comes from God, such as deliverance from demons, danger, sickness, and death.

6. The Word of God. Sixth, we must take the "sword of the Spirit, which is the word of God" (Eph. 6:17). The Word of God is one of the Pentecostal pastor's most powerful spiritual weapons. We can arm ourselves with God's Word by diligently studying and memorizing Scripture (Psa. 119:11). Further, we must faithfully proclaim God's Word to all who will listen (2 Tim. 4:2).[2]

The Word of God can be used for both offensive and defensive battle. It can be used as an offensive weapon when the Word is used in prayer, as well as when it is preached and taught under the anointing of the Spirit. And it can be used as a defensive weapon to counter the attacks of Satan, as did Jesus in the wilderness (Luke 4:1-13).

---

[2] For more on the Pentecostal pastor's relationship to the Bible, see Chapter 9: "Believes the Bible."

Part 5: The Public Ministry Of The Pentecostal Pastor

The "word of God" mentioned in this passage could also be a personal or *rhema* word that a disciple of Christ may receive from the Spirit. This could be a specific biblical passage the Lord impresses on one's heart. Or it could be a revelation from God to meet a specific need, such as a word of knowledge or a word of wisdom (1 Cor. 12:8).

7. Prayer in the Spirit. Finally, we must take up the weapon of prayer in the Spirit. Such prayer is a powerful spiritual weapon. Paul thus exhorts believers to "pray in the Spirit on all occasions with all kinds of prayers and requests" (Eph. 6:18). This means we should often allow the Holy Spirit to anoint and direct our prayers. This kind of praying includes intercessory prayer in tongues (1 Cor. 14:14; cf. Rom. 8:26).

Seven Other Spiritual Weapons

The Bible speaks of seven additional powerful spiritual weapons the Pentecostal pastor can use to defeat the enemy:

1. The weapon of fasting. When used alongside prayer, fasting is a powerful spiritual weapon (Mark 9:29 KJV).

2. The weapon of praise. Great spiritual power is generated through Spirit-anointed praise. When God's people praise Him, walls fall down (Josh. 6:16-20), armies are defeated (2 Chron. 20:1-26), and prison doors are opened (Acts 16:25-26).

3. The weapon of love. Genuine love has amazing power in directing men and women to Christ (Rom. 5:5). Some, who cannot be won by our logical arguments, or even our manifestations of power, can be won to Christ through simple demonstrations of Christian love (12:20-21).

4. The weapon of Spirit baptism. Jesus promised His followers power when the Holy Spirit came upon them (Acts 1:8). He was speaking about an experience He called the baptism in the Holy Spirit (Luke 3:16; Acts 1:5; 2:4).[3]

---

[3] For more on Spirit baptism, see Chapter 20: "Guiding Believers into Spirit Baptism."

5. The weapons of the gifts of the Spirit. One reason the Spirit gives His gifts to the church is that believers might be equipped for spiritual warfare (1 Cor. 12:8-10).[4]

6. The weapon of Jesus' name. All of the authority of heaven stands behind Jesus' name (Phi. 2:9-11). When we use His name as He has directed, the powers of hell must yield (John 14:13-14; Acts 3:6; 9:27; 16:18).

7. The weapon of the gospel. Paul called the gospel "the power of God for the salvation of everyone who believes" (Rom. 1:16). The gospel is the message of salvation in Christ. The message of the gospel has the power to create faith in the hearts of those who hear it preached (Rom. 10:17). We must not fail to faithfully preach the gospel at every opportunity (1 Cor. 9:16).

ENGAGING IN SPIRITUAL WARFARE

The question arises, "How can the Pentecostal pastor (or, for that matter, any Spirit-filled disciple) confront and cast evil spirits out of a person held in demonic bondage?" Here is a three-step procedure you can use to minister deliverance to those held in demonic captivity.[5]

The Interview

The first step in ministering deliverance to the captives is the interview, if this is possible. During this step, you will talk with the individual needing deliverance. Your goal is to gain greater insight into the person's condition. At this point, through the gift of discerning of spirits, you may discover the demonic presence. Or the demons may become agitated by the presence of God and expose themselves (Mark 1:23; 5:6-7).

---

[4] See Appendix 2: "The Manifestation Gifts of 1 Corinthians 12:8-10."
[5] For more information on challenging and defeating demonic spirits, see the Africa's Hope Discovery Series textbook, *Power Ministry: How to Minister in the Spirit's Power,* Chapter 11: "How to Cast Out Demons" and Chapter 12: "Defeating Territorial Spirits."

When possible, you should lead the sufferer in a prayer of repentance and confession of sin. This is especially important when the person's sins are closely related to his or her spiritual bondage. In this prayer, the sufferer should renounce the demonic infestation and the accompanying works of the flesh in his or her life.

Ministry Engagement

The second step of the deliverance process is the ministry engagement. This is the actual power encounter with the demonic forces. You should begin the engagement by calling on the name of Jesus and inviting the Holy Spirit to come and manifest His presence and power. Once you sense the presence of God, you can proceed to casting out (or in some cases, driving away) the demons. As the Spirit leads, you may use one or more of the following biblical procedures:

- You may bind the demons in the name of Jesus (Matt. 16:17-19; 18:18).
- You may command the demons to come out, be gone, or to release their hold on their victim (Luke 4:35).
- You may command the demons not to reenter the person (Mark 9:25).

Sometimes the demons will resist, and a struggle will result (Luke 8:29; 11:14). In such cases, you should persist in faith until the victory comes. Deliverance is often accompanied by physical manifestations (Mark 7:30; Luke 4:33-35; 9:42). When this happens, you should not be intimidated or distracted. Rather, you should continue to move in the power of the Holy Spirit, order the demons to be quiet (Mark 1:25), and in the authority of Jesus' name, command them to come out and stay out (Mark 9:25).

After-Prayer Counseling

The final step in the deliverance process is after-prayer counseling. This step is very important to a person who has been under the control of demons. He or she will need prayer and emotional support after their deliverance. If the person is not born again, you should

Chapter 22: Engaging in Spiritual Warfare

immediately lead them to faith in Christ. In addition, you should immediately lead them into the baptism in the Holy Spirit. Jesus warned about neglecting these essential matters (Matt. 12:43-45). You, or someone you delegate, should maintain close contact with the person until he or she is completely free from their bondage.

As a Pentecostal pastor, Christ has commissioned you to engage in spiritual warfare (Mark 16:15-16). You can confront the devil and his demonic forces with great confidence, knowing that the One who dwells inside you is infinitely greater than the one who is in the world (1 John 4:4).

~ Part 6 ~

The Pentecostal Pastor as Shepherd

~ Chapter 23 ~

Understanding Pastoral Ministry

It is quite possible for a person to be actively involved in a religious activity, and deeply committed to that activity, and at the same time not really understand what they are doing or why they are doing it. The Spirit once directed Philip to a sincere and deeply committed Ethiopian nobleman. The nobleman was dutifully reading Scripture. However, he did not understand what he was reading (Acts 8:29-31). On another occasion, Paul encountered some equally sincere and committed men in Athens. These men worshipped an "UNKNOWN GOD." However, they did not understand who they were worshipping or why (Acts 17:22-23). They needed an explanation.

Many Pentecostal pastors in Africa find themselves in a similar situation. They are actively involved in pastoral ministry, and they are deeply committed to fulfilling their role as pastors. However, in truth, they understand little about what they are doing or why they are doing it. Like the Ethiopian nobleman, they are pleading, "How can I know unless someone explains it to me?" This chapter is written to

Chapter 23: Understanding Pastoral Ministry

answer this plea. It will lay a foundation of understanding for pastoral ministry, a foundation on which a solid ministry can be built.

THE CONTEXT FOR PASTORAL MINISTRY

Pastoral ministry occurs in the context of a local church. The Greek word translated church in the New Testament is *ekklesia,* which means those who have been called out and set apart. Thus, a local church is a group of people who have been set apart by Christ to serve and worship Him. It is made up of those who have been born of God's Spirit and washed in Jesus' blood (John 3:3-7; Acts 20:28).

Three things can be said about the Church: First, the Church belongs to God. Jesus referred to the Church as "my church" (Matt. 16:18). Paul called it "God's household...the church of the living God" (1 Tim. 3:15). Second, the Church is God's dwelling place. Paul speaks of the Church as a "holy temple" which has "become a dwelling in which God lives by his Spirit" (Eph. 2:22). Finally, the Church is "the pillar and foundation of the truth" (1 Tim. 3:15). In other words, it is the spiritual structure that supports and sustains the truth. One primary mission of the Church is to preserve and proclaim truth (Matt. 28:19; 2 Cor. 2:14). As a Pentecostal pastor, you must be fully aware that you carry out your ministry in this context.

THE CONCEPT OF MINISTRY

It is also essential that you understand the biblical concept of ministry. The Scriptures teach that Christ appoints ministries in the Church to enable it to fulfill its God-given mission. The Church's mission is to proclaim the good news to all people in the power of the Holy Spirit before the soon coming of Christ (Mark 16:15-16; Acts 1:8). Then, it is to take those who believe and make them into obedient disciples, shaping them into the image of their Lord (Matt. 28:19; Col. 3:10).

The word *ministry* further carries with it the concepts of service and function. Paul elaborates on the idea of ministry. In Ephesians 4, he speaks of three types of ministry:

Part 6: The Pentecostal Pastor as Shepherd

The Ministry of Jesus

First, Paul speaks of the ministry of Jesus, the Messiah (Eph. 4:8-10). Through His redemptive work on the cross (including His death, burial, resurrection, and ascension to the Father), Jesus inaugurated the New Covenant. While on earth, Christ ministered as an apostle (Heb. 3:1), prophet (Luke 24:19), evangelist (Luke 19:10), pastor (John 10:11-16), and teacher (John 3:2; 13:13). He thus became the "chief cornerstone" of the Church, ensuring its stability and endurance (Eph. 2:20).

The Ministry of Believers

Second, Paul speaks of the ministry of believers (Eph. 4:11-16). Jesus entrusted His ministry to the Church. Therefore, any ministry in the Church is an extension of His ministry. The goal of ministry is that every member of the church becomes mature "attaining to the whole measure of the fullness of Christ" (Eph. 4:13). Those who have become mature should then turn and strengthen others, causing the whole church to grow and prosper.

Leadership Ministries

Third, Paul discusses the leadership ministries Christ gave to the Church. He writes, "Christ himself gave the apostles, the prophets, the evangelists, the pastors and teachers" (Eph. 4:11). These ministry roles should not be viewed primarily as offices or titles, as so many do. They should rather be thought of as ministry *functions*. They are not offices from which leaders rule over the church. Rather, they are functions given to servant leaders to "equip [God's] people for works of service" (Eph. 4:12), as follows:

- *Apostolic function:* The apostle serves the Church and God's purposes by advancing God's kingdom into unreached areas and among unreached peoples in the power of the Holy Spirit—and by equipping others to do the same.
- *Prophetic function:* The prophet serves the Church and God's purposes by speaking messages from God in the power of the Holy Spirit—and by equipping others to do the same.

- *Evangelistic function:* The evangelist serves the Church and God's purposes by announcing the gospel to the lost in the power of the Holy Spirit—and by equipping others to do the same.
- *Pastoral function:* The pastor serves the Church and God's purposes by ministering to God's people in the power of the Holy Spirit—and by equipping others to do the same.
- *Teaching function:* The teacher serves the Church and God's purposes by teaching the Word of God in the power of the Holy Spirit—and by equipping others to do the same.

These ministry functions often overlap, with individuals operating in multiple roles. For example, an individual may function as an apostle and prophet at the same time. Another may function as a teacher and an evangelist, and so on. As mentioned above, Jesus functioned in all five of these roles, as did the apostle Paul. By his wording of verse 11, Paul seems to join the roles of pastor and teacher into one function of pastor-teacher.

Within this framework, Paul introduces himself as a "servant of Jesus Christ, called to be an apostle" (Rom. 1:1; cf. Titus 1:1). Likewise, Peter introduces himself as a "servant and apostle of Jesus Christ" (2 Pet. 1:1). Note how both men first declared themselves servants. Only then could they be true apostles. It should be the same today for anyone serving in any of the five leadership ministries. Above all else, they are to consider themselves as servants of God and His people (cf. John 21:15-17; 1 Pet. 5:2-4).

These five "ascension gifts of Christ" further serve as expressions of Christ's authority within the Church. Their purpose is to guide the Church towards divine objectives. Paul taught that these ministries have two functions, planting and watering (1 Cor. 3:6). Planting ministries could include apostles and evangelists. Watering ministries could include prophets, pastors, and teachers. Collaboration between planters and waterers ensures the progress of God's work.

Service Ministries

Along with leadership ministries, God has placed certain service ministries in the Church. These ministries include elders, deacons, and deaconesses (cf. Acts 6:1-6; 14:23; 1 Tim. 3:1-10). The Hebrew word for elder is *zaqen*, which denotes a person of experience and authority (Num. 11:16). The Greek word for elder is *presbyteros*, which means much the same. An elder in the church is one who has authority to serve as an overseer (*episkopos* in Greek) (Acts 20:17, 28). Thus, a pastor is both an elder and an overseer (Acts 20:17, 28; 1 Tim. 3:1-2; Titus 1:5-7). To effectively lead the church, the Pentecostal pastor must be spiritually mature, and he or she must have a thorough knowledge of the Word of God (1 Tim. 3:6; 2 Tim. 4:2).

The Greek word for deacon is *diakonos,* which means "one who serves." In Acts 6, seven Spirit-filled men were chosen to serve tables so that the apostles could "give [themselves] continually to prayer, and to the ministry of the word" (Acts 6:2-4). Two of these men, Stephen and Philip, became powerful witnesses for Christ. In Romans 16:1, Paul introduced Phoebe as a deaconess in the church in Rome.

THE WORK OF THE PASTOR

The biblical term "pastor" comes from the Greek word *poimēn,* which literally means "shepherd." As a pastor, your role is to shepherd the flock of God (Acts 20:28). And as a shepherd, you are to serve as a leader, mentor, and protector of God's people (1 Pet. 5:1-4).

Pastoral Responsibilities

Among your pastoral responsibilities are caring for the flock (John 21:15-17; 1 Pet. 5:2-3), strengthening the body (Eph. 4:11-12), counseling God's people (1 Tim. 5:14), and guarding the sheep (Acts 20:28). Other responsibilities include preaching (2 Tim. 4:2), teaching (1 Tim. 3:2; Titus 2:1), leading (Heb. 13:17), administrating (Acts

Chapter 23: Understanding Pastoral Ministry

20:28), disciple-making (Matt. 28:19), evangelizing the lost (2 Tim. 4:5), and mobilizing the church for missions (Acts 13:1-4).[1]

In the early days of the Church, soon after the Day of Pentecost, the apostles assumed the role of pastors. They led the Church as Jesus had led them, emphasizing what He had emphasized. Several of their emphases are revealed in Luke's description of the Church in Acts 2:38-47.

This remarkable passage, along with the verses that precede it, reveals ten pastoral emphases of the apostles. As a Pentecostal pastor, you would be wise to follow the apostles' example, allowing these ten emphases to serve as a template for your own ministry today.

1. Proclamation of the gospel. Freshly empowered by the Holy Spirit, Peter stood and boldly proclaimed the gospel. In his sermon on the Day of Pentecost, Peter emphasized the death and resurrection of Christ (Acts 2:23-24, 32; cf. 1 Cor. 15:1-4). He concluded his message by calling on the people to repent and believe the gospel (Acts 2:36-40). This emphasis continued throughout Acts (cf. 3:19; 20:21; 26:20). In like manner, gospel proclamation should be at the core of your pastoral ministry today.[2]

2. Empowering of the Holy Spirit. Peter also emphasized the need to be empowered by the Holy Spirit (Acts 2:38-39; cf. 2:17-18). Those who receive Christ should immediately be given the opportunity to be filled with the Holy Spirit. Like gospel proclamation, this emphasis continued throughout Acts (8:14-17; 9:17-18; 10:44-46; 19:1-7). As a Pentecostal pastor in Africa, you must do the same. You must preach and teach often on the baptism in the Holy Spirit with

---

[1] For more on the Pentecostal pastor's responsibilities, see Chapters 23-27.

[2] For more on the Pentecostal pastor's preaching ministry, see Chapter 16: "Spirit-Anointed Preaching."

the goal of seeing every member empowered as a witness to the lost (1:8).[3]

3. Teaching the Word of God. Further, Luke tells us that the Jerusalem believers "devoted themselves to the apostles' teaching" (Acts 2:42). The apostles thus emphasized teaching the Word of God. Years later, Paul would testify, "You know that I have not hesitated to preach anything that would be helpful to you but have taught you publicly and from house to house" (20:20). This was Paul's method of operation wherever he went (cf. 11:26-26; 15:35; 28:31). You too should ensure that God's Word is accurately, clearly, and widely taught in the church God has called you to lead.[4]

4. Celebrating the sacraments. In obedience to the commands of Jesus (Matt. 28:19-20; Luke 22:19), the apostles emphasized water baptism and Holy Communion (Acts 2:38-41). Water baptism testifies to the believer's experience of new birth. Holy Communion testifies to their ongoing relationship with Christ. As a Pentecostal pastor, you must ensure that these two sacred rites are faithfully administered in the church.[5]

5. Leading in prayer. The apostles further emphasized prayer. Luke tells us that the people "devoted themselves…to prayer" (Acts 2:42). Devoted prayer forms the foundation for the believer's personal piety and witness. It also ensures the presence and power of the Spirit in the church and in the lives of believers (cf. 4:31). As a Pentecostal pastor, you too must lead the people in prayer through teaching and by personal example.[6]

---

[3] For more on the empowering of the Holy Spirit, see Chapter 20: "Guiding Believers into Spirit Baptism."

[4] For more on the Pentecostal pastor's teaching ministry, see Chapter 17: "Effective Teaching."

[5] For more on administering the sacraments, see Chapter 42: "Conducting Sacraments, Dedications, and Installations."

[6] For more on the Pentecostal pastor and prayer, see Chapter 8: "The Priority of Prayer."

6. Expecting signs and wonders. The apostles further contended for a demonstration of God's presence and power in the church. Luke writes, "Everyone was filled with awe at the many wonders and signs performed by the apostles" (Acts 2:43). Demonstrations of God's presence and power should also characterize your ministry as a Pentecostal pastor today.[7]

7. Promoting unity. Also, the apostles promoted unity in the body. Luke writes, "All the believers were together and had everything in common" (Acts 2:44). The people's togetherness spoken of here, was more than physical. They had a unity of heart and purpose that propelled the church forward in mission.

8. Encouraging generosity. Additionally, the apostles promoted generosity. As a result, church members "sold property and possessions to give to anyone who had need" (Acts 2:45). Such generosity was born out of a loving relationship with one another and with their Lord. Like the apostles, you too must lead your people in generous giving to the work of God.

9. Organizing for worship. Luke writes, "Every day they continued to meet together in the temple courts....praising God and enjoying the favor of all the people" (Acts 2:46-47). The apostles knew how important it was for the people to come together for worship, training, and encouragement.[8]

10. Mobilizing for witness. Finally, the apostles emphasized personal witness. They mobilized the people for mission, encouraging them to share the message of Christ with others. As a result, "The Lord added to their number daily those who were being saved" (Acts 2:47).[9]

---

[7] For more on ministry in the supernatural, see Chapter 21: "Ministering in the Spirit's Power."

[8] For more on leading the church in worship, see Chapter 18: "Leading Worship."

[9] For more on mobilizing the church for witness, see Chapter 37: "Evangelizing the Lost."

Part 6: The Pentecostal Pastor as Shepherd

These ten emphases of the apostles in the church in Jerusalem can serve as a model for you as a Pentecostal pastor today. They will help you to align your ministry with the ministries of Jesus and the apostles. And they will help ensure that the church you pastor is a spiritual force in your own community and in the world.

Pastoral Motivations and Accountability

As a Pentecostal pastor, *what* you do is important; *why* you do it is even more important. Peter wrote about the proper motivations for pastoral work (1 Pet. 5:2-3). Pastors are not to do their work out of a feeling of obligation, or for financial gain, or out of a desire to rule over people. Rather, they are to genuinely care for God's people and lovingly serve them. Those pastors who serve out of noble motives will be rewarded. Peter encourages faithful pastors with a promise: "And when the Chief Shepherd appears, you will receive the crown of glory that will never fade away" (v. 4).

As a Pentecostal pastor, you must never forget that you will one day stand before Christ to give an account of how you fulfilled your calling. Paul tells us, "We must all appear before the judgment seat of Christ, so that each of us may receive what is due us for the things done while in the body, whether good or bad" (2 Cor. 5:10). The faithful pastor will be rewarded (Matt. 25:23); the unfaithful pastor will be held accountable (v. 26).

Throughout Scripture, those shepherds who fail to care for God's people are condemned. For example, God spoke through Jeremiah saying, "Woe to the shepherds who are destroying and scattering the sheep of my pasture!...Because you have scattered my flock and driven them away and have not bestowed care on them, I will bestow punishment on you for the evil you have done" (Jer. 23:1-2; cf. Ezek. 34:1-10).

ENABLEMENT FOR MINISTRY

Pastoral ministry is a deeply spiritual endeavor. To effectively evangelize the lost and equip the saints, the Pentecostal pastor must learn to rely on divinely-supplied resources. Pastoral ministry further involves spiritual warfare that must be waged with spiritual weapons (Eph. 6:12; 2 Cor. 10:4-5).[10]

One of these spiritual weapons is the power you received when you were baptized in the Holy Spirit. Before returning to heaven, Jesus commanded His disciples to remain in Jerusalem to be empowered by the Holy Spirit (Acts 1:4-8). They were not to begin their ministries until they had been "clothed with power from on high" (Luke 24:49). They received that power on the Day of Pentecost when "all of them were filled with the Holy Spirit and began to speak in other tongues as the Spirit enabled them" (Acts 2:4). Like the apostles, you cannot properly fulfill your role as pastor without divine empowering. And like them, you must ensure that everyone who comes to Christ is soon baptized in the Holy Spirit and empowered as Christ's witness.[11]

---

[10] For more on spiritual warfare, see Chapter 22: "Engaging in Spiritual Warfare."

[11] For more on leading new believers into the baptism in the Holy Spirit, see Chapter 20: "Guiding Believers into Spirit Baptism."

~ Chapter 24 ~

Caring for the Sheep

Some Pharisees once criticized Jesus for associating with lost people. "This man welcomes sinners," they murmured. "He even eats with them!" Overhearing their remarks, Jesus asked them, "Suppose one of you has a hundred sheep and loses one of them?" He then told them the story of the shepherd who discovered one of his sheep was missing. The faithful shepherd left the ninety-nine in the open field and set out to search for the one lost sheep. When he found it, he put it on his shoulders and carried it home. As he entered his village, he called out to his friends and neighbors, "Rejoice with me, for I have found my lost sheep!" (cf. Luke 15:4-6).

Before David was a king and a psalmist, he was a shepherd, caring for his father's sheep. In the process, he learned to love each one of them. He came to understand that God loved him and cared for him just as he cared for his sheep. He wrote, "The Lord is my shepherd, I lack nothing. He makes me lie down in green pastures, he leads me beside quiet waters, he refreshes my soul" (Psa. 23:1-2).

Jesus claimed for himself the title of Shepherd. "I am the good shepherd," He said, "I know my sheep and my sheep know me...and

I lay down my life for my sheep" (John 10:14-15). The writer of Hebrews calls Jesus the "great Shepherd of the sheep" (Heb. 13:20). His sheep are those who have chosen to follow Him. Jesus further states that He is the owner of the sheep. Unlike the hireling, who runs when the wolf comes to ravage the sheep, the true shepherd will stand His ground to defend them. He is even prepared to lay down His life for them.

As a Pentecostal pastor, you must take Jesus as your model. You must shepherd God's people as Jesus himself would shepherd them if He were here in the flesh. This chapter will discuss the Pentecostal pastor's responsibility to care for the flock of God.

THE SHEPHERD'S HEART

As shepherds of God's flock, Pentecostal pastors must be compassionate, faithful, and dependable, as follows:

Compassionate

Speaking of God, Isaiah wrote, "He tends his flock like a shepherd: He gathers the lambs in his arms and carries them close to his heart" (Isa. 40:11). Like their Lord, authentic Pentecostal pastors are compassionate. They genuinely love people. This includes those inside and outside the church. Jesus demonstrated His love for people. The Bible says of Him, "When he saw the crowds, he had compassion on them, because they were harassed and helpless, like sheep without a shepherd" (Matt. 9:36). In like manner, you must truly love the people God has called you to serve.

Faithful

Further, as a Pentecostal pastor, you must prove yourself to be faithful. You must be willing to forsake all and fully follow your Lord (Matt. 19:21; Mark 8:34-35). Christ has placed His people in your hands as a sacred trust. You must therefore freely relinquish your own personal rights. And you must faithfully serve those whom Christ has placed under your care. Paul wrote concerning ministers of the gospel, "It is required that those who have been given a trust must prove faithful" (1 Cor. 4:2).

Dependable

Finally, to faithfully shepherd God's flock you must be dependable. You must not be like a hired hand, who when trouble comes, abandons the sheep and runs away (John 10:12-13). Rather, you must be steadfast and reliable. Both God who called you, and the people you serve, must be able to rely upon you, knowing that, whatever comes, you can be counted on to stand and fulfill your responsibilities.

THE SHEPHERD'S WORK

As God's shepherd, every Pentecostal pastor bears two solemn responsibilities: to care for the sheep and to organize the church as a caring community. Let's look at these two responsibilities:

Caring for the Sheep

First, you must care for the sheep. To do this, you will need to fulfill at least six responsibilities:

1. Feeding the sheep. Jesus' message to Peter was, "[If you love me] you will...feed my sheep" (John 21:17). God promised Israel, "I will give you shepherds after my own heart, who will lead [or feed] you with knowledge and understanding" (Jer. 3:15). So must you feed the people of God. You must faithfully teach them the Word of God. This practice will cause the people to grow and become strong in the faith. It will also cause the church to be built up and become mature in Christ (Eph. 4:11-16). This is, no doubt, one reason Paul encouraged Timothy to "preach the word; be prepared in season and out of season; correct, rebuke and encourage—with great patience and careful instruction" (2 Tim. 4:2).

Not only must you faithfully preach and teach the Word of God yourself, you must also establish a comprehensive teaching program in the church. You must ensure that the Bible is systematically taught to those of all ages—children, youth, and adults.[1]

2. Protecting the flock. Paul urged the Ephesian elders, "Keep watch over yourselves and all the flock of which the Holy Spirit has made you overseers" (Acts 20:28). He then warned them, "I know that after I leave, savage wolves will come in among you and will not spare the flock. Even from your own number men will arise and distort the truth in order to draw away disciples after them. So be on your guard!" (vv. 29-31).

You must therefore be on guard against false prophets and false teachers who seek to prey on the church. You must identify these "wolves in sheep's clothing" and boldly confront them. If necessary, along with the leadership of the church, you must expel them from the congregation. You must do the same with persistent troublemakers who cause division in the church (Rom. 16:17).

In addition, you must protect God's people from false teaching and false teachers by showing them the truth. They will then "no longer be infants, tossed back and forth by the waves, and blown here and there by every wind of teaching and by the cunning and craftiness of people in their deceitful scheming." Instead, they will "grow to become in every respect the mature body of him who is the head, that is, Christ" (Eph. 4:14-15).[2]

3. Reaching out to the hurting. Jesus reached out in compassion to hurting people (Matt. 9:36; 15:32-38). As a Pentecostal pastor, you must do the same. You must reach out in love to the weak and suffering in your church and community. This could include widows and orphans (James 1:27). It could also include the sick, the poor, those in prison, and others in need (Matt. 25:38). Jesus encourages us,

---

[1] For more on the Pentecostal pastor's responsibility in teaching the Word of God, see Chapter 17: "Effective Teaching."

[2] For more on protecting the church, see Chapter 27: "Guarding the Flock."

"Truly I tell you, whatever you [do] for one of the least of these brothers and sisters of mine, you [do] for me" (v. 40).

You will also need to visit in the homes of those who are sick, discouraged, backslidden, or harassed by demons. There, you will minister to them according to their need. You should also visit church members who are hospitalized or imprisoned. You must take time to pray with them and encourage them. You may also want to schedule specific office hours in which you receive people with problems or counseling needs. There, you will listen attentively to their problems, pray with them, and help them find solutions in God's Word.[3]

4. Strengthening the weak. In every congregation are those who are spiritually weak. Because of this, their walk with the Lord is unsteady. Some, because of their spiritual immaturity, or for other reasons, are in danger of drifting away from the Lord. You should be constantly on the lookout for those in this perilous condition. You should find ways to encourage them and strengthen them in their walk with the Lord. One way to do this is to assign a strong Christian to befriend and encourage them. Another way is to ensure that they have been filled with the Holy Spirit. The Spirit will become to them a helper, comforter, and guide.[4]

5. Seeking the lost. Jesus testified that He had come "to seek and to save the lost" (Luke 19:10). He commanded His disciples to do the same (Mark 16:15-16; Luke 14:23). As a Pentecostal pastor, you must follow the Lord's example. You must witness to the lost, and you must lead your people to do the same. Further, you must organize your church for Spirit-empowered evangelism, church planting, and missions.

To do this you will need to preach and teach often on people's need to know Christ as Savior. And you must frequently remind God's people of their responsibility to reach out to the lost with the

---

[3] For more on the Pentecostal pastor's counseling ministry, see Chapter 26: "Counseling God's People."

[4] For more on leading church members into the fullness of the Spirit, see Chapter 20: "Guiding Believers into Spirit Baptism."

gospel. You should also institute programs and initiatives to inspire and equip the people for witness. Someone has rightly said, "The best way for a pastor to inspire his people to witness is to be a witness himself." As the people observe their pastor winning the lost to Christ, and bringing them to church, they will be inspired to do the same.[5]

6. Disciplining the wayward. Discipline is an important part of caring for the sheep. It is a biblically prescribed way of calling the straying back into the fold. When wayward members commit flagrant sin, they must be warned. If they repent, a brother or sister has been restored to Christ. If they refuse to repent, they must be disciplined (Matt. 18:15-17). This practice will accomplish two things. It will serve to awaken the backslider, and it will serve to warn others in the church.

Remember, the goal of discipline is always redemptive. You must perform it in a spirit of humility and love. Paul wrote, "If someone is caught in a sin, you who live by the Spirit should restore that person gently. But watch yourselves, or you also may be tempted" (Gal. 6:1).

Creating a Caring Community

As a Pentecostal pastor, not only must you personally care for people, but as suggested above, you must inspire the church to do the same. You must strive to develop your church into a truly caring community. Being a caring community means that the members' hearts are filled with compassion for the hurting. Because they are filled with God's love, they naturally reach out to those in need. When they see a hurting brother or sister, they immediately respond with compassion. This is what Jesus did when he encountered a man with leprosy. The man said to Jesus, "If you are willing, you can make me clean." The Bible tells us, "Jesus was filled with compassion and

---

[5] For more on reaching the lost, see Chapter 37: "Evangelizing the Lost" and Chapter 39: "Planting New Churches."

reached out his hand and touched the man. 'I am willing,' he said. 'Be clean!'" (Mark 1:40-42, margin).

One way to shape God's people into a caring community is to ensure that they have been filled with the Holy Spirit and that the Spirit is working powerfully in their lives. Love is a fruit of the Spirit (Gal. 5:22). The Bible says, "God's love has been poured out into our hearts through the Holy Spirit, who has been given to us" (Rom. 5:5). Also, as the people observe the compassion displayed in the life of their pastor, they will become compassionate themselves.

As the situation demands, and as the Spirit leads, you will want to lead the church in instituting compassionate programs. This could include feeding, housing, and other programs.[6]

THE SHEPHERD'S ACCOUNTABILITY

As mentioned above, Pentecostal pastors must see themselves as stewards, or caretakers, of Christ's church. They must never forget that the church does not belong to them; it belongs to Jesus. As stewards of His church, they are accountable to Him. They must faithfully discharge their duties, for one day when Christ returns they will give account as to how they managed His property (Luke 12:42-43; 1 Cor. 4:2).

Those pastors who selfishly care for themselves and neglect the flock will be judged severely. In both the Old and New Testaments, the Bible strongly condemns such pastors. For example, Ezekiel prophesied against the shepherds who fattened themselves at the expense of the sheep: "You have not strengthened the weak or healed the sick or bound up the injured. You have not brought back the strays or searched for the lost" (Eze. 34:4). Then, speaking through the prophet, God declared, "I am against the shepherds and will hold them accountable for my flock" (v. 10). On another occasion, God charged the shepherds of Israel, "Because you have scattered my

---

[6] This is discussed in more detail in Chapter 38: "Serving the Community."

flock, and driven them away, and have not bestowed care on them, I will bestow punishment on you for the evil you have done" (Jer. 23:2).

In the New Testament, James warns, "Not many of you should become teachers, my fellow believers, because you know that we who teach will be judged more strictly" (James 3:1). Peter writes concerning false prophets and teachers, "They will secretly introduce destructive heresies, even denying the sovereign Lord who bought them—bringing swift destruction on themselves" (2 Pet. 2:1).

While God will judge unfaithful pastors, He will generously reward those who faithfully care for the sheep. Jesus said, "Who then is the faithful and wise servant, whom the master has put in charge of the servants in his household to give them their food at the proper time? It will be good for that servant whose master finds him doing so when he returns. Truly I tell you, he will put him in charge of all his possessions" (Matt. 24:45).

Writing to the elders of the churches, Peter admonished, "Be shepherds of God's flock that is under your care, watching over them—not because you must, but because you are willing, as God wants you to be; not pursuing dishonest gain, but eager to serve; not lording it over those entrusted to you, but being examples to the flock" (1 Pet. 5:2-3). He then encouraged them, saying, "And when the Chief Shepherd appears, you will receive the crown of glory that will never fade away" (v. 4).

Serving Christ as a shepherd of His flock is both an honor and a sacred duty. Pastors who faithfully fulfil their responsibilities can look to the future with great joy and expectation. One day they will hear the words of their Lord, "Well done, good and faithful servant! You have been faithful with a few things; I will put you in charge of many things. Come and share your master's happiness!" (Matt. 25:21).

~ Chapter 25 ~

Strengthening the Body

A celebrated preacher conducted a large evangelistic campaign in a Central African country. Tens of thousands attended the campaign, and thousands responded to the invitation to receive Christ as Savior. There was great rejoicing in the city where the campaign was held.

Three years later, a follow-up survey was conducted. It was discovered that, of the thousands who made professions of faith during the campaign, only a few remained in the churches. Upon hearing this, one church leader responded, "My heart was troubled at the report. Deep in my spirit I felt that the church in Africa must revisit the discipleship methods of Jesus. The Pentecostal church in Africa must come to understand that proclaiming the full gospel includes the task of discipleship training."

The Pentecostal church in Africa is well known for its evangelistic successes. It must now become well known for its discipleship programs. Evangelism and discipleship go hand in hand. Not only must the Pentecostal pastor concern himself or herself with growing the church, they must commit themselves to strengthening the body. This chapter will discuss ways you, as a Pentecostal pastor, may strengthen the body of Christ.

Chapter 25: Strengthening the Body

THE PENTECOSTAL PASTOR'S RESPONSIBILITY

A chief duty of every pastor is to build up and strengthen the church he or she leads. Every Pentecostal pastor must therefore aim at leaving the church stronger than when they found it. The primary way a pastor can achieve this goal is through discipleship training. This task is at the heart of the Great Commission, where Jesus commanded His followers, "Go and make disciples of all nations" (Matt. 28:19). He was telling them to do with others what He had done with them. Like Him, they were to focus their time and energy on building a team that would impact the nations. Paul emphasized this strategy of Jesus when he instructed his disciple, Timothy, "The things you have heard me say in the presence of many witnesses entrust to reliable people who will also be qualified to teach others" (2 Tim. 2:2).

Strengthening the Church

Paul took Jesus' command to make disciples seriously. A significant part of his apostolic ministry was dedicated to strengthening the churches he had planted. This was why he appointed pastors in the churches (Acts 14:23), revisited the churches he had planted (15:41), and wrote follow-up letters to them instructing them in the ways of the Lord. Paul further testified that the Lord had given him his apostolic authority to build up the churches (2 Cor. 10:8; 13:10). As a Pentecostal pastor, you must view your ministry in the same way. You must see yourself as the chief disciple maker in the church Christ has given you to lead.

In his letter to the Christians in Ephesus, Paul said that Christ gave pastors (along with the other four ministry gifts) to strengthen the body of Christ (Eph. 4:11-16). In this passage, the apostle notes that these ministers' primary responsibility is "to equip [Christ's] people for works of service" (v. 12). They are to do this "so that the body of Christ may be built up until we all...become mature" (vv. 12-13). Then, Paul explained, the church will "grow to become in every respect the mature body of him who is the head, that is, Christ" (v. 15).

Disciple making is thus crucial to the health of any church. If the leadership of the church fails to make disciples, much of their efforts in evangelism and church planting will be in vain.

Understanding the Terms

To better understand the disciple-making process, it is necessary that we understand the terms being used. Let's look at three of those terms:

1. Disciple. A disciple is a committed learner. He or she is one who sits attentively at the feet of a master teacher drinking in their words. Like an apprentice, a disciple learns his or her trade by imitating a skilled craftsman. A disciple of Christ is a person who has committed his or her life to Jesus Christ and is daily following Him, learning from Him, and pursuing His mission.

2. Discipleship. Discipleship is the lifelong process of becoming like Jesus. It begins the moment a person commits his or her life to Christ and continues until death. The concept of discipleship is a major New Testament theme. While the word *Christian* appears only three times in Acts, and the word *believer* occurs a scant 35 times in the Gospels and Acts, the word *disciple* occurs 289 times in the Gospels and 13 times in Acts.

Discipleship requires commitment to Christ and His mission. Jesus warned the crowds who followed Him, "Whoever does not carry their cross and follow me cannot be my disciple" (Luke 14:27). He told them that they should count the cost before becoming His disciples. He cautioned, "Those of you who do not give up everything you have cannot be my disciples" (v. 33).

3. Disciple maker. A disciple maker is one who is committed to obeying Christ's command to "make disciples of all nations" (Matt. 28:19). He or she is a mature follower of Jesus Christ who has devoted themselves to fully following their Lord and leading others to do the same. Effective Pentecostal pastors understand that their job is not to just make converts. Their job is to develop believers into fully committed disciples of Christ.

Chapter 25: Strengthening the Body

WAYS OF STRENGTHENING THE CHURCH

Christ never intended for the work of God's kingdom to be done by professional clergy alone. He rather gave the five ministry gifts to the Church to train normal, everyday Christians in kingdom living and service. The purpose of apostles, prophets, evangelists, pastors, and teachers is to develop Christians into soul winners, and then to teach them how to care for one another and develop one another into effective servants of Christ (Eph. 4:11-16).

Therefore, as a Pentecostal pastor, you must teach that every follower of Christ has been called and empowered to participate in advancing God's kingdom in the earth. While few are called to be apostles, all are called to participate in missions. While few are called to be prophets, all are called to stand up for what is right and good. While few are called to be evangelists, all are called to share their faith with others. While few are called to be teachers, all are called to teach others how to serve Christ. While few are called to be pastors, all are called to lovingly care for others. As a pastor, your job is to teach these things to God's people and to develop a strong discipleship training program in the church.

Let's look at six strategies you can use to strengthen your church:

Modeling Discipleship

First, you can strengthen the church by modeling what it means to be a real disciple of Christ. With your own life, you can show what a true disciple looks like. As church members observe their pastor's godly lifestyle, they will be encouraged to live the same way. They too will want to become disciples of Christ. As a result, the church will grow strong and prosper, and God's kingdom will be advanced.

This discipleship strategy is especially important in establishing new churches in formerly unevangelized places. In these circumstances, new Christians have little concept of what it means to live for Christ. The only models they have of Christian living are the lifestyles of the pastor and his or her family. Like Paul, you must be prepared to say to the people, "Follow my example, as I follow the example of Christ" (1 Cor. 11:1).

Preaching and Teaching

Second, you can strengthen the body through strategic preaching and systematic teaching of God's Word. To strategically preach God's Word is to prepare and preach biblical messages with a clear aim in mind. To do this, you must first determine, through prayer and meditation on the Word, the direction the Holy Spirit is leading the church. As you wait in prayer, the Holy Spirit will speak to your heart, saying, "This is the way; walk in it" (Isa. 30:21).[1]

Once you have discerned God's direction for the church, you must begin to prepare and preach sermons aimed at moving the church in that direction. At the same time, you must ensure that the "whole will of God"—that is, the entire Word of God—is being taught in the church (Acts 20:27). These practices will ensure that God's people understand God's Word and His will for their lives.[2]

In addition, your teaching and preaching must include frequent messages on the mission of God, along with the church's responsibility to participate in that mission. The mission of God, sometimes called the *missio Dei,* is God's eternal plan to redeem and call unto himself a people from every tribe, language, and nation on earth (Rev. 5:9; 7:9). Jesus underlined the Church's responsibility in fulfilling God's mission in His Great Commission (Matt. 28:18-20; Mark 16:15-18; Luke 24:46-49; John 20:21-22; Acts 1:8).

---

[1] For more on this topic, see Chapter 15: "A Strong Devotional Habit."
[2] For more on this topic, see Chapter 16: "Spirit-Anointed Preaching" and Chapter 17: "Effective Teaching." The "Living the Truth" and "Roots of Faith" discipleship curricula can be downloaded for free at www.africaatts.org/resources.

Chapter 25: Strengthening the Body

Empowering the People

Third, you can strengthen the body by ensuring that church members have been empowered for service. This empowering for service includes both spiritual and psychological empowering:

Spiritual empowering. You must work to see that every church member has been empowered by the Holy Spirit. This was Jesus' final command to the Church. Just before He ascended into heaven, He ordered His disciples, "Do not leave Jerusalem, but wait for the gift my Father promised, which you have heard me speak about. For John baptized with water, but in a few days you will be baptized with the Holy Spirit" (Acts 1:4-5). Jesus then gave His disciples an amazing promise: "But you will receive power when the Holy Spirit comes on you; and you will be my witnesses in Jerusalem, and in all Judea and Samaria, and to the ends of the earth" (v. 8). The disciples obeyed Christ's command, and Jesus fulfilled His promise. The Bible tells us,

> "When the day of Pentecost came, they were all together in one place. Suddenly a sound like the blowing of a violent wind came from heaven and filled the whole house where they were sitting. They saw what seemed to be tongues of fire that separated and came to rest on each of them. All of them were filled with the Holy Spirit and began to speak in other tongues as the Spirit enabled them." (Acts 2:1-4)

This divine empowering is the key to effective evangelism and missions in the church. You must therefore preach often on the topic and pray with your people to be filled with the Holy Spirit.[3] You must further teach them how to live and walk in the Spirit's power. And

---

[3] The book, *Proclaiming Pentecost: 100 Sermon Outlines on the Power of the Holy Spirit,* can be downloaded for free in PDF e-book format from the www.DecadeofPentecost.org website. For further discussion on how to pray with believers to receive the Spirit, see Chapter 20: "Guiding Believers into Spirit Baptism."

you must encourage them to cultivate the fruit of the Spirit and manifest the gifts of the Spirit in their lives and ministries (Gal. 5:22-23; 1 Cor. 12:8-10).[4]

Psychological empowering. As pastor, you must also work to ensure that your church members have been psychologically empowered for ministry. Members are psychologically empowered when they believe the door is open for them to participate in the ministries of the church. They have been given the confidence that they can succeed in their chosen ministry. As a Pentecostal pastor, it is your job to instill such confidence in the people.

If you will do this, church members will be encouraged to volunteer for ministry. However, if you fail to do this, they will be reluctant to volunteer. You must therefore avoid giving the impression that you are the only one in the church qualified for ministry. Rather, you must emphasize that there is a place of ministry for everyone. And you must instill in the people's hearts an assurance that they can effectively minister for Christ.

Mobilizing Workers

Once the people have been empowered, they must be mobilized for ministry. This is the fourth way you can strengthen the church. The process of mobilizing workers involves the following activities:

Identifying the need. You begin the mobilization process by identifying a need you want to address. Does the church want to launch a new children's ministry, plant a new church, improve the church's worship services, or accomplish some other task? You must begin the mobilization process by clearly defining what you want to see accomplished.

Creating job opportunities. You must then determine what positions need to be created to staff the new ministry. You should develop a job description for each new position. The job description should

---

[4] For definitions of the spiritual gifts, see Appendix 2: "The Manifestation Gifts of 1 Corinthians 12:8-10."

include the qualifications for the job and the duties of the one holding the position.

Praying. All along, you should pray to the Lord of the Harvest, asking Him to raise up the needed workers (Luke 10:2).

Sharing the vision. At the proper time, you should share the vision with the church. You should tell the people about the new ministry, explaining how it will bless the church.

Recruiting workers. You must then ask for volunteers. You should be specific about what the job will involve. You may want to identify particular individuals who you think may do the job well and ask them to pray about volunteering. You should seek to match the person's gifts with the job requirements.

Training. You should develop a training program for those who volunteer.

Deploying. Once you have chosen the new workers, and once you have properly trained them, you should install them into their positions. You should then stay in touch with the new workers, monitoring their progress and encouraging them in the work. The church should also provide these workers with the resources they need to fulfill their responsibilities.

Training for Ministry

As just mentioned, when mobilizing members for ministry, you should be prepared to provide training for those who volunteer. People are more likely to volunteer if they know they will be trained for the task. Training will also greatly increase their prospects for success. This training can be done in special seminars or through on-the-job training. The training should cover both the *why* and the *how* of the job. The new workers must be taught why the ministry exists and what it seeks to accomplish. They must also be taught how to best do the work. The pastor may want to consider starting a School of Ministry in the church.[5]

Mentoring Those Who Show Promise

A final way you can strengthen the body is by identifying and thoughtfully mentoring those who show promise. As pastor, you should take note of those members who demonstrate an exceptional zeal for God's work. You may sense God's hand on these individuals. When this occurs, you will want to establish a mentoring relationship with them, just as Jesus did with His disciples. You will then spend time with these individuals, praying with them and inviting them to join you in certain ministry tasks.

Some have noted that Jesus' method of discipleship involved three processes: First, Jesus ministered to others while His disciples watched. Sometimes He would take them aside and explain to them what He had done and why He had done it. Second, the disciples ministered as Jesus watched. He would then evaluate their work. Finally, Jesus sent out the disciples to minister on their own and to develop other disciples as He had developed them. He promised to send the Holy Spirit to empower and enable them in ministry.

Some of those you are mentoring may sense a call into ministry. When this happens, you will want to nurture that call. And you will want to guide them through the ministerial credentialing process.

The Bible teaches that the church "grows and builds itself up in love, *as each part does its work*" (Eph. 4:16, emphasis added). The best way for a Pentecostal pastor to strengthen the church is to develop a strong discipleship program aimed at turning believers into disciples and disciples into effective ministers of the gospel.

---

[5] This ministry is discussed in Chapter 17: "Effective Teaching."

Chapter 25: Strengthening the Body

~ Chapter 26 ~

Counseling God's People

A church member is contemplating divorce after many years in an abusive relationship. A young widower is struggling with the loss of his wife. A single mother is coping with a cancer diagnosis. Distraught parents are trying to control their rebellious teenaged son. These are some of the hundreds of issues faced by the members of our Pentecostal churches across Africa. Add to the list those struggling with demonic oppression, endemic poverty, unemployment, addictive habits, and much more.

God created men and women in His own image. He created Adam and Eve perfectly whole in body, mind, and spirit. They were "God's masterpieces," living in complete harmony with Him and with one another. However, when they transgressed, their relationship with God, and with each other, was affected (Gen. 3:6-24; Rom. 5:12). Brokenness and suffering became a part of the human condition.

Pastoral counseling is at the heart of pastoral ministry. Christ has called His Church to be a loving, caring community. He wants it to be a place where God's people partner with Him and with the Holy Spirit to bring healing and wholeness to broken people. It should be a place where the lost can experience transformation, reconciliation, and hope (2 Cor. 5:18-19). God has commissioned the Pentecostal pastor to ensure that this task is carried out.

This chapter will examine the counseling ministry of the Pentecostal pastor in Africa. It will discuss the distinctive characteristics of pastoral counseling and lay a biblical foundation for the same. It will further examine the role of the Holy Spirit in counseling. Finally, it will briefly discuss the types, principles, and ethics of pastoral counseling.

THE PASTOR AS COUNSELOR

Christ calls every Pentecostal pastor to carry out the missional mandate of the Church. He has given him or her to the Church to mold believers into effective disciples (Eph. 4:11-12). In addition to preaching, teaching, and leading, Christ has placed on the pastor the responsibility of providing godly counsel and support to members who are seeking to fully follow Christ.

A Shepherd of God's Flock

As His ministry was drawing to a close, Jesus charged Peter, "Take care of my sheep" (John 21:16). In his farewell address to the elders of the church in Ephesus, Paul emphasized the need for pastors to "keep watch over…all the flock of which the Holy Spirit has made you overseers." They were to "be shepherds of the church of God, which he bought with his own blood" (Acts 20:28). In like manner, Peter called upon the elders of the church to "be shepherds of God's flock" (1 Pet. 5:2). They were to take care of the hurting, struggling, and wounded sheep.

The Pentecostal pastor's calling as a counselor is not a career choice; it is a divine appointment. When church members (and in certain instances, non-members) struggle with emotional, social, and spiritual issues, they should be able to turn to their pastor for help. Just as a shepherd feeds, guides, and defends his sheep, Pentecostal pastors must care for those Christ has placed under them.

Part 6: The Pentecostal Pastor as Shepherd

A Unique Relationship

When compared with other mental health professionals, the pastor's counseling ministry is unique. People often regard pastors as representatives of God. They see them as being anointed and equipped as instruments in the healing process. Unlike other mental health professionals, the pastor's goal is to see God's people "grow in the grace and knowledge of our Lord and Savior Jesus Christ" (2 Pet. 3:18).

In addition, pastors have an established trust relationship with their members. They are involved in various areas of their members' lives, including their crises, milestones, and achievements. They are called upon to officiate marriage ceremonies, child dedications, and funerals. Because of this unique relationship, members can more easily share their brokenness with their pastor without fear of being turned away.

In addition, pastors are more accessible than other mental health professionals. Many communities do not have skilled counselors. Even when they do, their services are often unaffordable. The people's only hope is a pastor. In addition, like their Lord, pastors are moved by compassion for the "harassed and helpless" (Matt. 9:36). They view counseling as an opportunity to share God's love with the hurting.

Pastoral Counseling

Across Africa today, a number of counseling models are in use. Each seeks to deal with the complex nature of the human condition. And each is based on a certain worldview and belief system. These include, among others, a secular worldview, a traditional African worldview, and a Christian worldview.

Secular psychological counseling is scientific in its worldview and approach, often denying the truth of Scripture. This approach uses various techniques and therapies to treat mental, emotional, and behavioral disorders. In some African countries, indigenous African healing methods are also recognized and allowed to operate alongside western forms of therapy. These traditional approaches are based on

Chapter 26: Counseling God's People

an African worldview which ascribes life and wellness to unseen spiritual powers.

The Pentecostal pastor's approach to counseling is different from a secular or traditional African approach. The Pentecostal pastor's approach is Bible-based, Christ-centered, and Spirit-led. Pastoral counseling is thus rooted in the authority of Scripture. It holds that the Bible is the Word of God and that it is "useful for teaching, rebuking, correcting and training in righteousness" (2 Tim. 3:16). As God's Word, the Bible contains the answers to all of life's dilemmas.

BIBLICAL BASIS FOR PASTORAL COUNSELING

The Pentecostal pastor believes that the Bible is the revealed Word of God. As such, it is the definitive guide for counseling. Like no other diagnostic tool, the Bible lays bare the deep mysteries of a person's heart (Heb. 4:12). It deals with the roots of mankind's brokenness, and it presents Jesus Christ as the solution to all human problems.

This means that, as a Pentecostal pastor, you should saturate yourself with the truths found in God's Word. You should further allow these truths to guide you in your counseling ministry. If you choose to borrow from secular theories to enhance your counseling skills, you should ensure that these theories are consistent with biblical truth and Christian values.[1]

Old Testament Leaders

The Old Testament contains many examples of leaders offering godly counsel. For instance, Moses spent long hours judging and counseling God's people. Sometimes, he counseled them in large groups. At other times, he counseled just one or two at a time (Exod. 18:13-27). However, the time came when Moses himself needed

---

[1] For more on the Pentecostal pastor's relationship with the Bible, see Chapter 9: "Believes the Bible."

counseling. His father-in-law, Jethro, noticed that he was overburdened with his work. So he counseled Moses to choose capable men to help him. Moses followed Jethro's advice and the work prospered.

David is another example of a godly counselor. He counseled the people in his Psalms. There, he offered many excellent strategies for dealing with the issues of life. The same can be said of Solomon in Proverbs and of the prophets in their writings.

The Ministry of Jesus

Jesus himself was a counselor. Isaiah calls Him "Wonderful Counselor" (Isa. 9:6). He often gave counsel to people who struggled with spiritual issues. Three notable examples are Nicodemus (John 3:1-21), Zacchaeus (Luke 19:1-9), and the woman caught in adultery (John 8:1-11). Jesus declared, "I have come that they may have life, and have it to the full" (John 10:10).

At times, Jesus ministered to those who were troubled emotionally. When Mary and Martha lost their brother Lazarus, Jesus came to them. He showed empathy and walked with them through their grief (John 11:17-44). The night before He was crucified, Jesus spent much time with His disciples preparing them for the impending ordeal (John 14-16).

Jesus' counseling ministry touched people from all walks of life. It touched the educated and illiterate, the refined and commonplace, the rich and poor, men, women, and children. Jesus' love for people drove Him to cross all economic, social, and cultural barriers to fulfill His mission of seeking and saving the lost (Luke 19:10).

The Ministry of Paul

Sections of Paul's letters can be read as counseling sessions. They demonstrate the apostle's pastoral concern for God's people. In them, he counsels those who are coping with the issues of life. For instance, he wrote to the believers in Philippi telling them, "Do not be anxious about anything." If they would pray, they would experience God's peace (Phi. 4:6-7). Another example of Paul's counseling ministry is the way he came alongside his protégé Timothy, to assist him in dealing with his personal insecurities and self-esteem issues (2 Tim. 1:3-14; 2:15).

In his letter to the Christians in Corinth, the apostle addressed certain negative attitudes and behaviors that were threatening to destroy the church there. In his letter to Philemon, the apostle seeks to mend the broken relationship between Philemon and his runaway slave, Onesimus, who was now a Christian brother. A comprehensive review of Paul's letters reveals that his counseling method was Christ-centered, Spirit-guided, instructive, supportive, reconciling, and sometimes confrontational.

THE ROLE OF THE HOLY SPIRIT IN COUNSELING

As a Pentecostal pastor, you have a strong ally in your counseling ministry. That ally is the Holy Spirit. You must not fail to rely on Him. Imagine a soldier who goes to battle without his weapon. He may know all the rules of engagement and warfare strategies, but without his weapon, the outcome will be disastrous. It is equally foolish for the Pentecostal pastor to venture into spiritual battle without the power of the Holy Spirit.

The Helper

Four times Jesus referred to the Holy Spirit as the *Paraclete,* which means "Helper" or "Counselor" in Greek (John 14:16, 26; 15:26; 16:7). As our heavenly Counselor, the Holy Spirit stands ready to help us in every step of the counseling journey. If invited, He will guide, strengthen, and support the counselor. And He will help the counselee deal with his or her pain and struggles (John 14:1; 16:8).

Counseling often involves spiritual warfare (Eph. 6:12). Only the Spirit of God is strong enough to truly "bind up the brokenhearted" and "proclaim freedom for the captives" (Isa. 61:1; cf. Luke 4:17-18). The Bible therefore encourages us to "be strong in the Lord and in his mighty power" (Eph. 6:10).

Part 6: The Pentecostal Pastor as Shepherd

Honest, faith-filled prayer is an essential part of the counseling process. The Holy Spirit will help in this area. The Bible says, "The Spirit helps us in our weakness. We do not know what we ought to pray for, but the Spirit himself intercedes for us through wordless groans" (Rom. 8:26). Jesus said that the Heavenly Father would give the Holy Spirit to anyone who would ask (Luke 11:9-10, 13).[2]

Jesus is the perfect role model for the Pentecostal counselor. The Bible says that He was anointed by the Holy Spirit to "[heal] all who were under the power of the devil" (Acts 10:38). Through this anointing, He announced good news to the poor, proclaimed freedom to the prisoners, and set the oppressed free (Luke 4:18). Paul is another excellent role model for the Pentecostal counselor. Despite his great education and achievements, he depended on the power of the Holy Spirit (1 Cor. 2:4-5). In like manner, the Pentecostal pastor needs the help of the Holy Spirit to be an effective counselor.

The Revealer of Truth

Jesus further taught that the Holy Spirit is the revealer of all truth (John 16:13). He will help us to understand and interpret God's Word. He will also give us insights into both God's thoughts and the thoughts of those we are counseling (1 Cor. 2:11-12). This is important because a person's behavior is determined by his or her thoughts and by the interpretations they place on the events of life. A person who believes that the mishaps surrounding his or her life are due to evil forces and angry ancestors will act accordingly. The Holy Spirit will help them to know the truth that will set them free (John 8:32).

The Giver of Gifts

Mental health problems are diverse, complex, and culture-bound. They involve both natural and spiritual components. The gifts of the Holy Spirit are therefore essential to the counseling process (1 Cor.

---

[2] For more on helping believers receive the Holy Spirit, see Chapter 20: "Guiding Believers into Spirit Baptism."

12:8-10). Through the revelation gifts, the Holy Spirit can give the Pentecostal counselor insight into the needs of the counselee. Through the gift of discerning of spirits, the Spirit can reveal the presence and activity of demonic spirits. And, through the prophetic gifts, the counselor can speak inspired words of hope and healing. The Pentecostal pastor must therefore remain full of the Holy Spirit and sensitive to His working during each step of the counseling process.[3]

TYPES OF PASTORAL COUNSELING

The Pentecostal pastor should be prepared to offer the following types of counseling:

Spiritual Counseling

Spiritual counseling focuses on the counselee's relationship with God, and God's will for his or her life. Here, the Pentecostal pastor's chief concern is that the counselee be brought into a living relationship with Christ. Another concern is that that relationship be healthy and growing. Other related counseling issues include the following:

- The person's understanding of God as a loving, caring Father
- The person's understanding of the true meaning and nature of salvation
- The person's ongoing walk with Christ
- Deliverance from bondages and the need for inner healing
- Reconciling Christian values with day-to-day living.

In the African context, the counselor may also need to deal with the counselee's attempt to blend their former Islamic or animistic practices with the Christian walk. These practices could include the use of charms or amulets to ensure protection against evil powers and curses.

---

[3] For more on spiritual gifts, see Appendix 2: "The Manifestation Gifts of 1 Corinthians 12:8-10."

Marriage and Family Counseling

Marriage and family counseling aims at promoting Christian values and godly living in members' families. This kind of counseling could include individual or group counseling in seminars. It involves the following:

- Pre-marital counseling for couples planning to be married
- Marriage enrichment counseling for married couples wanting to deepen their relationship with one another
- Marriage counseling for couples experiencing challenges in their marriages
- Counseling for Christian parents
- Family group counseling to assist family members who are struggling with interpersonal relationships
- Counseling relating to family rituals such as marriages, childbirth, death, and funerals.

Supportive and Crisis Counseling

Supportive and crisis counseling is aimed at helping people through the traumatic events of life. Those events include the following:

- Terminal illness or death of a loved one
- Droughts, famines, pandemics, and natural disasters
- Being a victim of crime or abuse
- Unemployment and poverty.

During these difficult times, members may need someone who will listen to them as they work through their pain. If a pastor is not equipped to deal with life-threatening conditions like suicide and major depression, he or she should refer the sufferer to a qualified counselor.

Growth Counseling

Growth counseling is aimed at empowering people to succeed in life. Its goal is to help them decide on the best way forward. The

Psalms and Proverbs offer numerous words of wisdom and counsel (e.g., Psa. 32:8; Prov. 15:22).

COUNSELING PRINCIPLES

A thoughtful investigation of Jesus' encounter with the Samaritan woman in John 4 reveals four important counseling principles the Pentecostal pastor will want to employ:

Establishing Trust

Jesus began the counseling process by establishing trust between himself and the woman. He displayed non-judgmental respect for her and demonstrated unconditional love and acceptance. He further reached out to her by moving beyond the existing cultural barriers (John 4:7-9, 17-18).

Active Listening

Jesus sought to gain insight into the woman's condition by asking probing questions. He then listened closely to what she had to say and responded appropriately. His responses clearly communicated His understanding of her deep spiritual needs. Jesus further challenged those blind spots in her thinking that were keeping her from accepting the truth and finding freedom in Him (John 4:9-16, 21-24).

Speaking the Truth in Love

When necessary, Jesus lovingly confronted her dishonesty and challenged her with the truth (John 4:16-18; cf. Eph. 4:15).

Remaining Focused

Throughout the process, Jesus remained focused on His goal of helping the woman discover her true purpose for living (John 4:10, 13-14, 16-18, 21-24). The woman admitted her sin and acknowledged Him as the Messiah. She then ran to tell others about Him (John 4:28-29).

COUNSELING ETHICS

As representatives of Christ and caretakers of His people, Pentecostal pastors must be men and women of integrity. You should consider the following ethical issues in counselling. Adherence to these principles will protect both you and the counselee:

Understanding One's Limitations

You must be honest about your abilities and limitations in counseling, and you must not attempt to move beyond these limitations. In certain countries, professional counselors are required to be board certified.

Referring

You must know when you have reached your limits. If you have not been trained or qualified to give counseling in specific areas, you should be prepared to refer your members to certified Christian counselors. You should also be prepared to refer them when a dependent relationship is developing between you and the counselee, or when a counselee is no longer benefitting from your counseling.

Sexual Integrity

As a pastor, you should take special precautions when counseling those of the opposite sex. If an emotional attraction begins to develop between you and a counselee, the counseling sessions should be ended and the person should be referred to another counselor.

Confidentiality

Information shared in confidence should be respected and never discussed with others.

As a Pentecostal pastor, you must never shrink from your responsibility of serving as a counselor to God's people. Rather, with Jesus Christ as your example, and the Holy Spirit as your helper, you must eagerly embrace this vital ministry.

Chapter 26: Counseling God's People

~ Chapter 27 ~

Guarding the Flock

Throughout history, evil leaders have committed unspeakable crimes against humanity. These crimes include genocides, ethnic cleansings, and unjust wars. Some are guilty of carrying out these brutal acts; others are guilty of doing nothing to stop them. Sadly, Africa has had its share of such atrocities. A universal tenet of good governance is that every nation bears the responsibility to protect its people from evil doers. The same holds true for the Church. It bears the responsibility of protecting God's people from the attacks of the devil and his demonic legions.

Jesus warned of false prophets, of whom He said, "come to you in sheep's clothing, but inwardly they are ferocious wolves." He advised, "By their fruit you will recognize them" (Matt.7:15-16). Paul issued a similar warning to the Ephesian elders. He told them, "Savage wolves will come in among you and will not spare the flock. Even from your own number men will arise and distort the truth in order to draw away disciples after them. So be on your guard!" (Acts 20:29-31).

Chapter 27: Guarding the Flock

This chapter will discuss the Pentecostal pastor's solemn responsibility of guarding the flock of God against these agents of Satan. It will answer the questions: "What does the Bible say about the Pentecostal pastor's responsibility to protect the flock?" and "How does he or she go about fulfilling this responsibility?"

THE NATURE AND VALUE OF THE FLOCK

The Bible uses the picture of a shepherd and sheep to describe the relationship between a pastor and his or her people. To better understand the Pentecostal pastor's responsibility to their congregation, one needs to understand the nature and value of the sheep.

The Nature of the Sheep

A pastor once lamented, "Leading my people is like herding cats!" Herding cats is impossible. They are stubborn and refuse to go in the direction you want. Not so with sheep. Sheep are submissive. They are ready to follow the shepherd wherever he leads. This is good. However, this character trait poses a danger for the sheep. They sometimes foolishly follow the wrong person. They therefore need care and protection.

True Christians willingly submit themselves to the Good Shepherd. They are ready to follow Him wherever He leads (John 10:27). However, some Christians are immature, and like sheep they sometimes confuse spiritual wolves with true shepherds. They blindly follow those who are not true men or women of God.

Further, sheep have no natural defenses. Because of this, they are vulnerable and need a shepherd to protect them. And they tend to wander away from the security of the flock and the care of the shepherd. When this happens, they become easy prey for predators. The same is true of many Christians. They tend to wander away from the care of their pastor and the security of the church. They need the care and protection of a true shepherd.

Part 6: The Pentecostal Pastor as Shepherd

The Value of the Sheep

In biblical times, sheep were of great value to the shepherd. They were often the family's main source of livelihood. They provided meat for food, milk for drink, wool for clothing, and sheepskin for shelter and other purposes. Christians are of even greater value to the Good Shepherd. This is true for at least two reasons:

First, Christians are valuable to Christ because of the high price He paid for their redemption. Jesus said of himself, "I am the good shepherd. The good shepherd lays down his life for the sheep" (John 10:11). Peter reminds us of our value to Christ: "For you know that it was not with perishable things such as silver or gold that you were redeemed...but with the precious blood of Christ" (1 Pet. 1:18-19).

Further, Christians are valuable to Christ because of their special relationship to Him. They were once "separate from Christ, excluded from citizenship in Israel and foreigners to the covenants of the promise, without hope and without God in the world." However, they have now been "brought near by the blood of Christ" (Eph. 2:12-13). Peter reminds us that God's people are "a chosen people, a royal priesthood, a holy nation, God's special possession" (1 Pet. 2:9). As God's chosen flock, His people deserve special care.

THREATS AGAINST THE FLOCK

As a faithful Pentecostal pastor, you must be ever vigilant to protect your people from the threat of false prophets and false teachers.

Recognizing False Prophets and False Teachers

A false prophet is anyone who claims to speak for God, yet, in reality, he or she speaks in their own name or in the name of a false god or demonic spirit (Jer. 23:16). The Bible warns that God is against such false prophets, and that they must not be allowed to dwell among God's people (Ezek. 13:9). Jesus warned that false prophets sometimes even "perform great signs and miracles" and that they threaten "to deceive, if possible, even the elect" (Matt. 24:24). Paul called them "savage wolves" who "distort the truth in order to draw away disciples after them" (Acts 20:29-30). He wrote that they teach myths and say what people want to hear (2 Tim. 4:3-4).

False teachers are akin to false prophets. While a false prophet pretends to speak for God, a false teacher recklessly twists God's Word to say something other than what it really means. They often do this for personal gain (Titus 1:11). The Bible says that these people are ignorant and unstable and that they distort the Scriptures to their own destruction (2 Pet. 3:16).

There are two ways we can recognize false prophets and false teachers in the church today:

1. By observing their lives. Jesus taught His disciples, "Watch out for false prophets. They come to you in sheep's clothing, but inwardly they are ferocious wolves. By their fruit you will recognize them" (Matt. 7:15-16). They pretend to be something they are not. They dress and behave like saints; they use all the latest religious jargon, and they pray impressive prayers. Some may even perform mighty miracles. Outwardly, they appear to be holy and anointed. However, inwardly they are extortioners, liars, and adulterers. The fruit of their private lives reveals their hypocrisy. No man or woman who lives an ungodly life is a true prophet of God.

Jesus challenged the false teachers of His day: "Woe to you… hypocrites! You are like whitewashed tombs, which look beautiful on the outside but on the inside are full of the bones of the dead and everything unclean.…On the outside you appear to people as righteous but on the inside you are full of hypocrisy and wickedness" (Matt. 23:27-28). These rebellious men and women refuse to submit themselves to the authority of God and the Church.

2. By noting their motives and methods. A second way we can recognize false prophets and false teachers in the church is by taking note of their motivations and methods. The false prophet's primary motive is to further his or her own selfish interests. To do this, they gladly distort the Word of God. They often take texts out of context, interpreting them to conform to their own agenda. Their objective is "to draw away disciples after them" (Acts 20:30). They are little concerned about their followers' salvation or growth in Christ. They are more concerned about their own personal gain and glory.

False Teachings in Africa

Sadly, in many Pentecostal churches across Africa, false teachings and false prophecies seem to be the order of the day. These teachings promise blessing while ignoring the need for committed faith and repentance from sin. Focusing mostly on people's temporal needs, they ignore their spiritual development and growth in grace. In doing this, they fail to win the lost to Christ and prepare saints for eternity (Mark 8:36). The Bible strongly warns against such teachings (1 Tim. 4:1).

Two false teachings are especially prevalent in Africa:

1. The prosperity gospel. The first such teaching is the so-called "prosperity gospel." The prosperity gospel is the teaching that all believers have a covenant right to the blessings of health, wealth, and prosperity. These blessings can be acquired through faith, positive confession, and by sowing "seeds of faith."

While it is true that God does bless those who faithfully follow Him, the gospel of prosperity is not the gospel Jesus and the apostles preached. Jesus commanded the people, "Repent and believe the good news!" (Mark 1:15). Peter declared, "Repent...and turn to God, so that your sins may be wiped out, that times of refreshing may come from the Lord" (Acts 3:19). Paul warned, "In the past God overlooked such ignorance, but now he commands all people everywhere to repent" (Acts 17:30).

The true Pentecostal church must reject the gospel of prosperity because it is self-centered rather than Christ-centered. It focuses on people's material desires rather than on God's redemptive mission. The emphasis of the prosperity gospel is on blessing rather than service. It is a distorted gospel that has damaging effects on Christians. Paul's warning to the Galatian Christians applies: "I am astonished that you are so quickly deserting the one who called you to live in the grace of Christ and are turning to a different gospel—which is really no gospel at all....But even if we or an angel from heaven should preach a gospel other than the one we preached to you, let them be under God's curse!" (Gal. 1:6-8).

2. Syncretism. Another destructive practice in Pentecostal churches in Africa is syncretism. Syncretism is the mixing of the Christian faith with elements of African traditional religions. False prophets and false teachers sometimes use this strategy in an attempt to attract more people to their church. Many examples of syncretism can be found across Africa. In West Africa, examples include

- the offering of the prophet
- the redemption offering
- the sacrificial offering
- the selling and unscriptural use of anointed oils
- the selling and use of holy water
- the selling and use of honey and milk
- the selling of pictures of the "man of God"
- the use of the holy broom (to sweep away one's enemies)
- the use of mud from the Dead Sea
- the use of water from the Jordan River
- paid prophetic consultations.

These practices are an attempt to "Christianize" traditional religious practices. They revolve around money and the promise of blessing and protection for those who accept them. They must be rejected and challenged in favor of "the true message of the gospel" (Col. 1:5-6).

As a Pentecostal pastor, you must never forget that you hold in your hands the eternal destinies of those to whom you minister. Therefore, you must carefully consider what you do and teach. If you fail to teach the truth, and surrender to teaching lies, the people will be led astray, the church will be damaged, and you will be judged by God.

Results of False Teachings and Prophecies

There are five ways false teaching harms the church:

1. False teaching promotes ungodliness. Truth sanctifies and motivates Christians to godly living (John 17:17). On the other hand, false doctrines corrupt the mind and the heart, and they encourage immorality (1 Cor. 15:33).

2. False teaching produces ungodly leaders. Truth produces godly servant leaders; however, false teaching produces ungodly, dictatorial leaders. The true Christian leader "must hold firmly to the trustworthy message as it has been taught, so that he can encourage others by sound doctrine and refute those who oppose it" (Titus 1:9).

3. False teaching enslaves people. Truth sets people free (John 8:32). Heresies, however, enslave people (Gal. 4:9). Paul urged the Galatians, "It is for freedom that Christ has set us free. Stand firm, then, and do not let yourselves be burdened again by a yoke of slavery" (Gal. 5:1).

4. False teaching produces weak Christians. Christians who are taught false doctrines and heresies do not grow in grace. They remain spiritual infants. Even if the church grows in number, it remains weak and ineffective.

5. False teaching leads to judgment and destruction. The Bible speaks of "ignorant and unstable people [who] distort...Scriptures, to their own destruction" (2 Pet. 3:16).

GUARDING THE FLOCK

As a shepherd of God's flock, you must constantly watch over the sheep. You must even be willing to lay down your life for them (John 10:11; cf. 1 Sam. 17:34-35). Here are five ways you, as a faithful Pentecostal pastor, must stand guard for the people of God:

By Praying for the Sheep

First, you must often kneel before the Father on behalf of the congregation. In doing this, you will receive from Him the strength and wisdom you need to care for and safeguard the flock. In addition, your prayers will ensure that God's protecting hand remains on His people.

By Exercising Spiritual Discernment

Second, you must exercise spiritual discernment. The Bible warns of "deceiving spirits and things taught by demons" (1 Tim. 4:1). You should therefore ask God for the gift of discerning of spirits to help you uncover any teaching or spiritual manifestation that does not come from God. This spiritual gift will enable you to know whether someone in the church is acting under the influence of the Holy Spirit or a demonic spirit.[1]

By Teaching Sound Doctrine

Third, you must faithfully preach and teach sound doctrine (2 Tim. 4:2; Titus 1:9). This practice will strengthen the sheep and immunize them against false teachings. It will help to keep them on the path of purity (Psa. 119:9-11).

By Identifying False Prophets and False Teachers

Fourth, you must alert the church to false prophets and false teachers. The Bible speaks of three ways to identify these wolves in sheep's clothing:

1. Their prophecies do not come to pass. If their prophecies do not come to pass, they have not heard from God. They are false prophets (Jer. 28:9).

2. They point people away from the truth. Even if their prophecies do come to pass, if they point people away from the true message of the gospel, they are false prophets (Deut. 13:1-3; Gal. 1:6-9).

3. They live unholy lives. Even if their prophecies come to pass, and they perform miraculous signs, if they live ungodly lives, they are false prophets (2 Pet. 2:10-15). Jesus warned, "By their fruit you will recognize them" (Matt. 7:15-16; cf. vv. 22-23).

---

[1] For more on spiritual gifts, see Appendix 2: "The Manifestation Gifts of 1 Corinthians 12:8-10."

Part 6: The Pentecostal Pastor as Shepherd

As a faithful shepherd, you must guard the sheep from predators, and as the Lord does with you, you must guide them along the right paths (Psa. 23:3).

By Exposing False Teachings

Finally, you must protect the flock of God by identifying and correcting false teachings and false prophecies in the church. Paul wrote, "Do not treat prophecies with contempt." However, he quickly added, "But test them all; hold on to what is good, reject every kind of evil" (1 Thess. 5:20-22). Therefore, as a shepherd of God's flock, you will need to remain constantly aware of what is being taught in the church. There are three ways you can do this:

1. By monitoring what is being taught. False teachings can sometimes creep into the church through small groups or Bible studies. The person in charge of a group begins teaching something he or she has heard or read. In short time, the heresy has spread throughout the church. Therefore, you must closely monitor what is being taught in Sunday school classes, baptism classes, cell groups, home fellowships, and other groups to ensure that truth is being taught.

2. By being aware of what people are listening to. Today, the airways are flooded with all kinds of teaching and preaching. Our people are listening to these men and women. While many media preachers are faithfully spreading the good news, some are teaching error. You must be aware of what the people are listening to so you can point them to the truth of God's Word.

3. By being the "keeper of the gate." As pastor, you must stand as the gatekeeper to your church. In other words, you must carefully monitor who you allow to speak to the congregation. No matter how famous or charismatic a preacher may be, if he or she is not a person of the highest character, or if they have veered from the truth, you should not allow them in your pulpit.

The Pentecostal pastor who faithfully guards the flock of God will bring blessing to both the church and to themselves. The sheep will thrive under the protection of their shepherd, and they will develop into mature disciples of Christ. The shepherd will also be blessed. He or she will be rewarded with the satisfaction of knowing that they have been good and faithful servants.

Peter spoke of the faithful shepherd's reward: "Be shepherds of God's flock that is under your care, watching over them—not because you must, but because you are willing, as God wants you to be; not pursuing dishonest gain, but eager to serve; not lording it over those entrusted to you, but being examples to the flock. And when the Chief Shepherd appears, you will receive the crown of glory that will never fade away" (1 Pet. 5:2-4).

~ Part 7 ~

The Pentecostal Pastor as Leader

~ Chapter 28 ~

Pentecostal Leadership

Paul and his missionary team left Galatia heading westward into the province of Asia. However, the Holy Spirit, prevented them from continuing in that direction. So they decided to journey northward into the province of Bithynia. Again, the Spirit prevented them. So once more, they turned to the west. Eventually, they arrived at Troas, a city on the northwestern coast of the Aegean Sea. There, something extraordinary happened.

During the night, the Holy Spirit gave Paul a vision. In the vision, the apostle saw a man from Macedonia standing and pleading with him, "Come over to Macedonia and help us" (Acts 16:6). When Paul shared his vision with his team, they all agreed that it was from the Lord. Luke explains: "After Paul had seen the vision, we got ready at once to leave for Macedonia, concluding that God had called us to preach the gospel to them" (v. 10). (Other examples of Paul being led by the Spirit are found in Acts 13:1-5, 15:28, and 20:22.)

Paul is a good example of a Pentecostal leader. He led others by first allowing the Holy Spirit to lead him. In doing this, he was following the example of Jesus, who himself ministered under the anointing and direction of the Holy Spirit (Luke 4:1; John 5:19; Acts 10:38).

This chapter will discuss Pentecostal leadership. It will present a leadership model based on the methods of Jesus and the apostles. First, it will define what it means to be a Pentecostal leader. Then, it will discuss some of the qualities and activities of authentic Pentecostal leaders.

DEFINING PENTECOSTAL LEADERSHIP

While it is true that Pentecostal pastors employ many of the same leadership methods as do non-Pentecostal pastors, there are some important differences. The Pentecostal pastor's approach to leadership is significantly shaped by his or her experience with the Spirit. Their unique understanding of how the Spirit works in their lives and the lives of others profoundly affects the way they lead.

A Pentecostal leader is a God-chosen man or woman who has been filled with the Spirit and consciously seeks the Spirit's wisdom and guidance. His or her goal is to influence a specific group of God's people to faithfully and effectively fulfill their God-ordained role in advancing His mission in the earth. Let's break down this definition into its four component parts.

Called by God

First, a truly Pentecostal leader has been called by God to lead His people. Because of this, he or she closely identifies with Paul, who described himself as "a servant of Christ Jesus, called to be an apostle and set apart for the gospel of God" (Rom. 1:1).

Full of the Spirit

Next, the Pentecostal leader has been filled with the Spirit and seeks to live his or her life "in step with the Spirit" (Gal. 5:25). They take seriously Christ's command to "stay in the city until you are clothed with power from on high" (Luke 24:49), and Paul's instruction to "be filled with the Spirit" (Eph. 5:18).

Seek God's Guidance

Third, the Pentecostal leader proactively seeks the Spirit's guidance in all he or she does. They understand that their chief duty is to carry out God's will as revealed in Scripture and by the Holy Spirit. The authentic Pentecostal leader will therefore spend much time in Bible study and prayer.

Influence God's People

Finally, the Pentecostal leader seeks to influence a specific group of God's people—such as a national or local church—to faithfully and effectively fulfill their God-ordained role in advancing God's mission in the earth.

QUALITIES OF THE PENTECOSTAL LEADER

What qualifies a man or woman to be a Pentecostal leader? At a bare minimum, the authentic Pentecostal leader must be born of the Spirit, filled with the Spirit, and able to lead others into the Spirit-empowered walk. They must be able to discern the voice of the Spirit and be proficient in the ministry of spiritual gifts. They must understand and be committed to the mission of God. And they must be prepared to lay down their life for the cause of Christ, should such a sacrifice be required.

As a Pentecostal leader, your life and ministry should be marked by six essential qualities:

Integrity

Above all else, you must strive to live a godly, Christ-honoring life. In God's work, nothing is more important. Sadly, however, far too many Pentecostal churches and organizations are plagued with corrupt men and women who, because of their strong personalities, have achieved celebrity status in the movement. These "wolves in sheep's clothing" bring shame on the church (Matt. 7:15).

The Bible speaks of such godless people. For example, Paul warned the Ephesian elders of "savage wolves" who would come in and ravage the flock of God (Acts 20:29). In the same message, he reminded them of how he had led them with integrity. "I have not coveted anyone's silver or gold or clothing," he said (Acts 20:33). In similar manner, He reminded the Thessalonians of his godly conduct among them, saying, "You are witnesses, and so is God, of how holy, righteous and blameless we were among you who believed" (1 Thess. 2:10). Paul not only led with authority and ministered with power, he lived with godly integrity. We must do the same today.

Understanding

Second, as a Pentecostal pastor, you must clearly understand your God-given responsibilities. You must faithfully serve Christ and His church by leading God's people to advance His mission in the power of the Holy Spirit. You can gain this understanding from two sources: from God's Word and from God's Spirit. By faithfully studying Scripture, you will come to understand God's mission to redeem the nations. By praying and being attentive to God's voice, you will come to understand your unique role in fulfilling that mission.

Jesus clearly understood His place in God's redemptive plan. He often spoke of His mission (Mark 10:45; John 6:38; 18:37). He declared, "For the Son of Man came to seek and to save the lost" (Luke 19:10). In similar fashion, Paul understood his unique role in God's work. He wrote, "I was appointed a herald and an apostle…and a true and faithful teacher of the Gentiles" (1 Tim. 2:7).

Through daily prayer and Bible study, you, like Jesus and Paul, can gain greater understanding of God's mission, and your personal role in fulfilling that mission.[1]

Commitment

Third, as a Pentecostal leader, you must not only understand God's mission, you must be fully committed to doing your part to fulfill that mission. God's mission, sometimes referred to as the *missio Dei,* is His purpose and work in the world in relation to fallen

---

[1] For more on the mission of God, see the Africa's Hope Discovery Series book, *A Biblical Theology of Missions,* by Paul York.

humanity. He works through His Church to call unto himself a people out of every tribe, tongue, and nation on earth (Rev. 5:9; 7:9).

While other people's thoughts may wander from the mission, your attention must remain focused on doing God's will. All your thoughts and actions must move in the direction of God's mission. As a Pentecostal leader, you must grasp the bigger picture—God's redemptive plan for the nations. You must further understand where your church fits into that grand plan. Then, you must steadfastly move the church in that direction.[2]

Anointing

Fourth, as a Pentecostal leader, you must cherish the Spirit's anointing, and you must endeavor to maintain the touch of the Spirit on your life through committed prayer, holy living, and humble service. You must rely strongly on the Holy Spirit to anoint, enable, and guide you in ministry. And you must take seriously the Master's parting words to His disciples, when He commanded them not to begin their ministries until they had been empowered by the Holy Spirit (Acts 1:4-5; cf. Luke 24:49).

Humility

Fifth, as a true Pentecostal leader, you must see yourself as a servant of God and His people. You must seek to follow the example of your Lord, who humbled himself and became a servant, even to the point of dying on the cross (Phi. 2:7-8). And you must be ever mindful of Jesus' words: "Whoever wants to become great among you must be your servant, and whoever wants to be first must be slave of all. For even the Son of Man did not come to be served, but to serve, and to give his life as a ransom for many" (Mark 10:43-45).

This kind of leadership is known as servant leadership. Conversely, the leader who exalts himself or herself and seeks to exploit God's people can never be called a true Pentecostal leader. They are

---

[2] For more on leading the church into God's mission, see Chapter 31: "Missional Leadership."

rather "wolves in sheep's clothing" (Matt. 7:15-16; Acts 20:29-30). The Bible tells us, "Have nothing to do with such people" (2 Tim. 3:5).[3]

Competency

Finally, as a true Pentecostal leader, you must strive for competency. You must understand that, while being a good person is essential, it is not enough. Africans are known for being good, humble, and hospitable. To be a good leader, however, will require that you develop certain skills. These skills include the ability to teach, to cast vision, to motivate others, and to organize the work.

Further, you must understand that, ultimately, leadership ability comes from God. Paul was acutely aware of this. He explained to the Corinthians, "Not that we are competent in ourselves to claim anything for ourselves, but our competence comes from God. He has made us competent as ministers…of the Spirit" (2 Cor. 3:5-6). As a Pentecostal leader, you must constantly look to God for such competency.

ACTIVITIES OF THE PENTECOSTAL LEADER

The Pentecostal pastor must not be like the pastor who was seen running behind his congregation shouting, "Wait for me, I'm your leader!" On the contrary, he or she must go ahead of the people, bidding them to follow. They must be like Jesus, who beckoned His disciples, "Come, follow me, and I will send you out to fish for people." The Bible tells us, "At once they left their nets and followed him" (Mark 1:17-18).

As a Pentecostal pastor, Christ has appointed you to initiate Spirit-inspired programs and strategies in the church. You must then inspire God's people to follow you in the work. At the same time, as a godly leader, you must be a devoted follower. You must faithfully follow God's Spirit. And you must humbly submit to those whom the

---

[3] For more insight on servant leadership, see Chapter 29: "Servant Leadership."

Spirit has placed over you. You must lead your church to fulfill God's mission in three important ways:

Vision Casting

First, you must lead your people by casting a vision of a preferred future for the church. In other words, you must help them to envision the wonderful future God has planned for them. Then, you must influence them to move in that direction. You do this with your words, your actions, and your attitudes, that is, with what you say, what you do, and how you present yourself to the people.

Your God-inspired vision must so consume you that you cannot let it go. As a result, you will constantly talk about the vision. Your passion will flow from your life and affect the people, causing them to share the vision. As an authentic Pentecostal leader, you must never promote your own vision of the future. You must rather promote God's vision as revealed in His Word and by His Spirit.

The Bible tells us, "Where there is no revelation, people cast off restraint" (Pro. 29:18). Or, as one translation reads, "Where there is no prophetic vision the people are discouraged." Such discouragement often results in self-absorption, decline, and eventually destruction. However, a well-communicated vision will cause the people to understand five things:

1. *Who they are.* They are God's Spirit-empowered missionary people, commissioned by Christ to do His bidding in the earth.

2. *Where they must go.* They are to move together to fulfill God's mission by winning the lost, planting new churches, and participating in sending missionaries to the nations.

3. *What they must do.* They must be empowered by God's Spirit and committed to doing their part in fulfilling His mission.

4. *How they are to do it.* The pastor must articulate a specific plan or program of how to accomplish the work. He

or she must then show the people how they can engage in the work.

5. *How they must begin.* The effective Pentecostal pastor will assign individual tasks to help the people begin well.

Sadly, many God-given dreams die in the heart of the pastor. You, however, must not let this happen. You must faithfully cast the vision of a preferred future for the church. You must stand tall and confidently tell the people, "This is the way; walk in it" (Isa. 30:21).[4]

Supervising

Second, between discovering where God wants your church to be and arriving at that destination, there is a pathway you must walk. As God's representative, you must guide the church along that pathway. Not only must you cast a vision of God's preferred future, you must supervise the fulfillment of the vision.

This is what Jesus did. He cast the vision, and then He implemented a strategy to fulfill the vision. His strategy was to call men and women to His side, train them, commission them, empower them, and then to deploy them to the work. As a Pentecostal leader, you must do the same. You can do this through Spirit-inspired planning, mobilization, and supervision.

Thus, as a Pentecostal pastor, you are not only to inspire your people, you are to oversee the work (1 Tim. 3:1-2; Titus 1:7). As an overseer, you are to organize the church for Spirit-empowered mission. You must manage the tactics and activities necessary to execute the plan. These activities include recruiting, planning, training, and sending workers to the field. In all of this, you must look to the Holy Spirit for insight and direction.

Perpetuation

Finally, as a leader of God's people, you bear the responsibility of expanding and perpetuating the church's missionary vision. One

---

[4] For more on vision casting, see Chapter 30: "Visionary Leadership."

way you must do this is by raising up other visionary Pentecostal leaders. If this is not done, the vision will die, and the mission will fail. How sad that so many God-ordained ministries have died with their founders because these men and women failed to adequately instill the vision in others.

Jesus, however, was serious about passing on His vision to others. Soon after He began His ministry, He started calling disciples. The Bible says, "He appointed twelve that they might be with him and that he might send them out to preach" (Mark 3:14; cf. 1:16-17; 2:13-14; 3:13-19). These men would carry on the work after He was gone. He therefore trained them, empowered them, and sent them out to "go and make disciples of all nations" (Matt. 28:19). In other words, Jesus expected them to do with others what He had done with them.

Paul followed Jesus' example. He did not carry out His missionary ministry alone, but invited others to join him. He then mentored and trained them, just as Jesus had done with His disciples. Paul's disciples included John Mark, Timothy, Titus, Luke and others. Paul instructed Timothy to do with others as he had done with him. "The things you have heard me say," he wrote his son in the faith, "entrust to reliable people who will also be qualified to teach others" (2 Tim. 2:2). If we want to perpetuate the vision in others, we must follow in the footsteps of Jesus and Paul.

Paul admonished the believers in Thessalonica, "You yourselves know how you ought to follow our example," because, he said, "we offered ourselves as a model for you to imitate" (2 Thess. 3:7, 9). If we really want to perpetuate the vision of Pentecostal missions today, like Paul, we must be the kind of person others will want to emulate. That is, we must be people of honor, integrity, and vision.

As God's appointed leader of a local church, you must the best leader you can be. As a faithful Pentecostal pastor, you must work hard to develop the leadership skills necessary to fulfill this role.

Chapter 28: Pentecostal Leadership

~ Chapter 29 ~

Servant Leadership

One day a group of Jesus' disciples approached Him with a question. They asked, "Who, then, is the greatest in the kingdom of heaven?" (Matt. 18:1). These disciples had been arguing this point among themselves (cf. Matt. 20:20-28; Mark 9:33-37; 10:35-45; Luke 22:24-27). Some of them were ambitious and wanted to become leaders among the disciples.

Knowing their hearts, Jesus called a small child to come and stand in their midst. He then said to His disciples, "Truly I tell you, unless you change and become like little children, you will never enter the kingdom of heaven. Therefore, whoever takes the lowly position of this child is the greatest in the kingdom of heaven" (Matt. 18:3-4). On another occasion, Jesus explained, "You know that the rulers of the Gentiles lord it over them, and their high officials exercise authority over them. Not so with you. Instead, whoever wants to become great among you must be your servant, and whoever wants to be first must be your slave" (Matt. 20:25-27).

Chapter 29: Servant Leadership

Jesus was talking about the kind of leadership He would require in His newly forming Church. Leaders in His Church would be expected to lead much differently than leaders in the world. Rather than being served, these new leaders would serve others. Rather than ruling over the people, they would lovingly care for those they led. This kind of leadership has come to be known as servant leadership. It is the kind of leadership God demands of Pentecostal pastors in Africa today.

SERVANT LEADERSHIP DEFINED

Leadership is the ability to influence people to act in a certain way or move in a certain direction. For the Pentecostal pastor, leadership is the God-given ability to influence God's people to seek God's kingdom first (Matt. 6:33). It is the ability to inspire God's people to fulfill their God-ordained role in advancing God's mission in the earth.

Like all leaders, servant leaders are concerned with the mission. However, servant leaders are also concerned with the growth and well-being of the people they lead. They serve God's people with humility and compassion, and strive to influence through love rather than coercion.

The mindset of the servant leader is the opposite of the "chieftain mentality" often seen in Africa. The ungodly chieftain rules through intimidation; the servant leader leads through love and compassion. The chieftain demands obedience; the servant leader inspires confidence. The chieftain exploits the people; the servant leader seeks to bless them.

Jesus could have ruled as a chieftain; however, He chose to lead as a servant (Matt. 20:28). At any time, Jesus could have ordered legions of angels to carry out His will (26:53). However, He chose to humble himself and submit himself to His Father's will (26:39, 42). His sacrifice on the cross is the ultimate example of what it means to be a servant leader. Like their Lord, true Pentecostal pastors are servant leaders. Rather than exploiting their followers, they gladly and lovingly serve them.

God's kingdom has been described as an "upside-down kingdom." This is because leadership in God's kingdom works differently than leadership in the world's system. In worldly organizations, the leader is expected to be the one on top. He or she controls others and receives most of the glory and benefits. However, in the kingdom of God, the leader is the one on the bottom. He or she strives to serve and bless others.

CHARACTERISTICS OF A SERVANT LEADER

Six characteristics should be found in any Pentecostal pastor who wants to be a servant leader:

Humility

First, as a servant leader, the Pentecostal pastor should lead with humility. He or she should not waste time seeking personal recognition or power. Rather, they should follow the example of John the Baptist, who said of Jesus, "He must become greater; I must become less" (John 3:30). And they must remember the words of their Lord: "The greatest among you will be your servant. For those who exalt themselves will be humbled, and those who humble themselves will be exalted" (Matt. 23:11-12).

There is a troubling tendency among some African pastors to claim lofty titles for themselves. Jesus warned against this practice. He told His disciples, "You are not to be called 'Rabbi,' for you have one Teacher, and you are all brothers. And do not call anyone on earth 'father,' for you have one Father, and he is in heaven. Nor are you to be called instructors, for you have one Instructor, the Messiah. The greatest among you will be your servant" (Matt. 23:8-11). Small-minded men and women often seek big titles. Truly great leaders, however, are content to be viewed as servants of Christ.

The night before Jesus was crucified, He met with His disciples in an upper room in Jerusalem. There He taught them a lesson on servant leadership. After finishing the Passover meal, the Savior rose, removed His outer clothing, and wrapped a towel around His waist. He then filled a basin with water and began to wash His disciples' feet. When He had finished, He asked them, "Do you understand what I have done for you?"

Jesus then explained to them, "You call me 'Teacher' and 'Lord,' and rightly so, for that is what I am. Now that I, your Lord and Teacher, have washed your feet, you also should wash one another's feet. I have set you an example that you should do as I have done for you" (John 13:13-15). Jesus was teaching His disciples that the greatest leaders in His kingdom are the ones who assume the position of the least servant in the household.

As a Pentecostal pastor, you must therefore firmly resist the corrupting influences of power and pride. As a true servant leader, you must never seek to exploit God's people. Rather, you must seek to serve and bless them.

Empathy

Second, as a true servant leader, the Pentecostal pastor should empathize with those he or she has been called to lead. To empathize with someone is to closely identify with them and to share their feelings, hurts, and joys. The Bible says that Jesus is our Great High Priest who is able to "empathize with our weaknesses" (Heb. 4:15). He empathized with Mary and Martha when He wept with them at Lazarus' tomb (John 11:35). Like Jesus, as a servant leader, you must learn to "rejoice with those who rejoice" and "mourn with those who mourn" (Rom. 12:15).

Transparency

Third, as a servant leader, the Pentecostal pastor must strive to be transparent in his or her dealings with people. This means that they do not try to hide their true selves from others. They do not pretend to be something they are not. Paul reminded the Corinthians of his own transparency. "In our relations with you," he wrote, "[we have conducted ourselves] with integrity and godly sincerity" (2 Cor. 1:12). He later added, "We have spoken freely to you, Corinthians, and opened wide our hearts to you" (2 Cor. 6:11).

Such transparency will open the lines of communication between you and your church members. The people will begin to see you as an honest, credible person. As a result, they will be encouraged to trust and confide in you. And they will be happy to follow your leadership.

Trust

Fourth, as a servant leader, the Pentecostal pastor will trust God's people. He or she believes that the same Holy Spirit who indwells, empowers, and guides them, indwells, empowers, and guides their members. Because of this, the Pentecostal pastor is able to trust God's people, and he or she is willing to delegate ministry to them. This is what Jesus did with His twelve disciples (John 20:21). And it is what Paul did with Timothy (2 Tim. 2:2). Instead of trying to do ten jobs, the effective pastor will empower ten members to do those jobs.

Therefore, as a faithful servant leader, you must take note of God's gifts in others. And you must spend time with them, enabling them and training them to do the work. As these emerging leaders grow in their understanding and ability, you will want to delegate to them more and more responsibility. And you must give to them the authority they will need to effectively fulfill their new roles.

A great leader is not threatened by the success of others. On the contrary, his or her greatest joy comes from raising up others who will participate in fulfilling the mission.

Communication

Fifth, as a servant leader, the Pentecostal pastor must learn to communicate well with those they lead. Good communication involves both speaking wisely and listening perceptively. The Bible exhorts, "Let your conversation be always full of grace, seasoned with salt" (Col. 4:6). It also instructs us to be "quick [or ready] to listen" (James 1:19). Therefore, as an effective servant leader, you must invest much time and energy into becoming an effective communicator.

Anointing

Finally, as a servant leader, the Pentecostal pastor must seek the anointing of the Holy Spirit. He or she must ensure that other leaders in the congregation do the same. The anointing is received when one is baptized in the Holy Spirit as were the disciples on the Day of Pentecost (Acts 2:4). It is maintained by walking in the Spirit (Gal. 5:25).

Jesus is the supreme example of what Spirit-anointed servant leadership looks like. As Jesus was beginning His ministry, He announced that the Holy Spirit had anointed Him to serve others by ministering to their needs (Luke 4:18-19). Peter described Jesus' servant ministry like this: "God anointed Jesus of Nazareth with the Holy Spirit and power, and…he went around doing good and healing all who were under the power of the devil, because God was with him" (Acts 10:38).

Like Jesus, we should never attempt to do God's work in our own strength or ability. Rather, we should rely on the power and anointing of the Spirit (Luke 24:49; Acts 1:8).

EXAMPLES OF SERVANT LEADERSHIP

The Bible contains many examples of servant leadership. Let's look at four of those examples. Two are found in the Old Testament, and two are found in the New Testament.

Moses: Delegated Ministry

Moses is a good example of a servant leader who was humble enough to delegate ministry to others. God bestowed upon Moses great authority by choosing him to lead His people (Exod. 3:1-10). God often spoke with Moses "face to face, as one speaks to a friend" (33:11). And God used Moses to perform great signs and wonders among the people (4:21; Acts 7:36). However, Moses did not become proud. Rather, he chose to lead God's people with humility (Num. 12:3).

The Bible tells the story of how Moses' father-in-law advised him to carry out his work (Exod. 18:13-27). When Jethro saw Moses doing all the work himself, he advised his son-in-law, "What you are doing is not good….The work is too heavy for you; you cannot handle it alone" (vv. 17-18). Moses followed Jethro's advice and delegated much of the work to trustworthy men. As a result, Moses found relief, the work prospered, and the people were blessed.

David: Promoted Others

Another good example of a servant leader is King David. God referred to him as "a man after my own heart" (Acts 13:22; cf. 1 Sam.13:14). Because David was secure in his position as king and as a servant of God's people, he was able to invest time and energy in building up others.

Being a humble servant leader, David did not fear other people's success as did his predecessor, Saul. David confidently surrounded himself with those whose exploits rivaled his own (1 Chr. 11:10-47). And he honored those who served under him, encouraging them to succeed (vv. 17-19, 25). God used David's willingness to promote others to ensure his success and to bless those who served under him.

Paul: Godly Mentor

A third example of a humble servant leader is the apostle Paul. Although God chose him to be an apostle, he viewed himself as a mere servant of Christ (Rom. 1:1; Titus 1:1). Paul once described himself as "the least of the apostles" (1 Cor. 15:9). He was himself mentored by Barnabas (Acts 9:26-27; 11:25-26). In turn, he diligently mentored others. His letters reveal how he constantly sought to build up others.

Two of Paul's greatest successes were Timothy and Titus. He mentored Timothy (Acts 16:1-5), and in time he trusted his "son in the faith" to lead the church in Ephesus (1 Tim. 1:2-3). He also mentored Titus and appointed him to lead the churches in Crete (Titus

1:5). Had the apostle not taken the effort to mentor Timothy, Titus, and others, his influence and his work would have been greatly diminished.

Jesus Christ: Supreme Example

The Lord Jesus Christ stands as the supreme example of servant leadership. He taught that true kingdom leaders selflessly serve others (Luke 22:24-27). Then, He demonstrated this concept in His own life and ministry. Speaking of himself, Jesus said, "The Son of Man did not come to be served, but to serve, and to give his life as a ransom for many" (Mark 10:45). Paul described Jesus' servant leadership style like this:

> "In your relationships with one another, have the same mindset as Christ Jesus: Who, being in very nature God, did not consider equality with God something to be used to his own advantage; rather, he made himself nothing by taking the very nature of a servant, being made in human likeness. And being found in appearance as a man, he humbled himself by becoming obedient to death—even death on a cross!" (Phi. 2:5-8)

Paul thus urged all Christians, including Christian leaders, "Do nothing out of selfish ambition or vain conceit. Rather, in humility value others above yourselves, not looking to your own interests but each of you to the interests of the others" (Phi. 2:3-4).

AREAS OF SERVANT LEADERSHIP

The attitude of servant leadership must manifest itself in three areas of the Pentecostal pastor's life and ministry: in the home, in the church, and in the community.

Servant Leadership in the Home

As a Pentecostal pastor, your first area of servant leadership is your home. Before serving your congregation, you must faithfully serve your spouse and children. Paul said of the overseer, or pastor, "He must manage his own family well and see that his children obey him, and he must do so in a manner worthy of full respect" (1 Tim.

Part 7: The Pentecostal Pastor as Leader

3:4). Paul then added, "If anyone does not know how to manage his own family, how can he take care of God's church?" (v. 5).

Thus, as a Pentecostal pastor, you must be ever aware that your first area of servant leadership is your family. You must be willing to humble yourself and serve your spouse and children well. In a sense, your family is your "first church," and the church you are leading is your "annex church." The attitude with which you serve your family will inevitably be the attitude with which you serve your church. You must be a servant leader to both.

Servant Leadership in the Church

Your second area of servant leadership is the church. You should view yourself as Christ's gift to the church (Eph. 4:11-12). Further, you must realize that Christ has called you to shepherd God's people. Peter wrote to elders: "Be shepherds of God's flock that is under your care, watching over them—not because you must, but because you are willing, as God wants you to be; not pursuing dishonest gain, but eager to serve; not lording it over those entrusted to you, but being examples to the flock" (1 Pet. 5:2-3).

As a true servant leader, you must shepherd the flock of God by feeding them the Word of God, by strengthening the weak and feeble, and by praying for those who are sick and afflicted. You must also protect the sheep from predators (Acts 20:28-31). Further, you must be an example of godly service by showing the people of God how to care for one another, and by urging them to do the same.[1]

Servant Leadership in the Community

As a Pentecostal pastor, your third area of servant leadership is your community. You should therefore see yourself, not only as the shepherd of your family and the church you pastor, but as shepherd of the village or community in which you reside. Jesus taught that we are to be the "salt of the earth" and the "light of the world" (Matt.

---

[1] For more on shepherding God's people, see Chapter 24: "Caring for the Flock" and Chapter 27: "Guarding the Flock."

5:13-16). Therefore, you must closely identify with the people of your community, pray for them, serve them, and faithfully share Christ's love with them.[2]

Jesus set the standard for servant leadership in the Church. He told His disciples, "For even the Son of Man did not come to be served, but to serve, and to give his life as a ransom for many" (Mark 10:45). The Pentecostal pastor must follow in the footsteps of his or her Lord. And they must be ever mindful of His words: "Anyone who wants to be first must be the very last, and the servant of all" (9:35).

---

[2] For more on caring for one's community, see Chapter 38: "Serving the Community."

~ Chapter 30 ~

Visionary Leadership

After much prayer and soul searching, Pastor Emmanuel sensed that God was calling him to leave his comfortable church in the capital city and move his family into the country's densely forested interior. There, he was to launch a church planting movement. The pastor recalls, "It was the least evangelized province in my country, but that was where God wanted my family and me to go." He was certain that God had placed the vision in his heart.

The Holy Spirit directed Pastor Emmanuel to a certain village. Although the place was strategically located, it was known to be steeped in witchcraft. From the moment of their arrival, the pastor and his wife received threats from local witchdoctors. The couple nevertheless persevered, faithfully proclaiming the gospel to all who would listen. People were saved and filled with the Spirit, and the church began to grow and mature.

Pastor Emmanuel often shared his vision of launching a Spirit-empowered church planting movement with his members. Soon, others began to catch the vision, and in time leaders began to emerge, whom Pastor Emmanuel trained for ministry. He often took these emerging leaders with him to evangelize and establish churches in the surrounding area. Over the years, they planted many churches. They even trained missionaries and sent them out to plant churches among the unreached tribes to the north.

Today, Pastor Emmanuel's church is thriving. The people have embraced their purpose and have so identified with the vision of their pastor that they continue to plant new churches in the region. Pastor Emmanuel truly embodies what it means to be a visionary leader.

To lead a church into effective mission, a Pentecostal pastor must clearly understand God's purpose for the church. He or she must also have a clear-cut vision of how their church is to participate in fulfilling that purpose. When the pastor casts a clear vision of where the church should go, the people are inspired to follow. When he or she fails to cast such a vision, the church flounders (cf. Pro. 29:18). This chapter will discuss the necessity of vision in leading a local body of believers.

VISIONARY LEADERSHIP DEFINED

A visionary pastoral leader is a man or woman who leads God's people from where they are to where God wants them to be. These Spirit-led leaders are able to see beyond the present into the future. They are able to accurately assess the present condition of the church, understanding its strengths and weaknesses. And they are able to see what the church can and should become. They are further able to map out a pathway forward for the church to achieve its God-inspired goals. Finally, the visionary Pentecostal leader is able to inspire the church to boldly move forward in fulfilment of those goals.

CHARACTERISTICS OF VISIONARY LEADERS

Let's look at eight characteristics of visionary leaders as revealed in Scripture:

Spirit-led

First, a truly visionary leader is Spirit-led. Before a Pentecostal pastor can lead his or her church into God's purposes, they must themselves be full of the Holy Spirit and able to follow His leadership (cf. Gal. 5:25). They must be willing to abandon their own plans to passionately pursue God's plans.

Faith-filled

Second, visionary leaders are faith-filled. They possess the ability to believe God and trust Him in the face of difficulties and negative circumstances (Heb. 11:1-37).

Authentic

Third, visionary leaders offer an authentic model for the church to follow (Phi. 3:17). They have a faithful record of proven ministry, which attests to their right to lead the church. They truly personify how God expects the church to respond to its God-given vision.

Future-focused

Fourth, visionary leaders are future-focused. Their minds are fixed, not on yesterday's accomplishments, but on tomorrow's opportunities. Paul exemplified this character trait when he testified, "One thing I do: Forgetting what is behind and straining toward what is ahead" (Phi. 3:13).

Prophetic and Practical

Fifth, visionary leaders are, at the same time, both prophetic and practical. They are prophetic because they see what can be accomplished. They are practical because they realize what needs to be done to reach the goal. While envisioning the future, a visionary leader must be able to pragmatically lead the church through the challenges of the present.

Trustworthy

Sixth, visionary leaders are trustworthy. They have a proven record of reliability in the past. Because of this, God's people are willing to follow them into the future.

Influential

Seventh, visionary leaders are influential. They have a God-given ability to inspire others to act. They possess the gifts and skills needed to positively influence the attitudes, choices, and actions of others.

Courageous

Finally, visionary leaders are courageous. They are bold enough to walk into an uncertain future. When Pastor Emmanuel left the familiarity and comfort of the capital city, he did not know what lay before him. However, he courageously led his family into the unknown, trusting God to meet their needs.

EXAMPLES OF VISIONARY LEADERS

In many ways, the Bible is the story of men and women whom God raised up and anointed as visionary leaders. These leaders exemplify the aforementioned leadership traits. The following six men are typical of those leaders:

Abraham: Faith-filled Vision

Abraham was a faith-filled visionary leader. By faith he looked into the future and saw a "city with foundations, whose architect and builder is God" (Heb. 11:10). Then, by faith, he led his family to an unknown land, believing that God would fulfill His promise to him (Heb. 11:8). In doing this, he became the "father of all who believe" (Rom. 4:11).

Joseph: Prophetic Insight

Joseph led through prophetic insight. God gave him insight into the meaning of Pharaoh's dream (Gen. 41:15-24). Joseph then offered the king practical advice on how he should respond to this prophetic insight (vv. 25-36). As a result, many were saved from starvation. Pharaoh saw God's Spirit in Joseph and promoted him to a high position of leadership, second only to Pharaoh himself (vv. 37-44).

Joshua and Caleb: Courageous Vision

Joshua and Caleb's courageous vision enabled them to press forward in faith when others were withdrawing in fear (Num. 14:6-9). Rather than surrendering to their fears, Joshua and Caleb chose to put their faith in God. When the people refused to follow their lead, they stayed true to their commitment and kept the vision alive for forty years, preparing the next generation to enter the Promised Land.

Nehemiah: Singleness of Purpose

Nehemiah led God's people to rebuild the walls of Jerusalem with singleness of purpose. He did this in the face of great opposition. He was sustained by his vision of what could be accomplished if God's people would remain focused on their God-given task.

Haggai: Selfless Attitude

Haggai's selfless attitude inspired God's people to turn from their own selfish concerns and to put God's work first. He called on them to stop investing all their resources into building their own houses. Rather, they were to invest themselves in building God's house. The prophet told God's people that, if they would move together with unified purpose, the work would be completed.

Jesus: Our Ultimate Example

Our Lord Jesus Christ is the ultimate example of a visionary leader. He clearly understood why He had come, where He was going, and what He must do to get there. He is the perfect example of one who saw the pathway forward and then fully committed himself to following that path (cf. Heb. 12:2). He then enlisted, trained, and inspired others to join Him in the work.

Paul: Missional Vision

Second only to Jesus, Paul was the greatest missional leader of all time. Paul was driven by a heavenly vision to take the gospel to the Gentile nations. He imparted his vision to others, and he gave

Chapter 30: Visionary Leadership

them a reproducible model for evangelism, church planting, and missions. Toward the end of his ministry, Paul was able to testify, "I was not disobedient to the vision from heaven" (Acts 26:19).

LEADERSHIP DYNAMICS

To become a truly visionary leader, you will need a basic understanding of the dynamics of leadership. And you will need a clear grasp of what visionary leadership looks like in actual practice.

Mission and Vision

To begin with, you must understand the relationship between mission and vision. In the kingdom of God, vision grows out of mission, and not vice-versa. The Church's mission has already been decided by God. God's mission, sometimes called the *missio Dei,* is to redeem and call unto himself a people from every tribe, tongue, and nation on earth before Christ returns. Jesus spoke of this in His Great Commission: "Go and make disciples of all nations, baptizing them in the name of the Father and of the Son and of the Holy Spirit, and teaching them to obey everything I have commanded you" (Matt. 28:18-20; cf. Mark 16:15-18; Luke 24:49; John 20:21; Acts 1:8). The Church exists to fulfill God's mission.[1]

Christ has commissioned every Pentecostal pastor and church to fully participate in His mission. He has ordained that every church become a missional church. As such, it must actively engage in evangelism, discipleship, and church planting. In addition, every Pentecostal church must cultivate a vision to raise up and send out missionaries and other Christian workers. It must further commit to supporting these workers with its prayers and finances.[2]

Vision speaks of a congregation's Spirit-inspired perception of their role in fulfilling God's mission. It is prophetic in nature, focusing not only on today's tasks but also on tomorrow's opportunities.

---

[1] For more on missional vision, see Chapter 31: "Missional Leadership."
[2] For more on mobilizing your church for mission, see Chapter 40: "Developing a Local Church Missions Program."

Vision bridges the gap between what a church is today and what God wants it to become tomorrow. It is a Spirit-inspired mental image of what the church, with God's help, can become.

As you and the church you lead begin to embrace God's mission, God will give you a vision of what He wants you to accomplish. This God-inspired vision will always align with God's mission, as described above. This is why it is so important that you have a clear understanding of the mission of God and how that mission relates to the missional purpose of the local church.[3] Out of mission comes vision, out of vision come goals, and out of goals comes action.

Cultivating Vision

Just as a field must be cultivated to produce a good crop, vision must be cultivated to produce a harvest of divinely-inspired strategies. You can cultivate vision in your own heart and in the church you pastor by employing three strategies, as follows:

1. Reflective Bible reading. First, you can cultivate vision in your own heart through reflective Bible reading. You can prayerfully read the stories of great leaders in Scripture whom God used to advance His kingdom. As you read, ask yourself the following questions:

- What vision did God place in this leader's heart?
- How did this leader come to know the vision?
- How did he or she act to fulfill the vision?
- What is God saying to me through this story?

Write your answers in a notebook and prayerfully ponder them in your heart. In time, you may want to develop sermons from these thoughts and share them with your congregation. In this way, you and your people can grow together in your understanding of God's mission and your church's role in fulfilling that mission.

2. Waiting on God. Second, you can cultivate vision in your heart by waiting on God in prayer. Begin by drawing near to Him through

Chapter 30: Visionary Leadership

earnest thanksgiving and praise (James 4:8). Once you sense God's presence, you should pray, "Lord, show me your will. Let me see your heart." You should then linger in God's presence, praying in the Spirit and listening for His voice (Rom. 8:26-27; Eph. 6:18).

As you pray in this manner, you should take note of recurring thoughts or insights that the Holy Spirit puts into your heart or mind. Over time, some of these insights will grow more and more compelling. They may eventually develop into a burden. With the burden will come a deep understanding that God is leading the church in a certain direction (Isa. 30:21). You will also want to lead the congregation in times of seeking direction from God.

3. Observing the need. Finally, you can cultivate vision by prayerfully observing the needs of the people in your community or in some other chosen place (cf. John 4:35). As you look, ask God for insight, praying, "Lord, help me to see beyond the surface into the deep inner needs of the people" (cf. 2 Cor. 4:18). You should further pray, "Lord, which of these needs do you want our church to address?" After praying, be still and listen for God's response.

The Role of the Holy Spirit

We are living in the last days, when God is pouring out His Spirit on all people (Acts 2:17-18). God has given us His Spirit to empower and guide us in the work. As a true Pentecostal leader, you should remain dependent on the Spirit's leadership at all times. While contemporary leadership techniques and church growth strategies have their place, you must never rely too heavily on these humanly conceived approaches. As a visionary spiritual leader, you must always seek the Spirit's guidance and follow His leading, remembering the words of the prophet, "'Not by might nor by power, but by my Spirit,' says the Lord Almighty" (Zec. 4:6).

Vision Casting

While individual vision is essential, it is not enough for you to have a vision and keep it to yourself. You must be able to communicate that vision to the church. And you must do it in a way that will inspire and motivate God's people to follow. This process is known as vision casting. Much of Jesus' work with His disciples involved vision casting. He was constantly sharing His vision with them and challenging them to follow Him. Likewise, it is important that you communicate your vision to the church and call on members to "follow [your] example, as [you] follow the example of Christ" (1 Cor. 11:1).

For this to happen, the vision must inspire the people's imagination. It must be both challenging and attainable. In other words, the vision should not be so large that it overwhelms the people. Neither should it be so small that it fails to inspire them. If the vision is too large for the people to grasp, the pastor must break it down into bite-sized pieces, with achievable short-term and long-term goals.

It is sometimes wise to roll out the vision in stages. First, you may want to share the vision with your spouse or an inner circle of friends and trusted leaders. You can then discuss it, pray over it, and receive a witness from the Spirit that you should proceed. Next, you will want to share the vision with the church board and staff, getting their buy-in. It takes a team to implement a vision. It is therefore essential that all members of the team be on board.

When the time comes to share the vision with the church, you may want to plan a "Vision Sunday." This event will provide you with a platform to clearly explain the vision to the people. You must then talk often about the vision and preach on it regularly. This approach will help to implant the vision in the people's hearts.

Further, you must work to ensure that the whole church is moving together to fulfill the vision. You must encourage everyone to give, go, work, serve, and sacrifice to see the vision accomplished. Along the way, you may want to call on certain individuals to share testimonies about how the vision is being fulfilled. These testimonies will help to inspire the people and keep the church on track.

Overcoming Obstacles

You should not be surprised when the implementation of the vision is tested. Any church that seeks to pursue God's vision will

Chapter 30: Visionary Leadership

encounter obstacles and demonic opposition. Paul wrote to the Christians in Thessalonica, explaining, "For we wanted to come to you...but Satan blocked our way" (1 Thess. 2:18).

Such opposition can never permanently stop the progress of the church. It will be necessary, however, for you and the church to hold tightly to the vision. If you will remain focused on the vision that God has given you, He will bring it to pass. Jesus promised, "I will build my church, and the gates of Hades will not overcome it" (Matt. 16:18).

In the story told at the beginning of this chapter, Pastor Emmanuel was faithful to the vision God gave him. Through obedience and faith, he persevered until the vision was fulfilled. The same can be true for you. If you will discover God's vision for your church, and if you will press through seasons of difficulty, you too can see the fulfillment of your vision. You can confidently claim the promise of God to Habakkuk: "For the revelation [of the vision] awaits an appointed time...Though it linger, wait for it; it will certainly come and will not delay" (Hab. 2:3).

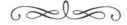

~ Chapter 31 ~

Missional Leadership

One day Jesus was walking by the Sea of Galilee. There, He met Peter and Andrew casting their nets into the sea. He said to them, "Come, follow me, and I will send you out to fish for people." The Bible says, "At once they left their nets and followed him" (Mark 1:16-18). People are naturally drawn to leaders with a strong sense of mission. They are instinctively moved to follow them, just as Peter and Andrew were moved to follow Jesus.

This chapter will focus on the Pentecostal pastor's role as a missional leader. It will discuss his or her responsibility to lead their churches to serve God's mission in the earth. It will further discuss how they can inspire others to follow them in this great cause.

THE MISSIONAL PASTOR

Jesus himself was a missional leader, and He calls the Pentecostal pastor to be the same. He is looking for men and women with the necessary spirit, commitment, and faith to lead His people in mission (cf. 2 Chr. 16:9).

Chapter 31: Missional Leadership

Essential Qualities

Missional leaders know where they are going, and they know how they intend to get there. As a result, they are able to inspire others to join them on the journey. Missional pastors possess three essential qualities:

1. Understanding. Missional pastors understand God's mission. They recognize that God is a missionary God and that He is on a mission to redeem and call unto himself a people from every nation on earth (Matt. 24:14; Rev. 5:9; 7:9). This concept is known as the *missio Dei,* which is Latin for the "mission of God." The missional pastor understands that the church exists to fulfill God's mission in the earth. He or she further understands that one of their primary roles as pastor is to mobilize the church to fulfill God's mission.[1]

2. Commitment. Beyond understanding God's mission, the Pentecostal pastor must be committed to leading his or her church to fully participate in fulfilling that mission in the power of the Holy Spirit. He or she must be prepared to do whatever is necessary to carry out this great responsibility.

3. Competence. Finally, the Pentecostal pastor must be committed to developing the attitudes and skills needed to mobilize the church to pursue God's mission. The true Pentecostal pastor realizes that, ultimately, his or her competency in ministry comes from God through the power of the Holy Spirit (Acts 1:8; 2 Cor. 3:5-6).

Jesus' Example

Jesus was the definitive missional leader. He clearly understood why He had come to earth. He announced, "For the Son of Man came to seek and to save the lost" (Luke 19:10). In another place, He declared, "I have come down from heaven, not to do my will, but to do the will of him who sent me" (John 6:38). Jesus once referred to His

---

[1] For more on the mission of God, see the Africa's Hope Discovery Series textbook, *A Biblical Theology of Missions,* by Paul York, available from Africa Theological Training Service (ATTS), www.africaatts.org.

mission as His "food" (John 4:34). Just as food energizes and nourishes the body, Jesus was energized and nourished by doing the will of His Father. This commitment ultimately led Him to the cross (Matt. 20:28).

Before He returned to heaven, Jesus handed over His mission and ministry to His Church. He said to His disciples, "As the Father has sent me, I am sending you" (John 20:21). Just as Jesus found His mission in the will of His Father, the Pentecostal pastor finds his or her mission in the will of Christ. And just as Jesus' commitment to doing His Father's will sustained Him in His mission, the same will sustain the Pentecostal pastor in his or her mission (Matt. 26:36-44; Matt. 28:19-20; John 14:16).

Being Before Doing

As a Pentecostal pastor it is essential that you understand that missional leadership is more about being than doing. Remember, Jesus promised Peter and Andrew, "Follow me, and I will make you *become* fishers of men" (Mark 1:17, ESV, emphasis added). By following Jesus and being filled with His Spirit, the disciples' very being would be transformed. They would *become* like their Teacher (Luke 6:40; Acts 4:13).

Not only would the Spirit enable them to minister with power, He would impart to them Christ's passion for the harvest. The Holy Spirit would so transform them that all their ambitions, desires, and talents would come under Christ's lordship. They would join Christ in fulfilling God's redemptive mission. A powerful spiritual experience, known as the baptism in the Holy Spirit, would form the foundation for their future missional leadership (Luke 3:16; Acts 1:4-5).[2]

The same can happen to us today. If we will allow God's Spirit to fill us and work in us, He will transform us into Christ's image (cf.

---

[2] For more on being baptized in the Holy Spirit, see Chapters 10, 11, and 20.

2 Cor. 3:18). And He will impart to us the same passion for the harvest that was in Jesus.

Becoming Missional

The Lord Jesus called men and women to follow Him and to carry on the work He had begun. He then invested His time and energy in training them and molding them into missional leaders. One way Jesus did this was by sending them out on short-term missions trips. He instructed them, equipped them, and then sent them out (Luke 9:1-6; 10:1-16). When they returned, He debriefed them on their work (10:17-20).

Jesus' twelve disciples were not born leaders. Neither were they naturally missions-minded. They were ordinary working-class men. However, they were willing to put their lives in the hands of Jesus to be molded by Him. Through His life and teaching, Jesus imparted to them His global vision. He commanded them, "Go and make disciples of all nations" (Matt. 28:19). He further insisted that they be empowered by the Holy Spirit, just as He had been (Luke 4:18-19; Acts 1:8).

In one of Peter's early encounters with the Lord, he ruled himself out as a possible leader. He begged Jesus, "Go away from me, Lord; I am a sinful man!" (Luke 5:8). Peter felt disqualified by the person he was. However, Jesus knew Peter's potential. So He answered Peter, "Don't be afraid; from now on you will fish for people" (v. 10). As Peter walked with Jesus, he was transformed into the powerful missional leader we read about in the book of Acts.

The Bible says, "Jesus appointed twelve apostles that they might be with Him and that He might send them out to preach" (Mark 3:14). By spending time with Jesus, listening to His teachings, and observing His actions, the disciples became like their Lord. Jesus molded them into missional leaders, each in a unique way for a unique task. Because He did this, the Church He founded continues until today. As aspiring Pentecostal pastors, we would do well to spend time with effective missional leaders. As we follow close to Jesus, and associate with others who are doing the same, we will be changed.

Part 7: The Pentecostal Pastor as Leader

The baton of leadership has been passed to us. We too must strive to become true missional leaders. Like Jesus and the apostles, we must work to develop others. Paul wrote to Timothy, "You then, my son, be strong in the grace that is in Christ Jesus. And the things you have heard me say in the presence of many witnesses entrust to reliable people who will also be qualified to teach others" (2 Tim. 2:2).

MISSIONAL AMBITION

Missional action rises out of missional ambition. An ambition is a strong desire to achieve something significant. The Psalmist spoke of God's ambition for His Son—and for the nations. "Ask of me," the Father said to the Son, "and I will make the nations your inheritance, the ends of the earth your possession" (Psa. 2:8). As God's sons and daughters, we can join the Son in this missional prayer. Doing this will create in us a strong desire to see our friends and neighbors come to Jesus. At the same time, it will create in us the ambition to see the nations reached with the good news of salvation in Christ.

As a Pentecostal pastor, you must make God's ambition your own. That is what Abraham did. Though he was old and childless, God told him, "Look up at the sky and count the stars….So shall your offspring be" (Gen. 15:5). Abraham believed God's promise and shared His ambition. As a result of his obedience, he became the father of all who believe (Rom. 4:11). Ask God to impart to you His passion for the nations. Then allow this passion to move you to mobilize your church to participate in God's mission.

MISSIONAL ACTION

While missional ambition is essential, it alone is not enough. As a Pentecostal pastor, you must work to turn ambition into reality. Paul is an example of this truth. He had an ambition to see the Gentiles turn to Christ (Acts 22:21; Rom. 10:1). This ambition compelled him to labor tirelessly for their salvation. He testified, "I worked harder than all of them—yet not I, but the grace of God that was with me"

Chapter 31: Missional Leadership

(1 Cor. 15:10). In like manner, you too must turn your missional ambition into missional action. You must strive to develop your church into a truly missional church.

Instilling Missions Vision

A major responsibility of every Pentecostal pastor is to instill a passion for the lost into the hearts of God's people. The people must become keenly aware of the lostness of those outside their church's walls. They must also sense the lostness of those unreached peoples dwelling in unreached places throughout Africa and around the world. For this to happen, you will need to preach, teach, and model missions before your congregation. And you will need to persevere until every member of the church understands his or her responsibility to participate in the *missio Dei*.

Missions vision is instilled in the hearts of God's people in two ways: by the Spirit of God and by the Word of God. It took a powerful move of the Spirit and a timely word from the Lord to change Peter's attitude concerning the Gentiles (Acts 10:9-16, 19-20). As a missional leader, you must ensure that the same dynamic is present in your church. You must ensure that the Spirit is moving powerfully in your services, and you must strive to see that every member has been genuinely filled with the Spirit. All along, you must explain to the people why God's Spirit is moving. As God's missionary Spirit, He is preparing them to participate in God's mission.

At the same time, you must teach the people what the Bible says about God's mission. And you must show them how they should respond to the Spirit and the Word. They must commit themselves to praying zealously for the lost, giving generously to missions, and faithfully sharing the good news with those around them. Finally, you must challenge them to commit themselves to God's mission.

As a true missional leader, you must lead your church from being self-centered to being others-centered, from being focused on their own wants and needs to being focused on the needs of the lost world around them. This missional journey will require a strong sense of intentionality on your part. It will also require that you make adjustments in your church's programs and changes in the purpose and content of your meetings.

Sharing Missionary Stories

One proven way you can develop a missions-minded church is to share missionary stories with your people. You can do this by incorporating these stories into your preaching and teaching. Many of these stories are found in the Bible. The story of Jesus is the greatest missionary story ever told. And the book of Acts is full of exciting missionary stories. You can also glean stories by reading missionary books and by listening to missionaries speak. In addition, you should not hesitate to share your own missionary stories with the congregation.

Scheduling Missions Services

You will also want to regularly schedule missionaries to speak to your church. You can invite them to come for a special missions service or for a missions awareness weekend. When missionaries do come, you must not forget to cover their travel expenses. And you will want to give the congregation an opportunity to participate in the missionary's ministry by receiving a generous offering for them. The church should also consider supporting the missionary on an ongoing basis.[3]

Creating "Cycles of Success"

Another effective way to instill a missions vision in the hearts of the people is through "cycles of success." This idea comes from the story of David. Before he became king over Israel, he led a number of small successful military campaigns. The people honored David, saying, "You were the one who led Israel on their military campaigns" (2 Sam. 5:2). Or, more literally, "It was you who led out and

---

[3] To learn more about mobilizing your church for missions, see Chapter 40: "Developing a Local Church Missions Program."

brought in Israel." The phrase "led out and brought in" speaks of cycles of success, and suggests the idea of leading short-term, achievable missions ventures. Each success will encourage the people to set successively more ambitious goals.

For instance, at first you can plan a "Pray for Your Neighbors" campaign. Get the names of neighbors and let the church pray for them. As the people begin to taste success, they will be encouraged to move beyond the church walls. Small successes will open their hearts to becoming even more missional. They will be encouraged to reach beyond themselves in ever-increasing cycles of success.

These successes can lead to increased mission funding and training. In time, the church can deploy short-term missions teams to other towns and villages for evangelism and church planting campaigns. Some may even be mobilized to travel to other countries to assist missionaries or plant churches there. As these teams report back to the church, the people will be inspired to greater missions participation.

THE LOCAL MISSIONS TEAM

Remember the old African adage, "If you want to go fast, go alone; if you want to go far, go together." You will want to create a local missions committee, or missions team, to assist you in the work. These visionary men and women will help you mobilize the church for missions.

A missional church can be compared to a football team. In this analogy, the pastor is not viewed as the star player, but the coach. And the missions team is his coaching staff. The church members are not the fans in the stands; they are the players on the field. The job of the pastor and missions team is to recruit players, train them, inspire them, and send them out as a winning team.

Before Jesus chose the Twelve, He spent the night in prayer to God (Luke 6:12). In the same way, you will want to choose your missions team prayerfully. You should look for people who are full of faith and the Holy Spirit, people with the right attitude and skills to bless the work. You will then want to meet with the missions team regularly to pray and plan. Together, you will develop the church's evangelism, church planting, and missions programs. You will establish strategic priorities and develop the church's missions budget.

As Jesus was about to return to heaven, He left His Church with a final command and a final promise. His command was, "Do not leave Jerusalem, but wait for the gift my Father promised, which you have heard me speak about. For John baptized with water, but in a few days you will be baptized with the Holy Spirit" (Acts 1:4-5). His promise was, "You will receive power when the Holy Spirit comes on you; and you will be my witnesses in Jerusalem, and in all Judea and Samaria, and to the ends of the earth" (v. 8).

With these words, Jesus was reminding His disciples that the experience they were soon to receive on the Day of Pentecost would be closely linked to His mission to redeem the nations. Thus, by extension, to be Pentecostal means to be missional. It follows that to be a true Pentecostal pastor one must be a zealous missional leader. As a missional leader, the Pentecostal pastor has been appointed by Christ to lead His church into Spirit-empowered mission at home and to the ends of the earth.

Chapter 31: Missional Leadership

~ Part 8 ~

The Pentecostal Pastor as Administrator

~ Chapter 32 ~

Managing Records, Finances, and Properties

Jesus told the story of a rich man who discovered that the manager of his properties was squandering his possessions. He called the unfaithful manager in and demanded that he give an account of how he had cared for his employer's business (Luke 16:1-2).

The Bible teaches that every follower of Christ is a manager of God's property. That is because everything he or she owns actually belongs to God (Psa. 24:1; James 1:17). The Bible further teaches that God will one day require every Christian to give an account of how he or she has managed God's property. Paul warns, "For we must all appear before the judgment seat of Christ, so that each of us may receive what is due us for the things done while in the body, whether good or bad" (2 Cor. 5:10).

This same principle applies to the Pentecostal pastor. He or she must be mindful of the fact that the church they lead belongs to Christ. They merely manage Christ's church, and they will one day answer to Him for how they managed His property.

Chapter 32: Managing Records, Finances, and Properties

THE PENTECOSTAL PASTOR AS A MANAGER

Paul wrote to the Christians in Corinth, saying, "Now it is required that those who have been given a trust must prove faithful" (1 Cor. 4:2). As God's appointed overseer of the church, the Pentecostal pastor must faithfully and effectively manage God's household. This includes both the spiritual and temporal matters of the assembly. The pastor must carefully watch over the people's souls. At the same time, he or she must faithfully manage the business affairs of the church. This includes the church's records, finances, and properties.

Along with the gifts of apostles, prophets, teachers, miracles, and others, God has given to the church the gift of "guidance," or, as some versions translate it, the gift of "administrating," to help build up the body of Christ (1 Cor. 12:28). Paul wrote that "an overseer manages God's household" (Titus 1:7). It is thus the pastor's responsibility to manage the church of God well. Paul told Titus that, among other things, an overseer must be "blameless...upright...and disciplined" (v. 8). Each of these traits are characteristics of a good manager.

While the administrative issues discussed in this chapter may seem mundane to some, and far from the Pentecostal pastor's calling, they are nevertheless very important. The way a pastor handles these issues can greatly affect his or her pastoral ministry. Pentecostal pastors who fails to handle the church's temporal matters well may disqualify themselves from handling its spiritual matters. Peter admonished, "Each of you should use whatever gift you have received to serve others, as faithful stewards of God's grace in its various forms" (1 Pet. 4:10).

While the church is more than a business, it is nonetheless a business. To a large extent, the success of any business lies in how well it is organized and managed. Some have argued that since the church is an organism and not an organization, it therefore requires no organizational structure. This statement is only half true. It is true that the church, as the body of Christ, is a living organism. However, it is untrue that it needs no organization. In fact, every living organism is by nature highly organized. For instance, in a human body, the head has its place, as does the torso, the arms, the legs, and so forth.

Organization speaks of order, and it implies united effort. A truckload of furniture may be a valuable asset, but it is of little practical use until it is unloaded from the truck and placed in a house in an orderly fashion. In like manner, for a church to reach its full potential, it needs to be carefully organized.

Every Pentecostal pastor must strive to develop his or her administrative skills. And every church should have workable systems in place to guide its business affairs. As a church develops and grows, its organizational structure will become more complex and its record-keeping systems more thorough. Three managerial responsibilities of every Pentecostal pastor are (1) keeping church records, (2) managing church finances, and (3) maintaining church properties. The remainder of this chapter will address these pastoral responsibilities.

KEEPING CHURCH RECORDS

The effective Pentecostal pastor will invest the time and energy needed to maintain accurate, up-to-date church records. These written records will benefit the pastor and church in at least four important ways:

First, a well-organized record-keeping system will make it possible for the pastor to find vital information when needed. And because the records are well maintained, the data will be trustworthy.

Second, well-kept records can help the pastor to manage and protect church properties. They can serve as legal proof of the church's holdings and financial dealings. For example, if someone challenges the church's ownership of lands, the pastor will be able to quickly produce the deed to the property and prove his or her case.

Third, good records provide the Pentecostal pastor with the background information he or she needs to make wise decisions about the future of the church. For instance, by examining attendance data from past years, the pastor can project the growth of the church into the future. This information could help the leadership make decisions on future building and staffing needs. In the same way, by examining how many marriages were celebrated during previous years, the pastor can estimate how many marriages he or she will perform in the coming year. He or she can thus use data from the past to predict trends for the future.

Fourth, good records provide the pastor and church with a connection to the past. They help inform the pastor and members of what went before them. This historical record will help them to appreciate their predecessors, and it will give them a sense of belonging and permanency.

Principles of Good Record Management

The time will come when every pastor will be asked to hand over the reins of leadership to a successor. The faithful Pentecostal pastor will prepare the church for this inevitable occurrence. One way he or she can do this is by keeping accurate church records. Here are five principles of good record-keeping:

1. *Accurate.* All records and documents must be accurate. They must represent a true record of what has occurred.
2. *Organized.* Church records should be well organized. They must be arranged into logical categories, thus providing efficient access to information when needed.
3. *Timely.* Records must be kept current and up-to-date. All financial transactions should be posted immediately. Other events, such as baby dedications, baptisms, and weddings, should be recorded in good time.
4. *Complete.* Church records must be complete. All pertinent facts regarding an event or transaction should be recorded.
5. *Secure.* All records must be kept in a secure place, safe from thieves and inclement weather.

Accurate Minutes

The Pentecostal pastor should ensure that accurate minutes are kept of all official church meetings. This includes monthly board

Part 8: The Pentecostal Pastor as Administrator

meetings, annual church business meetings, and special called business meetings. Minutes of each meeting should be kept by the appointed secretary and presented at the next meeting for approval. Once approved, they should be signed by the secretary and the pastor and placed in the church files for future reference.

The Events Register

Every Pentecostal pastor should keep an up-to-date events register. This register will include a record of church members, water baptisms, weddings, baby dedications, and church attendance, as follows:

Church memberships. The church's events register should include a list of church members. All new members' full names should be added to the list when they are officially received as members. The listing should also include the date they were received and any other pertinent comments concerning their reception. When any member dies or leaves the church, these events should be noted. It is good to issue a membership certificate or card to new members as part of their reception ceremony. Duplicates should be kept in the church files.

Water baptisms. The events register should also contain a list of those who are baptized in water, along with the date of their baptism and their age when they are baptized. A baptism certificate should be issued to each candidate.

Weddings. The church's events register should include a record of all who are married in the church. This record should include the date of the wedding and the full names of the bride and groom. It should further include the name of the minister (or ministers) officiating the ceremony, along with a list of all others who officially participated in the event. The pastor may also want to record the date the couple officially announced their engagement to the congregation. Following the wedding ceremony, a marriage certificate should be presented to the couple. The pastor must adhere to all civil laws concerning marriages.

Baby dedications. The Pentecostal pastor should also register all baby dedications occurring in the church. While Pentecostal churches do not baptize infants, they do practice baby dedications. Hannah's dedication of her son, Samuel, provides a good example of this practice (1 Sam. 1:21-28). After the dedication ceremony, the pastor should write the baby's full name in the events register, along with the child's date of birth, where the child was born, and the date of the ceremony. The listing should also include the names of the father and mother, the parents' address and contact numbers, and other pertinent observations. The pastor should give a dedication certificate to the parents.

Church attendance. The pastor should also keep track of the church's weekly attendance. This record should include the date and number of people attending each Sunday School class, Sunday morning worship service, Sunday evening service, as well as any children's, youth, and mid-week services. These records should be kept by the pastor or church secretary.

Sermon registry

In addition to a church registry, you will want to keep a personal record of the sermons you preach. Each time you deliver a sermon, teach a lesson, or speak publicly in any forum, you will want to record the event in the sermon registry. Each entry in this registry should include the date, the occasion, and the place the message was delivered. It should also include the Scripture text used, along with the title of the message. You may also want to include pertinent observations, such as the response of the people to the message. This registry will help you keep track of your messages, and it will help you to evaluate your preaching program. You will also want to keep your preaching notes in a secure place for future reference.

MANAGING CHURCH FINANCES

The Pentecostal pastor must further ensure that accurate and timely records are kept of all financial transactions related to the church. This practice will ensure that the church's finances are always handled properly. It will also help protect the pastor and church leaders from charges of mishandling church funds.

Part 8: The Pentecostal Pastor as Administrator

Receiving and Handling Offerings

Most Pentecostal churches in Africa are funded primarily through tithes and offerings received during their Sunday morning worship services. While these offerings may be received according to local church traditions, the pastor must ensure that every offering is handled with utmost honesty and transparency.

To do this, he or she will need to ensure that offerings are always collected and counted by two or more trustworthy church officers. After counting the offering, these same officials should complete an offering form. On the offering form should be places to fill in the current date, the kind (or kinds) of offering(s) received, and the names and signatures of those counting the money. The offering form should also have individual lines to record each kind of offering received. For instance, one line is labeled "tithes," another is labeled "undesignated offerings," another "building funds," another "missions," and so forth. The counters should ensure that the amount of each offering received is placed in its proper category.

These offering forms should be produced in duplicate, with one copy going to the church treasurer and the other going to the pastor. The treasurer will then recount the money and enter each amount received in the church ledger under its proper category. He or she will then deposit the money in the bank. (If possible, every church should have a bank account. When this is not possible, the money should be kept in a safe or locked cabinet.) The treasurer should retain the bank deposit receipt for the church records.

Keeping Financial Records

Accounting records can be kept on a paper ledger or on a computer. If a computer is used, it would be wise to produce paper reports each week to place in the file, since computers sometimes crash. Any time money is received or disbursed, the transaction is recorded on a cash receipt. This receipt is then given to the church treasurer who records it in the cash journal.

Every Pentecostal pastor must learn to read and analyze a cash journal. This skill will allow him or her to keep track of the financial dealings of the church and to know how much money is available in each fund at any given time. This practice will enable the pastor and church leaders to make wise financial decisions. And it will help to ensure that the church's financial records are being handled well.

Disbursing Church Funds

Any offering given to the church should be used only for the purpose it is given. It is unethical, for example, to take money given for the building fund and use it to purchase a car for the pastor. Whenever money is disbursed or transferred from one person or program to another, it must be receipted, and the receipt should be given to the treasurer for proper accounting. All receipts should be retained in the church's accounting files.

Financial Reports

At the close of each month, the church treasurer should prepare a financial report for the pastor and church board. This report will provide the church leadership with an accurate record of income and expenditures during the previous month. This will help them to make wise decisions concerning the church's finances. In addition to the monthly financial reports, the church treasurer should produce an annual financial report and present it to the pastor and church board. The pastor and board will in turn present the annual financial report to the church membership in the annual business meeting.

Budgeting

It is important that the Pentecostal pastor know how to prepare and follow an annual church budget. This practice will help them to better steward church funds. A budget is a financial plan. It is an estimate of the church's income for the coming year and a plan for distributing that income. A good budget will reflect the church's mission and priorities. For example, if a church prioritizes missions and church planting, the budget should reflect that priority. In this way, the budget can be viewed as a strategic missional document.

Preparing a church budget requires that the pastor and church board examine the church's financial dealings during previous years.

Then, using that information, they can make strategic decisions concerning how the church will distribute its funds during the coming year. This practice will help ensure that the church's funds are not wasted on trivial items, while more important items are left unfunded.

The budget consists of two main parts: projected income and projected expenses for the coming year. The projected income will include tithes, special offerings, and other sources. The projected expenses will include fixed expenses (such as salaries, mortgage payments, and utilities) and variable expenses (such as office supplies, Sunday school materials, promotions, and building maintenance). The church should also budget for unexpected and emergency expenses. At first, developing the budget will be challenging. However, after two or three years of faithfully tracking the church's income and expenditures, the budgeting process will be much easier. It will then become a great asset to the efficient functioning of the church.

MAINTAINING CHURCH PROPERTIES

As a steward of God's properties, the Pentecostal pastor must further ensure that church assets are well maintained. These assets include important church documents as well as the church's building, grounds, and other holdings.

Preserving Legal Documents

The pastor must ensure that the church's legal documents are kept in order and stored in a secure place. If possible, these documents should be kept in a safe or in a safety deposit box at a bank. A list of items in the safety deposit box should be kept in the church's files.

Caring for Church Properties

The Pentecostal pastor is also responsible to see that the church building and grounds are well maintained. He or she may want to appoint a maintenance and grounds committee to oversee this responsibility. This committee will ensure that the church properties are cared for as befits the house of God. Floors and grounds must be

Chapter 32: Managing Records, Finances, and Properties

swept and kept free from litter. Walls should be painted and washed. Windows should be kept clean and in good condition. Funds for building and grounds maintenance should be part of the church's budgeted expenses.

The same goes for the church's furnishings and equipment. Church furnishings, such as the pulpit, chairs, desks, office furniture, and the sound system should be kept clean and in good repair. When repairs are needed, they should be done in good time.

~ Chapter 33 ~

Mobilizing Lay Leaders

In Africa, it is not uncommon to see children playing football in an open field. Some play with a real ball. Others, in more rural settings, play with a homemade ball sometimes made of plastic bags wrapped into a ball and tied with strings. What a joy to see them running, laughing, and giving their best for their teams.

Some children are fortunate enough to play on a community team. There, they learn the values of teamwork and fair play. Team members learn that each player is significant and of value to the team. For the team to succeed, every player must give his or her very best. Even in defeat, everyone pulls together to encourage one another. The children learn that the success of the team is largely determined by the attitude of the players. This includes both those who are on the field and those on the sidelines. The church can learn a lot from a well-managed football team.

Someone once described a professional football match as twenty-two people who desperately need rest, being watched by ten thousand others who desperately need exercise. Sadly, this scenario describes many Pentecostal churches in Africa today. While a few members grow weary carrying the load of ministry, most of the congregation contribute very little. These churches have become a "spectator sport" where a few players are cheered on by many spectators. This unworkable and unbiblical situation is crippling the church's effectiveness in fulfilling God's mission. For any church to prosper, the pastor must learn to mobilize the laity for kingdom service.

This chapter will highlight this challenge. First, it will lay a biblical foundation for lay leadership in the church. Then, it will give practical advice on how you, as a Pentecostal pastor, can effectively mobilize the laity for ministry in the church and community.

WHAT THE BIBLE SAYS

From the beginning of the Church, the apostles saw the need to mobilize everyone for Spirit-empowered ministry. After all, had not Jesus promised, "But you will receive power when the Holy Spirit comes on you; and you will be my witnesses in Jerusalem, and in all Judea and Samaria, and to the ends of the earth" (Acts 1:8). This promise was not just for the apostles. It was for every Christian, clergy and layperson alike. Jesus' plan for the Church was that every member be filled with the Spirit and that each one participate in fulfilling God's mission.

The Early Church

Immediately after the outpouring of the Spirit at Pentecost, the early church began to organize for effective evangelism and discipleship training. The Bible says, "They devoted themselves to the apostles' teaching and to fellowship" (Acts 2:42). It then adds, "Every day they continued to meet together in the temple courts….praising God and enjoying the favor of all the people. And the Lord added to their number daily those who were being saved" (vv. 46-47). Leaders were needed to care for these quickly emerging home groups. The apostles undoubtedly began to train some of these new believers for leadership and service.

Part 8: The Pentecostal Pastor as Administrator

As the church grew and prospered, others began to join the leadership team. These men and women served under the apostles and assisted them in their work. Today, we call these people deacons. The apostles stipulated that these lay leaders needed to be full of the Spirit and wisdom. Their job would be to organize the feeding program for the Greek-speaking widows who had come to the Lord (Acts 6:1-7). No doubt, the responsibilities of these men changed as other needs arose. At least two of them, Stephen and Philip, became powerful proclaimers of the gospel.

Years later, after the organization of the church had developed, Paul explained to the Ephesians the leadership structure of the church. The church was to be led by apostles, prophets, evangelists, pastors, and teachers (Eph. 4:11). However, these leaders were not to minister alone. Their job was "to equip [God's] people for works of service" (v. 12). They were to raise up lay leaders to assist them in the work. If they would do this, the church would become strong and effective (vv. 11-16).

The Priesthood and Prophethood of All Believers

The Bible teaches the "priesthood of all believers." This means that every follower of Christ is a priest before God. As a priest, he or she has the right to read and interpret Scripture and to share God's grace with others (1 Pet. 2:5, 9). The Bible further teaches the "prophethood of all believers." This means that by virtue of being born again and filled with the Holy Spirit, every believer has become part of God's last-days prophetic community (Num. 11:29; Joel 2:28-29; Acts 2:17-18). By giving them His Spirit, God has empowered them as Christ's witnesses "in Jerusalem, and in all Judea and Samaria, and to the ends of the earth" (Acts 1:8).

At Pentecost, Peter began his sermon by declaring, "This [outpouring of the Holy Spirit] is what was spoken by the prophet Joel: 'In the last days, God says, I will pour out my Spirit on all people. Your sons and daughters will prophesy'" (Acts 2:16-17). Peter ended his sermon by commanding the people, "Repent and be baptized, every one of you, in the name of Jesus Christ for the forgiveness of your sins. And you will receive the gift of the Holy Spirit." Peter then issued an amazing promise: "The promise is for you and your children and for all who are far off—for all whom the Lord our God will call" (vv. 38-39). Peter was saying that the day had arrived when all of God's people would serve Him as Spirit-empowered ministers.

The empowering of the Spirit thus qualifies all people, no matter how humble or marginalized, to speak and to minister for Christ. The Pentecostal pastor must recognize this fact, and he or she must encourage their people to be empowered by the Spirit and to become active participants in the ministry of the church.

THE NEED FOR LAY LEADERS

For a church to flourish and grow as God intends, it must have strong pastoral leadership. It must also have strong lay leadership.

A critical challenge facing many Pentecostal churches in Africa today is that most members are not adequately discipled. This has greatly weakened the church. Because the people are not properly trained, pastors are performing tasks that should be done by others. As a result, pastors often become so busy with the small tasks that they have neither the time nor the energy to carry out the large tasks effectively.

The story of Jethro and Moses illustrates this point (Exod. 18:13-26). Moses had led the people of Israel out of Egyptian bondage. Now, they were coming to him to settle their disputes. So many came that Moses sat judging them from early morning until late evening. This went on day after day. In time, Moses became weary.

When Moses' father-in-law, Jethro, saw what was happening, he advised Moses, "What you are doing is not good....The work is too heavy for you; you cannot handle it alone" (vv. 17-18). Jethro then said to Moses, "Select capable men from all the people...and appoint them as officials....Have them serve as judges for the people at all times, but have them bring every difficult case to you....That will make your load lighter, because they will share it with you" (vv. 21-

22). Moses followed Jethro's advice. As a result, the people were better served and Moses found rest.

As a wise Pentecostal pastor, you must do the same. You must choose godly men and women to help you with the work. You must then train them and appoint them to carry out their jobs. If you will do this, you will be freed from the everyday tasks of the church. And you will be able to focus on the tasks that only you can do. As a result, the church will grow and prosper.

A Shift of Focus

To do this will require a shift in focus. You must move from seeing yourself as the star player on the team to seeing yourself as the coach. Your job is not so much to score goals, but to teach the people how to score goals. Your job is not to counsel all the people, but to see that all of the people receive wise counsel (Exod. 18:21-22). Your job is not to feed all the Grecian widows yourself, but to see that all the Grecian widows are properly fed (Acts 6:1-3). In other words, as pastor, your job is to "equip [God's] people for works of service" (Eph. 4:11-12). From the onset of your ministry in any church, you should begin equipping members for ministry. The church's lay leadership team will emerge from those being discipled.

Mobilizing Lay Leaders

As pastor, you must identify, train, and release lay leaders into ministry. You should view your church members as a team composed of people with different gifts and skill sets who can be mobilized for kingdom ministry. For the team to succeed, each player must do his or her part. A lay leader is anyone who has assumed the leadership of any ministry in the church. This includes deacons, lay elders, Sunday school administrators and teachers, cell group leaders, men's and women's ministry leaders, youth leaders, children's ministry directors, choir directors, worship team leaders, missions committee members, and others.

Chapter 33: Mobilizing Lay Leaders

QUALIFICATIONS FOR LAY LEADERS

While every church member is called to serve, not all have qualified themselves. To serve as a leader in the church, one's life must align with the standard set in God's Word. Paul said of deacons, "They must first be tested; and then if there is nothing against them, let them serve" (1 Tim. 3:10).

The apostles in Acts laid down two basic qualifications for lay leaders: they must be "full of the Spirit and wisdom" (Acts 6:3). In 1 Timothy 3 and Titus 1, Paul lists qualifications for church leaders. While most of these qualifications relate to pastors and elders, they are still useful in considering the qualifications of any leadership role in the church.

From these lists, we can deduce five categories that must be considered when appointing leaders in the church. These five categories are (1) the candidates' moral character, (2) their spiritual experience, (3) their temperament, (4) their day-to-day conduct, and (5) their testimony in the community. The pastor should appoint to leadership only those who are Spirit-filled, godly, committed, teachable, and willing to serve under the pastor as lay leaders.

RECRUITING AND TRAINING LAY LEADERS

Just as a football coach would search for qualified men or women to play on his team, as God's appointed leader of the church, you must search for qualified individuals to lead the ministries of the church. When there are no qualified leaders, you must develop them. Jesus did this with His disciples, and Paul did it with Timothy, Titus, and others. Let's look at these two parts of mobilizing lay leaders in the church: recruiting workers and developing leaders.

Recruiting Workers

The process of recruiting lay workers requires much discussion among the current leaders of the church. It also requires much prayer, seeking God for His guidance. This is what Jesus did. Throughout His ministry, He continually sought His Father's direction (Luke

5:16). For example, before choosing His twelve disciples, Jesus "went out to a mountainside to pray, and spent the night praying to God" (6:12).

Once you have received direction from the Lord, you must determine which workers will be needed to accomplish the work. You should then share the vision with the congregation and begin asking for volunteers. When asking for volunteers, it is important to promise training for the job. This will encourage more people to respond. Leaders often emerge out of those who volunteer for service. You should constantly ask yourself, "Who in this group has leadership potential?" You may want to approach certain individuals personally and talk with them about fulfilling a specific leadership role.

Developing Leaders

Once potential lay leaders have been identified, they must then be developed. This is the responsibility of every Pentecostal pastor. As previously stated, Paul indicated that the pastor's job was "to equip [God's] people for works of service, so that the body of Christ may be built up" (Eph. 4:12). You can do this in three ways:

1. On-the-job training. This kind of leadership training is also known as apprenticeship or internship training. The pastor assigns the emerging leader to an experienced leader. The experienced leader then takes the new leader under his or her wing and teaches them how to lead a particular ministry.

2. Seminars. You will want to conduct occasional seminars, workshops, or retreats to train new leaders.

3. Mentoring. You may want to individually mentor some who show special promise. To do this you will need to spend time with these promising leaders teaching them about ministry. This is what Jesus did with His disciples (John 3:22). He cultivated a deep relationship with them, pouring His life into theirs. Over time, they became more and more like Him (Acts 4:13). Jesus explained, "Everyone who is fully trained will be like their teacher" (Luke 6:40).

Chapter 33: Mobilizing Lay Leaders

CULTIVATIVING A TEAM SPIRIT

For the church to do well, there must be a sense of unity and common purpose among the people. The people must feel that they are part of something bigger than themselves. They must believe that their church is part of God's great redemptive mission, and that it exists to play a significant role in fulfilling that mission.

This is especially true of lay leaders. For them to do their best, they must feel that they are an important part of a team. They must feel that they are moving together with likeminded colleagues to achieve a noble end. As pastor, you must work to cultivate such a team spirit among leaders.

Create a Common Vision

As pastor of the church, you are the keeper and chief promoter of the vision of the church. It is up to you to nurture a common vision in the hearts of the church's leadership team. The vision should be compelling enough for the people to want to follow. Jesus' vision was so compelling that it moved Peter, Andrew, James, and John to leave everything to follow him (Matt. 4:18-22).

In like manner, you must be able to clearly and convincingly communicate the vision. Echoing the ancient prophet, you must be able to say, "This is the way; we must walk in it" (cf. Isa. 30:21). Like the current of a mighty river, this common vision will move everyone in the same direction.[1]

Create a Sense of Camaraderie

In addition to cultivating a common vision among lay leaders, you must seek to create a sense of camaraderie among them. For people to work well together they must genuinely like one another and enjoy being in one another's company. The Bible tells us that one reason Jesus chose the twelve apostles was "that they might be with him" (Mark 3:14). And one might add, He chose them *that they might*

---

[1] For more on vision casting, see Chapter 28: "Visionary Leadership."

Part 8: The Pentecostal Pastor as Administrator

be with each other. As the Twelve spent time with Jesus, and with one another, they grew to love each other. Together, they became a powerful force in the earth.

In like manner, you as a Pentecostal pastor, must strive to engender a strong sense of camaraderie between yourself, your staff, and your lay leaders. This can be done only by spending quality time together. Time can be spent together in three significant ways:

1. Time together in prayer. First, you and your lay leadership team should spend time together in prayer. You will want to set a convenient time each week when you and your lay leaders can come together for prayer. These prayer times must remain focused. While time can be spent praying for personal needs, the bulk of the time should be spent praying for the vision and ministries of the church.

2. Time together in ministry. Next, you and your lay leaders must spend time together in ministry. Each Sunday morning before church, call the leadership team together for prayer and remind them that you are working together as a team. Another way that the lay leadership team can minister together is that they could form the core of the church's church planting team. Each year, they could go together to plant a new church in a needy place.

3. Time in fellowship. Third, you and your lay leaders must spend time together in fellowship. Your lay leaders should be encouraged to visit in one another's homes. A monthly fellowship meal could go a long way in cementing the bond of fellowship between the families of your leadership team. After Jesus had spent much time with His disciples, He said to them, "I no longer call you servants....Instead, I have called you friends" (John 15:15). In like manner, you and your lay leaders should be able to call each other friends.

For a church to thrive, it must have a strong core of lay leaders committed to advancing the mission and vision of the church. The wise Pentecostal pastor will, therefore, set as one of his or her main goals in ministry to build a strong lay leadership team. He or she will

Chapter 33: Mobilizing Lay Leaders

intentionally invest time and energy identifying, recruiting, and developing lay leaders to serve with them in advancing God's kingdom.

~ Chapter 34 ~

Directing Church Departments

As a baby develops in its mother's womb, day by day its body becomes more and more complex. At the moment of conception, the new human being is made of just one fertilized cell. And yet, amazingly, its genetic makeup is already complete. Within 24 hours, the egg begins to rapidly divide into many cells. In three weeks, the first nerve cells have formed. By the end of the first three months, although the baby is only about 10 centimeters (four inches) long, all of its organs and limbs are present. However, for the baby to become a fully functioning person, and able to live outside its mother's womb, its organs will need to develop. After six more months, the baby is ready to be born. This is the precious child the mother and father will soon hold in their arms. No wonder David exulted, "I am fearfully and wonderfully made!" (Psa. 139:14).

A new church can be compared to a newly fertilized egg. It is already fully a church; however, it needs to develop certain systems before it can become a viable, fully functioning body of believers.

Some of these systems are known as church departments. This chapter will discuss the Pentecostal pastor's role in implementing, developing, and managing these departments.

THE PURPOSE AND FUNCTION OF CHURCH DEPARTMENTS

Church departments are ministries of a local assembly designed to address specific needs in the body. Their purpose is to enable the church to more effectively carry out its mission of reaching the lost and developing disciples into the image of Christ. Church departments can further be viewed as pillars supporting the ever-expanding ministry structure of the church. As new departments are added, the church's capacity to minister is expanded.

The Purpose of Departments

To properly understand the purpose and function of church departments, the Pentecostal pastor must first understand the mission of the Church. The Church exists to carry out the Great Commission and fulfill the Great Commandment of Christ. The Great Commission is Christ's command to "go and make disciples of all nations" (Matt. 28:19). The Great Commandment is the Lord's mandate to "love the Lord your God with all your heart and with all your soul and with all your mind" and to "love your neighbor as yourself" (Matt. 22:37-39).

These awesome responsibilities cannot be discharged by the pastor alone, or even by the paid pastoral staff. The task requires many hands. Church departments exist to enable the church to more effectively fulfill its mandate of establishing God's kingdom in the earth.

Seven Functions of Departments

Church departments enable the church to better carry out seven key ministry functions:

1. Reaching the lost. First, departments exist to help the church fulfill Christ's command to "go into all the world and preach the gospel to all creation" (Mark 16:15). Every department in the church must do its part to mobilize the church for this essential task. They should encourage members to personally share the good news with others and inspire them to participate in the evangelism and missions programs of the church.

2. Making disciples. Jesus further mandated that the Church "make disciples of all nations...teaching them to obey everything I have commanded" (Matt. 28:19-20). Teaching is at the heart of disciple making. Systematic instruction is essential to the spiritual growth of God's people and the development of the church. Departments help serve this purpose.

3. Encouraging worship. The Church also exists as a place where God's people can gather and worship Him "in the Spirit and in truth" (John 4:23). A well-organized department of worship and music can help ensure that such worship occurs.

4. Promoting prayer. Further, the Church exists to inspire and teach God's people to pray (Acts 2:42). Jesus declared, "My house will be called a house of prayer for all nations" (Mark 11:17). The local church is to be a place where Christians lift up their voices together and call on God, expecting Him to answer their prayers (Matt. 18:19-20; Acts 4:24). Departments help the church to fulfill this function. Each time a department in the church gathers, it should emphasize prayer.

5. Providing fellowship. Additionally, the Church exists to promote fellowship among brothers and sisters in Christ. Departments help the church to achieve this goal. As God's people gather in departmental meetings, they grow in affection for one another. As a result, they naturally want to support and care for each other. This dynamic serves to unify and strengthen the body. It also helps to attract new people to the church.

6. Mobilizing for mission. The Church further exists to fulfill the mission of God. It exists to take the good news about Christ to "every tribe and language and people and nation" before He returns from heaven (Matt. 24:14; Rev. 5:9). Departments help the church to mobilize itself for evangelism, church planting, and missions.

7. Developing leaders. Finally, Jesus commissioned the Church to train leaders. He commanded His disciples to go and make other disciples (Matt. 28:19). When He ascended into heaven, He gave ministry gifts to the Church "to equip his people for works of service, so that the body of Christ may be built up" (Eph. 4:11). Paul instructed Timothy, "The things you have heard me say in the presence of many witnesses entrust to reliable people who will also be qualified to teach others" (2 Tim. 2:2). Departments help the church to more effectively carry out this function.

POSSIBLE CHURCH DEPARTMENTS

As the church grows and develops, you and your leadership team will need to prayerfully departmentalize its ministry structure. You will begin by establishing one or two departments. Then, as the Spirit leads, you will organize other departments and programs. Possible departments and ministries include the following:

Christian Education

The Christian Education Department is the primary training arm of the church. This department exists to make believers into disciples by teaching them the Word of God and by applying its principles to their lives. In most Pentecostal churches, the Sunday School is the heart of the Christian Education Department and the primary disciple-making ministry of the church. It is normally the only department in the church that ministers to every age group, from small children through senior adults.

The Pentecostal pastor must therefore prioritize developing this department. It must be one of the first departments a new church begins. The church may also want to organize home cell groups where people are discipled and taught the Word of God. Further, every department must be involved in Christian education on some level.[1]

---

[1] Africa's Hope (the publisher of this book) has developed two powerful discipleship resources for Pentecostal churches in Africa. The first is the

Women's Ministry

The Women's Ministry Department is often one of the most powerful departments in the Pentecostal church. Its purpose is to reach women for Christ and to provide them with fellowship and ministry opportunities. Through this ministry, women are encouraged to reach out to their family members, friends, and neighbors and win them to Christ. Women are also encouraged to get involved in discipleship, church planting, missions, and other ministries.

Men's Ministry

The Men's Ministry Department exists to reach men for Christ, to provide them with Christian fellowship, and to challenge them to be leaders in their homes and communities. It further exists to mobilize men for Spirit-empowered ministry. Through this ministry, men are challenged to get involved in evangelism, church planting, and other core mission activities of the church.

Youth Ministry

The purpose of the Youth Ministry Department is to reach young people for Christ and develop them into mature, Spirit-filled Christian adults. It further exists to teach them to live godly, Christ-honoring lives, and to mobilize them for meaningful ministry to other young people.

Children's Ministry

The Children's Ministry Department aims at reaching children for Christ, leading them into the Spirit-filled life, and training them up in the ways of the Lord. It is not meant to replace the parents'

Living the Truth series, a Sunday School curriculum that takes students through the entire Bible in seven years. The other is the *Roots of Faith* series. This is a topical curriculum dealing with critical issues concerning the Christian life, such as "First Steps: Your New Life in Christ," "Bible Doctrines," "Life in the Spirit," and others. These series are offered in several African languages. You can find out more about these resources at https://africaatts.org/resources/.

efforts but to supplement them (Prov. 22:6). The scope of this ministry includes Children's Church and other children's discipleship ministries such as boys and girls clubs.

Worship and Music

The purpose of the Worship and Music Department is to enlist and develop musicians, worship leaders, and choirs who will lead the assembly into Spirit-anointed worship (John 4:23). The department also works with the Missions Committee in conducting evangelism and church planting outreaches. Members of the worship team must pray together often, and they must be taught how to respond to the Spirit's presence and to minister in His power.[2]

Prayer Ministry

A well-organized Prayer Ministry Department is an essential component of every Pentecostal church. This ministry provides spiritual support to the church by interceding for its pastors and members. It also intercedes for unsaved people at home, throughout Africa, and around the world. This ministry may take several approaches, such as regular prayer meetings, prayer retreats, prayer walks, prayer teams, and the ministry of individual prayer warriors.[3]

Missions Department

The Missions Department is tasked with the responsibility of keeping the church focused on spreading the gospel to all people everywhere. Its responsibilities include planning and carrying out evangelistic events and church planting missions. Evangelistic events

---

[2] The worship ministry of the church is discussed in greater detail in Chapter 18: "Leading the Church in Worship."

[3] For more on the prayer ministry of the church, see Chapter 8: "The Priority of Prayer."

could include revival services, open-air meetings, door-to-door witnessing campaigns, literature distribution efforts, and other creative evangelistic methods.[4]

The department is further responsible for developing and promoting the church's missions program. Through this vital program, the church is mobilized to support missionaries with their prayers and finances. The ministry does this by teaching the people about God's mission and exposing them to missionaries. Some churches will want to have separate evangelism, church planting, and missions departments.[5]

Compassion Ministry

Jesus cared about the physical needs of people. A truly Pentecostal church will do the same. James wrote, "Religion that God our Father accepts as pure and faultless is this: to look after orphans and widows in their distress and to keep oneself from being polluted by the world" (James 1:27). Through its Compassion Ministry, the Pentecostal church extends the hand of Christ to needy and hurting people.[6]

Single Adults Ministry

Through the Single Adults Ministry, Christian singles are equipped to grow strong in their faith and to embrace an active role in the life of the church. This ministry helps the church to recognize the value of having single adults participate in the activities of the church. It seeks to tap the immense resources of this often ignored group.

---

[4] For more on mobilizing the church for evangelistic outreach, see Chapter 37: "Evangelizing the Lost."

[5] For more on developing the church's missions program, see Chapter 40: "Developing a Local Church Missions Program."

[6] For more on compassion ministry, see Chapter 38: "Serving the Community."

Chapter 34: Directing Church Departments

College Students Ministry

If your church is located near a university or college campus, you should prayerfully consider launching a College Students Ministry. The purpose of this ministry is to reach out to the college or university campus, seeking to win students to Christ. This ministry will then train and mobilize these students to reach even more students with the gospel. If your national church has a university ministry department, you will want to work closely with that organization.[7]

Media and Technology

The Media and Technology Department handles all the technology issues for the church. It sets up, operates, and maintains the church's sound and video projection equipment. It further publishes and maintains the church website and social media presence on the Internet. This department is also responsible for publishing church services and events through such media as radio, television, and the Internet.

Ushering and Hospitality

The purpose of the Ushering and Hospitality Department is to welcome and assist those attending church functions. This ministry endeavors to create an environment of warmth and acceptance for all. It welcomes attenders, directs guests to their seats, distributes materials, and collects offerings. It also promotes safety, handles distractions, and keeps order in the church.

Building and Grounds

The Building and Grounds Department is responsible for the maintenance of church properties. It ensures that the buildings and grounds are kept clean, neat, and in good repair.

---

[7] Resources for developing a ministry to college students can be found on the Internet at https://chialpha.com/resources/.

Part 8: The Pentecostal Pastor as Administrator

DEVELOPING DEPARTMENTS

The question arises, "How can a Pentecostal pastor develop new departments and ministries in the church?" Of course, it is not possible to begin all of the above departments at once. Rather, new departments should be started prayerfully and strategically. Starting new departments must be viewed as an ongoing step-by-step process taking many years.

Starting a new department or ministry often involves a bold step of faith on the part of the pastor and church board. They must see the need, sense the leadership of the Spirit, and then move in faith to launch the new ministry.

Beginning the Process

You and your church board should begin the process by seeking God. You should ask Him, "Lord, what new ministries are most needed in the church at this time?" You can then create a short list of those departments and ministries you sense the Spirit is leading you to start. After you create the list, you should prioritize it, deciding which department will be started first, which will be started second, and so forth.

You should then turn your attention to the department at the top of your priority list. You should meet with your leadership team and discuss the following:

- What steps must we take to begin this new department?
- What resources will be needed?
- Who will lead and staff the program?
- When will it begin?

You should write down your decisions and continue to pray over them. Then, when the time is right, you can begin to implement your strategy. It is advisable to start small, making use of available resources. For instance, if you want to start a new Sunday School department, you may want to begin with just three classes: adults, youth, and children. You may want to appoint someone to serve as Sunday School superintendent, or you may want to serve in this role yourself, at least in the beginning. As the ministry grows, you can start new classes and appoint new leaders.

Choosing Leaders

The key to the success of any new departmental ministry is well-chosen and properly trained leaders. When choosing leaders, you should look for individuals with leadership potential, those whom you can develop into leaders. These individuals should be "full of the Spirit and wisdom" (Acts 6:3). Further, they must be full of faith, and they must fully embrace the vision of the church.

Training Workers

Quite often, qualified leaders are not available. Therefore, an effective pastor will be constantly developing new leaders. This is what Jesus did. He prayerfully chose twelve men whom He would develop into apostles (Luke 6:12-13). Though they were ordinary men, Jesus saw leadership potential in them. He bade them, "Come, follow me…and I will send you out to fish for people" (Matt. 4:19). As they followed Him, He developed them into great leaders.

When recruiting new departmental leaders and staff, it is important that you promise training. Tell the people, "We will walk beside you and teach you how to fulfill your ministry." This ministry training can be done in several ways: through seminars, one-on-one mentoring, and other creative means. If a church is going to have a steady supply of leaders, the pastor must be intentional about leadership training.[8]

Creating Team Spirit

For departmental ministries in the church to thrive, you must create a sense of purpose and loyalty among leaders and workers. This team spirit will motivate them to work together and to give their best to do their jobs well. You can nurture this team spirit by frequently

---

[8] For more on training workers for ministry in the local church, see Chapter 33: "Mobilizing Lay Workers."

reminding them of the church's vision, and by showing them the important role they play in fulfilling the vision.

You should meet often with departmental leaders and workers to encourage them and share victories and goals with them. You should also publicly recognize faithful workers and honor them for their achievements (Rom. 13:7).

Church departments play an essential role in a Pentecostal church's ability to effectively fulfill Christ's Great Commission and His Great Commandment. The effective Pentecostal pastor will therefore work to develop strong ministry departments in his or her church.

Chapter 34: Directing Church Departments

~ Chapter 35 ~

Overseeing Church Membership

Imagine a public school that has no clear idea of who is and who is not a student in the school. The school never takes roll, and it keeps no records of student achievement. Clearly, such a school would have little chance of success. Much the same could be said about a church. A church that has no clear idea of who is and who is not a member, and fails to take note of their spiritual progress, has little chance of becoming a strong church.

As a Pentecostal pastor, you must ensure that the church you lead is well managed. One important area of managerial concern is the church's membership roll. A well-managed membership roll will help the church to better fulfill its God-given responsibilities of caring for the sheep and evangelizing the lost. This chapter will address your duty of overseeing the church's membership rolls.

Chapter 35: Overseeing Church Membership

THE BIBLICAL MANDATE FOR MEMBERSHIP

While the Bible does not speak directly about formal church membership as it is known in the church today, it does support the idea.

Biblical Foundation for Membership

The concept of church membership has its origin in the Old Testament. There, God shared a unique relationship with the nation of Israel. They were His people, and He was their God. In the wilderness, God initiated a plan to organize His people. He commanded Moses, "Take a census of the whole Israelite community by their clans and families, listing every man by name, one by one" (Num. 1:2). Moses and Aaron then used this census to select those who would lead, serve, and defend God's people.

In the New Testament, Stephen spoke of Israel as "the assembly [Greek: *ekklesia*] in the wilderness." Throughout the New Testament the word *ekklesia* is translated "church." It speaks of a gathering of people called out of the world to follow Christ and advance His mission in the earth.

Jesus declared, "I will build my church" (Matt. 16:18). He began that process by inviting people to follow Him (Matt. 4:19). From these followers, Jesus appointed some to be apostles (Mark 3:13-14). The apostles in turn appointed deacons to serve under them. They were organizing the church for success. As a result, "the number of disciples in Jerusalem increased rapidly" (Acts 6:1-7).

For a local church to function as it should, it is essential that everyone knows who is, and who is not, a member. The early church understood this. For them, there was a well-defined "in" and "out" of church membership. For instance, on one occasion, Paul instructed the church in Corinth to expel a sinning member, removing him from the church roll (1 Cor. 5:5, 13). A well-managed membership roll will help the Pentecostal pastor to strengthen believers and advance the mission of the church.

Part 8: The Pentecostal Pastor as Administrator

Biblical Concept of Membership

One should not, however, think of church membership in terms of membership in a secular club or society. It goes much deeper than that. Paul compares the Church to the human body, calling it "the body of Christ" (1 Cor. 12:27). Each member of the Church is thus part of Christ's body, and "each member belongs to all the others" (Rom. 12:5). Just as the human body is organized, and each member of the body has a specific function, so it is with Christ's Church.

QUALIFICATIONS FOR MEMBERSHIP

In the Old Testament, God established standards for His people to live by. These standards are summed up in the Ten Commandments (Exod. 20:1-17). In like manner, as the early church grew and scattered beyond Jerusalem, the apostles were guided by the Holy Spirit to establish qualifications for Gentile inclusion in the church (Acts 15:19-20, 28-29). As pastor of a Pentecostal church, you must likewise ensure that anyone received into the church as a member meets certain qualifications, including the following:

The New Birth

The local church should be a reflection of the universal Church. The universal Church includes all people of all nations who have put their trust in Jesus Christ and been saved. It includes only those who have been truly born of the Holy Spirit (1 Cor. 12:13). Therefore, before a person can become a member of a local church, he or she must have first become a member of the universal Church. The Lord himself must have added them to His Church (Acts 2:47). It follows that, to become a member of a local church, one must be truly born again (John 3:3-7).

Water Baptism

A second requirement for church membership is water baptism by immersion. Jesus commands His Church to "go and make disciples of all nations, baptizing them in the name of the Father and of the Son and of the Holy Spirit" (Matt. 28:19; cf. Acts 2:38). Water

Chapter 35: Overseeing Church Membership

baptism is a public testimony that one has passed from death to life (Rom. 6:4).[1]

Shared Belief

A final qualification for church membership is full agreement with the teachings and policies of the church (cf. 1 Cor. 1:10). This requirement will ensure that the church remains unified and focused on its God-given mission. These issues should be dealt with in a new members' class.

RECEIVING NEW MEMBERS

As pastor, you must ensure that the church has a well-defined procedure for receiving members. This procedure should include three elements:

Encouraging Membership

You should regularly encourage new believers to join the church. To do this, you should take time in church services to explain the benefits of church membership and invite new Christians to join. You may also want to speak personally to prospective members. These actions will ensure that members are constantly being added to the church. (This is, of course, assuming that new people are coming to Christ as a result of the church's evangelistic outreach.[2]) In addition, you should ensure that membership application forms are readily available.

Preparing for Membership

It is important that your church has some means of preparing people for church membership. One way to do this is through a new members' class. This should be an ongoing class. It can be offered on

---

[1] For more on water baptism, see Chapter 42: "Conducting Sacraments, Dedications, and Installations."

[2] For more on reaching out to the lost, see Chapter 37: "Evangelizing the Lost."

Sunday mornings during the Sunday school hour or at any other appropriate time. In this class, prospective members will learn about the benefits and responsibilities of church membership. Much of what is discussed in this chapter can be taught in the class.

Receiving Members

Once approved by the church board, new members should be joyously received into the church in a public ceremony on a designated Sunday morning. The candidates should be gathered in front of the church. You can then publicly welcome them as members and pray over them. The church will then extend to them the "right hand of fellowship" (Gal. 2:9). At this time you should present a certificate of membership to each new member. You will then add their names to the church membership roll.

In addition, it would be good for someone on the pastoral team to visit these new members in their homes. This will help them to know how much the church appreciates their decision to join. Finally, you should connect the new members with the ministries of the church, such as cell groups, women's ministry, men's ministry, youth group, and others.

RESPONSIBILITIES OF MEMBERSHIP

As pastor of the church, you must ensure that new members are made aware of the responsibilities and privileges of membership.

Responsibilities of Members Toward the Church

With membership comes responsibility. Those responsibilities include the following:

1. Regular church attendance. The writer of Hebrews warned Christians that they were not to neglect meeting together. Instead, they were to regularly come together to encourage one another. This was especially important in light of Jesus' soon coming (Heb. 10:25). In like manner, church members today are expected to be faithful in their church attendance. There, they will be encouraged, worship

God, pray together, receive teaching, give to God's work, and develop lasting relationships with other committed Christians.

2. A Spirit-filled walk. Every member of a Pentecostal church should be committed to the Spirit-filled walk (Gal. 5:25). If they have not yet been baptized in the Holy Spirit, they should be earnestly seeking the experience (Acts 1:4-5; Eph. 5:18). If they have been filled with the Spirit, they must be committed to continuing in the Spirit-filled walk (Gal. 5:16, 25).[3]

3. Consistent witness. Every church member is expected to be a witness for Christ (Acts 1:8). They must faithfully share Christ with their family, friends, neighbors, and coworkers. Jesus commands us, "Let your light shine before others, that they may see your good deeds and glorify your Father in heaven" (Matt. 5:16).

4. Holy living. One way the Pentecostal Christian witnesses for Christ is by living a holy life (1 Pet. 1:15; 2:9). In doing this, they demonstrate their love for God. At the same time, their lives testify to a lost world what it means to be a disciple of Christ (Phi. 2:15).

5. Faithful giving. Every church member is expected to faithfully support the church financially (1 Cor. 16:2). By giving their tithes and offerings they strengthen the body and help to advance God's kingdom in the earth. In addition, cheerful giving pleases God and opens the door to His blessings on their lives (2 Cor. 9:7-8; Luke 6:38).

6. Active service. Further, every member is expected to find his or her place of service in the church. As each member does his or her part, the church becomes strong. As pastor, you must work to ensure that members understand their unique giftings and that they commit themselves to using these giftings to serve Christ and the church.

7. Fervent prayer. One mark of a truly Pentecostal church is fervent prayer. Every member can be expected to pray regularly for the pastor, the church, the community, and for other church members.

---

[3] For more on leading believers into the Spirit-filled walk, see Chapter 11: "Promotes Pentecostal Experience and Practice" and Chapter 20: "Guiding Believers into Spirit Baptism."

Part 8: The Pentecostal Pastor as Administrator

You will want to encourage some to join specially formed intercessory prayer groups.

8. Cooperative attitude. Finally, members are expected to maintain a cooperative attitude. Such an attitude will contribute to the unity of the church (Eph. 4:3). It will ensure that the church is not distracted by pointless bickering, but remains focused on fulfilling its God-given mission.

Responsibilities of the Church Toward Members

Not only do church members bear certain responsibilities toward the church, the pastor and church bear certain responsibilities toward members. Those responsibilities include the following:

1. A warm welcome. First, you must ensure that new members are warmly welcomed and fully integrated into the life of the church. Some will have left behind people and things to which they are accustomed. They may have entered into a new world they know little about. You should ensure that these new members are helped to adjust to their new environment. And you must make every effort to ensure that they feel like they are truly members of God's family.

2. Quality worship services. Second, as pastor, you are responsible to church members, both old and new, to provide them with truly edifying worship experiences. In other words, you must ensure that the church's worship services are well planned and of the highest quality. To do this, you must make every effort to prepare and preach biblically sound and inspiring messages. You must further ensure that each part of the service is carried out in a dignified and professional way. This includes worship, giving, announcements, or any other part of the service. In addition, you and your leadership team must bathe the church services in prayer to ensure that the Holy Spirit is powerfully present.[4]

---

[4] For more insight on planning worship services, see Chapter 18: "Leading Worship."

Chapter 35: Overseeing Church Membership

3. Pastoral care. Further, as shepherd of the flock, you are obligated to see that each member of the church is valued and cared for. You must imitate Jesus who called himself the "good shepherd… [who] lays down his life for the sheep" (John 10:11). You must be prepared to serve even the lowliest church member (Luke 15:1-7).[5]

4. Sincere prayer. Next, as a Pentecostal pastor, you must faithfully pray for your church members. It would be good to create a list of their names to serve as a prayer guide. You could then use the list to pray daily for each member. Further, during their times of crisis, you and your leadership team should be prepared to go to hurting members to encourage them and pray for them.[6]

5. Biblical teaching. Further, as a faithful Pentecostal pastor, you must ensure that your church members receive sound biblical teaching. This teaching should be practical and relevant to their lives. It will help them to grow and become mature Christians. You should also monitor the teaching in Sunday school classes and cell groups to ensure that it is biblically sound and edifying.[7]

6. Protection from false prophets. As pastor, you are further obligated to watch over the flock of God and protect them from false prophets and teachers (cf. Acts 20:28-29). One way you can do this is by consistently teaching the truths of God's Word. Another way is to point out specific false prophets and teachers, noting the error of their ways. Further, you can protect your members from false prophets and teachers by never allowing these "wolves in sheep's clothing" behind the pulpit of your church (Matt. 7:15).[8]

---

[5] See Chapter 24: "Caring for the Sheep."

[6] For more on the Pentecostal pastor and prayer, see Chapter 8: "The Priority of Prayer."

[7] For more on the Pentecostal pastor as teacher, see Chapter 17: "Effective Teaching." The *Living the Truth* and *Roots of Faith* curricula are excellent Pentecostal discipleship resources. They are available from Africa Theological Training Service (ATTS) at https://africaatts.org/resources/.

[8] For more on protecting the church from false prophets, see Chapter 27: "Guarding the Flock."

Part 8: The Pentecostal Pastor as Administrator

7. Opportunities for service. You should also provide new members with opportunities for service in the church. You should immediately invite them to help out in some simple way. This will help bind them to the church. It will also help them to understand from the beginning that serving God is more than just attending church events. It also involves active service.

8. Performing weddings and funerals. Finally, as their pastor, you are obliged to walk with members through the great transitioning events of life. You should provide them with marital counselling and perform wedding ceremonies for them. You should also conduct funerals and provide support and encouragement to grieving family members.[9]

MEMBERS' MEETINGS

Members' meetings are an important part of Pentecostal church life. In these meetings, members come together to discuss the business of the church. There, the pastor and other leaders share reports concerning the church's progress, challenges, and needs. Members' meetings should be conducted annually. In addition, specially called meetings can be scheduled as the need arises.

Members' meetings are an excellent time to discuss upcoming events and to share your vision with the church. These meetings also give church members an opportunity to discuss their hopes and dreams for the assembly. You will want to make the most of these meetings. You can do this by preparing well. You should always come to these meetings with a carefully prepared agenda and accurate reports.

In addition to members' meetings, you will want to meet with your leadership team (lay elders and deacons) at least once per month to discuss issues relating to the church. During these meetings, you will pray with your leadership team. Together, you can transact

---

[9] For more on conducting weddings and funerals, see Chapter 41: "Performing Weddings and Funerals."

Chapter 35: Overseeing Church Membership

church business, cast vision, and develop strategies for the growth of the church.

Further, you will want to meet often with the church's ministry leaders, such as those who lead the Sunday school department, home cell groups, men's and women's ministries, youth ministry, missions committee, church planting committee, evangelism committee, intercessory prayer groups, and others.[10]

DISCIPLINING WAYWARD MEMBERS

The time may come when it is necessary to discipline a wayward church member. Such discipline is an exercise of scriptural authority for which the church is responsible (Matt. 18:15-20; Luke 17:3; John 20:23; 1 Cor. 5:1-5; Eph. 5:11; 1 Tim. 5:19-20). As pastor of the church, you must not shrink from this responsibility. Rather, when the occasion arises, you must act with both courage and compassion, knowing that the purpose of the discipline is twofold, to purify the church (Acts 5:9-11) and to restore the offender (Gal. 6:1).

When you and the leadership of the church determine that discipline is necessary, you should follow the procedure set forth by Jesus in Matthew 18:15-20. This procedure consists of three steps. First, the pastor or a designated church leader goes to the offending member to discuss the charges and plead with them to repent. If this attempt does not resolve the matter, the member is then called to meet with the pastor and church board. If the sinning member still refuses to repent, the matter is taken before the membership of the assembly in a specially called business meeting. Only active members of the church should be allowed to attend this meeting. The decision of the church shall be final. If found guilty, the offending member will be dismissed from membership in the church (Matt. 18:17). However, in certain cases, lesser disciplinary measures may be more appropriate.

---

[10] For more insight on working with ministry leaders, see Chapter 33: "Mobilizing Lay Leaders" and Chapter 34: "Directing Church Departments."

~ PART 9 ~

THE PENTECOSTAL PASTOR IN MISSION

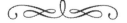

~ Chapter 36 ~

Understanding New Testament Strategy

The Bible tells the exciting story of God's ongoing mission to redeem lost humanity. It further tells how He bids all who follow Him to join Him in His mission. Every Pentecostal pastor must therefore commit himself or herself to this all-important task. We must each ask ourselves, "How can I best lead my church to do its part in fulfilling God's mission at home, across Africa, and around the world?" The answer is that we must follow the missions model established by Jesus and the apostles.

Through His life and ministry, Jesus presented the definitive model of how the Church is to fulfill God's mission. The apostles understood this, and imitated Jesus' model. As Pentecostal pastors, and heirs of Christ's mission, we must do the same. This model is sometimes called the "New Testament Strategy of the Spirit." This chapter will carefully examine this strategy. It will also make recommendations on how you, as a Pentecostal pastor in Africa, can implement the strategy into the life of your church.

Chapter 36: Understanding New Testament Strategy

THE MISSIONAL PURPOSE OF ACTS

Luke wrote the book of Acts with missional purpose. He wrote to call the church of his age—and ultimately the church in every age—back to its Pentecostal and missionary roots. By telling his readers how the Church began, and how, even in the midst of severe persecution, they triumphed in the power of the Spirit, Luke hoped to encourage them to do the same. Luke thus wrote Acts to present a missionary strategy that will work in every culture and in every age until Jesus returns.

Luke's primary purpose in writing is revealed in Acts 1:8, where Jesus tells His disciples, "But you will receive power when the Holy Spirit comes on you; and you will be my witnesses in Jerusalem, and in all Judea and Samaria, and to the ends of the earth." These words of Jesus are the key to understanding the missions model presented in Acts. They introduce a pattern that is repeated throughout the book:

> *The Empowering of the Holy Spirit*
> *— always results in —*
> *Spirit-empowered Witness.*

This pattern has been called Luke's "empowerment-witness motif." A motif is a pattern of words, concepts, or events repeated throughout a book. In Acts, this pattern is repeated over and over. Every time the Spirit is poured out, the result is Spirit-empowered witness. There are no exceptions.[1]

The promise of Acts 1:8 still applies to us today. Like those first disciples, we too can receive power when the Holy Spirit comes upon us. And like them, we can be Christ's Spirit-empowered witnesses at home and to the ends of the earth.

THE NEW TESTAMENT STRATEGY

---

[1] For more on this subject, see the Africa's Hope Discovery Series book, *Acts: The Spirit of God in Mission,* by Denzil R. Miller.

Part 9: The Pentecostal Pastor in Mission

Let's look at how Paul implemented this Acts 1:8 strategy in the Roman city of Ephesus (Acts 19:1-11). In doing this, we will discover that Paul's strategy was a carbon copy of the strategy Jesus used in mobilizing His Church. It is a strategy that we as Pentecostal pastors must use today in mobilizing our churches for evangelism, church planting, and missions.

Exemplary Ministry in Ephesus

By telling the story of Paul's ministry in Ephesus, Luke presents the fullest example of the strategy Paul used in his missionary work. It is meant to be a lasting strategy for church planting and missions. Let's look at how Paul applied this Strategy of the Spirit to plant the church, not only in Ephesus, but in all of Asia Minor.

The Ephesian Outpouring (Acts 19:1-7)

Paul arrived in Ephesus with a well-defined goal in mind. His goal is revealed in verse 10, where Luke tells us that after just two years "all the Jews and Greeks who lived in the province of Asia heard the word of the Lord." Paul's goal was to reach Ephesus and all of Asia Minor with the message of Christ. Paul also had in mind a clear strategy for achieving his goal. This strategy becomes clear through a thoughtful examination of his ministry in Ephesus found in Acts 19:1-11. With this in mind, let's look at what Paul did in Ephesus.

When Paul arrived in the city, he found twelve disciples. These men were likely leaders in the emerging church in Ephesus (Acts 18:24-27). Immediately Paul asked them, "Did you receive the Holy Spirit when you believed?" (19:2). The apostle asked this question to discover if these men were spiritually equipped to participate in the mission of reaching Ephesus and Asia with the gospel. He was applying the teaching of Jesus in Acts 1:4-8 (cf. Luke 24:49).

After a brief conversation, Paul laid his hands on the twelve disciples, and "the Holy Spirit came on them, and they spoke in tongues and prophesied" (Acts 19:6). The phrase, "the Holy Spirit came on them" reminds us of Jesus' promise in Acts 1:8, where He said, "You will receive power *when the Holy Spirit comes on you;* and you will be my witnesses" (emphasis added). This insight helps us understand what is happening in this passage. The Holy Spirit "came upon" these men just as He had come upon the disciples at Pentecost, to empower them for witness "in Jerusalem, and in all Judea and Samaria, and to the ends of the earth."

As soon as the Holy Spirit came upon and filled the Ephesian twelve, "they spoke in tongues and prophesied," thus indicating that Christ had empowered them to speak on His behalf.

The Ephesian Campaign (Acts 19:8-11)

Once these twelve men had been empowered by the Holy Spirit, Paul launched his evangelistic and church planting campaign. This campaign continued for two years and resulted in "all the Jews and Greeks who lived in the province of Asia" hearing the good news about Christ (v. 10). What an amazing accomplishment! In just two years, everyone in Asia—even those of various cultures and ethnic backgrounds—heard the gospel. In addition, many churches were planted. This number likely included the seven churches of Asia mentioned in Revelation 2-3.

Strategy of the Spirit

Luke included the story of Paul's ministry in Ephesus as his most complete example of the apostle's missionary strategy. It, in effect, sums up his missionary strategy demonstrated in his first and second missionary journeys. It is a strategy that we, as Pentecostal pastors, must employ in our own evangelistic and church planting efforts today. Let's look more closely at this Strategy of the Spirit. Paul's strategy included three key "pillars," as follows:

1. Pillar One: Empowering. The first pillar of Paul's missionary strategy was empowering. This empowering was twofold. First, it involved the empowering of *the missionary* himself. Then, it involved the empowering of *the church,* or churches, being planted. Let's look at each of these essential elements:

Part 9: The Pentecostal Pastor in Mission

Paul entered Ephesus full of the Holy Spirit. He thus ministered as a Spirit-empowered witness in accordance with Jesus' prescription in Acts 1:8. The fact that he was able to lay hands on the twelve disciples encouraging them to be filled with the Holy Spirit shows that he himself was full of the Spirit. Further, throughout Acts, Luke offers many examples of Paul's Spirit-empowered ministry (e.g., Acts 9:17-20; 13:4-5, 9-11; 14:8-10; 15:12).

Paul, however, understood that it was not enough for him alone to be full of the Spirit. He knew that, if the work was to prosper, the church in Ephesus must also be empowered by the Holy Spirit. Therefore, upon arriving in the city, Paul's first order of business was to ensure that the believers in that city had been baptized in the Holy Spirit. That is why he asked the twelve disciples, "Did you receive the Holy Spirit when you believed?" And that is why he immediately prayed with them to receive the Spirit. Thus, the two essential components of the first pillar of Paul's missionary strategy are the empowering of the missionary and the equally important empowering of the church.

Thus empowered, the church in Ephesus could become a powerful center of missionary activity, reaching into every corner of the province. These same two components, the empowerment of the pastor and the empowerment of the church, must be a part of our missions strategy today. Paul's Strategy of the Spirit is charted below:

THE NEW TESTAMENT "STRATEGY OF THE SPIRIT"

(Acts 19:1-11)

Pillar 1: Empowering: *Pillar 2: Witness:*   *Pillar 3: Mobilization:*

- Of the missionary
- Of the church

- Proclamation
- Demonstration

- Training
- Sending

Chapter 36: Understanding New Testament Strategy

. Pillar Two: Witness. The second pillar of Paul's missionary strategy was witness. This is to be expected, since bold witness is the expected result of being baptized in the Holy Spirit (Acts 1:8; 4:31). As with empowering, witness also has two components: proclamation and demonstration (see Figure 1).

First, Paul bore witness to Christ through powerful *proclamation* of the gospel. This proclamation began when the twelve "spoke in tongues *and prophesied."* Using Acts 1:8 as our interpretative key, we understand that their prophesying was in the form of Spirit-empowered proclamation of the gospel to the lost, as was Peter's prophetic proclamation on the Day of Pentecost (2:14).

Luke then tells us that Paul "entered the synagogue and spoke boldly there for three months, arguing persuasively about the kingdom of God" (Acts 19:8). In Acts, to proclaim the kingdom of God is equivalent to proclaiming the good news about Christ (8:12; 28:23, 31). In addition to proclaiming Christ in the synagogues, Paul "taught...publicly and from house to house," and he "declared to both Jews and Greeks that they must turn to God in repentance and have faith in our Lord Jesus" (20:20-21). Paul's spoken witness in Ephesus was accompanied by *demonstrations* of kingdom power through signs following (19:11-20).

Thus, like the first, this second pillar of Paul's Strategy of the Spirit had two components, the bold proclamation of the gospel and a demonstration of kingdom power through accompanying signs. No doubt, the witness of Paul's newly Spirit-filled colleagues included the same two components, proclamation and demonstration. These two components should characterize the witness of every Pentecostal church in Africa today.

3. Pillar Three: Mobilization. The third pillar of Paul's missionary Strategy of the Spirit was mobilization. Once the church had been empowered by the Spirit—and as the gospel was being preached—Paul began mobilizing the church for regional missions. This mobilization is indicated in Acts 19:10: "This went on for two years, so that all the Jews and Greeks who lived in the province of Asia heard the word of the Lord." Without leaving Ephesus, Paul was able to reach the entire province of Asia with the gospel in just two short years. This could only have been accomplished by effectively mobilizing the disciples in Ephesus.

The text indicates that Paul mobilized the Ephesian church in two ways, training and sending (see Figure 1). First, Paul *trained* workers and church planters in the school of Tyrannus (Acts 19:9). The wording of the text suggests a cause-and-effect relationship between Paul's leadership training and the fact that in only two years everyone living in Asia heard the word of the Lord. The school's curriculum likely included a strong practical emphasis on evangelism and church planting. In addition, the atmosphere of the school must have been saturated with the presence of the Spirit.

Paul's training procedure also seems to have included on-the-job mentoring. This is hinted at in Acts 19:8-9, where Paul included the newly Spirit-filled disciples in his evangelistic ministry. This mentoring relationship is further evidenced by the way that he remained in close company with the disciples in Ephesus (v. 9; 20:1, 17-18). Paul likely mentored his students in his missionary methods. He later wrote to Timothy in Ephesus, and instructed him, "The things you have heard me say in the presence of many witnesses entrust to reliable men who will also be qualified to teach others" (2 Tim. 2:2).

Once the disciples had been filled with the Spirit and trained—or more likely, while they were still being trained—Paul sent them into every corner of the province to preach the gospel and plant Spirit-empowered missionary churches. Undoubtedly, they employed the same missionary strategy as their mentor. The application of this strategy resulted in a spontaneous multiplication of churches throughout the entire region (Acts 19:10). It is also clear that Paul's strategy included reaching people from various ethnic and cultural backgrounds, for Luke says that "both Jews and Greeks" were presented the gospel.

Chapter 36: Understanding New Testament Strategy

The Example of Jesus

It is important to note that Paul's strategy for Ephesus and Asia Minor was not original with him. He was simply following the example of Jesus when He sent His church into the world.

Jesus mobilized His disciples by *training* them and *sending* them out (Mark 3:13-15). As they went, they were to *preach* the gospel and to *demonstrate* its power with signs following (Mark 16:15-18). Before they did any of this, however, they were to wait in Jerusalem to be *empowered* by the Spirit (Luke 24:49; Acts 1:4-8) just as Jesus himself had been empowered by the Spirit (Luke 4:18-19; Acts 10:38). The disciples' empowering occurred on the Day of Pentecost and on many other occasions in Acts. Paul, in his Ephesian campaign, was simply following the example of Jesus in sending His Church into the world.

LESSONS FOR TODAY

As Pentecostal pastors, we can learn some important lessons from our investigation of Paul's Spirit-empowered ministry in Ephesus. Let's look at three of those lessons:

Be Empowered by the Spirit

First, we learn that we must never presume to do the work of God in our own human strength or abilities. On the contrary, like Jesus and Paul, we must minister in the power and anointing of the Holy Spirit. According to the book of Acts model, this divine empowering comes when we are baptized in and empowered by the Spirit of God. It remains as we daily walk in the Spirit.

We further learn that, if our churches are to become centers of effective evangelism, church planting, and missions, they must have within themselves the spiritual vitality necessary to achieve that goal. Therefore, as Pentecostal pastors, our first order of business must be to see that our churches are empowered by the Holy Spirit. We can achieve this aim by ensuring that those who come to Christ are immediately led into Spirit baptism and taught how to live the Spirit-filled life. In addition, we must lead these same people into Spirit-empowered witness.[2]

Employ a Biblical Strategy

Second, we learn the necessity of employing a biblically-based, Spirit-guided strategy in doing the work of evangelism, church planting, and missions. In Ephesus, Paul was guided by such a strategy. It was a strategy based on divine precedent rather than human wisdom. Paul was simply following the strategy Jesus had used in mobilizing His Church for global missions.

Paul further aimed at scattering Spirit-empowered missional congregations throughout all of Asia Minor. Each of these congregations would have within itself the vision and spiritual potency it needed to plant other Spirit-empowered missionary churches. In this way, churches would be multiplied throughout all Asia, and the gospel would be proclaimed in power to all who lived there—both Jews and Gentiles.

Today, we as Pentecostal pastors must do the same. Certainly, we must strive to get people saved. However, we must realize that evangelism, as necessary as it is, is not in itself sufficient. We must plant and develop Spirit-empowered missionary churches—churches where new believers are filled with the Spirit, discipled in the ways of Christ, trained to effectively advance the kingdom of God, and then mobilized and sent out to do the same in places near and far.

Move with Intentionality

Finally, in all we do, we must move with deliberate intentionality. Too much church activity is done without clear purpose. Too much is assumed. We cannot assume that people will come to our church simply because we open the doors each Sunday. We cannot assume

---

[2] For more on encouraging the church to seek the Spirit, see Chapter 19: "Leading a Church into Pentecostal Revival." For more on leading believers into the empowering of the Spirit, see Chapter 20: "Guiding Believers into Spirit Baptism."

that people are being born again just because we are leading them in the "sinner's prayer." We cannot assume that believers are being truly empowered by the Spirit simply because they exhibit some outward physical manifestation. We cannot assume that the church we are pastoring is Spirit-empowered just because it belongs to a Pentecostal or charismatic fellowship of churches. We cannot assume that our church will develop a missionary vision and zeal simply because its denomination believes in these things. On the contrary, we must have a clear idea of what we want to accomplish, and we must know how we will go about accomplishing our aim.

Intentionality must mark every decision and every move we make. We must personally seek God's face with the intention of being genuinely filled (or refilled) with the Holy Spirit. We must preach the gospel with the intention of seeing the lost repent and be truly born again. We must pray with believers with the intention that they be truly empowered by the Spirit of God. We must plant churches with the studied intention that they become Spirit-empowered missionary churches.

And all along, we must intentionally pass on our vision and strategy to the leaders whom God raises up in the church. We must then mobilize the church with the focused intention of reaching our city, country, region, and the nations with the gospel. This is what Jesus did, and it was how Paul reached all of Asia with the gospel in the space of only two years. This is what we must do today.

~ Chapter 37 ~

Evangelizing the Lost

How important is it to lead just one person to Christ? Of course, for that one person it is eternally important. However, this one act of Christian love could be eternally important to many others too, as the following story illustrates.

Edward Kimball was a simple store clerk in Detroit, Michigan, USA. He was also a Sunday school teacher at his church. In 1854, Kimball met a seventeen-year-old boy named Dwight and led him to Christ. The boy grew up to be the renowned evangelist D. L. Moody. Moody would become one of history's greatest soul winners. Moody further influenced F. B. Meyer to enter evangelistic and missions work, who in turn influenced J. Wilbur Chapman, who then mentored Billy Sunday as an evangelist. Anyone who has studied modern church history knows that all of these men were powerful evangelists. Together, they won millions to Christ. But the story does not end there.

A country preacher named Mordecai Ham was inspired by the ministry of Billy Sunday. Then, in 1934, Ham preached the message that moved Billy Graham to surrender his life to Christ. Billy Graham has likely preached the gospel to more people than any other person in history. Think of it, all of this resulted from a simple Sunday school teacher winning a street boy to Christ. The story of Edward Kimball demonstrates how important it is for the Pentecostal pastor to lead his or her church into effective evangelistic outreach. This chapter will discuss how they can best do this.

DEFINITIONS

As a Pentecostal pastor, you must have a clear understanding of what evangelism is and how it relates to church planting and missions. While all three activities flow from Christ's Great Commission (Matt. 28:18-20; Mark 16:15-16), there are some important differences.

Evangelism

Evangelism is the purposeful sharing of the gospel with the lost with the intention of winning them to Christ. It involves telling people about Jesus and His saving work on the cross, and calling them to faith in Him (Acts 16:31). At the heart of evangelism is the story of Jesus' death and resurrection (1 Cor. 15:1-4). Evangelism is more than a program in the church, it is the Church's reason for being. And it is the solemn responsibility of every Christian.

Church planting

While church planting includes evangelism, it involves much more. Church planting involves organizing those who have been saved into bodies of believers. These believers regularly gather for fellowship, prayer, and Bible study. Leaders are chosen who will disciple these believers, forming them into the image of Christ. New believers are taught how to leave behind their old sinful lives, live according to God's Word, and tell others about Jesus.

Missions

Missions often includes both evangelism and church planting. However, there are some significant differences. Missions involves

Part 9: The Pentecostal Pastor in Mission

winning the lost to Christ and planting churches across cultures. It requires that missionaries leave their homes, go to new places, learn new languages, and adapt themselves to life in their new environment. In that "foreign" context, they win the lost to Jesus and start new churches.

Paul is an example of a missionary. He crossed borders and cultures to proclaim Christ to the lost. As he did, he established churches and monitored their progress. To ensure that the churches prospered, Paul appointed elders and pastors to lead these congregations. Part of the pastors' responsibilities was to lead their churches to evangelize the lost and send out missionaries themselves. This would ensure that the work of evangelism, church planting, and missions continued (cf. 1 Thess. 1:8).

PASTORAL RESPONSIBILITY

Paul wrote to Timothy, his son in the faith and pastor of the church in Ephesus, telling him to "do the work of an evangelist" (2 Tim. 4:5). The work of an evangelist is to win the lost to Christ and to train others to do the same (Eph. 4:11-12). As a Pentecostal pastor, you too bear this responsibility. You must develop a plan to mobilize your church for effective evangelism. This mobilization plan should include three strategies: motivating, training, and deploying, as follows:

Motivating

As a Pentecostal pastor, your first job in mobilizing your church for evangelism is to instill in the hearts of God's people a passion for the lost. One way you can do this is by teaching them what the Bible says about the lostness of humanity. Apart from a saving relationship with Jesus Christ, all people are hopelessly and eternally lost. Their only hope in this life, and in the life to come, is knowing Christ. You must impress these awesome truths on the hearts and minds of your people. You must further remind them of their obligation to share the gospel with lost people.

To accomplish this, you will need to rely on God's missionary Spirit. You must ensure that church members have been filled with the Holy Spirit and empowered as Christ's witnesses (Acts 1:8). You must further ensure that the presence and power of the Spirit is manifested in church services. If given the opportunity, the Holy Spirit will move in the people's hearts, molding them and pointing them to the harvest.

Training

Another strategy you can use to mobilize your church for evangelism is training. This is what Jesus did. He instructed His disciples, "Come, follow me…and I will send you out to fish for people" (Mark 1:17). As Jesus' disciples followed their Master, listened to His teaching, and imitated His methods, they became powerful proclaimers of the gospel.

The same dynamic must occur in our Pentecostal churches today. We must teach our members how to evangelize the lost as did Jesus and the apostles. In doing this, we must teach them how to walk in the Spirit and discern the Spirit's voice as He directs them in witness (cf. Acts 8:29). As Pentecostal pastors, we must further teach our people how to yield to the Spirit's anointing, trusting Him to speak through them as they tell others about Christ.

In addition, we must ensure that the saints understand the gospel, and that they are able to clearly communicate it to others. They must further understand how to lead people to Jesus, calling them to repentance and faith. One way we can accomplish this is to conduct annual workshops on Spirit-empowered evangelism.

Deploying

Once God's people have been motivated and trained, they must be deployed. This is what Jesus did. As part of His training program, He sent His disciples out to preach the gospel. They then reported back to Him for His evaluation (cf. Luke 9:6; 10:1-20). Later, as His ministry on earth was about to end, He permanently deployed His disciples for witness "in Jerusalem, and in all Judea and Samaria, and

Part 9: The Pentecostal Pastor in Mission

to the ends of the earth" (Acts 1:8). As a Pentecostal pastor, you should do the same. You should model a life of evangelism before your people. You should then train them and deploy them in ministry.

EVANGELISTIC METHODS

As a faithful Pentecostal pastor, you must not be so foolish as to sit idle, hoping that the people in the community will come to your church. Nor should you assume that your members will suddenly become witnesses to their friends and neighbors. As pastor, you must set the example and lead the people into the harvest. You must further develop strategies and implement programs to mobilize the church for effective evangelism.

You can do this by employing diverse evangelistic methods. The choice of method will depend on the community context, the target audience, and the leadership of the Holy Spirit. Here are a few evangelistic methods you can use:

Regular Church Services

Evangelism must be at the heart of the church's regular Sunday services. You must at all times remain mindful of the lost people in your congregation. And you must faithfully proclaim the gospel to them. Like Paul, you must be determined to preach only "Christ and him crucified" (1 Cor. 2:1-2). How sad it is for a member to bring a lost friend to a church where the gospel is not preached. Every message you preach should include an explanation of the plan of salvation and an invitation to come to Christ.

Personal Evangelism

In addition to proclaiming the gospel in regular church services, you must ensure that your church members know how to share the gospel with those outside the church. This kind of evangelism is called personal evangelism. As pastor of the church, you will want to encourage the following kinds of personal evangelism.

Door-to-door evangelism. In a door-to-door witnessing campaign, church members are trained and then sent out to go from house to house, introducing themselves to the people and making them aware of the church's concern for them. They should offer to pray for their needs, and they should be ready to share the gospel with those who show an interest.

Friendship evangelism. You should also equip and encourage church members to pray for the salvation of their friends. They should ask God to open their friends' hearts and provide an opportunity for them to share the gospel with them. The church may want to schedule an annual "Friend Day" when members are encouraged to invite their friends to church. On that day, all the friends who attend will be honored. You will then preach an evangelistic message and give them an opportunity to receive Christ as Savior.

Lifestyle evangelism. You will also want to teach the people that, in reality, evangelism is not so much an event or program as it is a lifestyle. You will want to encourage them to witness with their lives and personal testimonies. They should remain open to opportunities to share the gospel with others amid the day-to-day events of life.

Evangelistic Campaigns

Evangelistic campaigns (sometimes called revival meetings) are another excellent way to lead people to Christ. An evangelistic campaign may proceed as follows: You and your church leaders schedule the campaign, and at the proper time, begin announcing it to the church and community. As the event approaches, the church begins to bathe the event in prayer. Members are encouraged to invite their family, friends, and neighbors to the meetings. As pastor, you must ensure that the one you invite to minister has a passion for the lost and a reputation for preaching the gospel. You must further ensure that the preacher faithfully proclaims the gospel in each service and gives people an opportunity to be saved.

Open-Air Services

You will also want to take the evangelistic campaign to the streets. You will want to organize and send out evangelistic teams to the markets or other places where large numbers of people gather.

There, they will conduct brief but powerful open-air services. These services should include singing to attract a crowd, personal testimonies of God's grace, and a brief gospel message followed by an invitation to receive Christ.

Literature Distribution

Another proven way to spread the gospel is through literature distribution. You can plan a day to send workers into a strategic location to distribute gospel literature. The literature you hand out should be carefully chosen. It must be attractive and well written, and it must clearly present the plan of salvation. It should also contain contact information, including the church's name, location, and phone number, as well as the church's website and e-mail addresses.

Prayer Walks

Prayer walks can be used to open up new areas for gospel witness. They can also be useful in creating a burden in the hearts of believers for reaching the area for Christ. The church can organize teams to walk, two-by-two, into selected neighborhoods. As they do, they will ask the Holy Spirit to move on the residents, opening their hearts to receive the gospel. They may also want to do spiritual warfare, challenging and binding demons that are holding people in spiritual and physical bondage.

As the teams walk through the neighborhoods praying, they should remain open to opportunities to pray with people and present the gospel to them. Prayer walks are an excellent way to prepare the soil for a new church plant.

Media Outreach

If your church is financially able, you may want to consider using mass media to spread the gospel. Mass media opportunities include radio and television broadcasts. The Internet and social media can also be used creatively to spread the gospel. In planning such an outreach, you should keep in mind that, if the programs are not of the highest quality, they could turn people away rather than attract them to the church.

Chapter 37: Evangelizing the Lost

Church Planting

Research has shown that church planting is, by far, the most effective method of evangelism. More people come to Christ in new churches than in old established ones. Through church planting, the church not only grows numerically, it spreads geographically.[1]

Other Creative Approaches

You will want to be open to other creative methods of evangelism. More importantly, as a Pentecostal pastor, you must at all times remain open to the direction of the Holy Spirit in creating and planning new outreach programs.

EVANGELISTIC OPPORTUNITES

Paul exhorted the Christians in Ephesus to "[make] the most of every opportunity" (Eph. 5:16). As circumstances change, new evangelistic opportunities will present themselves. As a Pentecostal pastor, you must therefore be led by the Holy Spirit and ready to respond to needs as they arise. Take for example these four typical opportunities:

Responding to Crises

Societal upheavals, such as wars, famines, epidemics, droughts, cyclones, insect infestations, and other natural disasters, offer enormous opportunities for the church to share the good news of Christ. During these times of crisis, people are looking for answers. As a result, their hearts are more open to the Lord. The Christian message of love offers hope to the wounded and afflicted in such contexts. At such times, you and your church should be prepared to reach out in love and compassion. You should look for ways to serve those in need. As you do, you should make the most of opportunities to share the gospel.

---

[1] Church planting is discussed in more detail in Chapter 39: "Planting New Churches."

Reaching the Muslim Community

The Muslim community is growing and spreading across Africa. Radical Islam is on the rampage, and it is ravaging certain parts of the continent. As a result, many Muslims are disappointed with their religion. Your church must develop credible missions strategies for evangelizing these disillusioned Muslims.

Using Relationship Networks

Relationship networks, such as family members, friends, neighbors, and coworkers, can serve as natural bridges for evangelistic outreach. This is particularly true in the rural settings of Africa. There, people live in close community and share many things in common. In such contexts, the conversion of one opinion leader in the community can lead to the conversion of others in his or her circle of relationships. Evangelism through relationship networks holds enormous potential for success in Africa.

Strategic Partnerships

Formation of strategic partnerships with like-minded churches and organizations can be another effective way of evangelizing the lost. This is especially true in carrying out a mutually-agreed-upon missions effort. Your church could partner with other churches and parachurch organizations to implement specialized programs aimed at reaching certain neglected segments of society, such as orphans, street children, or victims of natural disasters.

ESSENTIAL ELEMENTS

While there can be many approaches to evangelistic outreach, for the Pentecostal pastor, three basic elements must always be present: proclamation of the gospel, the power of the Holy Spirit, and earnest prayer.

Proclamation of the Gospel

To evangelize the lost, the gospel must be preached (Mark 16:15; 1 Cor. 9:16). Paul declared, "Everyone who calls upon the name of the Lord will be saved" (Rom. 10:13). He then asked a series of pointed questions: "How, then, can they call on the one they have not believed in? And how can they believe in the one of whom they have not heard? And how can they hear without someone preaching to them?" (v. 14). There is no salvation without hearing and believing the gospel. As a Pentecostal pastor, you should therefore be ready at all times to share the good news with the lost (Rom. 1:15-16). And you should equip your members to do the same.

The Power of the Holy Spirit

No evangelistic venture should be undertaken without the power of the Holy Spirit. Jesus commanded His disciples, "Go and make disciples of all nations" (Matt. 28:19). But first, they were to "stay in the city until [they had] been clothed with power from on high" (Luke 24:49; cf. Acts 1:4-8). This biblical pattern continues until today—first empowering, then proclamation.

The New Testament pattern of evangelism further involves anointed preaching accompanied by confirmatory signs and wonders (Matt. 10:7-8; Mark 16:17). Not only must the gospel be proclaimed, its power must be demonstrated. This is especially true in Africa. Most Africans come from a background of idolatry, witchcraft, and occultism. They look for a religion that promises power over the forces of darkness.

As a wise Pentecostal pastor, you must therefore emphasize the baptism in the Holy Spirit, power ministry, and the manifestation of spiritual gifts in evangelistic outreach. However, you must take care to ensure that the gospel message is not compromised in a quest for spectacular miracles.

Earnest Prayer

Finally, every evangelistic activity of the church should be bathed in earnest prayer. Such prayer is a key to evangelistic success. Every other evangelistic activity flows from this one. In prayer we call on God to empower the saints, direct their steps, anoint their preaching, perform signs and wonders, and to open the hearts of those who will hear the gospel proclaimed (cf. Acts 4:29-30).

Evangelism is at the heart of the Church's reason for being. No church can truly call itself Pentecostal while failing to reach out to the lost in the power of the Holy Spirit. Thus, as a true Pentecostal pastor, you must boldly lead your church in reaching the lost for Christ.

~ Chapter 38 ~

Serving the Community

The pastor of a small Pentecostal church in East Africa was moved by the Holy Spirit to start a primary school in his church's classroom block. He testified, "We just wanted to help the neighborhood kids with a better education. We wanted to do our part to eradicate illiteracy and ignorance in our community." Although he had no money, and no experience in running a school, the pastor believed God had spoken to him. So, in faith, he moved forward with his plan.

Realizing the school needed cabinets to store teaching supplies, the pastor removed the cupboards from his own house and moved them to the school. He sold other personal possessions to purchase desks, books, and building supplies. He then went to work implementing his vision. Because the school could not afford to pay a security guard, he volunteered to serve in that position himself. All along, he trusted God to sustain and guide him. Little by little, the school prospered and grew.

As people in the community watched the pastor, they were moved by his vision and genuine concern for their wellbeing. As a result, they began donating money to help the school. In time, God made a way for the church to build more classrooms. These new classrooms were built according to the government's standards for schools. More recently, the school has acquired additional land on which to further develop the school. The pastor announced, "We are planning to build more classrooms and a children's playground. We are not yet where God wants us to be, but God is faithful, and He is helping us move forward. Our school is now among the best schools in the area."

In all they did, the pastor and staff of the school remained true to Christ's mandate to share the gospel with the lost. Because of this, many of the students have become Christians. In addition, the goodwill generated by the school opened the hearts of several parents who gave their lives to Jesus. God has further used the school to open the door of witness to the surrounding Muslim community.

This is but one example of the many ways you, as a Pentecostal pastor, can lead your church into caring for your community. This chapter will examine this subject. It will lay a biblical basis for holistic ministry. Holistic ministry is Christian ministry that reaches out to serve the whole person, spirit, soul, and body. The chapter will also offer practical suggestions on how your church can get involved in community care.

THE BIBLICAL MANDATE

In missions discussions, the question is sometimes asked, "Which is more important, preaching the gospel to the lost or caring for the needy?" The answer is, while nothing is more important than leading sinners to Christ, the church must be involved in both evangelistic outreach and community care. Both are expressions of the coming of God's kingdom. While the Pentecostal church in Africa has excelled in leading people to Christ and planting new churches, it has been less effective in caring for the hurting.

As a true Pentecostal pastor, you must avoid two pitfalls. First, you must avoid preaching the gospel while ignoring the physical suffering of those around you. At the same time, you must avoid caring for people's physical needs without sharing the gospel with them.

Part 9: The Pentecostal Pastor in Mission

Someone rightly noted, "We have not fully preached the gospel until we have demonstrated the love of Christ, and we have not fully demonstrated the love of Christ until we have preached the gospel." Let's look more closely at what the Bible says about this vital topic.

Following Jesus' Example

Jesus is our model for ministry. He ministered to the whole person, spirit, soul, and body. As Jesus was about to begin His ministry, He stated its purpose. "The Spirit of the Lord is on me," He said, "because he has anointed me to proclaim good news to the poor. He has sent me to proclaim freedom for the prisoners and recovery of sight for the blind, to set the oppressed free, to proclaim the year of the Lord's favor" (Luke 4:18-19). Thus, Jesus' ministry was marked by proclaiming the good news and caring for the needs of people.

The church in the book of Acts followed the pattern established by Jesus. They preached the gospel, healed the sick, cast out demons, and cared for the needy. One example of their caring for the needy is the concern they showed for the Grecian widows in Jerusalem (Acts 6:1). Another example is the response of the church in Antioch to the famished saints in Jerusalem. Upon hearing a prophetic exhortation from Agabus, "the disciples, as each one was able, decided to provide help for the brothers and sisters living in Judea. This they did, sending their gift to the elders by Barnabas and Saul" (Acts 11:29-30).

Two Great Mandates

Jesus left His Church with two great mandates. One is called the Great Commission (Matt. 28:18-20); the other is called the Great Commandment (Matt. 22:34-40). As a faithful Pentecostal pastor, you must lead your church to obey both. In the Great Commission, Jesus has commanded us to "go and make disciples of all nations." In the Great Commandment, He has commanded us to love God supremely and to love our neighbors as ourselves. In the Parable of the Good Samaritan, Jesus taught that our neighbor can be anyone we encounter who needs our help—irrespective of tribe or religion. The

Good Samaritan proved to be a good neighbor by stopping and helping the wounded man. Jesus commands us, "Go and do likewise" (Luke 10:37).

Other Biblical Insights

In several other places, the Bible tells us to care for those in need. For instance, James writes, "Religion that God our Father accepts as pure and faultless is this: to look after orphans and widows in their distress and to keep oneself from being polluted by the world" (James 1:27). Jesus taught that by ministering to those in need (i.e., the hungry, the thirsty, the naked, the sick, the homeless, and the prisoner), we are ministering to Christ (Matt. 25:31-40). By failing to care for them, we are neglecting Christ (vv. 41-46). As you minister to people's physical needs, you must never forget that each one has an eternal soul that will live forever in either heaven or hell. You must not fail to share the gospel with them and give them an opportunity to be saved.

THE VALUE OF SERVING THE COMMUNITY

There are many values to the Pentecostal church serving the community. Let's look at two:

It Pleases God

God is pleased when His children serve their communities and reach out in compassion to those around them. When we do this, we are exhibiting the loving nature of God, and we are following the example of Jesus, who often healed all who came to Him (Matt. 8:16). In His Sermon on the Mount, Jesus said, "You have heard that it was said, 'Love your neighbor and hate your enemy.' But I tell you, love your enemies and pray for those who persecute you, that you may be children of your Father in heaven. He causes his sun to rise on the evil and the good, and sends rain on the righteous and the unrighteous" (Matt. 5:43-45). Jesus is saying that we should love and seek to bless everyone—even our enemies. If we will do this, we will be like our Heavenly Father, and our actions will please God.

It Opens Doors

Not only does community care please God, it builds goodwill between the church and the community. When God's people act kindly toward others, people take notice, and they begin to look with favor on the church. Jesus once healed a deaf and dumb man. When the people heard about this act of compassion, they exclaimed, "He has done everything well....He even makes the deaf hear and the mute speak" (Mark 7:37). When the people saw that Jesus cared for them, their hearts turned to Him. As your church begins to serve and bless its community, the people will say, "Those are good people." As outsiders begin to look at your church with favor, doors will be opened for evangelism.

IDENTIFYING THE NEEDS

Community service begins by identifying a need, and then moving to meet that need. Here are a few ways your church can serve its community:

Christian Schools

Christian schools are a proven way for the church to serve the community and to advance the gospel. Many Pentecostal churches across Africa are blessing their communities by operating schools. Some have established them to address the need of primary education in a neglected area. Others have started schools to provide a Christian alternative to the prevailing secular or Islamic model of education. Schools are especially effective in areas where people are resistant to the gospel. A church that cannot see its way to start a school could begin by enlisting capable church members to provide free tutoring to students who need help with their studies.

Community Service Projects

Some Pentecostal churches are blessing their communities through service projects. They see a need in the community and then organize themselves to address that need. For instance, a church might volunteer to give a local clinic a new coat of paint. Or they may want to repair the broken glass panes in the local primary school. Or they may want to repair a leaky roof on a widow's house. In one church, the men organized a group they called Saturday Samaritans. Every Saturday, church members went out to help widows and other needy people with various tasks. There are hundreds of ways a church can serve their community with such service projects.

Healthcare

Many communities across Africa lack adequate healthcare. To address this need, a church may want to build a clinic for the community. It can then use its influence to procure healthcare workers to staff the clinic. On a more basic level, you could encourage your members to be caring people. They could survey their neighborhoods looking for people with physical needs. They could then offer them healing prayer, comfort, and financial support.

Clean Water

Depending on its size and financial strength, your church may want to provide clean water to your community by sponsoring a water well. Or you may want to repair or rehabilitate an old nonfunctioning well.

Feeding and Childcare

Child malnutrition is a great challenge in many parts of Africa. It affects the physical and mental growth of millions of children and young people, and its effects last a lifetime. Some Pentecostal churches have instituted feeding programs, where children come once a day for a meal. Others have started affordable childcare programs. These programs allow parents to go to work knowing that their children are properly cared for. Such feeding and childcare programs offer the church an opportunity to share the gospel with both the children and the parents. They also afford the church an opportunity to teach the children godly values.

Part 9: The Pentecostal Pastor in Mission

Scholarship Programs

Many children and young people in Africa are intelligent and highly motivated; however, their parents are unable to pay their school fees. Your church may want to address this need by creating a scholarship program to sponsor deserving students by paying their school fees. This will enable them to pursue their dreams and to acquire the skills they need to develop themselves and the community at large.

Youth Development

Africa's young people represent the future of the continent. Sadly, however, many of them are drifting into drug use and other destructive behaviors. Your church could address this need by putting in place youth programs to provide positive activities for young people. These programs could include choirs, sports teams, and other wholesome activities. Workers can use these activities as a platform to teach principles of godly manhood and womanhood. These programs will also provide the workers with an opportunity to present the gospel to young people and lead them to Christ.

Adult Education

Many adults across Africa have missed the opportunity for a proper primary or secondary education. Your church could address this need by establishing adult education programs. These programs could include the following:

Literacy training. The church could start an ongoing class that teaches adults how to read and write. Learning these skills will increase their self-esteem and will help them to get better jobs. This will, in turn, enhance the life of the entire community. It will also prepare them to read the Bible and other Christian literature that the church may want to provide for them. The church may also want to start a class to help adults learn a second language such as English, French, or Portuguese.

Marriage enrichment. Many marriages across Africa are of poor quality, and the divorce rate is on the rise. Married couples need to know the biblical principles of marriage. This is true both inside and outside the church. To address this need, you may want to organize a marriage enrichment class or seminar and open it to the public. Your members could then invite their unsaved friends to join the class. This will help them discover God's purpose for their lives and for their marriages. During the class, the gospel should be presented, and couples should be given an opportunity to receive Christ as their Savior.

Entrepreneurial business principles. If feasible, your church may want to start a class to teach adult students how to start and build their own businesses. The class could also teach biblical principles of business and stewardship, including the importance of a strong work ethic.

Best farming practices. In rural settings, the church may want to start a class or conduct an annual seminar on best farming practices. An expert in the field of farming could be recruited to teach the seminar.

Other Initiatives

These are just a few of the ways your church can serve its community. The Holy Spirit may lead you to start other programs and service projects not mentioned here.

MOBILIZING THE CHURCH

You may be asking, "How can I, as a Pentecostal pastor, go about putting these community initiatives into action?" As God's chosen leader of the church, you will need to take the lead. You must initiate the vision, develop the plan, and oversee the implementation of the plan. To develop an effective plan of action, consider the following:

See the Need

Jesus first saw the need. He saw the suffering people around Him and "had compassion on them, because they were harassed and helpless, like sheep without a shepherd" (Matt. 9:36). He then implemented a plan. He urged His disciples, "Ask the Lord of the

Harvest, therefore, to send out workers into his harvest field" (v. 38). On another occasion, Jesus told them, "Open your eyes and look at the fields! They are ripe for harvest" (John 4:35).

Remember, before you will ever be able to implement your plan for community engagement, like Jesus, you must first see the need. Once you do, you can help your church members to do the same.

Determine God's Will

Once you have seen the many needs in your community, you must then ask God, "Which of these needs do you want our church to address?" If you will open your heart to the Holy Spirit, He will direct you. He will place a growing burden on your heart and show you which needs He wants your church to meet.

Keep it Simple

As you begin to develop a plan of action for your new program, it is important that you keep things simple—at least at the beginning. Normally, you will want to begin with a small, manageable project. As church members see the success of this small project, they will be inspired to take on more ambitious projects.

Take Action

When the Spirit indicates that the time is right, you should immediately take action and initiate the program, trusting God to lead you step by step.

Keep it Spiritual

As you lead the church to care for people's physical needs, you must ensure that you do not neglect their spiritual needs. Christ must remain at the center of every program and activity. You and your workers must pray often, ensuring that you remain full of the Holy Spirit.

Encourage Church-wide Participation

You should not attempt to do the work alone. You should, rather, mobilize your church members to participate. Everyone can get involved in some way. As pastor, you must encourage the people to give generously to the initiative, and you must inspire them to volunteer their time and energy. As a wise Pentecostal pastor, you must identify members' God-given gifts, and then encourage them to use their gifts to bless God's work.

Trust God for Provision

Finally, you must trust God to meet your needs. You must not wait until everything is in place before you move into action. If you do this, you may never begin. As did the pastor at the beginning of this chapter, you must do what you can with what you have, and then trust God to do the rest. If you will remain obedient to God, and faithful to the vision He has given you, He will meet all your needs (Phi. 4:19).

~ Chapter 39 ~

Planting New Churches

Charles was a ministerial student in a Bible school in East Africa. One day, he said to his teacher, "Before I die, I want to plant one hundred churches among my tribe." This burden for church planting was birthed in his heart as he traveled with the missions team from the Bible school. The team had planted several new churches in remote areas and among unreached people groups. During the trips, Charles learned some practical methods for planting new churches.

When the Assemblies of God first came to his country, they began their work among his people. However, many years later there were still only a few churches among them. He graduated from Bible school sixteen years ago. Today, Charles has personally planted more than thirty churches. Through his influence as a denominational leader, he has indirectly planted about fifty more, for a total of about eighty new churches. Now, Charles has revised his goal. He avows, "I intend to plant 200 new churches in the next ten years!"

Just as healthy mothers have babies, healthy churches plant other churches. Every church should be a church planting church. This chapter will look at the scriptural priority of church planting, church planting models, the church as an apostolic community, Spirit-empowered missionary churches, indigenous church principles, and practical ways for a Pentecostal pastor to plant churches.

SCRIPTURAL PRIORITY

Jesus said, "I will build my church" (Matt. 16:18). He also commanded, "Go and make disciples of all nations" (28:19). Someone has said, "Jesus never commanded us to plant churches; He commanded us to make disciples." However, notice how the above statements of Jesus relate to one another. How can one make disciples without planting a church, and how can one plant a real church without making disciples? Reaching the lost without grounding them in a church is like having a baby and leaving her in the bush. Church planting is essential to the permanence of the work and the development of believers.

The apostles, ministers, and church workers in the New Testament were serious about establishing churches. Peter, John, Philip, men from Cyprus and Cyrene, Barnabas, Paul, John Mark, Silas, Luke, Timothy, Priscilla, Aquila, Gaius, Aristarchus, Erastus, and Titus, among others, were all involved in planting churches. These men and women were following Christ's command to make disciples, and in doing this, they planted churches. As Pentecostal pastors, we must do the same.

CHURCH PLANTING MODELS

A young pastor once spoke to his district leader about planting a church in a certain town. The leader replied, "God has not told me to plant a church there, but if you want to do it, go ahead. If it succeeds, we will know it was God's will. If it fails, we will know it was not." Feeling the Spirit leading him, the young man went to that place and planted his first church. Since that time, he has planted more than twenty churches.

Across Africa, many men and women, sensing a call from God to plant a church, have done the same. They have successfully planted churches on their own, without much external support. This could be called the "sink or swim" method. It is like a father teaching his son to swim by throwing him into a deep pond with no previous instruction or training. While many churches have been started this way, it is not the best way. The church planter attests to this fact. "I definitely learned a lot from that first church plant," he testifies. "One thing I learned is that I never want to plant another church without a team of committed coworkers."

A supportive team model of church planting has many advantages. Imagine instead of sending out a team of two people to plant a new church, you send out ten or more. The team might consist of the new pastor and spouse, worship leaders, an older couple to provide maturity, and people to work with children and youth. Such a group would provide emotional and financial support to the church planters. The supportive team approach to church planting can help the church reach maturity more rapidly. It will more quickly become a church that itself plants other churches.

The team model of church planting can come in different forms. A mother church can give birth to a daughter church by sending an associate pastor and some of its people to a nearby community. It can then offer care and advice to the new church until it becomes established. Paul and his apostolic band of missionaries are an excellent example of a supportive team that traveled to unreached peoples and planted churches where Christ was not known.

Some have developed systems to support church planters for a year or two as they work to plant a new church. After that, their support is diminished and eventually discontinued as new believers are developed into committed disciples who will tithe to sustain the work. Church planting models include the following:

- *Parenting:* A mother church plants a daughter church as described above.
- *Pioneering:* Pioneer church planters are sent into new areas to plant churches.

- *Hiving off:* A group attending a church from a remote or culturally diverse area requests permission from the church to "hive off" and begin a new church.
- *Cell groups:* Cell groups meeting in another part of a city develop into churches.
- *Cooperating churches:* Sections, districts, or national churches cooperate to plant churches.
- *Bible school.* Bible schools mobilize students to plant new churches.
- *Other:* Other creative ways can be developed to plant churches.

Whatever model one uses, church planting is not easy. It takes commitment from the new pastor, his family, and his team to establish the new work. The enemy does not like new churches to be started because they encroach on his territory (Matt. 12:29). He will fight to oppose the church plant (Eph. 6:12). The Pentecostal church planter, however, has a Greater One living within to help him or her win the victory (1 John 4:4).

Like every other Pentecostal pastor, you must pray and plan how you can lead your church to plant new churches, whether close by, in an unreached area of your own country, or in in other countries across Africa and around the world.

APOSTOLIC COMMUNITY

A healthy church is a giving church. A healthy church is a theologically sound church. A healthy church is a missions-focused church. A healthy church is a witnessing church. A healthy church gives birth to other healthy churches. But how does one church give birth to another? How can you, as a Pentecostal pastor, go about planting another church?

The church at Antioch is an outstanding example of a healthy, missions-focused church. The church was founded by Jewish lay people from Jerusalem, Cyprus, and Cyrene who boldly shared their faith with others, including people of other cultures (Acts 11:19-20). They were a Spirit-empowered church (v. 21). They had good leadership (vv. 22-26). They were a giving church (vv. 27-30), and they prayed, fasted, and worshipped God (13:2).

Thus, when the Holy Spirit said to them, "Set apart for me Barnabas and Saul for the [missions] work to which I have called them," they did just that (Acts 13:1-2). They freely gave their best people to leave their church and go do what God was calling them to do. They sent out Barnabas and Saul as missionary church planters (vv. 3-4).

As a Pentecostal pastor, God wants to use you "to equip his people for works of service" (Eph. 4:12). He wants to use you to plant churches nearby, across your country, and around the world. God has given you the means and opportunity to create in your church a culture of missions and church planting. You can do this by teaching and modeling missional prayer, worship, leadership, giving, evangelism, and teamwork. In such an atmosphere, God will call and empower His people to go out and preach the gospel and plant new churches.

You must stretch your people to give generously to God's work, and you must allow God to do the same with you. God may ask you to give your best church members to become church planters. One of the greatest gifts you can give to God is to raise up people in their God-given gifts and then release them into ministry. Barnabas helped to raise up Paul (Acts 9:26-27; 11:25). He then released him to pursue his own ministry and develop his own missionary team (15:36-41).

As a Pentecostal pastor, the apostolic community you develop in your church will work like a magnet. An apostolic community is a group of people focused on fulfilling the Great Commission at home and around the world. When people see the Spirit of God moving in your church, they will want to be a part of what He is doing.

In Acts 6, a dispute arose concerning feeding some neglected widows. The apostles resolved the conflict by appointing seven Spirit-filled men to take care of them. This action pleased the people both inside and outside the church. As a result, "the word of God spread, [and] the number of disciples in Jerusalem increased rapidly, and a large number of priests became obedient to the faith" (v. 7).

When you develop your church into a loving apostolic community, people will be drawn to Christ and His mission. Church growth and church planting will naturally flow from such an atmosphere.

SPIRIT-EMPOWERED MISSIONARY CHURCHES

Acts tells the encouraging story of the empowering of the church in Jerusalem. When the Holy Spirit came upon and filled the 120 disciples, the crowd saw something miraculous. The disciples began to speak in tongues as the Spirit enabled them (2:1-4). It was a fulfillment of Jesus' promise in Acts 1:8. Amazed, the crowds drew near to the disciples. This gave Peter a perfect opportunity to proclaim the good news in the power of the Holy Spirit, resulting in 3,000 people coming to the Lord.

God often uses signs and wonders to stir up interest in hearing the message of the gospel. It is noteworthy that in the gospels and Acts, more miracles happened outside the place of worship than inside. In Acts, a miracle often set the stage for the proclamation of the gospel. This happened in Jerusalem with Peter (Acts 2), in Cyprus with Paul and Barnabas (13:4-12), in Ephesus with Paul and Silas (16:11-40), and on many other occasions (9:32-35; 9:36-43; 10:1-11:18; 14:1-7; 14:8-20; 19:1-20:1).

God wants those outside the church to see His miracle-working power and love, and turn to follow Him. Never waste a miracle. Any time God performs a miracle, use it as an opportunity to tell people about Jesus.

Jesus said to His disciples, "As the Father has sent me, I am sending you" (John 20:21). But how did the Father send Jesus? He sent His Son to minister in the Spirit's power. As Jesus began His ministry, He announced, "The Spirit of the Lord is on me, because he has anointed me to proclaim good news to the poor. He has sent me to proclaim freedom for the prisoners and recovery of sight for the blind, to set the oppressed free, to proclaim the year of the Lord's favor" (Luke 4:18-19). Jesus ministered in the Spirit's power (Acts 10:38), and He sent His disciples to do the same (Luke 24:46-49; Acts 1:8).

Part 9: The Pentecostal Pastor in Mission

As a Pentecostal pastor, you must be empowered by the Holy Spirit, and you must purposefully develop your church into a Spirit-empowered missionary body. In addition, you should intentionally plant Spirit-empowered missionary churches. A Spirit-empowered missionary church is the kind of church Jesus planted. It is the kind of church we read about in the book of Acts.

Jesus described the essence of this church in Acts 1:8, where He said, "But you will receive power when the Holy Spirit comes on you; and you will be my witnesses in Jerusalem, and in all Judea and Samaria, and to the ends of the earth." Thus, the Spirit-empowered missionary church has two primary characteristics: Its members are empowered by the Holy Spirit, and they are committed to the mission of God. It is a church that plants other Spirit-empowered missionary churches, and it is a church that is committed to reaching unreached people groups across the nation and around the world. This is the kind of church we must develop, and it is the kind of churches we must plant.

INDIGENOUS CHURCH PRINCIPLES

Around the world, the Pentecostal church has grown at an astonishing rate. Contributing to this growth is the movement's commitment to what is known as "indigenous church principles." This is the belief that every new church must soon become self-supporting, self-governing, and self-propagating. As you and your church go out to plant churches, you should ensure that they develop into churches that can support themselves, take care of their own affairs, reach out to the lost, and quickly be able to plant other Spirit-empowered missionary churches.

When a new baby arrives in a family, the parents care for its every need. However, as the child grows and matures, the parents teach the child how to take care of itself. The child is taught how to live and, over time, is given more and more responsibility in caring for itself. When the child eventually becomes an adult, the parents release him or her as a self-reliant, contributing member of society.

It is much the same in planting a new church. In the beginning, the parent church devotes much time and many resources in caring for the baby church. It may help the new church with leadership, finances, and workers. The new church, however, is expected to grow and mature. The aim is that, very soon, it too will become a self-reliant contributing member of the kingdom of God.

WHAT NOW?

You may be asking, "What can I do to implement these church planting principles in my own ministry and in the life of my church? How can I develop my church into an effective church planting body?" Consider taking the following steps:

Pray

Start with earnest prayer. Sincerely ask God to give you a vision for church planting. Ask Jesus, the Lord of the Harvest, to "open your eyes and look at the fields [that] are ripe for harvest" (John 4:35). Intercede for those communities around you that have no Spirit-empowered missionary church (Matt. 9:38). But do not stop there. Look farther away to unreached peoples and places in your country where there is little or no gospel witness. And do not forget to look to the nations. As you pray, ask God, "Which of these peoples and places do you want us to reach with the good news about Christ?"

Commit

Next, commit yourself and your church to God and to His mission. Decide once and for all that your church will become an effective church planting church.

Invest in People

Once you have committed to church planting, begin to develop your church members into fully-committed disciples of Christ. Preach, teach, and talk often about God's mission and about Christ's mandate to plant churches. Cast a vision for church planting in your church leadership and congregation. As you do, give potential leaders opportunities to minister and develop their God-given gifts.

Assemble a Team

At the proper time, assemble your church planting team. Choose who will serve as pastor of the new church. Also, choose those who will work with the pastor on the church planting team. Ensure that each member knows his or her particular responsibilities. Also, ensure that your team members have been empowered by the Holy Spirit. In addition, it is important that you develop a support team who will remain at home to support the new church with their encouragement, prayers, and finances.

Develop a Plan

Now, together with your team, begin to develop a plan of advance. In your plan, you will want to answer the questions: "When and where will we plant the new church? Who will be involved? What specific things will we do?" Your plan must also include a budget detailing how much money and what supplies will be needed and how they will be obtained.

Move into Action

Once you have prayed and developed your plan, move aggressively to implement your strategy. Act in faith, believing that the Spirit of the Lord will empower you and anoint your witness. Trust God to confirm the word you proclaim with miracles, signs, and wonders. As people are being saved, ensure that they too are filled with the Spirit and taught the basics of serving Christ. You will want to immediately mobilize them to reach their families and friends.

Evaluate

Finally, once you have concluded your church planting effort, bring your team together to evaluate the work. Ask, "What did we do well? What could we have done better?" There will always be things that did not go smoothly, but do not be discouraged. Use what you have learned to strengthen your next church planting mission.

Chapter 39: Planting New Churches

Developing your congregation into a church planting body will not only serve to advance Christ's mission in the earth, it will bring revival to the church. Your congregation will become excited that they are a part of planting new churches and seeing people come to know Jesus. Every Pentecostal pastor should happily commit himself or herself to planting new churches.

~ Chapter 40 ~

Developing a Local Church Missions Program

The time had come for Jesus to reveal who He was and why He had come. If His twelve disciples were to continue His mission after He left, they would need to understand these truths. Arriving at a secluded spot outside the city of Caesarea Philippi, Jesus sat down with them. Turning to them, He asked, "Who do people say that the Son of Man is?" One by one, the disciples answered, "Some say you are John the Baptist. Others say Elijah. And still others allege that you are Jeremiah or one of the prophets."

Jesus then asked them directly, "What about you? Who do you say I am?" In a flash of divine inspiration, Peter blurted out, "You are the Messiah, the Son of the living God!"

Looking deep into Peter's eyes, Jesus replied, "You are blessed, Simon son of Jonah, for my Father in heaven has revealed this to you." Jesus then added, "I say to you that you are Peter, and on this rock I will build my church, and all the powers of hell will not be able to stand against it" (cf. Matt. 16:13-20).

Jesus thus revealed to His disciples who He was: He was the promised Messiah, the Son of God. He also revealed to them why He had come: He had come to build His Church. He further revealed that the Church He was building would be more than a human institution; it would be a divinely commissioned movement. It would face fierce demonic opposition, but it would ultimately prevail.

CONNECTING WITH GOD'S MISSION

Our Lord's primary purpose for His Church is that it proclaims the good news of salvation in Christ to a broken world before He returns from heaven. Jesus put it like this: "This gospel of the kingdom will be preached in the whole world as a testimony to all nations, and then the end will come" (Matt. 24:14). This being true, every Pentecostal pastor is obliged to lead his or her church to fully participate in God's mission. This chapter will examine how you can best accomplish this central task of the Church.

Personal Preparation

Before attempting to connect your church with God's mission, you must prepare yourself for the task. You can do this in the following ways:

1. Understanding God's mission. First, you must make it your aim to gain a clear understanding of God's mission. To do this, you must know what God's mission is and how it relates to the Church. God's mission, sometimes called the *missio Dei,* is the unifying theme of Scripture. It is God's plan to redeem and call unto himself a people from every tribe, tongue, and nation on earth (Rev. 5:9; 7:9). It is God's plan that, in Christ, the seed of Abraham, "all peoples on earth will be blessed" (Gen. 12:3; 22:18; Gal. 3:16). The Bible is the story of God acting in history to fulfill this mission.

2. Understanding the Church's role. Further, as a true Pentecostal pastor, you must understand the Church's central role in fulfilling God's mission. Jesus connected the Church to God's mission when He commanded His followers, "Go and make disciples of all nations, baptizing them in the name of the Father and of the Son and of the Holy Spirit and teaching them to obey everything I have commanded you" (Matt. 28:19-20; cf. Mark 16:15; Luke 24:46-48; John 20:21; Acts 1:8). This command of Jesus is known as the Great Commission. Missions is not just a program of the Church, it is the purpose of the Church.

3. Accepting pastoral responsibility. Finally, as a true Pentecostal pastor, you must accept your responsibility of mobilizing the church to participate in God's mission. You must be that "faithful and wise servant" whom the master has commissioned to care for His household "to give them their food at the proper time" (Matt. 24:45). Remember, you will one day give account to God for how you have managed Christ's church (Luke 16:2).

A Biblical Model

The Bible gives us a clear example of what a truly Pentecostal church should look like. It should be a missional church. A missional church is a church that is committed to advancing God's mission in the earth. The church in Antioch, Syria, was such a church (Acts 11:19-20; 13:1-4). Luke included the story of this church in Acts as a lasting model of how a church can best connect with God's mission. It is an example of how a Pentecostal church should function today. An examination of these two passages reveals seven characteristics of a truly missional church:

1. The presence and power of the Spirit. A truly missional church will value the presence and power of the Holy Spirit. The Bible says of the church in Antioch, "The Lord's hand was with them" (Acts 11:21). This is another way of saying that the Holy Spirit was powerfully at work in their midst (cf. 2 Kings 3:15; Ezek. 3:14). As a result of the Spirit's working in and through the believers in Antioch, and their focus on winning the lost, "a great number of people believed and turned to the Lord."

2. Godly, anointed, faith-filled leadership. A truly missional church is led by godly, Spirit-anointed, faith-filled leaders such as Barnabas and Saul (Acts 11:22-26). The Bible says that Barnabas was "a good man, full of the Holy Spirit and faith" (v. 24). Saul, who also led the church in Antioch, was also full of the Holy Spirit and faith (13:9; cf. 9:17-18).

3. Visionary outward focus. A truly missional church intentionally reaches out to the residents of its city or village. This is what the church in Antioch did. Further, their outreach was multiethnic, focusing on both Jews and Gentiles (Acts 11:19-21). The church in Antioch also planted other churches in the region (15:41). In addition, they sent missionaries to the nations (13:1-4). Then they stayed connected to those they sent out (14:27).

4. Bold proclamation. A truly missional church will boldly proclaim "the good news about the Lord Jesus Christ" as did the church in Antioch (Acts 11:20). Bold proclamation of the gospel was a characteristic of disciples throughout the book of Acts (cf. 8:4-5; 16:30-32; 28:31).

5. Systematic missions-focused training. The truly missional church will systematically teach its members about the mission of God. The Bible says, "For a whole year Barnabas and Saul met with the church and taught great numbers of people" (Acts 11:26). They surely taught the basics of Christian living. Also, observing how the church in Antioch functioned, it is clear that they taught about God's mission and how Christians could effectively participate in that mission.

6. The free operation of spiritual gifts. A truly missional church will encourage the operation of spiritual gifts in their gatherings. The church in Antioch encouraged such manifestations (cf. Acts 11:27-28). The Christians there depended on God's Spirit to guide them into God's will. The manifestation of a prophetic gift in the church prompted the commissioning and sending of Barnabas and Saul as missionaries to the Gentiles (13:2).

7. Spirit-prompted generosity. The truly missional church is a generous church. In Antioch, the Christians gave generously to advance the work of the kingdom. They responded to Agabus' prophecy by giving to provide help for the brothers and sisters living in Judea

Part 9: The Pentecostal Pastor in Mission

Part 9: The Pentecostal Pastor in Mission

(Acts 11:29). This reminds us of what happened after the outpouring of the Spirit on the Day of Pentecost (2:44-45).

As a Pentecostal pastor, you should use the church in Antioch as a model. You should work to ensure that each of these seven traits of a missional church are cultivated in the church you lead.

IMPLEMENTING GOD'S MISSION

You may be asking, "How can I initiate an effective missions program in my church? What practical steps can I take to move my church from where it is today to where God wants it to be?"

To do this, you must understand that a truly missional church cannot be created in a moment. It is not as if you can flip a switch and immediately the "light of missions" comes on in the church. Creating a missionary vision in a congregation is a process that will take time and effort. It will require a plan. And that plan will need to be implemented.

Here are five effective strategies you can use to instill a missionary vision in your church. If you will consistently apply these strategies, in time, your church will move from being an inward-focused, self-centered church to being an outward-focused, missional church—the kind of church that pleases God.

Impassioned Preaching

The first strategy you can use to instill a missionary vision in your church is impassioned preaching. You must preach often on God's mission and the church's responsibility to engage in that mission. And you must let your passion for missions be communicated in how you deliver your message. The people will be moved as much by your passion for the subject as they will by your logical arguments. At the close of your message, be sure to challenge God's people to commit themselves to God's mission. Then call for a specific response to the message.[1]

Focused Prayer

A second strategy you can use to instill a missions vision in your church is missions-focused prayer. You must often lead your church in prayer for the harvest (cf. Matt. 9:37-38). You should allot time in each Sunday service for missionary prayer. In this time slot, you or a designated leader will lead the church in prayer for one of the missionaries or missions programs the church supports. You should also offer prayer for unreached peoples and places in your own country and around the world.

In addition, you must often lead your people in prayer for an outpouring of the Holy Spirit on the church. As more and more members are empowered by God's missionary Spirit, their hearts will be filled with His passion for the lost. And the Spirit will move them to do their part in reaching lost people at home and to the ends of the earth (Acts 1:8).[2]

Systematic Teaching

Third, you can instill a passion for missions in the hearts of God's people through systematic teaching on the mission of God. To do this, you will need to move through the Scriptures step by step highlighting how God has acted throughout history to fulfill His mission in the earth. This new perspective on the Bible will create in the people's hearts a clear understanding of the missionary nature of the Church.

---

[1] The book, *Proclaiming Christ to the Nations: 100 Sermon Outlines on Spirit-empowered Mission,* is available through the Africa's Hope, Acts 1:8 Initiative. It can be downloaded for free from the www.DecadeofPentecost.org website.

[2] For more on these topics, see Chapter 8: "The Priority of Prayer" and Chapter 11: "Promotes Pentecostal Experience and Practice."

This understanding will inspire them to participate more fully in God's mission.[3]

Purposeful Organization

A fourth way you can instill a missionary vision in your people is to purposefully organize (or reorganize) your church for missions involvement. To do this, you will need to thoughtfully evaluate each of the church's departments and ministries to ensure that their programs reflect your church's commitment to God's mission. You, along with the church's leadership team, should ask of each ministry in the church, "How is this program helping our church to fulfill the mission of God?" If the program does not help the church accomplish God's mission, it should be scrapped or revamped.

Strategic Partnering

A fifth strategy you can use to instill a missionary vision in your church is to strategically partner with reputable missionaries and missions organizations. No local church is capable of carrying out God's mission alone. Missions is something the entire Body of Christ must do together. Therefore, along with its local outreach programs, you must lead your church to cooperate with the missions program of your national church and other legitimate missions organizations. In doing this, you must lead your church to faithfully support its national church's missions program and the missionaries it endorses. As your church members see all that is being accomplished through this cooperative effort, they will be inspired to even greater involvement in missions.

Congregational Exposure

Finally, you can instill a missionary vision in your church by exposing your members to the mission field. Here are five effective ways you can do this:

---

[3] You can learn more about God's mission in the Africa's Hope Discovery Series textbook, *A Biblical Theology of Missions,* by Paul York.

Chapter 40: Developing a Local Church Missions Program

1. Missionary guests. One way you can expose members to the mission field is to invite missionary guests to come and preach to your congregation. These missionaries will share with the church their vision for reaching the lost, along with the nature of their work on the field. As the people listen to these missionaries, a passion for missions will be born in their hearts. When you invite a missionary to speak, you must ensure that your church blesses the missionary with a generous offering, a monthly financial commitment, and with ongoing prayer support.

2. Missions Sundays. Another effective way you can expose your church to missions is by designating one Sunday each month as "Missions Sunday." On Missions Sunday, you or a designated representative, will read reports from missionaries and pray for them. You will then preach a missions sermon and receive a missions offering. This strategy will ensure that your church maintains a healthy missions fund.

3. Missions conferences. You will also want to schedule an annual missions conference for the church. A missions conference is a series of church services designed to expose the church to missions and increase its burden to reach the lost. During the conference, you will invite missionaries to preach and share their ministries with the church. Also, during the conference, you will want to highlight the church's missions accomplishments along with its missions goals for the coming year. In addition, you will want to challenge the people to make monthly giving commitments to the missions program of the church.

4. Missions board. You can further expose the church to missions by creating an attractive missions board and displaying it in a prominent location in the church. On this board should be posted pictures of missionaries with descriptions of their ministries. Letters from missionaries, missions maps, and other missions-related information can also be posted.

5. Missions outreaches. Another way you can expose your congregation to missions is by encouraging your members to participate in church-sponsored missions outreaches. For example, the missions department of the church may want to plan an outreach to a neglected area or tribal group in your country. Or they may want to sponsor a program to plant a new church in an unevangelized area. This direct exposure to missions work will advance the kingdom of God, create a passion for missions in the people's hearts, and help members to understand the work of missions.

SUPPORTING MISSIONARIES

Paul reminded the church in Rome that, for missionaries to be able to go and preach the gospel to the lost, somebody must send them (Rom. 10:13-15). Therefore, a major part of any church's missions program is helping to send and support missionaries on the field. Three ways a church can do this is through faithful financial support, ongoing prayer support, and caring moral support, as follows:

Faithful Financial Support

First, your church must support its missionaries financially. Paul was talking about such support when he challenged the believers in Corinth, asking, "Who serves as a soldier at his own expense?" (1 Cor. 9:7). He further reminded them, "Those who preach the gospel should receive their living from the gospel" (1 Cor. 9:14).

For missionaries to remain on the field, they must receive faithful and sustained financial support from the home base. This support largely comes from individual donors and local churches. Most local churches give to missionaries through the missions department of their national church. As pastor, you must ensure that all missions offerings are handled with integrity and that they are used only for the purpose for which they were given.

Ongoing Prayer Support

Second, the church must provide ongoing prayer support for their missionaries on the field. Paul often reminded the churches to pray for him. For example, he entreated the Christians in Thessalonica, "Brothers and sisters, pray for us that the message of the Lord may spread rapidly and be honored" (2 Thess. 3:1). Other examples of Paul requesting prayer from Christians are found in Romans 15:30-32, Ephesians 6:19, Colossians 4:3-4, and 1 Thessalonians 5:25. Through their prayers, Christians can support missionaries on the field and help them fight the good fight of faith. Prayer for missionaries sometimes involves intense spiritual warfare (Eph. 6:11-18; Matt. 12:29).

Caring Moral Support

Finally, the Pentecostal church must provide its missionaries with moral and emotional support. Missionaries often live far from home and their support base. They sometimes feel isolated and lonely and need moral support. Christians at home can provide this support by writing encouraging letters and emails.

TARGETING THE UNREACHED

Paul's missionary ministry focused on unreached peoples. He wrote, "It has always been my ambition to preach the gospel where Christ was not known, so that I would not be building on someone else's foundation" (Rom. 15:20).

In the same way, every local Pentecostal church's missions program must include a focus on unreached people groups. An unreached people group is a tribe or ethnic group with no local, self-sustaining church movement. Researchers say there are more than seven thousand unreached people groups in the world today. These unreached peoples constitute more than three billion people who have no access to the good news about Jesus. Many of these unreached people groups reside in Africa. The African church must target these lost peoples for missionary outreach.[4]

---

[4] You can find out more about unreached people groups at the website www.JoshuaProject.net.

~ PART 10 ~

THE PENTECOSTAL PASTOR AND CEREMONIES AND SACRAMENTS

~ Chapter 41 ~

Performing Weddings and Funerals

Soon after graduating from college, Samuel asked Esther to marry him, and she accepted. Being godly young people, they committed themselves to remain sexually pure until they were married. Sadly, prior to the wedding, a civil war broke out in their nation. Each of their families fled to different countries for refuge. After two years of separation, Samuel and Esther returned to their home country and reconnected. Their wedding was simple; however, God's Spirit was clearly present during the ceremony. Since that time, Samuel and Esther have faithfully served the Lord and raised up godly children.

In another story, Christopher and Stephen were two very close brothers. When Stephen suddenly passed away, Christopher was heartbroken. Though he was not a Christian, his brother was. Stephen had faithfully served God as a deacon in his church. Because of the care the local church gave to Stephen's family, the dignity of the funeral service, and the follow-up ministry of the pastors, Christopher and his entire family gave their lives to Christ and became members of the church. Today, Christopher is a deacon in the church. He is serving in the same ministry position in which his brother Stephen once served.

This chapter will discuss what the Bible says about weddings and funerals and their value to the families, the church, and the community at large. It will also offer insights to Pentecostal pastors on preparing for, conducting, and following up on weddings and funerals. While the details of how a pastor is to conduct these sacred rites may vary from country to country, and from culture to culture, this chapter will provide some general guidelines for conducting these important ceremonies.

THE WEDDING CEREMONY

Nowhere does the Bible lay down specific guidelines concerning wedding ceremonies. It does, however, offer several examples of divinely sanctioned weddings. Principles learned from these examples can guide the Pentecostal pastor in preparing and officiating wedding ceremonies.

One example is the biblical account of how God brought Adam and Eve together as husband and wife (Gen. 2:18-25). After He created them, God brought them together in what may be rightly called the "first wedding ceremony." As a result of their coming together, the Bible says that they became "one flesh" (v. 24; cf. Matt. 19:5-6).

Later in Genesis, the Bible tells of the marriage of Isaac and Rebekah (Gen. 24:1-67). It describes how God led Abraham's servant to a beautiful Chaldean girl named Rebekah. After explaining to her why he had come, the girl agreed to return with him to Canaan to become Isaac's wife. When she first met Isaac, she respectfully took her veil and covered herself in keeping with the custom of the time. The servant then explained to Isaac how God had helped him find Rebekah. Isaac then took Rebekah into the tent of his late mother Sarah and married her. He loved Rebekah dearly and found comfort in her. This story of Isaac and Rebekah shows that if one will pray and seek God, He will lead them to a faithful spouse with whom they can share the joys and comforts of marriage.

Solomon declared, "He who finds a wife finds what is good and receives favor from the Lord" (Pro. 18:22). The reverse is, of course, also true: she who finds a husband finds what is good and receives favor from the Lord. Solomon expands on this truth in the Song of Songs, where he paints a beautiful picture of romantic love in marriage. To enter into a godly marriage is a blessed thing.

Jesus Blessed Marriage

Jesus had much to say on the sanctity of marriage (Matt. 5:31-32; Mark 10:1-12). He further showed how much He values wedding ceremonies by attending one in the village of Cana in Galilee. There, He blessed the event by miraculously turning water into wine, thus saving the hosts from public humiliation (John 2:1-11). The fact that this was Jesus' first miraculous sign in the gospel of John further emphasizes the importance He places on the rite of marriage.

Additionally, the Bible uses marriage and wedding metaphors to express God's intimate relationship with His people. For instance, in the Old Testament, the Bible characterizes Israel as the bride, or wife, of God (Isa. 62:5; Jer. 3:14). In similar fashion, in the New Testament, Paul describes the Church as the bride of Christ (Eph. 5:23-32). By using such word pictures, the prophets and apostles were declaring God's love and commitment to His people. And by implication, they were declaring how highly God values the institution of marriage.

The Value of the Wedding Ceremony

Church weddings enhance the couple's sense of belonging to the community of faith. They also enhance the couple's commitment to one another. God made Eve to solve Adam's loneliness. Concerning Adam, God declared, "It is not good for the man to be alone" (Gen. 2:18). The same is true of the newly married couple. It is not good for them to be alone, that is, separated from the community of believers.

Chapter 41: Performing Weddings and Funerals

Just as God is a relational being of Father, Son, and Holy Spirit, He created human beings to live in community.

In Africa, the wedding of a man and a woman is not a private matter. It is a public event to be joyfully celebrated by the entire community. The wedding demonstrates that the couple is part and parcel of the community of faith, the Church. If the husband or wife is from a distant home, the love and care exhibited by their new church family makes them feel welcome and accepted.

Christian weddings also deliver an ethical message to the broader community. Every young couple who is properly married in the church challenges their peers to follow their example. In the contemporary world, it has shamefully become a norm for a man and woman to live together as sexual partners without being married. The couple who gets married according to God's Word adds moral value to their community and sets a good example for their peers.

Preparing for the Wedding Ceremony

The success of the wedding ceremony depends largely on proper preparation. As a Pentecostal pastor, you should prepare yourself, as well as the bride and groom, in four ways:

1. Spiritual preparation. First, you should address the spiritual preparation of the wedding participants. Marriage is more than a mere social contract, as the world would have us believe. From God's standpoint, it is a sacred covenant between a man, a woman, and God. It is thus designed for a man and a woman who live in covenant relationship with their Lord. The wedding ceremony should reflect these sacred truths.

As pastor, you should counsel the couple to ensure that they understand the seriousness of the vows they are about to exchange. You should also ensure that both the bride and the groom are born again. If you discover that either of them has not been truly converted, you should seek to lead them to Christ. If they are saved, but are not living fully committed lives, you should lead them in recommitting their lives to Christ.

2. Cultural preparation. Second, as pastor, you must consider the issue of cultural preparation. Different African cultures have different customs and traditions surrounding weddings. For instance, in some African cultures, a proper marriage must be preceded by the settlement of a dowry payment. If you find yourself in such a context, you should ensure that the participants comply with customary requirements before the wedding day—so long as those requirements do not offend Scripture or church tradition. It can be embarrassing when unresolved cultural requirements are demanded during a church wedding.

3. Legal preparation. Third, you must ensure that you and the wedding participants have taken care of any legal matters required for the wedding. For example, you must ensure that the marriage license has been acquired from the proper governmental authority. You must further ensure that neither candidate has a living spouse. In some countries, legal action may be taken against any pastor who violates marriage laws.

One pastor overlooked this responsibility and brought embarrassment on himself and his church. During a wedding ceremony, he stated, "If anyone can show any just cause why this man cannot be married to this woman, let them speak now or hereafter forever hold their peace." To the amazement of everyone, a young lady raised her hand. She stated, "I do not want to stop the wedding, since my sister is the one getting married. However, the man she is marrying is the father of my child. He promised to marry me before changing his mind and moving on to her." After much confusion, the wedding was cancelled. This humiliating scene could have been avoided had the pastor done the proper background investigation.

4. Ceremonial preparation. Finally, as pastor, you must ensure that proper ceremonial preparation has occurred prior to the wedding. You should meet with the wedding participants to ensure that they understand that the Christian wedding ceremony is a worship service conducted in the presence of God.

The wedding attire of the pastor, bride, groom, and all attendants should be appropriate to the occasion. The groom and groomsmen should be dressed in a respectful manner. Suit jackets are not required, but they are recommended. The bride, bridesmaids, and female guests should be dressed beautifully yet modestly. If the couple and their attendants choose to dress in cultural attire, the pastor may need to adjust what he or she wears accordingly.

You should familiarize yourself with the wedding ceremony you will use.[1] You should also go over the ceremony with the bride and groom, discussing each part with them. In this way, they will clearly understand the commitments they will soon make to each other. Prior to the wedding, the church building and grounds should be cleaned and decorated.

Officiating the Wedding

The wedding ceremony is made up of three important parts: the sermon, the exchange of marital vows, and the signing of the legal documents, as follows:

1. The sermon. The sermon, or exhortation, should focus on the couple's devotion to God, their faithfulness to one another, and the raising of godly children. Although the marriage couple is the focus of the ceremony, the message is for all who are present, both married and unmarried. The message should be kept brief, taking no more than fifteen or twenty minutes.

2. The ceremony. The actual wedding ceremony, involving the exchange of vows and rings, should be marked by dignity and solemnity. Prior to the marriage service, you should rehearse the exchange of vows and the exchange of rings with the couple. This will help ensure that they avoid embarrassing mistakes during the actual ceremony.

3. The signing. As an ordained minister, the Pentecostal pastor's role in the wedding ceremony is both spiritual and legal. You should

---

[1] Wedding ceremonies can be found in *The Minister's Service Book,* compiled by Myer Pearlman. You should have a copy of this book or some other resource recommended by your denominational fellowship.

fulfill both roles in a professional manner. Prior to the ceremony, you must confirm that the legal documents are all in order. Those who are legally required to sign these documents should be informed ahead of time. You should ensure that these individuals are present and aware of their responsibility.

Finally, you should direct the signing of the register. Once every required signature is affixed, you should publicly deliver the documents to the groom, who bears the greatest responsibility for the success of the marriage. Once the documents have been presented, you can pronounce the couple husband and wife. You should then ask the couple to kneel before God, preferably on clean, soft pillows. You will then lay hands on them and pray a prayer of blessing over them. The ceremony is concluded with the groom kissing the bride and the benediction.

THE FUNERAL SERVICE

When Gertrude's death was announced, the whole town was shaken. Not only did her family grieve, but the entire community mourned her loss. Men, women, youth, and children all wailed. Gertrude was an Assemblies of God deaconess. Because of her Christian character and generosity, she was beloved by all.

During her funeral, the pastor delivered a message of comfort. He also shared the message of hope in Christ. At the end of the sermon, the pastor invited the people to come forward to receive Christ as Savior. Several responded and gave their lives to Christ. Because of Gertrude's life, and her pastor's wisdom in conducting the funeral service, great good came, not only from her life, but from her death as well.

The Value of the Funeral Service

Africans live their lives in community. Their individual values are defined and strengthened by those around them. Thus, when someone in the community dies, the funeral service brings everyone together. People from all walks of life, regardless of their religious background, gather to pay their last respects to the departed. They also come to show their solidarity with the grieving family.

The funeral service in Africa serves multiple purposes. First, it provides the family and friends with an opportunity to come together and mourn. As they do this, their hearts are comforted and strengthened. Next, the funeral service helps to give mourners a sense of closure. It provides them with a point in time when they are able to accept their loss, and in God's strength, move on with their lives. Finally, the funeral service affords an excellent opportunity for the Pentecostal pastor to share the message of Christ with those who do not know Him. Many who would never attend a regular church service will come to a funeral. The wise Pentecostal pastor will use this opportunity to tactfully, yet compellingly, share the message of salvation.

Ministering to the Bereaved

As a Pentecostal pastor, your ministry to the bereaved begins as soon as you learn of the person's death. You should be prepared to interrupt your schedule and immediately reach out to the loved ones of the deceased. This will be the first sign to the family that you care for them. While a few words of consolation are appropriate and helpful, at first you will probably want to keep your words to a minimum. You will simply want to sit and weep with the grieving family. Your presence, a few words of consolation, and a prayer are usually all that is needed at this point.

Later, you will want to visit the family again, this time with other church leaders. During this visit, you may want to lead a hymn or two, give a brief exhortation, and again offer prayer for the family. You may also want to read some appropriate Scripture texts. Further, you and your leadership team may want to offer financial assistance on behalf of the church. This is especially helpful when the bereaved family cannot afford the cost of the funeral.

Preparing for the Service

You and your leadership team should also take time to sit with the grieving family and plan the funeral service. During this meeting, you can make assignments for Scripture reading and the reading of the obituary (life sketch) of the deceased. You should respect the wishes of the family as to who will be assigned these tasks. The funeral sermon is normally delivered by the pastor of the deceased. However, if for some reason the family requests that another Christian minister preach the funeral sermon, you should be flexible.

The Funeral Service

The funeral service itself should include several key elements. First, appropriate hymns should be chosen for the occasion. Second, the ceremony should include a funeral sermon delivered by a qualified and respected minister. If the deceased lived an exemplary Christian life, the sermon may be biographical. Otherwise, a simple message should be preached emphasizing salvation and the reality of the afterlife.

Church members and friends should be allowed to pay their tributes in ways that will honor the memory of the deceased and console the family. Those who offer tributes should be encouraged to be brief so that the funeral service does not extend too long and become a burden rather than a blessing to the family.

You should also keep the interment ceremony brief. This ceremony normally includes an appropriate hymn, prayer, and the interment rite offered by an ordained pastor. You should monitor the time to ensure that the body of the deceased is interred well before dusk.

Follow-up Ministry

Your responsibility as pastor does not end with the funeral service. Following the interment, you and your church elders should accompany the family to their home. There, you will offer some final words of consolation and pray for them. As the days go by, you should occasionally visit with the bereaved family. And you should

Chapter 41: Performing Weddings and Funerals

look for opportunities to share the gospel with family members who do not know the Lord.

Weddings and funerals are excellent times for the Pentecostal pastor and church to show their love and concern for church members and others in the community. He or she should take great care in planning and conducting these rites with loving concern and dignity.

~ Chapter 42 ~

Conducting Sacraments, Dedications, and Installations

The Pentecostal pastor is often called on to administer the sacraments of the church and to conduct other sacred and celebratory rites. These acts must be performed with the skill and dignity they deserve. This chapter is offered to aid the Pentecostal pastor in this important area of ministry.

WATER BAPTISM

Water baptism is the first of two sacred ordinances instituted by Jesus. He himself was baptized in water, setting an example for those who would follow Him (Matt. 3:13-17). He further commanded His Church to go and make disciples of all nations, "baptizing them in the name of the Father and of the Son and of the Holy Spirit" (Matt. 28:19-20; cf. Mark 16:15-16).

The early church carefully followed Jesus' instructions by baptizing new believers in water soon after they were converted (Acts 2:37-41; 8:12-13, 36-38; 9:17-18; 10:47-48; 16:13-15, 31-33; 18:8; 19:5). Since water baptism is a divine command, it is not optional.

Therefore, as a Pentecostal pastor, you must prepare yourself to faithfully and competently carry out this ordinance.

The Meaning

Water baptism is an act of obedience on the part of both the minister and the new believer. It is a public confession of the new disciple's faith in Christ and his or her commitment to fully follow their Lord. Baptism in itself does not save. It is rather "the pledge of a clear conscience toward God" that one has already been saved (1 Pet. 3:21). Water baptism symbolizes the death, burial, and resurrection of Jesus (Rom. 6:3-11). It further symbolizes the new believer's death to the world and his or her resurrection to new life in Christ (2 Cor. 5:17). In addition, water baptism indicates the new believer's commitment to join Christ in fulfilling His mission (Matt. 3:15).

The Participants

Anyone who sincerely puts their faith in Jesus Christ as Lord and Savior can, and must, be baptized in water. The rite should be administered soon after conversion. However, before baptizing someone in water, you should first interview them to ensure that they have truly been born again, and that they fully understand the meaning of the sacrament.

The Method

The scriptural method of baptism is by complete immersion in water. The word "baptize" literally means to immerse or submerge. Further, immersion best fits the rite's symbolic meaning of death, burial, and resurrection (Rom. 6:2-4).

You can use the following procedure in baptizing new Christians in water. You enter the water with the candidate. You may want to ask the candidate to share a brief testimony of how he or she found Christ as Savior. You may then ask the candidate the following questions:

- "Do you freely confess that Jesus Christ is your Lord and Savior?"
- "Do you renounce the world, the flesh, and the devil, and totally commit yourself to Christ and His will for your life?"
- "Do you commit yourself before God and His Church to walk in newness of life in a manner worthy of the Lord?"
- "Will you fully commit yourself to Christ and His mission, seeking to lead others to faith in Him?"

The candidate should answer "yes" to each of these questions.

You will then submerge the candidate in water, saying, "Because of your confession of faith in Christ as your Lord and Savior, and because of your commitment to forsake all to follow Him, I baptize you, (full name), in the name of the Father, and of the Son, and of the Holy Spirit. Amen."

Biblical Passages

You may want to read some or all of the following biblical passages during the baptismal service:

- Jesus' baptism (Matt. 3:13-17; Mark 1:9-11)
- The Great Commission (Matt. 28:18-20; Mark 16:14-20)
- The Day of Pentecost (Acts 2:36-41)
- The Ethiopian eunuch (Acts 8:36-39)
- Paul's teaching on baptism (Rom. 6:3-11; Gal. 3:26-29; Col. 2:11-15).

HOLY COMMUNION

Holy Communion is the second of two sacred ordinances instituted by the Lord Jesus (Matt. 26:26-29; Luke 22:14-20; 1 Cor. 11:23-26). It is also called "the breaking of bread" (Acts 2:42) and "the Lord's Supper" (1 Cor. 11:20). The word "communion" comes from the Latin word *cena,* which means "evening meal." Jesus instituted this ordinance during His last meal with His disciples in the upper room. While water baptism is administered only once, and symbolizes the believer's entering into his or her new life in Christ, communion is administered regularly, and speaks of the Christian's ongoing walk with the Lord.

The Meaning of Communion

Communion reminds the believer of the sacrifice of Jesus on the cross. The broken bread brings to remembrance His broken body, and the cup His shed blood (Luke 22:19-20). In 1 Corinthians 11, Paul speaks of five things we are to do during the communion service:

1. We are to remember Christ's death on the cross (vv. 24-25).
2. We are to contemplate the meaning of the New Covenant (v. 25; cf. Matt. 26:28).
3. We are to anticipate His soon coming (v. 26; cf. Matt. 26:29; Luke 22:16-18).
4. We are to come together in unity, preferring one another (vv. 18-21, 33).
5. We are to commit ourselves to Christ's redemptive mission (v. 26).

The Participants

Most Pentecostal churches practice open communion. This means they welcome to the Lord's Table all who have truly received Christ as Savior and are faithfully serving Him. The participant is not required to be a member of that particular church or denomination. Some Pentecostal churches restrict communion to those who have been baptized in water. You should be clear concerning the policy of your national church on these matters, and you should follow that tradition. Everyone who receives communion should be instructed to examine their hearts in order to avoid God's judgment (1 Cor. 11:27-29).

Frequency

The Bible gives no specific instructions on how often a church should celebrate communion. It does, however, indicate that communion should be done regularly and often. Some churches celebrate the Lord's Supper every Sunday morning, while others do it monthly or quarterly. The main thing is that you should schedule the Lord's Supper in your church on a regular basis.

The Ceremony

Holy Communion is a sacred ceremony. Therefore, it should not be rushed, but should be carried out in an orderly and dignified manner. You will want to choose the most spiritual men and women in the church to assist. This could include church elders, deacons, or assistant pastors. You should instruct the servers ahead of time about how the communion ceremony will proceed.

You will begin the ceremony with a short exhortation or by reading an appropriate Bible passage. You will then pray and distribute the bread and the cup to the deacons. The deacons will then distribute the emblems to the congregation. Once everyone has received the bread and the cup, you will read the appropriate verses (i.e., 1 Cor. 11:23-26). The congregation will then eat and drink together.

Following Jesus' example in Matthew 26:26-29, you will want to include five elements in the ceremony: thanksgiving, Scripture reading, distribution of the elements, hymn singing, and prayer. The communion ceremony can take place at any appropriate time during the service.

Biblical Passages

You may read the following biblical passages during the communion service:

- Jesus institutes Holy Communion (Matt. 26:17-29; Mark 14:12-25; Luke 22:7-20)
- The practice of the early church (Acts 2:42-46; 20:7)
- Paul explains Holy Communion (1 Cor. 10:16; 11:18-31).

DEDICATION OF CHILDREN

Most Pentecostal churches in Africa practice the public dedication of children to the Lord. While it is not an ordinance of the church like water baptism or Holy Communion, it is a meaningful practice.

Chapter 42: Conducting Sacraments, Dedications, and Installations

In the Old Testament, children were presented to the Lord and circumcised according to the Law of Moses (cf. Exod. 13:2, 12-13, 15; 22:29; 1 Sam. 1:20, 24-28; 3:19). Hannah dedicated her son, Samuel, to the Lord, saying, "So now I give him to the Lord. For his whole life he will be given over to the Lord" (1 Sam. 1:28). Jesus' parents followed this ancient custom by consecrating Him to the Lord (Luke 2:22-38, 40). Jesus himself "took the children in his arms, placed his hands on them and blessed them" (Mark 10:16).

The Meaning

During the ceremony, it is important to stress that the dedication of children to the Lord is not the same as infant baptism. Baby dedication does not save the child, nor does it make the child a Christian. It is rather an act of consecration on the part of the parents in which they commit themselves to raise the child "in the training and instruction of the Lord" (Eph. 6:4).

Baby dedication is a public act of gratitude to God for the wonderful gift He has given to the parents. It is an occasion when the whole assembly can rejoice with the parents. Together they can commit themselves to surround the child with love and to mentor him or her in the faith.

The Ceremony

The child dedication ceremony may vary from church to church and from culture to culture. It normally takes place as part of a Sunday morning worship service. It can include four parts: (1) the pastor lays hands on the child and prays for God's blessing on him or her; (2) the pastor continues his or her prayer by asking God to grant wisdom to the parents in rearing the child to serve God; (3) the pastor delivers a charge to the parents, exhorting them to bring up the child to love and serve the Lord; and (4) the pastor calls on the church to support the parents in bringing up the child in the ways of God.

Biblical Passages

The following biblical passages may be read during the dedication of a child:

- God's promise to Abraham (Gen. 18:19)
- Train up a child (Pro. 22:6)
- Impress God's commands on the children (Deut. 6:6-9
- Hannah dedicates Samuel to the Lord (1 Sam. 1:20-2:26)
- Jesus blesses the children (Matt. 19:13-15; Mark 10:13-16; Luke 18:15-16)
- Mary and Joseph present Jesus (Luke 2:22-38, 40)
- Training children (Eph. 6:4).

INSTALLATION OF LEADERS

Both the Old and New Testaments speak of the installation of leaders into their offices. The Lord commanded Moses to consecrate Aaron and his sons to the priesthood (Exod. 29:1-27; Lev. 8:1-36; Num. 3:3). He later commanded Moses to do much the same with the Levites who would serve in the temple (Num. 8:5-22).

In the early church, the apostles laid hands on the first deacons to install them in their office (Acts 6:6). In similar manner, the church in Antioch laid hands on Barnabas and Saul commending them to the work of the Lord (Acts 13:2-3). In addition, Paul ordered Titus to appoint elders in the churches in various cities (Titus 1:5). The Greek verb translated "appoint" in this passage is *kathistēmi*, which means "to ordain" or "to install into office."

The installation ceremony will help the church to know who holds a particular office in the church. It will also help them to know the responsibilities of the office. It will further enhance the credibility of the new officer in the eyes of the congregation. The installation ceremony is also a time to remind the candidate that he is a servant of Christ, and because of this, His authority has been delegated to him. Therefore, he is not a ruler, but a servant of the Lord who owns the flock (1 Pet. 5:1-4).

The Ceremony

As pastor, you will begin the installation ceremony by calling the newly chosen officers to the front of the church. You will then read an appropriate Scripture passage and introduce the new officers to the assembly. You will want to briefly explain to the congregation the responsibilities of each office. You will then lay hands on the new officers, asking God to fill them with the Spirit and bless them in the performance of their ministries.

Laying on hands in this context can be more than ceremonial. In the New Testament, people were often filled with the Spirit when hands were laid on them (Acts 8:17; 9:17-19; 19:6). Paul reminded Timothy to "fan into flame the gift of God, which is in you through the laying on of my hands" (2 Tim. 1:6). The apostle was referring to the gift of the Holy Spirit that Timothy had received on that occasion. You should thus prepare the candidates beforehand telling them, "When I lay hands on you, open your heart to God to be filled (or refilled) with the Holy Spirit."

Biblical Passages

You may read one or more of the following biblical passages during the installation of church leaders:

- Choosing the Seven (Acts 6:1-7)
- The ministry gifts of Christ (1 Cor. 12:28-31)
- Stewards of God's gifts (1 Pet. 4:10-11)
- Do not neglect your gift (1 Tim. 4:9-16)
- Stir up the gift of God (2 Tim. 1:1-8).

DEDICATION OF BUILDINGS

Building dedication is the sacred act of setting a structure apart to God for His exclusive use. The practice of dedicating buildings to the Lord finds its meaning in Scripture. On a number of occasions, the Israelites dedicated structures to the Lord. In the wilderness, Moses and the congregation dedicated the tabernacle to Jehovah God (Exod. 40:1-38). They also dedicated the altar to the Lord (Num. 7:10-11, 84-88). Years later, Ezra "celebrated the dedication of the house of God with joy" (Ezra 6:16).

The dedication of the first temple in Jerusalem is possibly the best example of a dedication ceremony in the Bible. When Solomon had finished building the temple, he organized a massive celebratory feast

Part 10: The Pentecostal Pastor and Ceremonies and Sacraments

(1 Kings 8). During the feast, the king led a dedication ceremony in which he invited God to come and dwell in the building (1 Kings 8:13-53).

The Purpose

Today, when we dedicate church buildings to the Lord, we are setting them apart for Him and for His exclusive purposes as did Moses, Ezra, and Solomon. We are saying to God, "We dedicate this structure to You, and we will use it to bring glory to Your name and to advance Your work in the earth."

As Pentecostal Christians, we understand that the Spirit of the Lord indwells God's people (1 Cor. 3:16), and that He empowers them for service (Acts 1:8). However, we also understand that God's presence can at times come and fill buildings. This is what happened on the Day of Pentecost when "suddenly a sound like the blowing of a violent wind came from heaven and filled the whole house where they were sitting" (Acts 2:2). Christ has promised to manifest His presence when two or three gather in His name (Matt. 18:20).

The purpose of the dedication service is to thank God for the assistance He has given the church in enabling them to complete the new building. It is also to dedicate the use of the new building to Him and to His purposes. In the service, the congregation invites the Lord to come down and manifest His presence as He did in Scripture. In addition, the members of the church recommit themselves to God and His redemptive mission.

The Dedication Service

The dedication service should be chaired by the pastor or an invited denominational leader. It is good to have the ceremony on a special day when honored guests will be able to attend. The dedication service may include any or all of the following functions:

- Ribbon cutting
- A dedicatory prayer
- Recognition of special guests
- Scripture reading

Chapter 42: Conducting Sacraments, Dedications, and Installations

- Testimonies
- Celebratory worship
- A thanksgiving offering
- A sermon
- A tour of the new property
- A shared meal or refreshments.

Biblical Passages

The following biblical passages may be read during a building dedication ceremony:

- Dedication of the temple (2 Chr. 6:1-2, 17-20, 40; 7:1-5)
- The courts of the Lord (Psa. 84)
- Let us go into the house of the Lord (Psa. 122).

The observance of sacraments, the dedication of children, the installation of church officers, and the dedication of church buildings are each a vital part of Pentecostal church life. The Pentecostal pastor must conduct these rites and ceremonies with the dignity and solemnity they deserve.

APPENDICES

~ Appendix 1 ~
Statement of Faith of the World Assemblies of God Fellowship

This Statement of Faith is intended simply as a basis for belief, fellowship, and cooperation among us. The phraseology employed in this statement is not inspired, but the truth set forth is held to be essential to a truly Pentecostal ministry. No claim is made that it contains all biblical truth, only that it covers our need for these essential doctrines.

1. THE INSPIRATION OF THE SCRIPTURES

We believe that he Scriptures, both the Old and New Testaments, are verbally inspired of God and are the revelation of God to man, the infallible, authoritative rule of faith and conduct. Divine inspiration extends equally and fully to all parts of the original writings, insuring their entire trustworthiness (2 Tim. 3:15-17; 2 Pet. 1:21).

2. THE ETERNAL GODHEAD

We believe in the unity of the one true and living God who is the eternal, self-existent One, and has revealed Himself as one being in three persons: Father, Son, and the Holy Spirit (Matt. 3:16-17; 28:19).

a. God the Father. We believe in God the Father, the first person of the triune Godhead, who exists eternally as the Creator of heaven and earth, the Giver of the Law, to whom all things will be subjected, so that He may be all in all (Gen. 1:1; Deut. 6:4; 1 Cor. 15:28).

b. The Lord Jesus Christ. We believe in the Lord Jesus Christ, the second person of the triune Godhead, who was and is the eternal Son of God; that He became incarnate by the Holy Spirit and was born of the virgin Mary.

We believe in His sinless life, miraculous ministry, substitutionary atoning death, bodily resurrection, triumphant ascension, and abiding intercession (Isa. 7:14; Heb. 7:25-26; 1 Pet. 2:22; Acts 1:9; 2:22; 10:38; 1 Cor. 15:4; 2 Cor. 5:21).

c. The Holy Spirit. We believe in the Holy Spirit, the third person of the triune Godhead, who proceeds from the Father and the Son, and is ever present and active in the work of convicting and regenerating the sinner, and sanctifying the believer into all truth (John 14:26; 16:8-11; 1 Peter 1:2; Rom. 8:14-16).

3. THE FALL OF MAN

We believe that humankind was created good and upright. However, voluntary transgression resulted in their alienation from God, thereby incurring not only physical death but spiritual death, which is separation from God (Gen. 1:16-27; 2:17; 3:6; Rom. 5:12-19).

4. THE SALVATION OF MAN

We believe in salvation through faith in Christ, who died for our sins, was buried, and was raised from the dead on the third day. By His atoning blood, salvation has been provided for all humanity through the sacrifice of Christ upon the cross. This experience is also known as the new birth, and is an instantaneous and complete operation of the Holy Spirit whereupon the believing sinner is regenerated, justified, and adopted into the family of God, becomes a new creation in Christ Jesus, and heir of eternal life (John 3:5-6; Rom. 10:8-15; Titus 2:11, 3:4-7; 1 John 5:1).

5. DIVINE HEALING

We believe that deliverance from sickness is provided in the atonement and is the privilege of all believers (Isa. 53:4-5; Matt. 8:16-17; James 5:14-16).

6. THE CHURCH AND ITS MISSION

We believe that the Church is the body of Christ and the habitation of God through the Spirit, witnesses to the presence of the

Appendix 1: Statement of Faith

kingdom of God in the present world, and universally includes all who are born again (Eph. 1:22-23; 2:22; Rom. 14:17-18; 1 Cor. 4:20).

We believe that the mission of the church is to (1) proclaim the good news of salvation to all humankind, (2) build up and train believers for spiritual ministry, (3) praise the Lord through worship, and (4) demonstrate Christian compassion to all who suffer (Matt. 28:19-20; 10:42; Eph. 4:11-13).

7. THE ORDINANCES OF THE CHURCH

We believe that baptism in water by immersion is expected of all who have repented and believed. In so doing, they declare to the world that they have died with Christ and been raised with Him to walk in newness of life (Matt. 28:19; Acts 10:47-48; Rom. 6:4).

We believe that the Lord's Supper is a proclamation of the suffering and death of our Lord Jesus Christ, to be shared by all believers until the Lord returns (Luke 22:14-20; 1 Cor. 11:20-34).

8. SANCTIFICATION

We believe that sanctification is an act of separation from that which is evil, and of dedication unto God. In experience, it is both instantaneous and progressive. It is produced in the life of the believer by his appropriation of the power of Christ's blood and risen life through the person of the Holy Spirit. He draws the believer's attention to Christ, teaches him through the Word and produces the character of Christ within him (Rom. 6:1-11; 8:1-2, 13; 12:1-2; Gal. 2:20; Heb. 10:10, 14).

9. THE BAPTISM IN THE HOLY SPIRIT

We believe that the baptism in the Holy Spirit is the bestowing of the believer with power for life and service for Christ. This experience is distinct from and subsequent to the new birth, is received by faith, and is accompanied by the manifestation of speaking in tongues as the Spirit gives utterance as the initial evidence (Luke 24:49; Acts 1:8; 2:1-4; 8:15-19; 11:14-17; 19:1-7).

Appendix 1: Statement of Faith

10. THE GIFTS OF THE HOLY SPIRIT

We believe in the present-day operation of the nine supernatural gifts of the Holy Spirit (1 Cor. 12) and the ministry gifts of Christ (Eph. 4:11-13) for the edification and expansion of the church.

11. THE END OF TIME

We believe in the premillennial, imminent, and personal return of our Lord Jesus Christ to gather His people unto Himself. Having this blessed hope and earnest expectation, we purify ourselves, even as He is pure, so that we may be ready to meet Him when He comes (John 14:1-3; Titus 2:13; 1 Thess. 4:15-17; 1 John 3:2-3; Rev. 20:1-6).

We believe in the bodily resurrection of all humanity, the everlasting conscious bliss of all who truly believe in our Lord Jesus Christ, and that everlasting conscious punishment is the portion of all whose names are not written in the Book of Life (John 5:28-29; 1 Cor. 15:22-24; Rev. 20:10-15).

~ Appendix 2 ~
The Manifestation Gifts of 1 Corinthians 12:8-10

Revelation Gifts (Given to know the mind of God)

- *Word (message) of knowledge:* A Spirit-conferred revelation of a portion of God's knowledge
- *Word (message) of wisdom:* A Spirit-conferred revelation of a portion of God's wisdom
- *Distinguishing between spirits:* A Spirit-conferred revelation of what S(s)pirit is being manifested or motivating an action

Prophetic Gifts (Given to say the words of God)

- *Gift of prophecy:* A Spirit-inspired speaking forth of a message from God
- *Different kinds of tongues:* A Spirit-inspired speaking forth of a message from God, or a prayer to God, in a language not known to the speaker
- *Interpretation of tongues:* A Spirit-inspired speaking forth of the meaning of a message or prayer spoken in tongues

Power Gifts (Given to do the works of God)

- *Gift of faith:* A Spirit-energized surge of faith to accomplish a God-ordained task
- *Gifts of healing:* A Spirit-energized healing of diseases and infirmities
- *Miraculous powers:* A Spirit-energized release of divine power to accomplish a special work of God. (Note: This gift could more properly be called "works of power" or literally from the Greek (*energemata dunameon*) "operations of works of power."

~ Appendix 3 ~
Bible Book Abbreviations

Old Testament

Genesis	Gen.
Exodus	Exod.
Leviticus	Lev.
Numbers	Num.
Deuteronomy	Deut.
Joshua	Josh.
Judges	Judg.
Ruth	Ruth
1 Samuel	1 Sam.
2 Samuel	2 Sam.
1 Kings	1 Kings
2 Kings	2 Kings
1 Chronicles	1 Chr.
2 Chronicles	2 Chr.
Ezra	Ezra
Nehemiah	Neh.
Esther	Esther
Job	Job
Psalms	Psa.
Proverbs	Pro.
Ecclesiastes	Ecc.
Song of Solomon	Song
Isaiah	Isa.
Jeremiah	Jer.
Lamentations	Lam.
Ezekiel	Eze.
Daniel	Dan.
Hosea	Hos.
Joel	Joel
Amos	Amos
Obadiah	Oba.
Jonah	Jonah
Micah	Mic.
Nahum	Nah.
Habakkuk	Hab.
Zephaniah	Zeph.
Haggai	Hag.
Zechariah	Zec.
Malachi	Mal.

New Testament

Matthew	Matt.
Mark	Mark
Luke	Luke
John	John
Acts	Acts
Romans	Rom.
1 Corinthians	1 Cor.
2 Corinthians	2 Cor.
Galatians	Gal.
Ephesians	Eph.
Philippians	Phi.
Colossians	Col.
1 Thessalonians	1 Thess.
2 Thessalonians	2 Thess.
1 Timothy	1 Tim.
2 Timothy	2 Tim.
Titus	Titus
Philemon	Phm.
Hebrews	Heb.
James	James
1 Peter	1 Pet.
2 Peter	2 Pet.
1 John	1 John
2 John	2 John
3 John	3 John
Jude	Jude
Revelation	Rev.

Made in the USA
Columbia, SC
24 March 2025

2d67d95b-95b1-4bb3-8de1-985f06c2c3b0R02